Following God

Life Principles for

Following Christ

TWELVE PORTRAITS OF OUR SAVIOR

Life Principles for

TWELVE PORTRAITS OF OUR SAVIOR

RICK SHEPHERD

Advancing the Ministries of the Gospel

AMG Publishers

God's Word to you is our highest calling.

LIFE PRINCIPLES FOR FOLLOWING CHRIST

© 2004 by Richard L. Shepherd

Fifth Printing, 2009

ISBN: 0-89957-258-8

Editing and layout by Rick Steele
Proofreading by Jody El-Assadi
Cover design by Daryl Phillips at ImageWright Marketing and Design, Chattanooga, Tennessee

Printed in Canada
11 10 09 –T– 8 7 6 5

Acknowledgments

No work is ever done alone. So many encourage and challenge, give insight and fresh light. I am grateful to my wife Linda Gail for the walks and the talks, the prayers and the proofreading, and the patience during long hours of night writing. I am grateful for the prayers of my children. I thank the Lord for my son, Josh, and our conversations about the character and ways of God as well as his insights in Scripture. I thank the Lord for the prayer partners who continually lift me up to the Father as I write. I am continually grateful for the words of encouragement from pastors and from my coworkers at the Florida Baptist Convention. Thank you, Misael, for singing "I AM" on a certain Sunday in Okeechobee, Florida. It came at a time when I needed to be reminded about Who He is and what He is doing in my life. I am very grateful for the fellow laborers at AMG Publishers—thanks to Rick Steele, a truly insightful editor, to Jody El-Assadi for her attention to detail in proofreading, and to Trevor Overcash, Dale Anderson, Warren Baker, and Dan Penwell for their continued encouragement. Their patience, skill, and heart for ministry are much appreciated. I am also indebted to many whose knowledge of the life, ministry, and teachings of Jesus far exceed my own. I gladly acknowledge the helpful insights of fellow ministers Eddie Rasnake and Wayne Barber. I am also grateful for John MacArthur and his insights in *The MacArthur Study Bible*. Robert L. Thomas and Stanley N. Gundry have done an excellent job in their revised edition of *A Harmony of the Gospels* originally compiled by John A. Broadus and A.T. Robertson. Their edition contains many helpful insights on the content and chronology of Jesus' life and teachings. I am also thankful for William Hull and his insights on the process of Jesus' work with His disciples in *Jesus Christ, Disciplemaker* (retitled *Twenty-first Century Disciplemaking*). All these have helped make this work more complete.

I dedicate this work to those leaders who have encouraged me in following Christ by their words and the way they have followed Christ. Over the years there are several leaders I have worked with and served under. Senior pastors Paul Burleson and Wayne Barber have been an encouragement to me to focus on Christ and follow without reserve. Those I now serve under, David Burton and Dr. John Sullivan, continually call me and others to unquestioning loyalty to Christ, His Word, and His Commission to "make disciples of all the nations." None of these is perfect, but each is consistently pursuing, faithfully following Christ, and helping others, including me, to do the same.

 RICK SHEPHERD

About the Author

Richard L. Shepherd has been engaged in some form of ministry for over twenty-five years, focusing on areas of teaching, discipleship, and prayer. He has served in churches in Alabama, Florida, Texas, and Tennessee and now serves as Director of Prayer and Spiritual Awakening with the Florida Baptist Convention. For nearly seventeen years (1983–2000), Rick served as an associate pastor at Woodland Park Baptist Church in Chattanooga, Tennessee. The Lord's ministry has taken him to several countries, including Haiti, Romania, Ukraine, Moldova, Italy, Israel, England, and Greece, where he has been involved in training pastors, church leaders, and congregations. Rick has also lectured on college and seminary campuses. He graduated with honors from the University of Mobile and holds a Master of Divinity and a Ph.D. from Southwestern Baptist Theological Seminary in Fort Worth, Texas. He and his wife Linda Gail have four children and make their home in Jacksonville, Florida.

About the Following God Series

Three authors and fellow ministers, Wayne Barber, Eddie Rasnake, and Rick Shepherd, teamed up in 1998 to write a character-based Bible study for AMG Publishers. Their collaboration developed into the title, *Life Principles from the Old Testament*. Since 1998 these same authors and AMG Publishers have produced five more character-based studies—each consisting of twelve lessons geared around a five-day study of a particular Bible personality. More studies of this type are in the works. In 2001, AMG Publishers launched a different Following God category called the Following God™ Discipleship Series. The titles introduced in the Discipleship Series are among the first Following God™ studies to be published in a topically-based format (rather than Bible character-based). However, the interactive study format that readers have come to love remains constant with each new Following God™ release. As new titles and categories are being planned, our focus remains the same: to provide excellent Bible study materials that point people to God's Word in ways that allow them to apply truths to their own lives. More information on this groundbreaking series can be found on the following web page:

www.amgpublishers.com

Preface

Have you ever heard a symphony? Think of the many individuals with an assortment of instruments all playing together with incredible harmony and force, communicating a message—perhaps of adventure or mystery, sorrow or excitement, intense agony or great joy. The word "symphony" comes from two Greek words, *sun/syn* and *phonos*. *Sun* or *syn* means "together," and *phonos* means "to sound"—"to sound together." When various sounds are blended together, we have music that can best be described as a symphony. The Scriptures are a blended assortment of writings, a symphony of life, if you will—written from the heart of God the Father, revealed fully in God the Son, and orchestrated by God the Holy Spirit. This study, *Following Christ,* is meant to be a symphony of Christ who is our Life. Each lesson presents a melody or harmony of who Christ is, what He has done, what He is doing, and what He will ultimately do to fully express and display His glory and bring to us His full redemption and salvation.

Have you ever been captivated by a portrait? Something in the eyes, or the smile, or a certain look, or perhaps a serious countenance, or a beautiful face? *Following Christ* can be viewed as twelve portraits of Christ—seeing Him in His multifaceted glory, observing Him in His magnificent beauty, and experiencing Him in the magnitude of His power. Each portrait expresses something unique about His person and His work. Each conveys an avenue of worship and surrender, a point of love and adoration, a path of obedience to follow.

As we listen and look—as we participate in the symphony and view the portrait gallery—we will see "The Last Adam" and His creative design for each of us. We will see "The Seed" and the salvation He brings. We will look and listen to "The Angel of the LORD" and marvel at His power, wisdom, and skill to fulfill His will. We will stand before "The Lawgiver and Judge," listening carefully so that we might diligently apply all He says. We will bow before Christ the King, surrendering to His rule and gratefully following Him in His Kingdom. We will listen to Christ the Prophet, knowing that His words are "spirit and life." In seeing Christ our High Priest we will see the open door into pure worship and full fellowship with the Father. We will walk with "The Son of Man" as He reveals Himself in the pages of the New Testament. Our lives will be refreshed and energized as we walk with Christ in prayer. Wonder and awe await us as we look at Christ, the "I AM," and we will learn much about the ways and the will of God as we walk with and listen to Christ the Rabbi. The most magnificent portrait awaits us as we look at "The Lamb of God." In looking at Jesus the Lamb, we also hear the grand symphony of the Lamb, the symphony that has been sung and heard in the heart of God before time. This same symphony will resound for all eternity in our hearts alongside Him in our heavenly home.

This study will be an adventure, a challenge, a time for new steps of obedience, for new sounds of worship coming from our lips and our lives. Come meet with Christ. Listen to Him. Allow Him to teach you, to lead you, to show you what it means to follow Him. Let Him guide you in leading others to follow Him as faithful, loving disciples wherever He may take you in this world, to whatever nations He may send you. Follow Christ and in following Him discover why you were created and re-created in Him. Then, by His Life at work in you and through you, you will see His glory in greater ways. As you live Following Christ, you will experience more of the fullness of His will, you will delight more in the beauty of His holiness, and you will discover more of the wonders of His love. Come, join the journey.

Following Him,

Richard L. Shepherd

RICHARD L. SHEPHERD

Table of Contents

The Last Adam

CHRIST THE CREATOR—REVEALING AND FULFILLING HIS PURPOSES

Think of a blueprint, a design, a pattern, or a picture. What comes to mind? Something to build, something to work on, something that will take time, energy, skill, and resources. Think of the finished product: a building, a suit or dress, a machine or engine, or some other creation—something useful, beneficial, helpful. Now think of Genesis chapter 1. There we see the Architect and Builder of the universe at work. His design is awesome! His work is nothing short of amazing! And of course, there is the finished product—the Creation of the earth and all it contains, the sun, the moon, and the stars along with countless planets and galaxies. But with all the many creations of Genesis 1, none of them is the crowning creation; none can be called the most amazing of His works. That is found in the creation of man and woman. There we see a most unique part of the blueprint, for in the creation of Adam (the first Adam) is a design with an eternal purpose, a purpose fulfilled in Jesus Christ, the "Last Adam." What is that purpose?

Consider this: the Scriptures reveal that the Last Adam is the Creator of the First Adam. The Godhead desired to create **the first man, Adam** with a unique design and purpose—*"in Our Image, according to Our likeness."* What does that mean? What is the image of God? What is in Adam that reveals this "image of God"? Can we see that image today? Is what we see in men and women today what God designed, what God intended, or is something wrong, something out of place? And if all is not right, then how are things to be made right? How do we get back on track, back to God's design and back to His purposes for us?

We will seek to answer these and many other questions in this lesson. Our journey will take us back in time, even back into eternity before time. We will enter into the counsels of the Godhead—the Father, the Son, and the Holy Spirit—and see the heartbeat of God and His ultimate design for man. We will

In the creation of the First Adam is a design with an eternal purpose, a purpose fulfilled in the Last Adam.

see this is more than a generic design. This is personal. This is about the design of God for the expression of His greatness, wisdom, grace, and glory. It is the design of God for you and me as we follow, obey, love, and worship Him.

To see the fullness of this design and understand *"the Last Adam,"* we must delve into this matter of *"the first man, Adam."* What can we learn about Christ and what it means to follow Him? We begin by looking at the beginning.

"Before Me there was no God formed, and there will be none after Me. I, even I, am the LORD; and there is no savior besides Me."

Isaiah 43:10b–11

THE CREATOR'S GRAND DESIGN

Genesis means "beginning." Genesis 1:1 declares, *"In the beginning God created the heavens and the earth."* God wasted no time trying to prove creation. He simply states it as fact. He does not spend time defending that fact. He simply defines that fact so that we can understand who He is, who we are, and how we are to relate to Him. What has He revealed about this matter of creation, and, more particularly, what has He revealed about Himself as the Creator?

📖 What do you find about God and creation in these Old Testament scriptures? Write a simple summary statement after each verse.

Psalm 33:6, 8–9

_____

_____

_____

Isaiah 45:8, 12, 18

_____

_____

_____

_____

Jeremiah 10:1–13, 16

_____

_____

_____

_____

"Yet for us there is but one God, the Father, from whom are all things, and we exist for Him; and one Lord, Jesus Christ, by whom are all things, and we exist through Him."

1 Corinthians 8:6

It is clear that God declares Himself the Creator of all . . . of the heavens and the earth . . . of all we can see and all we cannot see. He spoke and created. Out of nothing He made everything. He is the Everlasting God, the Eternal God, beyond time, King of time, and ruler of the realm of men. He knows exactly what man needs and provides it throughout the earth. Unlike the lifeless, powerless, mindless, useless idols of other nations, He is awesome in power and might, wise and wonderful in His creativity, full of life and power. He is the creator of the clouds and lightning, the winds and rain. He is *"the Maker of all,"* worthy of our worship and obedience.

📖 What do you find in these New Testament scriptures? Write a brief summary statement after each passage of Scripture.

Acts 17:24–26

_____

_____

_____

1 Timothy 4:3–4

_____

_____

_____

The Lord *"made the world and all things in it"* and is clearly declared Lord of all. He needs nothing since He made all that is and He is the one who ever *"gives to all life and breath and all things."* He created man and orchestrates the times of men on earth and the places they live and travel. God created marriage and families, foods and feasts, and designed that we gratefully enjoy all of these gifts. All that God created is good, made for the well-being of men and women and for the enhancement of our relationship with God and one another. All we see should lead us to greater gratitude and worship of our Creator God.

📖 First Corinthians 15:45 speaks of the *"the Last Adam,"* Jesus Christ. We will discover much about Him in the days ahead, but for today, what part does Jesus Christ play in this matter of creation according to the New Testament Scriptures given below? Write your findings and insights in a concise statement.

John 1:1–3

_____

_____

_____

Colossians 1:15–17

_____

_____

_____

Hebrews 1:2–3 and 11:3

_____

_____

_____

John declared that *"the Word"* is God coming to earth as Jesus Christ. He was *"in the beginning"* and is the Creator of all that is. *"Apart from Him nothing came into being."* From miniscule molecules to majestic galaxies, He created it all. Paul acknowledged that He is Lord and *"by Him are all things."* Jesus is the manifest image of God, *"the first-born of all creation."* "Firstborn" does not mean born first, but is rather a title referring to the preemi-

Did You Know?

WHAT HOLDS ALL THINGS TOGETHER?

Scientists speak of the atom as the smallest unit of matter. It is made up of neutrons, electrons, and protons. But what holds all that together? What is the "glue" that keeps things in place? Scientists are unsure, but from Scripture we could say that the "glue-tron" is Jesus Christ. Colossians 1:17 says *"in Him all things hold together,"* and Hebrews 1:3 tells us He *"upholds all things by the word of His power."*

"*Upholds*" and "*prepared*" are two words used in Hebrews 1:3 and 11:3 respectively to reveal the work of the Creator. Hebrews 1:3 says that Jesus "*upholds all things by the word of His power.*" The Greek word *phérō* translated "*upholds*" refers to carrying or bearing something. It is in the present tense, meaning He is continually carrying or upholding all things, constantly carrying all things forward in line with His purposes. He does so by "*the word of His power,*" continually speaking forth His will and His purposes to see all accomplished. Hebrews 11:3 says "*the worlds were prepared*" by that same word of God. The Greek word *katartízō* means to outfit or prepare as in readying a wagon or backpack with everything needed for a journey. The perfect tense points out that our Creator put everything in place and it stands in place to fulfill all His purposes, including His purposes for you.

nent one, the one above all. Jesus is preeminent as Lord and Creator, creating "all things" in all places, in all dimensions. All was created "*by Him and for Him,*" and He is the one who holds it all together. Through Jesus, "*the world*" or "*the ages*" were created, those terms referring to all we know of this universe in this time frame. Not only did Jesus Christ create all, Hebrews 1:3 affirms He "*upholds all things by the word of His power.*" We continue to live by His sustaining word of command.

📖 Now that we see Christ as the Creator, we need to look at His creation. Read the account in Genesis 1:1–31 and then the conclusion and expanded version in Genesis 2:1–7. We find here a threefold purpose for the creation of man. Specifically, what do you find in Genesis 1:26–27?

_____

_____

_____

_____

📖 What two additional purposes do you discover in Genesis 1:28?

_____

_____

_____

After God had created all the essentials of earth and sky, water and land, plants and animals, He created Adam and Eve. The first purpose of the Godhead was the creation of man "*in Our image,*" the image and likeness of God. That included both male and female. He blessed them and commanded them to "*be fruitful and multiply, and fill the earth.*" Not only did God want them **bearing His image,** His first purpose, He also wanted them to **"be fruitful,"** bearing children who would carry that image throughout the earth, and in so doing fulfill the third purpose of **reigning** over the creation. He gave them oversight of the earth to "*subdue it*" and "*rule over*" all He had created, doing so with God's character and care, thus revealing the good and righteous image of God. God saw this creation and this design as "*very good.*"

📖 How would man fulfill this threefold purpose found in Genesis 1:26–28? First, what is unique about his creation? How did God uniquely make Adam according to Genesis 2:7–8?

_____

_____

_____

📖 In what daily activities would man engage in order to carry out his God-given purpose? In other words, what would man and woman do on the "playing field" to carry out God's "game plan"? Look at Genesis 2:15–17 and 2:18–25 and record your insights.

_____

_____

_____

On each of the six days of creation, God simply spoke, and the creation appeared—until He proceeded to create humanity, beginning with Adam. With Adam, He took a special, hands-on approach, forming him from the dust and then breathing into him the *"breath of life."* Adam was unlike any other creature. He came alive by the breath of God and bore God's image. He was **made for relationship**—a person-to-person, heart-to-heart, mind-to-mind, spirit-to-spirit relationship **with God**! God intended for mankind to bear His image and fruit, reign over all of His creation, and live in relationship with Him.

In addition, Adam had a specific assignment given him personally by the Lord. First, he was to cultivate, or **grow,** as well as keep and **guard** the Garden in which he lived. With that came the call to always choose **good** and never *"the knowledge of good and evil."* Here we see the relationship between Adam and God taking shape. The Garden of Eden was the "playing field" in which to begin fulfilling God's "game plan," His grand design. This would be a walk **with** God, a walk of work and rest, of challenge and creativity, of responsibility and accountability. God made sure it would not be a solo walk. Adam needed a companion. The Lord then created Eve and brought her to Adam as his wife, the companion *"suitable for him."* Together they could follow God, walking in His will, obeying His word, and enjoying the experience of bearing His image and fulfilling His purposes for their lives.

APPLY How well are you doing at fulfilling God's grand design in your life? Pause and talk to the Lord about His purposes for you. Ask Him to make His purposes clear as you walk through His Word this week.

_____

_____

_____

_____

_____

_____

God set the grand design in motion. God had prepared the Garden home as the place in which His purposes were to be carried out. How well did Adam and Eve carry out this design? We will begin to see in Day Two.

ADAM'S "GREAT DISCONNECT"

Adam and Eve were designed and directed to follow God. Together they could reflect the image of God, bear the fruit God desired and designed, and reign over creation, growing and guarding it as God directed. How well did they carry out their responsibilities? How well did they walk in their relationship with God? Today, we will see as the Tempter enters the Garden.

MADE FOR RELATIONSHIP

Man was made for relationship—a person-to-person, heart-to-heart, mind-to-mind, spirit-to-spirit relationship *with God!* Bearing God's image, bearing fruit, and reigning over the creation were meant to be done in relationship to God.

📖 Look at the events of Genesis 3:1–13. How did Adam and Eve handle the serpent's challenge? Record your insights about this encounter and its results.

_____

_____

_____

_____

Put Yourself In Their Shoes
CONSEQUENCES OF SIN

Sin shattered the fellowship Adam and Eve experienced with God. Instead of walking *with* God, there was division between God and Adam and Eve. Now Adam and Eve were running *away from* God. With Adam's disobedience, sin entered the human race. Instead of fullness of life and fellowship with God, they experienced death and separation.

The serpent came tempting Eve to eat of the forbidden tree that she knew to be off limits. She was *deceived* and ate and gave to Adam, who also **chose** to eat. As a result, both realized that they had sinned and that with their sin came guilt and fear, shame and blame, along with hiding and an attempted "cover up." Sin shattered the fellowship Adam and Eve experienced with God. They could no longer truly reflect His image. The image was marred, tarnished by their sin. Instead of walking **with** God, there was separation and running **away from** God. With Adam's **disobedience, sin** entered the human race. Instead of the fullness of **life** and **fellowship** with God, Adam and Eve experienced **death** and **separation.** Like a "great blackout," which leaves a city powerless and disrupts life, this "Great Disconnect" separated mankind from the life God intended. What would happen next?

📖 What happened after Genesis 3? How well did men and women fulfill the purpose for which God created them? Look at the following verses in light of God's design for man and record your insights.

Genesis 5:3

_____

_____

_____

Genesis 6:5–6

_____

_____

_____

Genesis 6:11–13

_____

_____

_____

In Genesis 3 and in the chapters following, Adam did not succeed in fulfilling God's design or obeying God's directions. His sin brought death into the world. Man began to show forth **his own image**, a fallen, self-centered image. The **fruit** he bore in his own character and in his children reflected this fallen image. Genesis 6:5 reveals the condition of man. Instead of reigning over life, man was enslaved to his selfish, sinful desires. Man was doing a poor job of cultivating life and guarding what had been given him. Instead of nurturing and growing life in goodness and purity, man had *"corrupted"* life. Instead of guarding life from harm, violence *"filled the earth."* There was no relationship or fellowship with God, and personal relationships were marked by evil toward one another instead of the good that God desired.

Genesis 6—7 records how God destroyed all life *except* for Noah, his family, and the creatures in the Ark. It was clear that God was not through with man nor His creation.

The image of God in man is flawed, marred by sin. That image is revealed in the deeds, words, and attitudes of men and women. The Lord reveals some crucial insights into the ways of man and His need for a change, for a reconnection to the Lord.

What do you discover about man and his relationship to God in Jeremiah 17:9–10?

_____

_____

_____

_____

What characteristics do you find about man in Jeremiah 9:23–24?

_____

_____

_____

The Lord reveals that the hearts of all men and women are *"deceitful"* and *"desperately sick."* Human beings are incapable of seeing just how sick their hearts are apart from God revealing that truth. God is ever searching the heart. He knows each heart in every detail, thoroughly understanding every motive and every move of the hearts and minds of men and women. He is looking at the words and deeds that flow from the heart and makes it clear that every man and woman will have to give account for the fruit of life, what he or she has done. We humans love to brag about our image: We are self-image conscious rather than God conscious. We are predisposed to tell about our wisdom—what we know; about our might—what we can do; about our riches—what we have. That is what often fills our hearts rather than the close, personal knowledge and understanding of the Lord and His ways, the knowledge that is part of a right relationship with God. For most men and women, a relationship with God is not on the priority list, or even on the list period. Something has to change.

How does the New Testament summarize "the Great Disconnect"? Write a description of our condition based on Romans 3:9–18.

_____

_____

_____

What additional insights do you find in Titus 3:3?

_____

_____

_____

All who have ever been born are born *"under sin,"* in a condition of unrighteousness, not seeking God or His will, not desiring to obey or follow Him in

Word Study
PRONE TO WANDER

Jeremiah 17:9 speaks of the heart of humanity, using two descriptions. "Deceitful" is a translation of the Hebrew word *aqob*, which literally means "swelling up" as a knoll or hill, something that slows one's journey, or uneven ground that can cause one to stumble. The word pictures anything crooked, fraudulent, or that which can trip up or trap. It is rooted in *aqab*, which refers to something swelling out as the heel of the foot. This word spoke of seizing by the heel, tripping someone, or throwing someone to the ground. It is the root for the name "Jacob" who was a heel-grabber at birth and deceitful in life. "Desperately sick" is the translation of *anash* which means to be frail, feeble, incurably sick, or *"desperately wicked"* (KJV). The condition of man is hopeless apart from the work of God on his behalf.

Christ came to die for man when he was in an enemy status. Romans 5:6–10 catalogs man's condition—"helpless," "ungodly," "sinners," "enemies." What an amazing love! What an awesome Lord and Savior!

"Through one man sin entered into the world, and death through sin, and so death spread to all men, because all sinned."

Romans 5:12

any way. Nobody in his or her own efforts seeks to do good **God's way**. Mankind's words and deeds reveal a heart disconnected from the life of God. Death, deceit, lies, and bitterness characterize all who have ever lived. Strife and turmoil are the constant companions of men and women on earth as they walk apart from God, ignoring His Word and His will. *"There is no fear of God before their eyes."* They show no respect for the true and living God and are ignorant of His desires and design for man. As a result, men and women continually make foolish choices, disobey the will of God, and deceive themselves and others with so many lies and temptations. Men and women are born enslaved, bound to their corrupt desires. This corrupt fruit shows up in attitudes and actions marked by malice, envy, and hate. From Old Testament times, to New Testament times, to our time—nothing has changed about the heart of mankind. The "Great Disconnect" is still great! A massive gulf exists between God's design and the human fulfillment of that design.

📖 What do you find about humanity and its condition in Romans 5:12? What is the bottom line?

_____

_____

_____

_____

_____

📖 What are some of the marks of this condition? In 1 Corinthians 15:42–44 we find a description of our physical condition because sin entering into the human race through Adam. What do you discover in those verses? List the characteristics you find there.

_____

_____

_____

_____

_____

Through Adam, sin entered the world, and with sin came death. All men and women have sinned and are thus spiritually dead—separated from the life of God—and therefore are bound for physical death. That is most evident as we consider the physical realm. We have bodies that are constantly decaying. We begin growing old the moment we are born. Eventually everyone reveals a body that is perishable, weak, without honor, and bound to the natural world. Even worse, unless something happens, our initial spiritual deadness will lead to eternal death—separation from God and His life forever. We need a Savior and Deliverer, someone who can deal with our sin, our spiritual and physical death, and our physical decay. So how can man fulfill God's grand design and walk in His purposes? We will see that in Day Three.

CHRIST'S GREAT DESCENT AND "THE GREAT CONNECTION"

What could man do to change his heart or to change his life to fit God's grand design? The Old and New Testament scriptures reveal that apart from God man is helpless and hopeless. Something has to change and the only way for change to become reality is for God to act as only He can act. That is where the Lord Jesus enters the scenario. He descended to earth through a virgin birth in Bethlehem some two thousand years ago. Then He began to reveal God's grand design in a greater way. God's design of mankind bearing His image, bearing His fruit, and reigning in life took on a whole new light.

📖 In John 1:14–18, the apostle John summarizes the way Jesus came and what He did. What do you find about Jesus in those verses? Whose image did Jesus reveal?

_____

_____

_____

_____

_____

Thinking of the matter of image, what additional insights do you glean from Hebrews 1:3?

_____

_____

_____

> *"And the Word became flesh, and dwelt among us, and we beheld His glory, glory as of the only begotten from the Father, full of grace and truth."*
>
> *John 1:14*

Jesus, who is God, is known as *"the Word,"* a picture of the clear expression and communication of God to man. To make Himself clearly understood He became flesh. He grew to manhood and dwelt among men and women, revealing the Father in all He spoke and all He did. He revealed the grace and truth of God in greater measure than ever before as He came to explain the Father and the Father's will. *"He is the radiance of His glory,"* a statement pointing to Jesus as the outshining or splendor-filled display of the Father's glory showing exactly what the Father is like. *"He is the exact representation of His nature"* or *"the express image,"* a second statement focusing on how Jesus revealed the image of God precisely. The Greek word translated *"exact representation"* is the word *charakter,* which literally refers to an impression such as one made by a die cut or a seal. It is an image corresponding exactly to a pattern. Jesus was the exact image of God the Father, being one with Him in every way and revealing what He is like to men and women wherever He went, whatever He did.

What kind of fruit did Jesus bear in revealing the Father? Read the sampling of verses listed below and summarize the kind of fruit that was evident in His life.

> *"Christ . . . is the image of God."*
>
> *2 Corinthians 4:4*

Luke 2:46–47 (age 12)

_____

_____

Luke 4:22, 31–32 (age 30)

_____

_____

_____

Luke 4:36, 40; 5:15

_____

_____

_____

Luke 5:17–26

_____

_____

_____

Luke 5:32

_____

_____

_____

Jesus bore abundant fruit in His words, His deeds, and in the numerous lives He encountered and changed day after day.

Even from boyhood Jesus amazed the Jewish teachers and leaders with *"His understanding and His answers"* in their discussions at the Temple. When Jesus spoke in the synagogues or to crowds outdoors, the people were amazed, *"wondering at the gracious words."* They marveled at His teaching and the authority with which He spoke. He had authority over unclean spirits and healed all kinds of diseases. Not only did He heal physically, but also spiritually, as He declared certain individual's sins forgiven. He gave hope to anyone willing to repent of sin and follow Him. The fruit He bore in words and deeds revealed God. The lives changed day after day became a testimony of the abundant fruit of His life. What we have recorded in the Gospels is a sample, a quick synopsis, as John 21:25 declares, *"And there are also many other things Jesus did, which if they were written in detail, I suppose that even the world itself would not contain the books which were written."* Jesus truly lived a fruitful life as evidenced in His character, conduct, and the lives He radically changed.

📖 Did Jesus reign in life like God intended for the first Adam? Read Luke 8:22–25 and note your insights.

_____

_____

_____

_____

Jesus ruled over the creation in ways greater than Adam could have ever ruled. On the Sea of Galilee, He spoke to the *"fierce gale of wind"* and the *"surging waves,"* and they stopped and became calm. The disciples were amazed at this demonstration of power and authority over the winds and water. Luke 9:12–17 records that later He multiplied five loaves and two fish and fed five thousand men plus women and children.

📖 What do you discover about Jesus reigning in life in Luke 4:1–13?

_____

_____

_____

_____

What additional insights do you find in Hebrews 4:15?

_____

_____

_____

Jesus began His ministry with forty days of fasting. In that time, the devil tempted Jesus, offering Him a variety of ways to fulfill His needs and establish His Kingdom. Jesus saw through all of Satan's overtures because He thought like His Father; He listened to His Father; and He knew His Father's Word. Therefore, Jesus conquered each and every temptation the devil launched. Throughout Jesus' life on earth, He faced a host of temptations, temptations just like the ones we all face. In every situation, every circumstance, every opportunity to choose between good and evil, between the Father's will and a counterfeit will, Jesus made the right choice. He was *"without sin."* He reigned in life.

📖 Jesus did more than conquer daily temptations. What do you find about His victories in Revelation 1:4–5, 17–18? Read those verses and record your insights about our Lord Jesus.

_____

_____

_____

_____

On the island of Patmos, the apostle John received a revelation from the risen Christ in which He revealed Himself as *"the faithful witness"* and *"the first-born of the dead, and the ruler of the kings of the earth."* He stood as the risen Lord, *"the living One,"* who once was dead. He not only conquered every temptation, but on the Cross He also endured the wrath of God to pay for our sins. He was buried but rose on the third day, revealing that He had overcome death's grip. He holds *"the keys of death and Hades,"* showing that He is in charge, never to be challenged again. He reigned in life, in death, and ever reigns in eternity.

Jesus perfectly revealed the image of the Father, bore the Father's fruit and reigned in life and death. What does this mean to us? What was His focus as He lived and ministered? Look at these verses and give a brief description of His mission in life.

> **"For we do not have a high priest who cannot sympathize with our weaknesses, but One who has been tempted in all things as we are, yet without sin."**
>
> **Hebrews 4:15**

Matthew 20:28

_____

_____

_____

Luke 19:10

_____

_____

_____

John 17:1–4

_____

_____

_____

> "For Christ also died for sins once for all, the just for the unjust, in order that He might bring us to God, having been put to death in the flesh, but made alive in the spirit."
>
> **1 Peter 3:18**

Jesus stated very clearly that He came to serve others and ultimately _"to give His life a ransom for many."_ We who could not reign in life, who were enslaved to sin and self-centered living, He bought off the slave block with the ransom of His own lifeblood. He came _"to seek and to save that which was lost,"_—lost to God's image, lost to good fruit of any kind, lost to reigning in life. He came to do the Father's will, to give Himself so that people could know His life, eternal life. That would mean an experiential knowledge of the Father through Jesus Christ. That was His mission and our salvation.

📖 One of Christ's disciples, Peter, came to know Jesus Christ and understand His heart and His mission. Summarize what you find in 1 Peter 3:18, especially considering humanity's disconnected state.

_____

_____

_____

Peter summed up the mission of Jesus in one verse. Jesus came to die for sins _"once for all."_ He is the just one, the righteous one who died for us, the unrighteous ones. Why? So that He might bring us to God by His Spirit. He suffered the just punishment for our "Great Disconnect" from God and in His death and resurrection provided for the "Great Connection" back to God. We can now be connected to Him and His life forever. What an amazing Lord and Savior! What an amazing salvation!

 Are you connected to God through a personal relationship with Jesus Christ? Is He your Lord and Savior? If not, or if you are unsure, you can settle this issue now. At the back of this book is a section entitled, "How to Follow God." Read this section and call on the Lord Jesus, asking Him to forgive you of your sins and come into your life as **your** Lord and Savior. Make sure you have made the connection.

📖 First Corinthians 15 contains an extensive discussion on the resurrection, first of Christ and then of those who belong to Him. Look at 1 Corinthians 15:45, where we are introduced to Christ—"the Last Adam." Read 15:45–49 and record what you find about "the Last Adam."

Christ is called *"the Last Adam," "the second man,"* and is referred to as *"the heavenly,"* which could be translated "the heavenly One." Jesus came to earth from heaven as a man, but not an ordinary man. He is "heavenly," marked by the characteristics of heaven in His person and nature. His most important designation is as *"a life-giving spirit,"* a phrase rich in meaning. The Greek word for *"life-giving"* is *zōopoíeō,* which is rooted in two Greek words, *zōós* or *zoē* and *poieo.* *Zoē* refers to the essence of life in the spirit and soul. It is more than physical life on which the Greek word *bios* focuses (as in "biology," "biography"). *Zoē* is a nobler word, referring to more than just physical existence. It is the kind of life God possesses that He gives to man, enabling man to relate to Him. It is the best life God can give because it is His own. It is *real* life. When one receives "life" or *zoe* from God it is heaven's kind of life, eternal, everlasting, and relational. It is a God-kind of life with the quality of life found in the Last Adam.

The second part of *"life-giving"* is *poíeō,* which means to make or to create. It is the root word of the English word "poem" and can refer to a work of art or a masterpiece. The word for *"spirit"* (*pneúma*) refers to wind or breath in its root meaning. Just as Christ the Creator breathed physical and moral life into the dust of the first Adam and made him a *"living soul,"* so Christ, the Last Adam, breathes into the heart of a sinner and creates new life, making the person *"a new creation,"* one *"born again"* or "born from above" by the Spirit of God (2 Corinthians 5:17, John 3:3–8, Titus 3:4–6) Thus in 1 Corinthians 15:45 the phrase *"life-giving spirit"* could be translated "life-creating spirit" or "life-making spirit," pointing to the resurrected Last Adam as the Creator not only of the first human from the dust, but also of the new creation in which men and women are born or created anew from above by the Spirit of God. By Christ's creative work, redeemed men and women come alive! He enters into a new dimension, a spiritual dimension of life, God's kind of life, His quality of life. The Last Adam is the eternal-life Creator. He gives eternal life to all who, in repentance and faith, place their trust in Him for salvation, who become followers of the Lord Jesus, the resurrected Last Adam.

Let's see if we can sum up what God was up to in sending Jesus to earth? Second Corinthians 5:17 states, *"therefore, if anyone is in Christ, he is a new creation; old things have passed away; behold, all things have become new"* (NKJV). What was God up to? In the coming of Jesus we see the inauguration of **a new creation**, a creation in which connection to Jesus Christ means a new life, God's way. This new creation surpasses the old creation in many ways. This new creation means new life, a new way. What is the full meaning of this *"new creation"*? What was God doing, and how did it fit with His grand design? We will see in Day Four.

"But may it never be that I should boast, except in the cross of our Lord Jesus Christ, through which the world has been crucified to me, and I to the world. For neither is circumcision anything, nor uncircumcision, but a new creation."

Galatians 6:14–15

THE "GREAT CONNECTION" AND THE NEW CREATION

Word Study
NEW CREATION

Kainós, the Greek word translated "new" in *"new creation"* (2 Corinthians 5:17 [NKJV]; Galatians 6:15), means new in nature, kind, and quality versus *neos* (also translated "new"). *Neos* points to something new in time, temporarily new. *Kainós* is used of all the new things in God's new creation. When Jesus spoke, the people recognized *"a new teaching with authority"* (Mark 1:27), new in nature and quality. The new creation is a new kind of creation. It is part of the *"new covenant"* (Luke 22:20; 1 Corinthians 11:25; 2 Corinthians 3:6; Hebrews 8:8, 13; 9:15; 12:24) in which we *"walk in newness of life"* (Romans 6:4) with a "new self" (Ephesians 4:24). We are part of a *"new man"* made up of Jew and Gentile (Ephesians 2:15). We come to God "by a new and living way" (Hebrews 10:20) and walk obeying *"a new commandment"* (1 John 2:7, 8; 2 John 1:5). *"We serve in newness of the Spirit"* (Romans 7:6). We look forward to a new home—*"the new Jerusalem"* (Revelation 3:12; 21:2), part of the *"new heavens and a new earth"* (2 Peter 3:13; Revelation 21:1), where we will have a *"new name"* (Revelation 2:17) and we will know Jesus' *"new name"* (Revelation 3:12). We read of the *"new song"* of the elders and of the 144,000 (Revelation 5:9; 14:3) and we have the promise that ultimately God will make *"all things new"* (Revelation 21:5).

God has always had a grand design for a family of sons and daughters, a body of believers, an army of soldiers, a temple of living stones, a flock of following sheep, and a bride made up of saints. Each of those metaphors pictures a gathering of people united in heart, surrendered to one leader, filled with His purposes and reflecting His goals and desires. That was the design in Genesis chapter 1—men and women living out God's image, bearing fruit throughout the earth, and reigning in life.

Adam sinned and all was marred, but God's design was not abandoned. He sent Jesus Christ to bring about the "great connection" and with it the new creation marked by life, *zoe.* God has created a new race of "*zoē* people," those marked by the very life of Christ given at the new birth. How does His "zoe-life" manifest itself? What does this new creation look like, and what part does the Last Adam play? We will see in today's lesson.

What are the characteristics of this "life" that Christ gives us, His life with which He comes to indwell us? These are the characteristics of the new creation. What marks this new creation, this display of Christ's life in and through us? Let's begin by looking at Romans 8:28.

📖 Romans 8:28 is a familiar verse to many and it has something to show us about God's grand design. Read that verse and summarize what you find.

_____

_____

_____

What is that purpose toward which God is working all things together? Look at the next verse, Romans 8:29, and record your answer.

_____

_____

_____

God is the sovereign Lord, ever at work to fulfill His purposes. In the lives of His children He is causing *"all things to work together for good."* That does not mean all things are "good," but that He uses all things to reach His ultimate and very good purpose. This is not for all people, but for those who love and follow Him, for *"those who are called according to His purpose."* What is that purpose? That those called become *"conformed to the image of His Son."* We who are called are destined to be like, think like, look like, and act like Jesus. Like brothers often look and act alike, we are Jesus' *"brethren"* following in the line of the preeminent, resurrected one, the *"first-born among many brethren."* Romans 8:22–23 reminds us that right now we *"groan"* as does all creation waiting for God to bring in the fullness of this design, *"the redemption of our body."* God is at work shaping and forming to conform us to the image of Jesus. His design is still on line, still on track. Ultimately, we will be glorified, part of the promised resurrection package found in 1 Corinthians 15.

  What about bearing fruit in this "new creation"? Look at Romans 7:4, especially the last half of that verse. What is God's design for us?

_____

_____

_____

What additional truths do you see in Ephesians 2:10 and Matthew 5:16?

_____

_____

_____

_____

> *"Let your light shine before men in such a way that they may see your good works, and glorify your Father who is in heaven."*
>
> *Matthew 5:16*

Before Christ came, mankind tried to bear righteous fruit through obeying laws, either God's Law or a man-made law, a cultural code, or some other form of rule or ritual. Of course, mankind has never been successful at adhering to laws, man-made or divine. Before Christ came, mankind only bore fruit for death. Through Christ's death, those who trust in Him die to themselves, and in so doing, they abandon any human efforts to live according to the Law. Now, because He is raised from the dead, we too are raised to newness of life and are united to Him by faith. In this new union with Christ, God has designed that we bear fruit according to His purposes, the kind of fruit that is pleasing to God because it is coming from the life of His Son living in and through us. The life of the Son is the mark of the new creation—His image, His fruit. This fruit is the *"good works"* He has always planned for us to do. When we let our light shine in obedience to our Father, people will see the good works, recognize a different image (His image), and give honor to Him. What about His Reign?

  Look at Romans 5:17. What do you discover about reigning?

_____

_____

_____

Through Adam's sin, death reigned throughout the earth. Christ now reigns over sin and death through His own righteous death and resurrection and graciously offers that reigning life as a gift by faith. *"Those who receive the abundance of grace and of the gift of righteous"* have the opportunity now to *"reign in life,"* in all of life, through Jesus Christ. As we follow and obey and depend on Him, trusting Him day by day and moment by moment, we discover His reigning life in the situations we face daily. Because He reigns and as He reigns over us, we reign in life.

  Romans 6:3–14 describes the new life that we experience when we trust Christ. List some of the drastic changes when we become believers. How do we reign as Christians?

_____

_____

_____

> *"Therefore do not let sin reign in your mortal body that you should obey its lusts, . . . but present yourselves to God as those alive from the dead, and your members as instruments of righteousness to God."*
>
> *Romans 6:12–13*

Through the death, burial, and resurrection of Christ, the Father has worked a miracle. As He raised Christ from the dead, He has raised us in Christ so that we can walk in *"newness of life,"* new creation life. Walking by faith in Christ, we are no longer slaves to sin. Sin does not have to reign over us. As we live *"dead to sin"* and *"alive to God,"* with Christ reigning over us, we reign over sin. How does that work? On a day-by-day basis we must present our *"members,"* all the parts of our body, anything we think or do, to Christ as *"instruments of righteousness"* for Him to use for His purposes. When a lust or unrighteous desire of any kind suggests we act or speak unbecomingly, we must reject such a desire. Instead we should obey God and do His will. What results when we live according to God's will? We bear His Image, we bear His fruit, and we reign in life—the new creation at work.

A day is coming when this work will be completely visible in each and every child of God—when we receive a perfect resurrection body, what Romans 8:23 calls *"the redemption of our body."* Until this day comes, we wait on that hope, with confident expectation that God will fulfill all His Word. What will this time of heavenly resurrection be like?

📖 We have a glimpse in 1 Corinthians 15. Read verses 42–44 and describe the resurrection body.

_____

_____

_____

Who is responsible for seeing this come to pass according to verse 45?

_____

_____

_____

_____

What is the promise we have in 1 Corinthians 15:47–49?

_____

_____

_____

As we saw in Day Three, the Last Adam is a *"life-giving spirit."* He gives His kind of life, eternal life, conquering-death kind of life. The resurrection body He will give each of His children is an imperishable body, incapable of decay or death. It is marked by power, not weakness or sickness. It is a spiritual body not bound to this natural world. Just as we now bear the *"image of the earthy,"* a body made of dust, one day we will bear the "image of the heavenly," a body made like Christ's resurrection body.

📖 What additional insight do you find in Philippians 3:20–21 and Colossians 3:4?

_____

_____

_____

Did You Know?

OUR RESURRECTION BODIES

When we receive our resurrection bodies, we will literally shine. Our spirits will then be under full control of the Holy Spirit, and our new bodies will be rid of all that mars and scars, all the tarnish of sin and its curse. With our bodies transformed and minds clear of all that clouds, we will experience Matthew 13:43, *"then THE RIGHTEOUS WILL SHINE FORTH AS THE SUN in the kingdom of their Father."* We will be like Jesus. At His transfiguration, Peter, James, and John received a brief glimpse of the Son of Man in His kingdom. *"His face shone like the sun, and His garments became as white as light"* (Matthew 17:2). Mark 9:3 says, *"His garments became radiant and exceedingly white."* Peter later testified, *"we were eyewitnesses of His majesty"* (2 Peter 1:16). He will make us like that, shining like the sun, majestic in splendor. That is our destiny, fully conformed to the image of Christ.

We are foreigners on earth, dwelling in our temporary tents. Our true citizenship is in heaven, our true home. From there we await the coming of our Lord Jesus. He is the Savior from sin and from the curse of this fallen body and this fallen earth. When He returns, He will transform *"the body of our humble state"*—the weak, failing, faltering body we have now—into *"conformity with the body of His glory"*—His strong, unfailing, never faltering resurrection body. He has the power to do so, since He reigns over all. We will be *"revealed with Him in glory"* for all creation to see. This is the promised *"redemption of our body"* found in Romans 8:23 and described in 1 Corinthians 15.

In 1 Corinthians 15:50–54, we find how God will transform our bodies. He has promised a new body as part of the new creation. Paul declares confidently, *"we shall all be changed."* How? Suddenly, when the Lord orders the last trumpet to sound, the dead will be raised and we who are alive will be raised and changed with them. At that point, death is totally vanquished, *"swallowed up"* in the victory of Christ over death. Then the image of God will be complete in each of His children. We will be fully conformed to the image of His Son in spirit, soul, and body along with all the rest of His family. What a wonder and what a joy to be part of such a family, such a new creation! Now fast-forward to the ultimate future in Revelation 22.

📖 Look at Revelation 22, the final chapter of the Bible. What do you find in verses 3–5 about the subject of our image, our fruit, and our reign? Note your insights below.

_____

_____

_____

What a glorious, majestic, wonderful reality we will experience in the New Jerusalem. We, His bondservants, shall serve Jesus Christ, the Lamb, **bearing the fruit** of His life within as we follow Him throughout eternity. We will live forever as His Bride by His side **bearing His image**; His name will be on our foreheads, a picture of our identity with Him in every detail. He owns us, claims us as His own, and displays us as His own. What a security we have in Christ! Walking in the light of His presence, we will **reign** with Him, a reign marked by His victory over death and darkness. The life of the Last Adam will be fully seen in His reign with His bride—His image fully revealed; His fruit multiplied a million-fold and more; His reign unquestioned and unconquerable; and His light unquenchable. What a Lord we follow and what a Life we can expect!

Word Study
TRANSFORM

The Greek word *metaschēmatizō* and *metamorphóō* are both translated *"transform,"* the first word being found in Philippians 3:21 and the second in 2 Corinthians 3:18. In Philippians 3:21, we find the transformation Christ will enact when He gives us resurrection bodies. This will be a transition from our weak, frail, dust-made bodies into conformity with His strong, lasting, resurrection body. The second word describes the transfiguration of Jesus when His countenance was transformed from an earthly one to a heavenly one—His face shone as the sun, and His clothes became bright white. The transformation spoken of in Romans 12:2 and 2 Corinthians 3:18 is also a translation of the second word. It refers to an internal transformation already begun on the inside. We are now being transformed into the image of Christ from one degree of glory to another.

FOR ME TO FOLLOW CHRIST

The Last Adam DAY FIVE

So what are we to do now? What is God up to now, today in your life and mine? How is He carrying out His grand design in each of our lives? How does His design apply in the day-to-day matters of work and school, bills and budgets, sports and hobbies, church and ministry, and all the other things that make up life on Planet Earth?

When we look in the Scriptures, we see two factors at work—we see God's **promise** to us and we see God's **process** with us. His **promise** is His guaran-

> *"And put on the new self, which in the likeness of God has been created in righteousness and holiness of the truth."*
>
> **Ephesians 4:24**

tee of the work He will do. The **process** is the place where we join Him and cooperate with Him. Both His promise and the process combine to bring the changes He desires. In the process, the changes take place. Let's look at those factors as they relate to **image**, **fruit**, and **reigning** in life.

We have already seen God's promise in Romans 8:28–29 about Him conforming us to the image of His Son. In another letter, Paul gave testimony of his amazement at the adequacy of God in touching and changing people by His Spirit. Second Corinthians 3:3–18 contains that testimony of the change that occurs when a person turns to the Lord Jesus and begins following Him. Verse 18 contains a **promise** of what God is doing.

📖 Read 2 Corinthians 3:3–18, especially verse 18 and record your insights into that promise.

_____

_____

_____

_____

_____

When a person turns to the Lord in repentance and faith, he or she changes from the bondage of law or religion or ritual to the freedom of a relationship with Christ. As the Spirit of God does His work of convicting and convincing and we surrender to Him, He changes us. That change lasts forever. As a believer walks through life, he or she experiences the Lord at work moving him or her from one level of glory to another level, making the image of Christ more and more evident and real in that person's life. This is the **promise** of the **new life** that goes with the **new covenant**. The **new covenant** is the agreement at the heart of the **new creation** God is bringing to pass. Because of His work in us, we can be confident of the changes He is bringing about in our lives, changes that assure His image will continue to show through more and more.

What is the **process** through which He is working to make that promise real in each of our lives?

_____

_____

_____

_____

📖 Look at 2 Corinthians 4:6–11. What are some of the things we go through, and how does God use that to reveal Himself to others?

_____

_____

_____

What is Paul's confidence (and our confidence) in 2 Corinthians 4:16–18?

_____

_____

_____

We are earthen vessels, simple jars of clay, in which God has placed the treasure of the life of Jesus. As weak vessels, we face a variety of pressure points, tight spots, and difficult circumstances, especially as we follow Christ. Yet each of these struggles is not the end of the story. We may be afflicted, but we are not crushed. We may be perplexed, but we do not have to despair in the face of the perplexity. We may be persecuted, but God never forsakes us. Even when we are struck down, we are never destroyed. In each of those situations, the life, the image of Jesus, the fruit of Jesus, and His reigning life can be seen and experienced as we yield and trust Him. While we see our outer bodies decaying, weakening, even struggling, we can know that God is doing a renewing work, making us newer and newer on the inside. Ultimately, Jesus will reveal the promised *"eternal weight of glory far beyond all comparison."* Then, all the "stuff" we endured for Christ's sake will be seen clearly as well worth it. Like Paul, we must walk in faith, keeping an eternal perspective knowing that all we see now and all we endure in this timeframe is not all there is. We are in the foyer of life—the grand design will be fully revealed in the grand celebration of eternity.

 What are some of the things you are facing now? Look at the chart below and list some of the matters you are dealing with. Then look for ways you see God working things together for good, ways you see Him working His image, His fruit, and His reign in you and through you. Perhaps you could write a prayer about the situation you are facing.

What God is Using to Shape His Image in Me Part of the "All Things" of Romans 8:28 What I am Facing	Ways I See God Working His Image, Fruit, and Reign My Prayer to God about This
"Afflicted" (tight spot/pressure point)	
"Perplexed" (confusion/unanswered questions)	
"Persecuted" (harassed)	
"Struck Down" (wounded in some way)	
Evidence of Decaying (physical weakness)	
"Momentary light affliction"(temporary tough spot)	

Colossians 3:10–11 also speaks of the **process** of Christ's **image** becoming real in our lives and the kind of **fruit** we should be bearing. There must be cooperation with the Lord in this matter of bearing fruit. Read through Colossians 3:1–14, especially verses 5–14, which reveal the part we play as we join Him in the process of bearing fruit. In the left column of the chart on the next page, list the "PUT OFF" elements of the old self, and in the right column list the "PUT ON" elements of the new life He has given us.

"For we who live are constantly being delivered over to death for Jesus' sake, that the life of Jesus also may be manifested in our mortal flesh."

2 Corinthians 4:11

BEARING CORRUPT FRUIT WHAT I SHOULD BE "PUTTING OFF"	BEARING GOOD FRUIT WHAT I SHOULD BE "PUTTING ON"

> "In reference to your former manner of life, …lay aside the old self, which is being corrupted in accordance with the lusts of deceit."
>
> Ephesians 4:22

 How is the Spirit of God working in your life to make the **reign** of Christ more real to you? Thinking of the Lord's **process** in your life, recall the truths we saw in Romans 5 and 6, and, in the space below, write some of the ways you have begun to *"reign in life through the One, Christ Jesus."* Look at the members of your body listed in the left column and fill in any others about which God speaks to you. In the right column, describe ways you have yielded or ways God is pinpointing you to yield to God—practical ways you can reign in life.

"THE MEMBERS OF YOUR BODY"	WAYS I AM YIELDING MY MEMBERS "AS INSTRUMENTS OF RIGHTEOUSNESS"
Eyes	
Ears	
Tongue	
Hands	
Feet	

As in the life of Jesus, so in our lives His Image, His Fruit, and His Reign should be seen in us **and** be working through us in . . .

- ❏ our **Character** (heart attitudes and direction of life),
- ❏ our **Conduct** (choices and actions), and
- ❏ in **Changed** lives (people touched with the Word of God), which includes:

    Converts (those who **come to Christ** or those still **considering** or those **refusing** what I have said or done) and

    Christians (encouraged and helped in their walk).

 In the spaces below, write some ways you have seen God bearing His fruit in your life.

Your character (attitudes, heart condition, choices)

_____

_____

_____

Your conduct (choices and actions)

_____

_____

Converts, or those considering coming to Christ or those refusing what I have said or done in my witness of the gospel

_____

_____

_____

Christians (encouraged and helped in their walk)

_____

_____

_____

Image, fruit, reign—three words that speak volumes about God's grand design and about the work of Christ as our Creator and the Last Adam as our Re-Creator. He is *"a life-giving spirit,"* or that could be translated "a life-creating spirit." Either way, He is our Creator at work, making His life real to us, for us, in us, and through us. We have begun the adventure of becoming like Him. Be encouraged! He is not finished working in your life. We have His promise, *"He who began a good work in you will perfect it until the day of Christ Jesus"* (Philippians 1:6). He is seeing to it that we bear fruit like that spoken of in John 15, where He reminds us that *"apart from Me you can do nothing,"* but connected and dependent on Him we can bear *"fruit . . . more fruit . . . much fruit."* We can also be confident that in our walk with the Last Adam, He will keep working so that His reign is more evident in additional areas of our lives. Trust Him. He is working as a life-giving spirit, and one day, He will bring to pass all His promises of a new body that will live in a new home—forever.

Spend some time talking to Him about these things.

Lord, I stand in awe of Your creation—the sun, moon, stars, and planets, the plants and animals, all that lives in the seas and sky, all the wonders of mountain and plains, rivers and lakes, deserts and polar ice caps. More than that I stand in awe of how You have worked in first creating me and then in re-creating me—destined to be fully in Your image. I praise You for the fruit You have produced in my life. I give You the honor and credit for all the good works You have done through me, because I know that apart from Your grace they would never have been done. I would have faltered and failed with counterfeit works. When all is said and done, those would have been useless to me, to others, or to You. Thank You also that You have begun Your reign in my life and that You are showing me what it means to reign in life through Your power and wisdom, through Your life at work in me. What a privilege to have You at work in me and to know how much You love and care for me, in each and every detail of each and every day. Even the tough times are orchestrated through Your careful wisdom—customized for my life. Thank You. I also thank You that one day I will be like You, as You have promised. *"It has not appeared as yet what we shall be. We know that, when He appears, we shall be like Him, because we shall see Him just as He is"* (1 John 3:2). Because I have that promise and my *"hope fixed"* on You, may I be diligent in purifying myself as You are pure (1 John 3:3) and be better prepared in heart and life for Your return and the fulfillment of the new creation that You as the Last Adam have brought to pass. In Jesus' name, Amen.

The Last Adam is our Creator at work, making His Life real to us, for us, in us, and through us.

In the space below, record your own prayer or a journal entry about the truths you have seen this week. Spend some time talking to the Lord about these things and what they mean to you.

_____

_____

_____

_____

_____

_____

_____

_____

_____

_____

Christ The Seed

CHRIST BRINGING THE FULLNESS OF GOD'S PROMISED SALVATION

God created men and women with the opportunity to walk in fellowship and oneness with Himself. Amos 3:3 asks the question, *"Can two walk together, unless they are agreed?"* (NKJV). This question sums up the essential factor for any relationship—two must agree in heart and mind to walk together. Adam and Eve walked together with one another and with the Lord at first, until they agreed with the Serpent. Then, they walked away from the truth of God's Word and the command of God's heart. At that point, their agreement with God shattered and their fellowship with one another turned to disagreement, shame, fear, and blame. Their broken fellowship with God made them run and hide from Him.

God still came looking for them, however, asking questions about their strange behavior, seeking to bring them to an honest answer about their sin. Here is an amazing truth. With His confrontation about their sin came a meeting with His mercy. He did not slay them the moment they sinned; His justice could have demanded that action if He chose. Instead, He had a word of mercy and grace. It is that word of mercy and grace that we will explore in this lesson.

What could God do to bring man back to where He wanted him to be? What would God do to accomplish that? What would it take? It would take a "seed"—planted, broken, dying, rising in new life, bearing new fruit. Our salvation is all about a "seed," the seed known as Jesus Christ, who He is, what He has done, and what He is now doing to bring us into the fullness of His redemption and His fruit. We will see this Seed and the salvation He brings as we walk through a many-century journey in the Scriptures. That journey will take us into the heart of God and into the awesome wisdom of His plan for the salvation of mankind and the exaltation of His Son. This will be a journey that can speak to any man or woman, for the Lord desires to bring His salvation to *"every tribe and tongue and people and nation"* (Revelation 5:9). In this lesson, we will see how God has chosen to bring the fullness of His salva-

Our salvation is all about a seed, the Seed Christ, who He is, what He has done, and what He is now doing to bring us into the fullness of Himself and His redemption.

tion through Christ the Seed to many, one heart at a time. Let's begin our journey at the very beginning of recorded time.

THE GENESIS CONNECTIONS— FROM EDEN TO EGYPT

From the start in Genesis, we find God revealing His purposeful design and His personal salvation. He wasted no time in bringing that revelation to Adam and Eve. Today, we will see Him at work in the Garden of Eden.

📖 Read Genesis 3:1–15 focusing on verse 15. What was God's promise in verse 15? Record your insights.

_____

_____

_____

_____

What are the two seeds?

_____

_____

What will happen to the seed of the serpent?

_____

_____

What will happen to the seed of the woman?

_____

_____

Word Study
ENMITY

"Enmity" is the translation of the Hebrew word *eybah* which refers to being an enemy, one hostile against another. It is rooted in the word *ayab* which means to hate, to treat another as hostile. *Eybah* is found five times in the Old Testament. In Numbers 35:21–22 it refers to someone who has murdered another out of hatred. In Ezekiel 25:15 God declares judgment on the Philistines for their *"everlasting enmity"* against Israel, seen in their *"revenge,"* their *"vengeance with scorn,"* and their desire and commitment to destroy. In Ezekiel 35:5, He speaks against Mount Seir, the place of the Edomites, for their *"everlasting enmity"* against Israel seen in their desire to destroy and conquer them (35:6–14). In verse 11, the Lord describes their enmity as marked by *"anger,"* *"envy,"* *"hatred,"* and the desire to consume and make *"desolate."* That is the kind of enmity between the seed of the woman and the seed of the serpent that began in the Garden of Eden.

A war has begun. Enmity would now exist between the serpent and the woman and between her seed and the serpent's seed. While the "seed" is singular referring ultimately to a man to come, in the scope of history it points first to two types of descendants—the seed of the serpent—all those who carry the nature of the serpent in their hearts, hating the Lord and hating those who follow Him—versus the seed of the woman. The seed of the serpent would be at enmity with the seed of the woman, which includes all who walk by faith and thus have a heart like God's—those who hate evil, love righteousness, and stand against the nature of the serpent. These obey the will and the word of God. Prophetically, the Lord was pointing to one offspring of woman, the Lord Jesus Christ, who would come to crush the serpent's head. The Lord made it clear that the seed of the woman would be a man—*"He shall bruise"* the serpent on the head, bringing a fatal blow to him. The serpent, on the other hand, would bruise the seed of the woman on the heel, inflicting a wound but not destroying that man, a picture of the coming crucifixion of Christ. He would die but rise again. His death and resurrection would result in the deliverance from sin and death as well as the destruction of Satan and all evil. We will see how this is worked out in other Scriptures.

📖 How did Eve understand this promise? Look carefully at Genesis 4:1–2 with 4:25–26 and record what you discover.

_____

_____

_____

_____

With the birth of her first son, Eve made a somewhat puzzling statement, *"I have gotten a man from the LORD"* (KJV) or *"I have gotten a manchild with the help of the LORD"* (NASB). Some translate the Hebrew for "gotten" (*qanah*) as "created" or "acquired." The "I" is emphatic, so this could be a statement of pride, **"I** have created a man." If her emphasis was on bearing a son *"from the LORD,"* she could be pointing to Cain as the Lord's fulfillment of His promise, the seed of woman now on earth to deliver them. However, Cain was not that "seed" who would crush the serpent's head. He was like the serpent, a murderer. Later, at the birth of Seth, she said, *"God has appointed* [placed] *me another offspring in place of Abel"* (4:25). Here is a word of hope. Her focus was on the gift God had placed in her life, on what God had done, not what she had created. The word "offspring" is literally "seed," a reference to Seth as the God-given seed in the line of the godly Abel. Luke 4:38 marks Seth as in the line of the seed through which Jesus came.

📖 The next time we see a reference to a "seed" is in God's call to a man named Abram in Ur of the Chaldeans. Read Genesis 12:1–7. What were God's promises in verses 1–3?

_____

_____

_____

_____

What did God say in verse 7? [Note that a literal translation of the term "your descendants" is "your seed."]

_____

_____

_____

_____

God promised Abram that He would make him *"a great nation," "bless"* him, and make his *"name great."* He promised blessings to those who blessed Abram and curses to those who cursed him. With that came the promise, *"in you all the families of the earth shall be blessed,"* quite a statement in light of the consequences of sin that had been handed to Adam and Eve. God promised Abram that his descendants would be given the land on which he stood, the land of Canaan. Remember that the translation of *"your descendants"* is literally "your seed." This distinction will be helpful as we look at other scriptures about Abram's "seed." It is important to understand some of the history that transpired after Abram

---

Put Yourself In Their Shoes

THE WAR

From the beginning, God said there would be enmity between the two seeds. That includes those in the line of each seed. Cain revealed the nature of the serpent and killed his brother, the righteous Abel who walked in faith. There are always two lines warring, the godly line who place faith in the Lord and those who do not. The godly line went through Seth, not Cain. Noah and his family were righteous and the rest of the world perished. Nimrod and Babel went astray. Abram was declared righteous by faith. The seed would go through Abraham. The line of the seed was promised through Isaac, not Ishmael, then Jacob not Esau, then through Judah, not the firstborn Reuben, and later through David, not the firstborn Eliab. When Jesus was born, the war continued—Herod tried to slaughter Him. The devil tried to derail and destroy Him. Even the disciples spoke against His mission of crucifixion. To Peter's objections, Jesus declared, *"Get behind Me, Satan."* Today, the war continues. Will the righteous seed ultimately prevail? Definitely, yes!

entered Canaan. As Abram walked with God, the Lord continued to assure him of His call and His promises to him. After Lot separated from Abram, God promised him once again that all the land of Canaan belonged to him and his descendants' seed (Genesis 13:15). Years passed, and Abram began to question how all this could be, since he and Sarai had borne no child. It was essential for Abram to have a son, if the promises were to come to pass.

In Genesis 15, God came to Abram once again and promised him a son and descendants as numerous as the stars of heaven. Abram believed God could and God would, and God counted his faith *"as righteousness."* In order to assure him further, God instructed Abram to cut several sacrifices in two and lay them in order. God then passed through them in the form of a smoking oven and flaming torch. God was confirming His promises with a covenant ritual used in Abram's day. He promised once again, *"to your descendants* [seed] *I have given this land"* (Genesis 15:18). When Abram was ninety-nine years old, this covenant was again affirmed (Genesis 17) and the promises repeated—a nation, a seed/descendants, a land, and God's blessing. In that meeting God changed Abram's name to Abraham and Sarai's to Sarah. He called Abraham to circumcise every male in his household as a sign of this covenant agreement and promise. A year after completing this sign of circumcision, Abraham and Sarah experienced God's gift of a son named Isaac, the promised son, the promised seed.

> Some twenty to twenty-five years after the birth of Isaac, God presented a test for Abraham and prepared him for the revelation of yet another truth about his seed. Read Genesis 22:1–18, focusing on verses 15–18. What do you find in verse 17 about Abraham's *"descendants"* or his *"seed"*?

_____

_____

_____

_____

What promise is made concerning the "seed" in verse 18?

_____

_____

On Mount Moriah on this momentous day, the Angel of the LORD had a word of revelation for Abraham concerning his descendants and his "seed." He promised to *"greatly bless"* Abraham and *"greatly multiply"* his seed or his descendents *"as the stars of the heavens, and as the sand which is on the seashore,"* a promise of a great nation greatly blessed. Then the Lord said, *"your seed shall possess the gate of their enemies."* There is an important truth found in the original Hebrew text that we need to see. The first instance of the word "seed" is plural, referring to *"descendants"* (22:17). The second instance of "seed" in verse 17 is masculine singular so that the phrase should read *"your* **seed** [singular] *shall possess the gate of* **his** [masculine, singular] *enemies."* The same is true in verse 18: *"in your* **seed** [masculine, singular] *all the nations of the earth shall be blessed."* What does this mean? The Angel of the LORD gave Abraham revelation concerning the seed that would be born to him. The "seed" that would come through his descendants would rule as a conqueror of all His enemies and would be a blessing to all the nations of the earth. Later, we will discover more about this Son of Abraham.

"And in you all the families of the earth shall be blessed."

Genesis 12:3c

Abraham knew that the selection of a wife for Isaac was a crucial choice in God's scheme concerning his descendants, his "seed." Genesis 24 gives the account of that choice, a remarkable picture of the ways of God in fulfilling His will. Concerning this matter of the "seed," we read in Genesis 24:60 the blessing of Rebekah's family spoken as she prepared to leave and join Isaac in Canaan. The Hebrew language uses the masculine, singular for "seed" in the last phrase of verse 60. Rebekah's family blessing is similar to the blessing spoken by God for Abraham and Sarah. There appears to be a prophetic word given in what they say. The last half of the verse literally reads, *"And may your seed possess the gate of those who hate him,"* pointing to one who would rule over his enemies. What more can we learn of the promised seed?

📖 What did God promise Isaac in Genesis 26:2–5?

_____

_____

_____

When Isaac thought of going to Egypt to escape the famine in Canaan, God appeared to him and warned him not to go. Instead, he was to stay in Gerar. God promised to bless him as He had promised Abraham—promising the land, multiplied descendants, and a seed through which all the nations of the earth would be blessed. The promise transferred to another generation; the hope remained strong. Even in the face of a famine and uncertain days ahead God called Isaac to keep looking to Him.

God blessed Isaac and Rebekah with twin sons, Esau and Jacob. How would this family turn out? Though questionable in how it happened, the birthright and the blessing went to the younger Jacob. As a result, conflict arose between Esau and Jacob, so Jacob left for Haran. On his way he stopped to spend the night. There the Lord met him in a dream.

📖 Read Genesis 28:10–22. What did the Lord promise Jacob according to Genesis 28:13–15?

_____

_____

_____

What was Jacob's response in Genesis 28:16–22?

_____

_____

_____

As the Lord had promised Abraham and Isaac, so He promised Jacob the land on which he was occupying, a great host of descendants to dwell in the land, and blessings to *"all the families of the earth"* through his seed. In addition, God promised to be with him, to guard and keep him, to bring him back to this promised land, and to accomplish all He had spoken. As a result, Jacob surrendered his life to the Lord to follow Him as God.

The Lord reminded Jacob of His promises when he was laboring in Haran (Genesis 31:3). Later in Genesis 35:9–12, when God called Jacob back to Bethel, He reaffirmed His promises as well as Jacob's new name "Israel."

"... and your seed shall possess the gate of [His] enemies. And in your seed all the nations of the earth shall be blessed."

Genesis 22:17b–18a

Jacob returned to Bethel, then moved south, and eventually moved to Egypt, where his twelve sons and their families would live for several generations. The promises of God for Abraham's descendants were beginning to be fulfilled in greater ways.

 APPLY God works in meticulous ways to fulfill His will. We see this in the lives of Abraham, Isaac, and Jacob. He does the same in each of His children's lives—including your life. What is God saying to you as you consider His ways and His words, not only in the past, but now, in **your** present? Stop and talk to Him about these things.

_____

_____

_____

_____

_____

We have seen much in Day One. What would be the story of the seed of woman, the seed of Abraham, Isaac, and Jacob in God's plan? Through which of the twelve tribes would "The Seed" (the Messiah) come? We will begin to see in Day Two.

DAY TWO

THE SEED OF JACOB, JUDAH, AND DAVID

When Jacob moved to Egypt with his eleven sons to join Joseph and his two sons, they were fulfilling a prophecy God had given to Abraham. His descendants would dwell in Egypt four hundred years and then return to the promised land of Canaan. How would the promised "seed" fit into all this? What is the common thread throughout the generations?

When Jacob was about to die, he gathered all his sons to bless and pass on the word God had given for each of them. In doing this, he declared prophetically what the final days would hold—*"what shall befall you in the days to come"* (Genesis 49:1). Of particular importance is what he said to Judah.

📖 Read Genesis 49:8–12. What promise did he declare in verse 8?

_____

_____

What do you find in verse 9?

_____

_____

_____

What added picture did Jacob give in verse 10?

_____

_____

Did You Know?

JUDAH

The Tribe of Judah was destined to rule over Israel. In the tribal order traveling through the wilderness, Judah led (see Numbers 10:14), and Judah was noted for being the largest tribe (see Numbers 1:26–27; 26:19–22). King David came from this tribe, as did his son Solomon and the succeeding kings who ruled over Judah—a line of kings lasting 425 years from David's reign beginning in 1011 BC until Judah was overthrown by the Babylonians in 586 BC. Even after this the line continued through leaders like Zerubbabel (see Haggai 2:20–23). His genealogy shows the line of Judah never ceased (Matthew 1:1–17; Luke 3:23–38). Jesus is **the Lion of the Tribe of Judah** (see Revelation 5:5).

What is the promise concerning "Shiloh"?

_____

_____

In Jacob's meeting with his sons, he declared that Judah's descendants would be a triumphant tribe, standing *"on the neck of* [his] *enemies"* and leading his brothers' tribes. Like a strong lion, Judah would rule. The ruler's scepter would be his permanently. Jacob also gave a prophetic word about "Shiloh" coming—*"to him shall be the obedience of the peoples,"* a clear picture of ruling fully and ruling well. What did this mean? In the context, *Shiloh* is a symbolic word pointing to the Messiah. He is the one the peoples will obey. Shiloh is Lord and Ruler.

Many years later, we read a further prophecy about the central role of Judah. Just before Israel went into the land of Canaan, Balaam prophesied and spoke of Israel ruling as a lion, devouring its prey (see Numbers 23:24). When he spoke of the king of Israel and his kingdom, he made it clear that both king and kingdom would be powerful (24:7). This king would come out of Egypt. He would be marked by great strength and reign over all his enemies. In Numbers 24:9, Balaam then quoted Jacob's prophecy (see Genesis 49:9) about the coming ruler who would rule *"as a lion."* What more can we learn about this ruler, and what connections can we discover regarding the Seed that will come from the tribe of Judah?

In the line of Judah, a most significant event occurred in the home of Jesse of Bethlehem, the birth of a son named David, the eighth son in the family. He became Israel's second king and ruled in great power. When David had won many battles and ruled unchallenged, he desired to honor God by building Him a permanent house to replace the portable wilderness Tabernacle (see 2 Samuel 7:1–3). The prophet Nathan encouraged David to pursue that desire, but God immediately told Nathan this was not to be; David's son Solomon would build the House, the Temple in Jerusalem (7:4–7). With this revelation, the Lord had another word for David.

📖 Read 2 Samuel 7:8–29 for the full story. What did the Lord promise David in verses 11–14? [Note that a literal translation from Hebrew for the word "descendant" in the NASB is literally "seed."] For additional insights look at Hebrews 1:1–5, especially verse 5.

_____

_____

_____

_____

What do you discover in verse 16?

_____

_____

_____

What was David's response according to verse 18?

_____

_____

Did You Know?
THE LION KING

All that Jacob prophesied about Judah being like a lion (see Genesis 49:9) is ultimately fulfilled in Jesus Christ. Revelation 5:5 reveals the Lamb who is also *"the Lion that is from the tribe of Judah."* It is Jesus Christ who has *"overcome"* and is able to rule and reign as *"the Root of David."*

Put Yourself In Their Shoes
GOD'S PROMISES FOR HIS PEOPLE

The promises of God are very special to His people. In Psalm 89 (especially verses 3–4, 24–29, and 36–37), one God-follower, Ethan the Ezrahite, wrote of the covenant faithfulness of God to establish David's seed forever and make his throne everlasting. He spoke in permanent terms—*"I will establish your seed forever, and build up your throne to all generations."* He used lasting images—*"his throne as the days of heaven," "endure . . . as the sun . . . established . . . like the moon, and the witness in the sky"* (89:29, 36, 37). The "son" of David would reign. The Psalmist and those who read his words could rejoice and sing praises in light of this truth because it rested in the unalterable oath of God (*"I have sworn"*) found in the LORD's covenant with David—if his descendants proved unfaithful, God would deal with them accordingly, but He also guaranteed that He would fulfill His covenant promises. Psalm 89 is ultimately a statement and prayer of hope.

What other insights do you glean from David's prayer, especially verses 25–29? What connection do you see to the promised seed?

_____

_____

_____

_____

_____

The Lord sent Nathan to David with a clear message and several promises. David would not build the Temple, but God would build him a house and a kingdom that would endure forever. Of special significance is the promise of a *"descendant"* or a *"seed," "a son,"* who would *"come forth from you"*—and the promise—*"and I will establish his kingdom . . . and . . . the throne of his kingdom forever."* That is a double reference to David's son Solomon **and** to his future seed, the son of David, the Messiah. Hebrews 1:5 contains a quote from 2 Samuel 7:14 that refers directly to the Son of God, Jesus. The kingdom and the throne that God would establish would endure forever. David heard all Nathan said and *"went in and sat before the Lord."* He prayed, thanking the Lord for His many blessings and His clear promises. David asked the Lord to fulfill all His Word, the fullness of His promise—*"do as Thou hast spoken"* (7:25). David praised the Lord and prayed for God's name to be exalted, for all His purposes for His people to be fulfilled. He asked that his household continue forever and know the blessing of God. The blessing of God makes life real and wonderful, and that blessing is found in the "seed" God would send. This "house" and the "blessing" would be inseparably tied to the "seed" of David.

Doctrine

THE SEED NAMED JESUS

One day, the Angel Gabriel would give fuller revelation of the Seed to come, declaring to Mary:

And you shall name Him Jesus. He will be great, and will be called the Son of the Most High; and the Lord God will give Him the throne of His father David; and He will reign over the house of Jacob forever; and His kingdom will have no end. (Luke 1:31b-33)

📖 Several psalms speak of David and God's promises about one who would sit on his throne. One of those is Psalm 132, where we find the hope of the coming and reigning seed of David. Read Psalm 132:10–12 and record your insights.

_____

_____

_____

_____

_____

The psalmist, thinking of God's promises to David, prayed that the Lord not turn His face away from His anointed. The Hebrew word for "anointed" is *mashchiyth,* the root word of "messiah," which in turn is translated in the New Testament Greek as *christos* or "Christ." In verse 11, he expressed his confidence in God to set on the throne of David *"the fruit"* of his body or his seed. Verse 12 adds that if David's other sons walk in obedience they *"also shall sit upon"* that throne. The Messiah, the fruit or seed of David, is guaranteed the throne of David.

📖 The writers of the Psalms were not alone in proclaiming the coming of this seed of David. Isaiah was one of the most vocal. Read the following verses from Isaiah and note your insights about the one who would come.

Isaiah 7:14

_____

_____

_____

_____

Isaiah 9:6–7

_____

_____

_____

_____

Isaiah 11:1–5

_____

_____

_____

_____

_____

God commanded King Ahaz to ask a sign from Him that would assure the king of protection from enemy forces (see Isaiah 7:1–13). Ahaz refused to ask, so God gave him a sign. A virgin would conceive and bear a son whose name would be Immanuel, meaning "God is with us," the promise of God's presence with him and the nation. A few verses later, Isaiah again focused on a promised son. This son would be a ruler with the government resting on His shoulders. His names would describe Him and His rule— Wonderful (or "a Wonder"—causing awe), Counselor (full of wisdom), Mighty God (overwhelmingly strong), Eternal Father (always leading and caring for His people as a compassionate Father), Prince of Peace (one who brings peace and maintains peace). This ruler will have the right and authority to reign on the throne of David in a kingdom of peace, justice, and righteousness—forever!

This son would clearly be a descendant of David, *"a shoot"* springing from the stem of Jesse, David's father, as a *"branch from his roots."* Isaiah 4:2 also mentions *"the Branch of the LORD."* This branch will bear fruit. He will have the anointing of the Spirit of the Lord resting or abiding on Him. He will be marked by wisdom and understanding, counsel and strength, knowledge and the fear of the Lord—all that is necessary to rule righteously. The prophets promised that the Messiah, *"Immanuel," "the Branch,"* would have heavenly perception for every earthly situation, always making righteous decisions based on absolute truth. This one will rule over the kingdom of God. One day, Jesus, the Messiah, will reign in full authority over Israel and the world, and He will bring about new heavens and a new earth. What a ruler, and what a kingdom God promised through His prophets!

What else do we find in the Scriptures about this "seed"? What connections do we find in the New Testament? We will begin to see in Day Three.

The prophets promised that the Messiah, "Immanuel," "the Branch," would have heavenly perception for every earthly situation, always making righteous decisions based on absolute truth.

"JESUS CHRIST, THE SON OF DAVID, THE SON OF ABRAHAM"

The New Testament opens with these words—*"The book of the genealogy of Jesus Christ, the son of David, the son of Abraham."* In one statement we find the connection between Jesus Christ and the promised seed of the Old Testament. The genealogy of Jesus in Matthew obviously highlights the fact that He is a descendant of Abraham and David (see Matthew 1:1, 17). Luke traces His genealogy back through David and Abraham, all the way to Adam (see Luke 3:23–38).

Many did not know these facts about Jesus at His birth, but they would later proclaim these truths with confidence. What can we learn from the New Testament account of the birth and life of Jesus? We will begin to see in today's lesson.

📖 When we turn to the pages of the New Testament, we see many of the Old Testament promises beginning to be fulfilled. Read Luke 1:26–38. What promise was given to Mary?

_____

_____

_____

_____

What connection to David do you find in verse 32?

_____

_____

_____

_____

What connection to Jacob do you find in verse 33?

_____

_____

_____

What connection to God do you find in verses 32 and 35?

_____

_____

_____

_____

The angel Gabriel told Mary she would supernaturally conceive and bear a son named Jesus. This would not be the seed of any man, but the seed of a woman, a virgin overshadowed by the power of the Most High, thus fulfilling Isaiah 7:14. Jesus would be conceived by the Holy Spirit. He would be

📖 *Doctrine*
WHY THE VIRGIN BIRTH?

Jesus had to be born of a virgin without an earthly father. Why? Through the seed of Adam comes the nature of fallen Adam, a sin nature bent toward sin and selfishness. Jesus was born through a human mother, the virgin Mary. No man was involved. Mary conceived through the supernatural work of God the Father, the Most High God, not the seed of a fallen man. Jesus had no fallen Adamic nature. He had the perfect nature of His Father—*"I and the Father are one"* (John 10:30, 33, 38; see also 14:7–10; 17:11, 21, 22). Because He was the perfect, sinless God-Man in His nature *and* in His conduct, He could be the sinless, spotless sacrifice for us (see Romans 5:12–21; 1 Timothy 2:5–6; 1 Peter 1:18–20).

the very Son of God, the Son of the Most High, and the Son of David—the promised seed in the lineage of Israel's great king, David. Jesus would rule on the throne of David as the promised seed. He would have an everlasting kingdom and *"reign over the house of Jacob forever,"* just as the Lord had promised hundreds of years before.

Soon after this, Mary traveled to her relative Elizabeth's home and stayed with her for three months. When she came into the home, the Holy Spirit moved greatly in the heart of Elizabeth and even in the heart of the child, John, whom she carried in her womb. Mary spoke in praise of God for His wondrous works. Her praise song is recorded in Luke 1:46–55. In verses 54 and 55 she reflects on the faithfulness of God to show His mercy to Israel. He had spoken to Abraham and his seed. Now He was bringing to pass the coming of the ultimate seed of Abraham, the Savior born to Mary and the redeemer of Israel and all other nations.

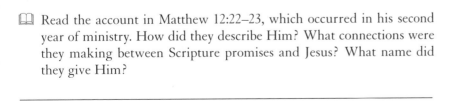 What additional insights do you glean from Matthew 1:18–25, especially in verses 20–23?

_____

_____

_____

_____

When Joseph found that Mary was expecting a child, he prepared to break their betrothal, thinking the worst of Mary, but an angel appeared to him with clear revelation from God about the child and Mary. This child was no mark of Mary's unfaithfulness. Rather, this child was conceived of the Holy Spirit. This was, in fact, the fulfillment of Isaiah's prophecy—a virgin would conceive and bear a Son, Immanuel—*"God with us."* Joseph obeyed the angel's instructions. When the child was born, they named Him Jesus, meaning "Jehovah is salvation," for this Son would *"save His people from their sins."* The seed of the woman, the seed of Abraham, Isaac, Jacob, Judah, and David had been born through Mary. Jesus was the holy Son of God, the God-Man, fulfilling the prayers and promises of the psalmists and prophets and bringing salvation to millions.

How would this child be received, and what would He do? As we put together the pieces of the puzzle, we begin to see the full portrait of Jesus as the Seed. Each piece of the puzzle helps us see the portrait more clearly and know Him more fully as our Lord and Savior, the Seed of Abraham and Seed of David.

As Jesus began to minister, heal, and teach, the crowds gathered in great numbers. They also talked a lot about what they were seeing and who this man could be.

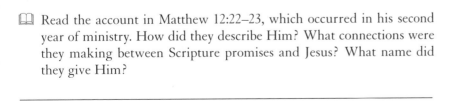 Read the account in Matthew 12:22–23, which occurred in his second year of ministry. How did they describe Him? What connections were they making between Scripture promises and Jesus? What name did they give Him?

_____

_____

_____

Doctrine
THE ROOT AND OFFSPRING OF DAVID

Jesus declared Himself to be *"the root and offspring of David,"* a title that conveys both His deity and His humanity (Revelation 22:16). He is the Root. He is God **before** David, the root that assures the fruit to come. He is the foundation for the throne and rule of David. He is the Offspring. He is Man **after** David as his seed, his descendant in the legal, royal line of David. He is legal heir to the throne of David and reigns forever on that throne.

Doctrine
GENEALOGIES OF JESUS

The Genealogies of Jesus given in Matthew and Luke present two viewpoints. Matthew looks at the royal or legal claims of Jesus to the throne of David and to the promises made to Abraham. Luke apparently traces Jesus' physical descent from Adam through David to Mary thus establishing His physical claim to the throne of David through Mary. Joseph is listed in Luke 3:23 but only as the "stand-in" in the genealogy. His name is the only one in the list given without the Greek article, showing he is not in the physical or biological line of Jesus. Jesus was *"supposedly,"* not actually, his son (Luke 3:23). Eli or Heli (3:23) is most likely Mary's father and Joseph, as Mary's husband, is given as the legal husband as in a customary Jewish genealogy. Joseph is not the bloodline son of Eli/Heli, but the legal son, or son-**in-law**. Jesus has a **legal** claim to the promises of Abraham and the throne of David through Joseph and a **physical** claim through Mary's descent from David.

📖 What do you find in Matthew 9:27–31? What did the two blind men think of this man Jesus?

_____

_____

_____

_____

_____

Did You Know?

A CANAANITE IN THE KINGDOM

Matthew 15:21–28 records the encounter of Jesus with a Caananite or Syro-Phoenician woman in the region of Tyre and Sidon north of Israel. She was a Gentile who recognized Him as the Messiah, crying out to Him, _"Have mercy on me, O Lord, Son of David…"_ Though Christ appeared to be reluctant to answer her, He in fact led her to confess her faith and trust in Him and His ability to heal her daughter. Seeing her humility and faith, Jesus did just that. Can a Canaanite come into the Kingdom? Certainly. Jesus is the Son of David, the Messiah and Lord of any and all who will believe in Him—Jew or Gentile (even Canaanite), man or woman.

A demon-possessed man , afflicted with both dumbness and blindness, was brought to Jesus. When Jesus healed him, the people marveled and began to consider whether He could indeed be the Son of David, a name associated with the promised Messiah. In Matthew 9, two blind men cried out to Jesus, _"Have mercy on us, Son of David!"_ They evidently believed that when the Son of David came, He would be able to heal, and this man Jesus certainly had the power to heal. He had shown His power time and time again. Jesus asked them if they truly believed He was able to heal them, and they responded with evident faith, _"Yes, Lord."_ Jesus touched their eyes and immediately they could see. The word about Him continued to spread.

Jesus revealed another piece of the puzzle during the Feast of Booths or Tabernacles celebrated each October. This feast looked not only to the past works of God and His dwelling with His chosen people, but to the future kingdom to come. At the feast that took place in His third year of ministry, Jesus declared that any who would come and believe on Him would discover Him to be the one who could quench their spiritual thirst, the one who could make the kingdom of God real, starting within, in the heart. He proclaimed Himself as the source and giver of living water (see John 7:37–39). When He did this, several in the crowds responded with various comments.

📖 Read John 7:40–43. What did the multitudes understand about the Christ who was to come?

_____

_____

_____

_____

_____

Some in the crowds thought Jesus was the great prophet who was to come, the one Moses described in Deuteronomy 18. Others clearly declared Him to be the Christ, the Messiah. Others were unsure since all they knew about Jesus centered on His home in Galilee rather than the prophesied birthplace of Bethlehem. They clearly acknowledged that the Messiah would be _"the offspring"_ or "the seed" of David. The crowd could not come to a unified conclusion, but it was evident that Jesus was revealing more and more of Himself as the Seed and Son of David, the promised Messiah through whom God's eternal kingdom would come.

As Jesus entered Jerusalem on Sunday, the people began crying out in triumph. It is known as Jesus' "Triumphal Entry." What did they say to Him?

📖 Read Matthew 21:1–11, noting especially verse 9.

_____

_____

_____

The next day, Monday, Jesus entered into the Temple area and cleaned out the moneychangers and sellers of doves and began healing many. He drew a response from the children there as well as from the religious leaders.

📖 Read Matthew 21:12–17 and record your insights, especially from verse 15.

_____

_____

_____

_____

The people considered Jesus to be the Messiah. They thought of Him as their king and expected Him to set up His earthly kingdom. As Jesus entered the city, they spread their garments and palm branches on the road, the welcome reserved for a king. They cried out to Him, *"Hosanna to the Son of David,"* pointing to the promised salvation and the strong kingdom He would bring. *"Hosanna"* means "save now" or "bring salvation now." The miracles He had done revealed Him as their Messiah, and they joyfully praised God and cried out *"blessed is the King,"* (Luke 19:38). When the Pharisees objected, calling Jesus to rebuke His disciples, He boldly declared, *"I tell you, if these become silent, the stones will cry out!"* The next day in the Temple, after Jesus cleansed the area of the greedy merchants and again began healing the blind and the lame, several children followed the lead of their parents and began crying out, *"Hosanna to the Son of David,"* once again acknowledging Him as their Messiah King. Though the Pharisees objected, this too was a fulfillment of prophecy, as these children offered the praise prepared for the True King.

In His final week on earth, many sought Jesus; some sought to believe in Him and others sought him to question and raise doubts about Him. In His interaction with the Pharisees, Jesus had a few pointed questions that related directly to who He was as the Son of David.

📖 What do you discover about Jesus' questions to these men as recorded in Matthew 22:41–46? What truths do you find about the Son of David in this question from the lips of Jesus?

_____

_____

_____

Nearing the final days of His earthly ministry, Jesus began to make razor sharp the distinction of who He was. The Pharisees and other religious leaders did not accept Him as the Messiah, the Son of David. He did not fit their preconceived mold. They agreed that the Christ or Messiah was the son of David, but they could not produce an answer to Jesus' probing question based on Psalm 110:1. Jesus asked, *"How does David in the Spirit call Him*

Did You Know?

THE MESSIAH AND THE SALVATION HE BRINGS

When the people cried out "Hosanna," they were calling for deliverance by the Messiah King. "Hosanna" means "save now" or "bring salvation now." That is what the people expected from the Messiah, though primarily focused on a political salvation. They wanted deliverance from the idolatrous Romans and their pagan ways and a restoration of the glorious kingdom of David under the Messiah, the Son of David. That salvation is more clearly revealed in the words of Zacharias in his song in Luke 1:68–79.

Jesus knew He was indeed the Seed and Son of David. He was also David's Lord, the eternal God and King who became man. He would rule as Lord and King.

'Lord' "? How can the Messiah be David's son and David's Lord? The religious leaders were dumbfounded at Christ's question. Jesus knew He was indeed the Seed and Son of David. He was also David's Lord, the eternal God and King of kings who became man. He would rule as Lord and king.

 We know from the Scriptures that Jesus is the Messiah/Christ, the Son of David, with all the qualifications and character to rule righteously forever. It is only right that we honor and obey Him as our Lord and master, ruler and king. Are you obediently following Him? Are you facing any points of disagreement or disobedience? Trust Him. Obey Him.

Three days later, Jesus was crucified, as the prophets and He Himself predicted. He died, was buried, and on the third day rose again from the grave. He appeared over the next forty days to His disciples, even to more than five hundred at one time. Then, He ascended from the Mount of Olives, where the disciples heard once again the promise of His return—the assurance of His reign as King of kings and Lord of lords. How did the early Church and the first Christians think of this Jesus, especially as the "seed"? What applications can we see for our lives today? We will see in Days Four and Five.

DAY FOUR

THE SON OF ABRAHAM, THE SON OF DAVID, AND THE SONS OF ABRAHAM

Doctrine
THE SEED OF DAVID IN THE GOSPEL

"...the gospel of God which He promised before through His prophets in the Holy Scriptures, concerning His Son Jesus Christ our Lord, who was born of the seed of David according to the flesh, and declared to be the Son of God with power according to the Spirit of holiness, by resurrection of the dead." Romans 1:1b–4 (NKJV)

God promised to bring the Seed of the woman, the Seed of Abraham and the Seed of David. He fulfilled that promise. In the New Testament, we read the clear revelation of Jesus Christ as the Son of Abraham and the Son of David. In his Pentecost sermon (see Acts 2), the apostle Peter quoted David and what he said about the coming Messiah. David spoke of *"the resurrection of the Christ,"* and of David's descendant being seated on the throne of David forever. Christ did indeed rise from the dead. Peter confidently declared in Acts 2:32, *"This Jesus God raised up again, to which we are all witnesses"*—it was an historical, experiential fact. Peter then quoted the same verse Jesus had used to question the Pharisees about the Messiah being both Lord and Son of David. Psalm 110:1 says, *"The LORD says to my Lord 'Sit at My right hand, until I make Thine enemies a footstool for Thy feet.'"* David prophesied, Peter proclaimed, and God revealed this Jesus for who He was—Lord and Christ, King and Messiah, the Seed and Son of David, and our Savior. In Romans 1:1–7, Paul pointed to Jesus as the clearly revealed Seed of David and Son of God. The gospel God called him to proclaim made it clear that Jesus was the Seed of David (see 2 Timothy 2:8). All the prophecies and promises of the Old Testament are wrapped up in this Jesus, and our salvation is inseparably tied to Him, impossible without Him.

Think of what the Seed means. As the Seed of the woman, of Abraham, David, and Mary, Jesus is fully man, completely able to understand and lead men and women in every aspect of life. Since He is the Son of God the Father, He is exactly like His Father. He has the perfect nature of God and the nature of a perfect man. Because He is fully man, He can relate to all men and women. Because He is fully God, He can touch and change any man or woman. He does so from the inside out. How so? God desired not only to bring the Seed into the world, but also to bring that Seed and His life into our hearts and lives. God wants to dwell in man, to bring forth the fruit of His Seed in each life. Today, we will see how He does that.

📖 In his letter to the Galatians, the apostle Paul is careful to spell out who Christ is and what it means to be connected to Him by faith. First, who is Christ according to Galatians 3:16?

_____

_____

_____

_____

What is our relationship to Christ according to Galatians 3:26 and 29? How do we enter into that relationship?

_____

_____

_____

_____

What do we have *"in Christ Jesus"* according to Galatians 3:6–14 and 4:4–7?

_____

_____

_____

_____

The promises God gave to Abraham and his seed were primarily focused on one man, the God-Man, Christ Jesus. Christ is **the** Promised Seed, the son of Abraham, the son of David, and the Son of God. When people place their faith in Christ Jesus as their God and Savior, there is a supernatural connection to Him—they become sons of God. With that sonship connection come the promises of God as part of His family. We belong to Christ, and God sees us as *"Abraham's offspring"* or "seed." Because of this family connection, we are heirs with Christ of all God has to give His Son. What a treasure to know Him!

How does this faith connection work? Abraham believed God—he believed in His person (who He is) and His promises (what He said). By faith, Abraham counted God's promise as settled truth. God counted Abraham as righteous by that faith. When anyone places faith in Jesus Christ as Lord and Savior, believing His word in repentance and faith, he or she becomes a child of God and, from God's point of view, a son of Abraham—one who has faith like Abraham. The family connection that happens for any who place faith in Christ, the seed of Abraham, is part of the blessing promised to the nations—to **anyone** from **any** nation. This blessing of salvation does not come from the Law or obeying the Law, since no one can do that perfectly. Christ paid the penalty and debt for the many ways we had broken God's Law. Now we can know the blessing of Abraham and *"the promise of the Spirit through faith"*—we can know the very presence of God to give life within and to guide and empower us in daily life. We can know Immanuel—

> **"But as many as received Him, to them He gave the right to become children of God, even to those who believe in His name."**
>
> **John 1:12**

BEING BORN FROM ABOVE

In John 3:1–21 Jesus spoke of being born again or born from above. Jesus focused attention on the absolute necessity of being born again in order to see and enter the kingdom of God. He was not talking about natural sight nor a natural birth, but supernatural seeing and a supernatural birth, one orchestrated by the Spirit of God, a birthing from above. In this birth, the spirit of a person is born anew by the work of the Spirit of God along with the word of God. First Peter 1:23 states, *"for you have been born again not of seed which is perishable but imperishable, that is, through the living and abiding word of God."* We listen to "the message of truth" from Jesus, we "believe" in Him, He saves us *"by the washing of regeneration and renewing by the Holy Spirit,"* and He seals us with His Spirit (see Titus 3:5; Ephesians 1:13). As Moses lifted the serpent in the wilderness for any to look upon and be healed, so any who will look in repentance and faith to Jesus Christ lifted on the cross and raised from the dead will find spiritual healing and new life (see John 3:14–16).

"God with us"—personally. Galatians 4:4–7 adds that we have received *"the adoption as sons"* and the Spirit of God, our personal connection to the Father, has been sent into our hearts crying *"Abba! Father!"* We are close-knit sons and certain heirs, not shackled slaves and condemned castaways.

The book of Genesis conveys a basic principle of life: a seed defines and determines the nature of something. Every seed in the plant kingdom determines the fruit of that plant whether tree or vine or bush. An apple seed will never produce oranges or bananas. So in the realm of mankind, each person has a certain nature, certain characteristics. The seed of a man and woman produces another man or woman, not a plant or animal or fish. In the spiritual realm, when a person is born of the seed of Christ, he or she is born from above, born again, a *"new person, created in God's likeness—righteous, holy, and true"* (Ephesians 4:24 NLT), given a new nature marked by *"newness of life"* (Romans 6:4). That means a person born of the Seed of Christ experiences a change, a different way of thinking and acting, and ultimately a different destiny. What can we expect in that person?

Recall that we asked several questions at the beginning of this lesson. What could God do to bring men and women back to where He wanted them to be? What could God do with a rebel heart, with an enemy opposed to Him and His Word, to make Him a loving, loyal follower? What would God do to accomplish that? What would it take? We have seen God's solution. He brought the Seed, Jesus Christ, to earth, to live and die for man and his sin, then to rise, ascend to heaven, and send the Holy Spirit to change, rearrange, and inhabit the repentant, faith-filled heart. He brings about a new birth; one is born again or born from above by the Spirit of God. God's very seed enters the heart of man to change him from the inside out, to give him a new nature, a new desire, a new will. God has committed Himself to work in the believer's heart *"to will and to work for His good pleasure"* (Philippians 2:13). What an amazing love! What a design! What a work He has chosen to do! But how does Christ's miraculous work accomplish itself in daily life? How does the seed of Christ make a difference in the believing child of God? What does this life look like?

📖 In the letter of 1 John, God reveals some further truths about the matter of being born into the family of God and links it to the matter of the "seed." Read 1 John 1:8–9 and 3:1–12. What do you discover about being a child of God in 3:1–9?

_____

_____

_____

_____

_____

📖 Does one born of God never sin? How does one deal with sins committed after being born again? Read 1 John 1:8–9 and record your insights.

_____

_____

_____

_____

In His great love, God the Father sent His Son, Jesus, to take away sins and destroy the works of the devil. He came to bring salvation, to bring to birth a family of righteous children. When we come to Christ, we are *"born of God,"* born into the family of God. God makes us His children, placing *"His seed"* in us. That means we receive His spiritual DNA, a new nature, and we become like Him in heart and action. When God makes us His children, He gives us a new nature. In Christ is no sin, no desire to sin and no sinful actions. When we are under His control, He is free to manifest Himself, and we can walk with His desires and choices. The one born of God has His desires as part of his or her life. This does not mean a Christian does not sin. It means that sin is neither the true desire nor the continual, habitual practice of one born of God. When a believer sins, he and the Spirit within are grieved, and God has provided a way to deal with that sin. First John 1:8–9 makes it clear that believers must walk in the light and be honest about sin, confessing it when they commit it and receiving God's forgiveness and cleansing. One born of God practices righteousness as a lifestyle—that is the fruit of the nature of God, His "seed," placed within.

📖 Thinking about all we have seen in Christ being the Promised Seed, what further insights do you glean about *"His seed"* in 1 John 3:9–12?

_____

_____

_____

_____

What do you discover in John's contrast of Cain and Abel in verses 11–12?

_____

_____

_____

_____

The children of God and the children of the devil are easily distinguishable by the habitual deeds of their lives. Those born of God practice righteousness and love others God's way. Those of the devil practice lawlessness (they oppose the things near to the heart of God) and do not love others God's way. Cain walked this way. He was *"of the evil one,"* having a heart that agreed with the serpent, the devil. He murdered his brother, Abel.

In 1 John 3:9–12, John contrasts the children of God, those *"born of God,"* with the children of the devil. The children of the devil do what they do out of a sinful nature, having no desire to obey God or do His will. Each is *"of the evil one,"* having his seed or his nature of disobedience and evil within the heart, a heart unchanged by the grace of God. Cain and Abel reveal the two seeds. Cain was *"of the evil one"*; *"his deeds were evil"*—deeds followed desires that came from a heart with an unrighteous nature. Abel, on the other hand, was marked by righteous deeds from a heart of faith, a heart made righteous by God. In his case, righteous deeds followed righteous desires from a righteous heart.

By faith in the Seed, Jesus Christ, we become the *"offspring of Abraham"* and an inheritor of the salvation and the promises made to him by God. With that faith connection comes the life of His "seed"—new life, a new nature, new desires, and a new direction of following Jesus. We can experience His

Doctrine
THE TWO SEEDS IN 1 JOHN

In Genesis 3:15, the Lord speaks of two seeds, the seed of the woman and the seed of the serpent, and how the two lines will forever stand opposed to one another. The seed of the woman would come and crush the serpent, a prophecy of Christ Jesus and His victory over sin, death, and the devil. That verse also speaks of two lines of people, one of the evil one and one who would seek God by faith. First John 3:10–12 gives Cain and Abel as examples of two with entirely different connections. Cain was *"of the evil one."* Abel walked in faith and was marked by righteousness. Those *"born of God,"* those with "His seed" abiding in them, walk in righteousness (3:9). The serpent opposed Abel. Throughout history the seed of the serpent has continually opposed the righteous seed. Christ came to destroy the works of the devil and establish the works of the Father. Jesus Christ has won. Ultimately, Christ the Seed of the woman and all who come to Him will be clearly revealed in His victory, the victory of the Cross, the Empty Tomb and the Eternal Throne.

new life within, empowering and changing us from the inside out. How does this work in daily life? What does it mean to walk following Christ; experiencing this new life He has given? We will see in Day Five.

Christ The Seed   **DAY FIVE**

FOR ME TO FOLLOW CHRIST

We have seen much about the Son of God—as the Seed of the Woman, the Seed of Abraham, and the Seed of David. How can we apply these truths to daily life? Remember, since Christ is the only begotten Son of God, He has the perfect nature of God and is able to touch and change any man or woman. Since He is the Promised Seed, He is able to understand and relate to all men and women. We asked at the beginning of this lesson, what it would take to bring man into all God wanted for him. The answer is—it would take a Seed—planted, broken, dying, rising in new life, bearing new fruit. Jesus is that Seed who was planted, broken, and dying for us on the cross, rising in resurrection life, and now bearing the fruit of His victory in new creation "seedlings"—all those who have come to Him by faith. Now, He is growing us up. He has implanted His seed in each believer giving His divine life so that each has His desires, His likes, and dislikes, and each is growing according to His workings. As we consider Jesus as the Seed and understand that now His seed is in us forever, we can apply these truths to our daily walk.

📖 Scripture is clear about the fact that the Christian life is a new birth into a new life. We have His seed implanted in us. What do you discover in 2 Peter 1:2–4 about this new life, especially in verse 4?

_____

_____

_____

In Christ, we have entered into a new kind of life; we experience God's grace and peace in greater and greater measure the more we get to know God the Father through his Son, our Lord and Savior, Jesus Christ. By His power, He has given us all we need to experience true life and walk in true godliness. He has given us many promises that assure us we can be a partaker of His divine nature rather than continually experiencing the rottenness brought by the deceitful lusts common in the world. Partaking of the divine nature does not mean being "little gods." Rather, it means we have like desires, interests, and inclinations. We think and act more and more like Him as He continues His work in us. For example, though the apostles Paul and Peter came from very different backgrounds, they had the same understanding as active participants in Christ's ministry. Paul expresses it this way in Philippians 2:13, *"for it is God who is at work in you, both to will and to work for His good pleasure."* That does not mean we are passive. Rather, we are active *"partakers"* and participants. Just one verse before (see Philippians 2:12b) Paul also said, *"work out your salvation with fear and trembling,"*— work out what God has worked in.

 What are we to do with these promises and these realities in our Christian walk? What are some ways we can work them out? Peter

Word Study
DIVINE NATURE

In 2 Peter 1:4, we are told that believers are *"partakers of the divine nature."* The word "nature" here is a translation of the Greek word *phúsis,* which refers to one's nature or disposition. It is rooted in *phúō* which means "to germinate" or "to spring up," that is, to bring forth what is in a seed. A related word is *phusikós,* "instinctive" or "natural," the root word for the English word "physical." Christians have a divine birthing with divine inclinations or instincts, the desires of the Spirit. The Christian no longer continually gravitates to the old desires. Though those desires may surface from time to time, it is not the habitual practice of one born from above, born of the Spirit. If a person continually returns to the old ways as a long-term lifestyle like the hogs and dogs of 2 Peter 2:22, that is evidence that the inner man, one's nature, has never changed.

gives clear direction for how this *"divine nature"* is to be lived out. Read 2 Peter 1:5–11. Look at the chart below and consider each of the actions Peter commands. Prayerfully evaluate how you are applying these principles. How are you in the **"all diligence"** department? God is at work, but He also calls us to cooperate, to live out the faith we say we have. In the space provided in the chart below, write how you have seen these things being worked out in your life or write some needed changes.

MARKS OF THE NEW LIFE HIS SEED AT WORK, HIS QUALITIES SEEN	HOW IS HIS SEED AT WORK IN ME? OR, HOW COULD HE BE AT WORK IN ME?
The Starting Point— *"Faith"* **or Trust in Christ**	Have I started right? What evidence do I see?
Generously add or input *"Moral Excellence"* **Doing Right with All My Might,** **Standing Out with Excellence in All I Do**	
Generously add or input *"Knowledge"* **Growing in Knowing Jesus and His Word**	
Generously add or input *"Self-control"* Self Restraint, literally "to hold oneself in," **Saying "No!" to "Self" by Saying "Yes!"** **to Christ and His Word**	
Generously add or input *"Perseverance"* or Endurance, literally "to bear up under," **Keeping on Keeping on**	
Generously add or input *"godliness"* or literally, "to worship well," "to wholeheartedly give all that is due to God in attitude and action" **Walking and Talking in the Fear of the Lord**	
Generously add or input *"Brotherly Kindness"* or brotherly love, show genuine friendship, think of one another and act like it **Being a Real Brother/Sister**	
Generously add or input *"Love,"* *agape*—wholehearted giving to meet needs **Giving-Living toward Others**	

If I am to grow in my walk with God, I must start with **faith** in Christ. Each of us must have a personal relationship with Jesus Christ—He must be Lord and Savior. Remember, He is the giver of a new heart and power for daily life. To walk as He desires, He calls each to generously add or input or abundantly supply certain qualities. Think of a garden and all that is needed to make it flourishing and fruitful or an army and all that is needed to make it mobile and victorious. A successful Christian life starts by being linked by faith to the Giver of Life, to the Commander and Lord. To that faith-walk one should generously add **diligence in doing the right thing**—showing excellence in all, whatever one does. This is faith in action.

To know the right way to do the right thing, each must supply a growing and accurate **knowledge** of Him and His Word, of His will and His ways.

With that must go an abundance of **self-control**, letting the Word of God guard and guide all relationships and every daily decision. That will take stick-to-it **endurance**—keeping on keeping on, never giving in or giving up. To do that, one must walk in the fear of the Lord, looking at all of life with a deep respect and **reverence** for God, living for His pleasure. Living focused on Him also means letting Him direct the path of **brotherly love**, letting Him give practical wisdom in meeting the needs of brothers and sisters and showing how to be considerate and kind to each other. Then, one must always make sure he or she is ready to show **love God's way**, to give abundantly, even sacrificially, as the needs of others come.

What happens when we live this way? If these qualities are indeed the lifestyle in which we walk—*"if these qualities are yours and are increasing,"* 2 Peter 1:8–11 promises a fruitful and stable life—growing in the knowledge of Jesus Christ. You will discover how wise and powerful, how loving and merciful He is, as you interact with Him along the way. God honors this diligent obedience and daily dependence on Him. As we walk this way, we will see more fruit in our lives and grow in our confidence in Christ. In addition, we will find a richer reward in eternity. This kind of living leads to a growing expectation of reward at the return of Christ, when we will see the fullness of *"the eternal kingdom of our Lord and Savior Jesus Christ"*—mission accomplished!

 First John 3:3 says, *"And everyone who has this hope fixed on Him purifies himself, just as He is pure."* One of the marks of biblical hope is diligence in holy, clean living like we have described in 2 Peter 1:4–11. Second Corinthians 7:1 says, *"Therefore, having these promises, beloved, let us cleanse ourselves from all defilement of flesh and spirit, perfecting holiness in the fear of God."* Pause and talk to the Lord about your walk. Is it clean? Ask Him to reveal any unconfessed sin, any impurity, anything displeasing to Him—then confess it, turn from it, and receive His forgiveness and cleansing. Remember, 1 John 1:9.

As believers, we have much for which to hope. First Peter 1:3 reminds us that God the Father *"has caused us to be born again to a living hope."* Titus 2:13 speaks of *"looking for the blessed hope and the appearing of the glory of our great God and Savior, Christ Jesus."* The apostle John spoke of the **hope** we have. Let's look at two final scriptures.

Read Revelation 5:5 and 22:16 and record what you find about Jesus **"the offspring,"** or **Seed,** and the hope He brings?

_____

_____

_____

_____

_____

When all is said and done, the Lord Jesus will be clearly revealed to all as the promised Lion of the Tribe of Judah, the Root of David who has overcome all obstacles, all sin, all evil, all opposition to reign unchallenged as Lord and Christ. Part of His last recorded words declare, *"I am the root and the offspring of David"* in whom all the promises of the Old Testament come to fruition. He is God, the root of David, the one before him, and He is Man, the offspring or Seed of David. He is **our hope**, the one who brings light in the midst

Did You Know?

THE MESSIAH IS UNDENIABLY GOD

Psalm 110 is a messianic psalm that portrays the victorious Messiah reigning as Lord, King, and Priest. Psalm 110:1 points to the deity of the Messiah, *"The LORD said to my Lord, 'Sit at My right hand, till I make Your enemies Your footstool.'"* (NKJV) This verse is quoted by Jesus in Matthew 22:44; Mark 12:36; and Luke 20:42–43, where He points out that the Messiah is Lord and also a man, the Son of David. Peter quotes Psalm 110:1 in his Pentecost sermon and applies it to Jesus being "both Lord and Christ" (Acts 2:34–36). Paul alludes to it in 1 Corinthians 15:25. The author of Hebrews quotes it in 1:13 and alludes to it in 10:12–13. Other verses mentioning Christ being exalted to the right hand of God include Ephesians 1:20; Hebrews 1:3; and 1 Peter 3:22. Psalm 110:4 speaks about the priesthood of Melchizedek being applied to *"my Lord"* (the Messiah) and in Hebrews 5:5–6 and 7:14, 21 that priesthood is applied to Jesus Christ. He is Lord, King, Priest, and Messiah/Christ.

of darkness. That is why He calls Himself **"the Bright and Morning Star,"** the star that signals the coming morning at the darkest part of the night. So too, in our lives Jesus signals His hope to us—look to Him, call on Him. The invitation of His Spirit and of His bride calls—*"Come . . . let the one who is thirsty come; let the one who wishes take the water of life without cost."* What a Lord and Savior! What a Friend! What a Hope!

 Are you in need of hope? The Son of David brings hope. He reigns in hope—not with "I hope so-maybe so" uncertainty, but "I hope so-know so" certainty. He is the Promised Seed who fulfilled all the Old Testament promises. His sovereign rule will bring to pass all He has promised. Turn to Him; talk to Him; hope in Him.

 Father, thank You for Your merciful promise of the Seed and the salvation He alone can bring. I praise You for Your power at work to insure that the Seed would come, for protecting the line of Abraham, Isaac, Jacob, Judah, David, and Mary. Thank You for Your provision of the Seed, Jesus, and the salvation He has purchased and brought to each one who places faith in Him. Thank You for Your mercy. I am so grateful that You are able to understand all I go through and able to save me in the midst of it all. Thank You for changing my heart, for continually changing me from the inside out, for giving me a new heart, new desires, new direction, and, ultimately, a new destiny in heaven with You. I praise and bless You for Your patience and Your continual work to see Your Life become more evident in and through me—my thinking, my choices, my relationships, and my everyday lifestyle. Thank You that one day, I and millions of true believers will be with You and made like You, changed into Your image—what a glorious, wonderful reality that will be. May I be faithful in telling others of this salvation You have brought and can bring to any heart who hears and believes and receives. May You be clearly seen, the fullness of Your "seed" evident in my life until I'm home with You. In Jesus' Name, Amen.

Record your prayer or a journal entry in the space provided.

_____

_____

_____

_____

_____

_____

_____

_____

_____

_____

_____

_____

_____

_____

May You be clearly seen, the fullness of Your "seed" evident in my life until I'm home with You.

Notes

The Angel of the Lord

CHRIST REVEALING HIMSELF AND LEADING HIS PEOPLE IN THE OLD TESTAMENT

When mention is made of the Angel of the LORD many pictures can come to mind—a winged, robed angel like those in medieval art or in a stained glass window, perhaps a strong warrior-like angel fulfilling God's plan, or simply one angel among many other angels mentioned in Scripture. None of these pictures is accurate. The Angel of the LORD is not just another angel. The word "angel" actually means "messenger"—one with a word or message from God. The Angel of the LORD is the Messenger of the LORD or the Messenger of Jehovah, but He is more than just an angel or simple messenger. He is not a created being like the host of angels active in heaven and earth. The Angel of the LORD is God Himself—and in His appearances in Scripture, we find that He is actually the pre-incarnate Christ.

What is the purpose of the appearances of this Angel, the Messenger of Jehovah/Yahweh? Why does God choose this as one of the ways He reveals Himself throughout the Old Testament? Why does He not appear this way in the New Testament? We will seek to answer these and many other such questions as we look at the Angel of the LORD. We will listen carefully to His words. The Scriptures record at least twenty-five encounters with or messages from this Angel, and each one gives clear revelation of who He is, of His ways, and particularly of His will for His people.

What He said, the way He said it, the steps He directed for His people, and His battles for His people are all instructive of **Christ's will for our walk** today. What can we learn from this heavenly messenger about God, about His plans, about His ways and His will for **each of us**? These questions and more are the focus of this lesson. As with so many other truths about Christ, we begin early in the book of Genesis. Come meet the Angel of the LORD.

Word Study
WHAT'S IN A NAME?

"The Angel of the LORD" could be translated "The Messenger of Jehovah" or "Yahweh." "Angel" is a translation of the Hebrew *malak,* which can also be translated "ambassador" or "messenger." The word "Lord" is a translation of the Hebrew *YHWH,* which we render "Jehovah" or "Yahweh." "Yahweh" means "the One who is" and is the primary name for God in the Old Testament. It is related to the name "I AM" revealed to Moses in Exodus 3. The Angel of the LORD is God and is considered a Christophany, a preincarnate appearance of Christ in the Old Testament.

The Angel of the Lord

DAY ONE

MEET THE ANGEL OF THE LORD IN THE DAYS OF ABRAHAM, ISAAC, AND JACOB

The Old Testament records at least twenty-five encounters with the Angel of the LORD. Today's lesson will focus on several encounters in Genesis. In each encounter we can see more about Christ as He reveals how He leads us, and how He expects us to follow Him. The first mention is found in the days of Abram.

📖 Genesis 16 gives us the first mention and encounter with the Angel of the LORD. Read Genesis 16:1–16. What problems are found in verses 1–5?

_____

_____

What was Abram's solution according to verse 6? How did Hagar respond?

_____

_____

✏️ *Did You Know?*

? NAMES OF GOD

In the Old Testament, names were not mere labels. Each name was descriptive. "Abram" means "exalted father" and "Abraham" refers to being "father of a multitude." Hagar called the Angel of the Lord "Elroi," which means "God sees." This is the first time in Scripture in which someone gave a name to God. It is not the last time. Time and again as the Lord revealed Himself to His people, they would give the Lord a name. Hagar experienced the Lord in His power and grace and praised Him, describing Him as the one who had seen her and in seeing, chose to act to help her and her child. Later, in his encounter with the Angel of the LORD on Mount Moriah, Abraham called the place "Jehovah Jireh" ("The Lord will provide"), thus combining a place name with the activity of Jehovah and giving the Lord another name.

God had promised Abram that he would have a son, the first of many descendants. Yet many years went by, and no son came. Ten years after the yet unfilled promise, Sarai suggested that Abram have a child through her Egyptian handmaid, Hagar. While this was a custom acceptable in the culture of that day, it is never condoned in the Word of God; it was neither God's design nor His desire. However, Abram agreed to Sarai's suggestion, and Hagar conceived. When she did, she became proud, and Sarai was despised in her eyes. Sarai became upset with Abram, and he in turn told Sarai to deal with the problem as she saw fit. She became harsh with Hagar, which resulted in Hagar's attempt to escape by running away.

The Angel of the LORD met her in the wilderness. What insights do you see in His encounter with Hagar in verses 7–8?

_____

_____

What instruction did the Angel give to Hagar in verse 9?

_____

_____

📖 In Genesis 16:10–12, what promises did He make to Hagar?

_____

_____

What was Hagar's response to this encounter according to verses 13–14? What actions did she take?

_____

_____

The Angel of the LORD was fully aware of who Hagar was and what she was going through. He knew she was Sarai's maid and addressed her as such. Then He asked about her life—*"where have you come from"*—her past—and *"where are you going"*—her future? She admitted she was running away. The Angel commanded her to return and submit to Sarai's authority, to bear with the situation. Then, He spoke to her about the future. He promised he would *"greatly multiply"* her descendants. She would bear a son whom she was to name "Ishmael," meaning "God hears." He would always be a reminder that the LORD gave heed to her in her affliction. The LORD also revealed the kind of man Ishmael would be—*"a wild donkey of a man,"* self-willed, antagonistic, and facing antagonism from others. With this message regarding Ishmael, the Angel of the LORD departed.

Hagar recognized this was the Lord who had spoken to her. She responded with wonder that she was still alive, and she gave the name *Elroi,* "God sees," to the LORD who had met her. Hagar exclaimed, *"Thou art a God who sees."* Thereafter, the name of that meeting place was called Beer-lahai-roi, "the well of the Living One who sees me" (NASB margin). Both names reflect praise to the LORD, who sees fully and acts with care and concern.

In Hagar's encounter, we clearly see two characteristics of the Angel of the LORD—He sees and He hears. He saw her in her situation with Sarai, and He heard her in the midst of her affliction in the wilderness. The word "affliction" speaks of depression or being abased, put down. God **saw** her and **heard** her in that situation and gave her direction in dealing with it. He does the same with us in our "situations." He is seeing every step, hearing every cry, and is willing to give us clear direction in every situation.

 What situation are you facing now? Is someone you know facing a difficult or depressing situation? Turn to the Lord who sees and hears. Perhaps you need to encourage someone with the message that God sees and hears and pray for him or her in this situation. Like Hagar, the place you are could take on a new name, a name that reveals the care and direction of the Lord.

Abram's visit with the LORD in **Genesis 17** is possibly another appearance of the Angel of the LORD, revealing Himself as God Almighty, promising a multitude of descendants and changing Abram's name to Abraham, "father of a multitude." Before he would have that son, God commanded Abraham to circumcise every male as a sign of the covenant. The LORD changed Sarai's name to Sarah and promised them a son to be named Isaac. After that meeting, the LORD simply *"went up from Abraham,"* an evident manifestation of His supernatural power.

Here again is testimony of the Angel seeing, hearing, and taking care to accomplish His will. He heard the specific need, gave Hagar a specific word, and provided exactly what they needed.

What do you discover about Abraham and the Angel of the LORD in Genesis 22:1–18 (note verses 11 and 15)?

_____

_____

_____

_____

Did You Know?
A VISIT WITH ABRAHAM AND SARAH

In what is possibly an appearance of the Angel of the LORD, Genesis 18 records the Lord's appearance to Abraham and Sarah, this time among three men (most likely the Lord and two angels). Abraham received the revelation that he and Sarah would bear a son named Isaac. At their ages, God promised the impossible—*"Is anything too difficult for the Lord?"* The Lord also gave Abraham word about the doom of Sodom and Gomorrah and, in answer to Abraham's prayer, promised to spare them if ten righteous men were found. The Lord is ever working to fulfill His will.

Put Yourself In Their Shoes
THE CARING ANGEL

The Angel of the LORD appeared again to Hagar and Ishmael in Genesis 21:9–21. With the birth of Isaac and the conflict with Ishmael, it was time for Hagar and Ishmael to part ways from Abraham, Sarah, and Isaac. Though this distressed Abraham, God assured him it was the right path to take. Though Abraham's descendants would be named through Isaac, God promised to take care of Ishmael because he was Abraham's son. Hagar and Ishmael began their journey and came to the wilderness of Beersheba where they ran out of water. Hagar expected both of them to die, but *"the Angel of God"* heard Ishmael's cry. The Angel called out, *"Do not fear,"* assuring her He had heard that cry and promised once again *"I will make a great nation of him."* God showed her a spring. She and her child were revived, continued their journey, and settled in the Wilderness of Paran. Here is testimony of the Angel seeing, hearing, and taking care to accomplish His will. He heard the specific need, gave a specific word, and provided exactly what was needed.

PROVIDING ISAAC'S BRIDE

In Genesis 24 we read the testimony of Abraham's arrangement of a bride for Isaac. Abraham sent his servant, Eliezer, to Haran to find a wife for Isaac. We find some evidence of the Angel of the LORD active in this mission. With confidence, Abraham assured his servant, *"the Lord . . . will send His angel before you."* When Eliezer reached Haran, he prayed, and the Lord arranged his meeting with Rebekah. He testified, *"the Lord has guided me in the way"* (24:27), and to Rebekah's family he repeated that testimony about being *"guided . . . in the right way"* (24:48). In addition, he noted his experience of how the Lord had sent *"His angel with"* him to make his *"journey successful"* (24:40). The Lord certainly guarded and guided Eliezer as He continually worked to assure His will in the life of Abraham and his descendants.

In a God-given test, Abraham and Isaac traveled to Mount Moriah to worship the Lord. God tested Abraham's trust, and Abraham trusted God in the test. He obeyed and willingly gave his son. When the Angel of the LORD saw the evidence of Abraham's trust—his obedient fear of the Lord and his not withholding his only son, He stopped him and showed him the ram caught in the thicket, which Abraham offered. The Angel called a second time from heaven, affirming his obedience and assuring him of the promised blessings for him, his descendants, and his "seed." This time, the Angel of the LORD had revealed Himself once again by fulfilling His will for His people—through necessary testing and training along His well-planned paths. He does the same for His children today.

We find another encounter of the Angel of the LORD in Genesis 28, this time in the life of Isaac's son Jacob. What do you discover in Genesis 28:10–22? [Note: Genesis 31:11–13 makes it clear that this was an appearance of *"the Angel of God."*]

_____

_____

_____

Jacob left Isaac and Rebekah in Beersheba to travel to Haran—temporarily escaping from Esau until a later day. When he encamped for the night, the Lord ("the Angel of God") spoke to him in a vision, promising him the land on which he was lying, many descendants to fill the land, and that they would be a blessing to all the nations. He promised His presence, His protection, and assured him he would return to Canaan. Convinced this was God, Jacob worshiped Him there, promising that this God would be his God and he would give a tenth of all he had to Him. These promises to Jacob were the same promises God had made to Abraham and Isaac. The Angel of God was continuing to guide His people and guarantee His plans through to the end.

Jacob lived in Haran twenty years and then at the direction of the Angel of the Lord left for Canaan. He arrived at the Jabbok River on the border of the land of Canaan where he found out Esau was coming with four hundred men—he was greatly afraid and distressed, but prayed. He then sent a present of several hundred head of livestock to Esau and settled his family safely across the Jabbok River.

Surveying Genesis 31:1–13, we see "the Angel of God" at work with Jacob in the land of Haran. He spoke to Jacob reminding him of their meeting at Bethel. He had seen all the ways of Laban and all that Jacob had gone through. He gave him unmistakable guidance to return to Canaan, to the land of his birth. Here we see the Angel of God very aware of all His followers are going through, understanding the struggles and questions, and giving practical counsel about the next steps to take. Jacob listened and obeyed.

What would happen next? Read Genesis 32:22–32. What occurred in this encounter?

_____

_____

_____

Record your insights about this man and His encounter with Jacob?

_____

_____

_____

_____

📖 What additional insights do you glean from Hosea 12:3–5?

_____

_____

_____

_____

_____

Jacob placed his family safely across the Jabbok River and went back to camp alone. Then a man wrestled with him—beginning a match that lasted all night. Hosea reveals that this man was the Angel of the LORD wrestling with Jacob. He touched and dislocated Jacob's thigh, leaving him weak and helpless for wrestling. Jacob held on, weeping and asking for the blessing of this man, but first Jacob had to admit who he was—"Jacob," the name that means "heel-grabber," "deceiver." Then the man blessed him there and gave him the new name "Israel" because he had held on to this man wanting only what God could give. Jacob knew he had encountered God face to face and was not only spared, but blessed by Him.

What is Jacob's testimony about this Angel in Genesis 48:1–16, especially verse 16? Thinking about all we have seen today, write any additional insights about the Angel of the LORD from what you read.

_____

_____

_____

_____

_____

Near the end of his life, when Jacob blessed the sons of Joseph, he also gave testimony to how *"God Almighty"* had worked in his life. Jacob applied that name to the Angel who had appeared to him at Luz (Bethel). In blessing Joseph and his sons, Jacob spoke of his God as *"the God before whom . . . Abraham and Isaac walked"* and *"the God who has been my shepherd all my life to this day."* He was confident in the Lord in his life and desired that Joseph's sons know that same blessing. He concluded by speaking of *"the angel who has redeemed me from all evil"* and then prayed for that one to *"bless the lads,"* something the "angel" could do only if He were God Himself. Jacob believed that. The testimonies of Abraham and Isaac confirmed that. The Angel of the LORD was God at work directing His people in His will.

What more can we learn about the Angel of the LORD in Scripture? In Day Two we will see how He led His people into the land of Canaan.

Word Study
GOD ALMIGHTY

When the Lord appeared to Abram in Genesis 17, He revealed Himself as "God Almighty" or *El Shaddai*. Jacob also gave testimony of God Almighty at work in his life. *Shaddai* may be related to the Akkadian word *shadu*, which can refer to "mountain," or it could be rooted in the Hebrew word *shad*, meaning "breast." Both ideas convey sustaining strength. God Almighty is the God of infinite sustenance who can give life and sustenance like a mother nursing an infant. He could give strength to Abraham and Sarah to have a child. God Almighty promised Abram, *"I will multiply you exceedingly."* The God who has all might, all strength, and all sustenance is able to bring His promise to pass. Jacob testifies in Genesis 48:3, *"God Almighty appeared to me at Luz in the land of Canaan and blessed me."*

"The God before whom my fathers Abraham and Isaac walked, The God who has been my shepherd all my life to this day, The angel who has redeemed me from all evil, Bless the lads. . . ."

Jacob's testimony in Genesis 48:15–16a

THE ANGEL OF THE LORD MEETING MOSES, LEADING ISRAEL

The children of Israel grew very numerous over the next four hundred years as they lived in the land of Egypt. During that time, the Egyptians made slaves of them and used them in various building projects. Through some unusual and supernatural circumstances, Moses grew up in the courts of Pharaoh. Around the age of forty, Moses had to leave Egypt after trying in his own power to settle some leadership issues between the Egyptians and the Hebrews. Forty years later, the Lord was ready to settle those issues His way, and He met Moses to talk to him about these things. That is where we pick up the story.

📖 Look at Exodus 3:1–2. What do you discover about the Angel of the LORD in verse 2?

_____

_____

_____

How did Moses respond to this encounter according to verse 3?

_____

_____

_____

What did God reveal about Himself in verses 4–9?

_____

_____

_____

The Angel of the LORD revealed Himself to Moses in a burning bush—a fire that did not stop and a bush that was not consumed. Moses focused his attention on this strange phenomenon. The Lord spoke out of the bush, instructing him to take his shoes off, *"for the place on which you are standing is holy ground,"* made holy by the presence of the Angel of the LORD. He was the God of Abraham, Isaac, and Jacob, the same God who appeared to each of them and spoke His covenant promises. As He had been aware of every need each of them had, so He was aware of the needs of the children of Israel in Egypt—their enslavement, oppression, and suffering. As He led and delivered the patriarchs in the past, so now He would deliver the Israelites out of Egyptian bondage into the promised land of Canaan.

What did God reveal about His mission for Moses in Exodus 3:10 and 12?

_____

_____

_____

_____

What was Moses' response to the Lord according to verses 11 and 13?

_____

_____

_____

_____

In directing Moses to lead the children of Israel out of Egypt, the Lord planned to send Moses to Pharaoh, but Moses was not at all sure about this plan. He lacked confidence in himself and was certain that Pharaoh would not listen. God assured him of His presence and guaranteed to bring him back to the ground on which they were then standing, to *"this mountain"* (Mount Horeb or Mount Sinai). Moses asked God how he should respond to his fellow Israelites when they asked the name of the God of their fathers. "What shall I say?" Moses pleaded. God revealed Himself to Moses.

What did God reveal to Moses about His name, about Himself, and about His plans for His people in Exodus 3:14–22?

_____

_____

_____

_____

_____

_____

First, the Angel of the LORD revealed Himself as "I AM WHO I AM," the name for God that reveals His timelessness and the fullness of His being. Then He spoke to Moses all He desired to do. He instructed Moses in how he and Aaron were to confront Pharaoh and the steps they were to take in delivering the people of God out of Egypt and bringing them into the land of Canaan. The Lord also promised that Pharaoh would resist, but that He as the one true God would miraculously deal with this oppressive king. Eventually, the people of Egypt would give the Hebrew children great wealth as they left the country.

In the New Testament, we find further revelation about what was going on in Moses' heart during these days. Read Hebrews 11:24–27, noting especially verse 27. What impact did the Angel of the LORD have on Moses?

_____

_____

_____

_____

Moses knew the LORD was the true God and chose to follow Him, even though it meant that he would experience difficulties rather than luxuries. Part of Moses' knowledge came through his encounters with the Angel of the LORD. God revealed Himself in such a way that Moses saw the true

Did You Know?

MOUNT SINAI

Mount Horeb and Mount Sinai are two names for the same mountain located in the land of Midian where Moses tended sheep for forty years. This is the mountain of the burning bush, the receiving of the Ten Commandments, and the meeting place of the Lord and Elijah years later. The apostle Paul referred to Mount Sinai as located in Arabia (see Galatians 4:25), which was part of the land of Midian in Moses' day.

"By faith [Moses] left Egypt, not fearing the wrath of the king; for he endured, as seeing Him who is unseen."

Hebrews 11:27

treasure of following the Christ/Messiah, even though it meant *"enduring ill treatment with the people of God."* By faith, he recognized *"the reproach of Christ,"* the things he would face in following Christ, ultimately would develop into *"greater riches than the treasures of Egypt."* His fixed focus was *"the reward"* that would come from the Lord. Moses walked and endured by faith *"seeing Him who is unseen."*

Over the next several weeks, the Lord led Moses and the children of Israel step by step, then plague by plague as God dealt one deathblow after another to the gods of Egypt. Finally, he dealt the deathblow to Pharaoh's family and the families of every Egyptian—anywhere the blood of the Passover lamb was not applied met God's judgment in the death of the firstborn of man and beast. Then the Lord led them out of Egypt on their way to the Promised Land. How did He lead them?

📖 What did God promise about His presence and His leading? What do you discover in Exodus 13:17–22?

_____

_____

_____

_____

_____

📖 Read Exodus 14 and answer the questions that pertain to that chapter.

What does Exodus 14:19 reveal about the Pillar of Cloud and the Pillar of Fire? Where does the Angel of the LORD fit into this?

_____

_____

_____

_____

_____

THE PILLAR OF FIRE AND CLOUD

"And it came about at the morning watch, that the Lord looked down on the army of the Egyptians through the pillar of fire and cloud and brought the army of the Egyptians into confusion. . . . so the Egyptians said, 'Let us flee from Israel, for the Lord is fighting for them against the Egyptians.'" (Exodus 14:24–25)

The Lord was careful to lead His people out of Egypt by a purposeful route toward the Red Sea. He knew that first He had to train them in following Him; then he would prepare them for war. God's people literally followed Him as they followed the Pillar of Cloud by day and the Pillar of Fire by night. The Angel of the LORD was in the Pillar leading them, going before the children of Israel as a shepherd guiding and protecting his flock.

What did Pharaoh do as the people left Egypt? Read the account in Exodus 14:1–12. What threat were God's people facing? How did they respond to this threat?

_____

_____

_____

_____

_____

What did God do in this situation according to Exodus 14:13–18?

_____

_____

_____

Who was leading the children of Israel according to Exodus 14:19–20?

_____

_____

_____

Pharaoh had a change of heart toward the Israelites, so he gathered his mighty army and began the chase. When the encamped Israelites realized the Egyptians were coming, they *"cried out to the LORD"* and complained to Moses. He focused their attention on their powerful Lord who would deal with the Egyptians. The Lord instructed Moses and the people to go forward, and He promised to divide the sea, providing the way of escape. The Angel of God stood as a defense separating the Israelites from the Egyptians—a protection for His people as He prepared the path through the sea.

How did the Angel of the LORD lead, and what did He do with Pharaoh's army? Read the account in Exodus 14:21–31 and summarize what happened. Include your insights about the Angel of the LORD.

The Lord led Israel through the sea to the other side. Moses described the work of the Angel of the LORD in picturesque form—He was looking down on the Egyptians *"through the pillar of fire and cloud"* and then *"brought the army of the Egyptians into confusion."* He *"caused their chariot wheels to swerve"* and *"made them drive with difficulty."* Then the Lord issued the order for the waters to cover the army, and they were drowned in the collapsing waters of the Red Sea, signaling a great victory for the people of God. The Angel of the LORD is indeed a great warrior. When the people sang about the victory He gave, they declared, *"the LORD is a warrior"* (15:3).

The Lord continued to guide the people through the pillar, and they set camp or broke camp *"at the command of the LORD"* according to Numbers 9:15–23. Whether staying a day, a week, or longer, the people followed the Lord.

What additional insights do you glean from Exodus 23:20–23?

_____

_____

_____

_____

_____

The Lord promised His guidance through the Angel in whom *"is My name."* He would go before them to guard them on the way and bring them into the land He had prepared. Israel was to obey His voice in every detail, and they would see the kind of victory He could bring.

 The Lord led Israel, guarding them and bringing them into *"the place which I have prepared"* (Exodus 23:20). Psalm 80:8–9 says God took Israel as a vine out of Egypt, cleared the ground, and planted it. As He led Israel, so He prepares the way before His children and places them with care to fulfill His will. How have you seen the Lord at work leading you? Talk to Him. Trust Him with His preparations and His placements in your life.

The Angel of the LORD led His people. Just so, the Lord Jesus Christ continues to lead His people. In Day Three we will see how He led them in conquering and ruling over the land of Canaan.

DAY THREE

THE ANGEL OF THE LORD CONQUERING AND RULING IN ISRAEL

The Angel of the LORD led the people of Israel from Egypt to Mount Sinai and then to Kadesh-Barnea and was prepared to lead them into the Promised Land. But entry into this region would be delayed because the majority of God's people refused to follow by faith, resulting in forty years of wilderness wandering though still being led by that Pillar of Fire and the Cloud of Glory. In the last days of Moses' leadership, toward the end of the forty years of wandering, the people again came near the land of Canaan and camped. We pick up their adventure there and discover some fresh insights into how the Angel of the LORD worked in leading His people, especially as we look at their entering, conquering, and ruling in Israel.

📖 Numbers 22—24 gives the account of Balak, king of the Moabites, approaching Balaam to hire him to curse the people of God. Balak considered Israel a threat to them, so he sought a defense against Israel. Read Numbers 22 and answer all questions pertaining to this chapter.

What was their plan according to Numbers 22:7–11?

_____

_____

_____

_____

What did God tell Balaam in Numbers 22:12? How did he respond (22:13–14)?

_____

_____

_____

_____

BALAAM'S BLESSING

"And God said, '. . . you shall not curse the people; for they are blessed'. . . . 'God is not a man, that He should lie, nor a son of man, that He should repent; has He said, and will He not do it? Or has He spoken, and will He not make it good? Behold, I have received a command to bless; when He has blessed, then I cannot revoke it.' "
(Numbers 22:12; 23:19–20)

Balak saw no way to engage and defeat Israel from a military standpoint so he chose to use pagan superstition. He sent his men to bring back Balaam, a professional diviner (soothsayer), to come curse the Israelites. God communicated to Balaam not to curse His people "for they are blessed." Having understood God's prohibition, Balaam refused to go.

Balak sent more honorable representatives the second time, and God permitted him to go with them (see Numbers 22:15–21). God instructed him to speak only the word He would give him and nothing more. Balaam went with the men, but on the way God confronted him. What was God's attitude toward Balaam according to verse 22? What did God do?

_____

_____

_____

_____

What transpired according to Numbers 22:23–27? How did God deal with Balaam?

_____

_____

_____

What miracle occurred next as found in Numbers 22:28–30?

_____

_____

_____

_____

According to verse 31, how was Balaam able to see the Angel of the LORD?

_____

_____

_____

As Balaam traveled with the men from Balak, God's anger burned against Balaam. The Lord knew the heart, motives, and desires of Balaam. The Angel of the LORD met Balaam and his donkey en route to Balak and stood in the way *as an adversary against him.* The donkey went aside and Balaam beat her. This happened not once but three times. Then the Lord made the donkey speak—not a prophecy, not a command, just a simple statement made by a simple donkey. It was enough to get Balaam's attention. Then the Lord opened Balaam's eyes. He saw the Angel of the LORD with His drawn sword ready to slay him. The Lord had his attention. Balaam bowed before the Lord with his face to the ground.

What did the Angel of the LORD tell Balaam (22:32–33)?

_____

_____

_____

_____

How did Balaam respond (22:34)?

_____

_____

Did You Know?
WHO WAS BALAAM?

Balaam appears in Numbers 22—24 as a soothsayer. Was he a follower of the one true God? Not according to the rest of Scripture. While in his oracles he spoke only what God told him, he did so out of necessity. Numbers 31:16 speaks of his wicked counsel that caused Israel to *"trespass against the LORD."* Deuteronomy 23:3–6, Joshua 24:9–10, Nehemiah 13:1–3, and Micah 6:5 mention the attempted curse on Israel. Joshua 13:22 calls him a "diviner" whom Israel killed. Second Peter 2:15–16 speaks of the wayward *"way of Balaam…. who loved the wages of unrighteousness."* Peter condemns him for his *"transgression"* and his *"madness."* Jude 11 mentions *"the error of Balaam"* and Revelation 2:14 notes the *"teaching of Balaam"* and his efforts to *"put a stumbling block before the sons of Israel,"* which included idolatry and immorality.

What final word did the Angel have for Balaam in verse 35? What did Balaam tell Balak when they finally met (22:38)?

The Lord confronted Balaam about his reckless way that was apparently contrary to the Lord in spirit and motive. Balaam was willing to turn back, but the Lord gave him instructions to proceed and to *"speak only the word which I shall tell you."* When Balaam met Balak, he told him he would speak only *"the word that God puts in my mouth,"* and that is what he did.

What does this encounter tell you about the Angel of the LORD? What does this reveal about His ways with His people?

_____

_____

_____

_____

The Angel of the LORD continually worked to protect and guide His people. He is a mighty warrior and able protector. As they neared the entry date into Canaan, His work continued in guiding and protecting. He would not allow Balaam to curse His people. Instead, He blessed them. They would succeed by Him and His power.

Balaam gave seven oracles or prophecies about the people of God and how God would fulfill His will in Israel in the days ahead. While he spoke the words that God gave him at this juncture, Balaam would eventually prove to be a great menace and detriment to the Israelites. According to Numbers 31:16, through Balaam's counsel, the Moabites and Midianites led Israel into idolatry and the immorality that went with it. This corrupted the people of Israel so that God's anger came against Israel (see Numbers 25). Israel finally responded in obedience and dealt in judgment with the Midianites (see Numbers 31) as they prepared to go into Canaan.

The children of Israel heard God's word through Moses before they came to the border of Canaan. His instructions were clear about following God and only God, not any of the idols of Canaan nor of any of the nations surrounding them. Joshua took command after the death of Moses. The Lord desired to lead him every step of the way. How would He do this? We see part of His plan in Joshua 5.

📖 Read Joshua 5:13–15. Who did Joshua face after the nation of Israel crossed the Jordan? Give a description of this *"man."*

_____

_____

_____

_____

📖 What instructions did *"the Captain of the Host of the LORD"* (or *"the Commander of the army of the LORD"* (NKJV) give to Joshua in Joshua 6:1–5?

_____

_____

_____

> **The Angel of the LORD continually worked to protect and guide His people. He is a mighty warrior and able protector.**

As Joshua stood looking at Jericho, he saw a man standing with sword drawn. It was the Captain of the Host of the LORD. He stood ready to lead Joshua and the people in conquering Canaan starting with Jericho, the gateway point. When He identified Himself, Joshua bowed before this man. He spoke to him words similar to those spoken to Moses some eighty years before, *"remove your sandals . . . the place you are standing is holy."* Joshua obeyed. The Captain assured him that He had given Jericho to Joshua and Israel. He instructed him in how to attack—march around the city once for six days and on the seventh day march around seven times, blow trumpets, shout, and go in and conquer. Joshua followed His orders to the letter, and God fulfilled His word to the letter. This Captain, an evident appearance of the Angel of the LORD, led His people in a victory over Jericho. As long as they followed the LORD, they found themselves victorious.

In the land of Canaan, Israel failed to conquer all the Canaanites. They began living in a cycle of conquest and blessing from the LORD, **compromise and sin—corruption—conquest** by **an enemy—crying out to the LORD—** and once again **conquering the enemy and blessing** from the LORD.

This cycle is repeated several times in the book of Judges. In one of the times of great distress, the LORD came to visit a man named Gideon. Read Judges 6. What do you discover about Israel in Judges 6:1–10?

_____

_____

_____

_____

_____

What occurred in Judges 6:11–12?

_____

_____

What was Gideon's response in Judges 6:13?

_____

_____

_____

In Judges 6:14, what did the Angel of the LORD propose as the answer to their dilemma?

_____

_____

_____

Read Judges 6:15–16 and record what you see in the interaction between Gideon and the Angel of the LORD?

_____

_____

_____

Put Yourself In Their Shoes

CONFRONTING DISOBEDIENCE

The Angel of the LORD dealt with disobedience. He confronted His people:

Now the angel of the LORD came up form Gilgal to Bochim. And he said, "I brought you up out of Egypt and led you into the land which I have sworn to your fathers; and I said, 'I will never break My covenant with you, and as for you, you shall make no covenant with the inhabitants of this land; you shall tear down their altars.' But you have not obeyed Me; what is this you have done?" (Judges 2:1–2)

The Lord confronts our disobedience through His Word and by the conviction of His Spirit.

The people of Israel failed to obey God, and He allowed the Midianites to oppress them. They cried out and He sent a prophet to recall who the true God is, what He had done for Israel, and how they were to fear Him and obey Him. Then the Angel of the LORD came to one man, Gideon the son of Joash. He encouraged him, *"the LORD is with you, O valiant warrior."* Gideon questioned that statement in light of the oppression of the Midianites. He considered Israel to be a people abandoned by the Lord. The Lord focused on His plan and instructed Gideon to lead the people out from under the hand of Midian. In spite of Gideon's objections and his apparent weaknesses, the Lord continued to exhort him in fulfilling His plans.

Gideon asked for a sign and suggested he bring an offering to Him. The Angel waited as Gideon prepared an offering. This account is given in Judges 6:19–27. In Judges 6:21, what did the Angel of the LORD do with the offering Gideon prepared?

_____

_____

_____

What occurred and what did Gideon do in response as found in verses 22–27?

_____

_____

_____

> *Gideon recognized the Angel of the LORD as God. He feared Him, honored Him, and obeyed Him. He treated Him as God.*

Gideon placed the offering before the Angel of the LORD on a certain rock. The Angel touched the offering, and fire sprang up and consumed the offering. The Angel of the LORD vanished. Gideon recognized this as the Angel of the LORD, as the *"Lord GOD"* Himself, and he began to fear for his life. The Lord spoke comfort to him. Gideon then built an altar to the LORD and named it *"The LORD is Peace"* (*Jehovah–shalom*). The Lord spoke to Gideon again later that night and instructed him to tear down the altar of Baal and *"build an altar to the LORD your God."* Gideon gathered ten men, and they did exactly as the Lord instructed.

What insights does this encounter with Gideon tell you about the Angel of the LORD?

_____

_____

_____

Gideon recognized the Angel of the LORD as God. He feared Him, honored Him, and obeyed Him. He treated Him as God. As a result of Gideon's feeble obedience, the Lord gave him a great victory over the Midianites (see Judges 6–8). Gideon's army of three hundred saw the vast enemy army totally overcome by the Lord's designs. The Angel of the LORD once again led His people in conquering and ruling in the Promised Land. His purposes were being carried out, even with the weakest of leaders. What a leader and commander the Angel of the LORD is!

 Are you like Gideon, fearful, unsure of the ways of God, unsure of what to do with the mess all around? Call on the Lord. He is willing to guide you as He rules in His kingdom day by day.

The Angel of the LORD was quite active in the days of the Judges. In Judges 2:1–6, we read of Him rebuking Israel for not dealing with the Canaanites as He had commanded. This disobedience and lack of faith on their part caused many heartaches and headaches through the years. In Judges 5:23, we find the Angel cursing the town of Meroz for not fighting alongside the people of God against the LORD's enemies in northern Israel. God wants His people wholeheartedly obeying and following Him—wherever He leads, however He leads. We see this in the encounter of the Angel of the LORD with the future parents of a child named Samson. You may want to read that account in Judges 13.

We have seen much today about how the Angel of the LORD acted in bringing His people to conquer the land of Canaan. We have observed Him ruling in the midst of His people, guiding them, at times rebuking, at other times encouraging. He is an able Conqueror and Ruler, a fierce Warrior and a just King. He knows how to lead His people and bring them into the fullness of His will. He does the same today. He is also a protector and provider for His people. We will see these truths highlighted in Day Four.

Extra Mile
SAMSON'S PARENTS

Manoah and "Mrs. Manoah," the parents of Samson, had an encounter with the Angel of the LORD, which included Him ascending in the fire of the altar. Read this account in Judges 13 and see what you discover about the Angel of the LORD.

THE ANGEL OF THE LORD: CORRECTING, PROTECTING AND PROVIDING FOR HIS PEOPLE

The Angel of the Lord | DAY FOUR

God never gave up on His people in spite of the numerous times they wandered from Him and His Word. More than wandering, they often ran from His will. He dealt with them according to His covenant promises and He revealed both His wrath and His mercy. The LORD is always as gentle as He can be and as forceful as He needs to be in accomplishing His will and leading His people. We will see how He continued to do that as the kingdom of Israel grew up.

📖 David knew the protecting hand of God and gladly gave testimony of this. One incident concerns his flight from Saul. Psalm 34 begins with an explanatory note, "A Psalm of David when he feigned madness before Abimelech, who drove him away and he departed." The account alluded to is found in 1 Samuel 21:10–15; 22:1. Read that account and describe what occurred.

_____

_____

_____

_____

📖 While those events were occurring, there were more things going on in the heart of David. After the event, we see David's reflection on that event and on the Lord's protecting hand. Read Psalm 34 especially verses 4–10 and record your insights.

_____

_____

_____

The LORD is always as gentle as He can be and as forceful as He needs to be in accomplishing His will and leading His people.

> **"This poor man cried and the LORD heard him, and saved him out of all his troubles. The angel of the LORD encamps around those who fear Him, and rescues them."**
>
> **Psalm 34:6–7**

When David was running from King Saul, he made his way into Philistine territory. In fear of the Philistine king, Achish, David chose to pretend insanity by scratching on the doors and drooling into his beard, a shameful and dishonorable practice. David then escaped and made his way to the cave of Adullam in the Judean wilderness. When David wrote of this incident, he recognized the Lord's protecting hand in spite of his fearful lack of faith. David confidently declared, *"This poor man cried and the Lord heard him, and saved him out of all his troubles. The angel of the LORD encamps around those who fear Him, and rescues them"* (Psalm 34:6–7). The Lord worked to accomplish His will in David's life, protecting and guiding. David also knew the correcting hand of the Lord.

📖 The Lord is faithful to deal with sin in the lives of His people. Read 1 Chronicles 21:1–30. What did David do according to verses 1–6?

_____

_____

_____

_____

_____

What was God's response to David's actions? Look at verses 7–15 and record what you find about the Lord and about David.

_____

_____

_____

_____

_____

God allowed Satan to tempt David to number Israel. While there appears to be a wrong motive on David's part, it is not specified. Most likely, pride in his military strength lurked here. A census provided a way to determine the number of able men for war and could have easily been a cause for boasting, and, even worse, a step toward self-dependence rather than God-dependence. Whatever David's sin, he knew he had acted foolishly and his heart condemned him. The Lord quickly dealt with it, sending the prophet Gad to give David three options—prolonged famine, three months of enemy attacks, or three days' plague. Gad noted this as *"the sword of the LORD"* with the Angel of the LORD dealing in judgment. Hoping for a measure of God's mercy, David chose the three days' plague, and seventy thousand died. In the parallel account of this incident, 2 Samuel 24:1 notes that the Lord was also angry at Israel for some unnamed sin. In His sovereign design, God allowed David to take a census that surfaced David's heart problem. Joab certainly recognized the problem. God dealt with both David's sinful heart and Israel's sin in this series of events.

What did David see, and how did he respond according to 1 Chronicles 21:16–17?

_____

_____

_____

📖 Summarize what you find about the commands of the Angel of the LORD and David's responses in verses 18–30 and 22:1.

_____

_____

_____

_____

What insights do you see about the Angel of the LORD in this encounter?

_____

_____

_____

_____

📖 What additional insights do you glean from 2 Chronicles 3:1?

_____

_____

_____

In this moment of judgment, David saw the Angel of the LORD with sword drawn over Jerusalem. He and the leaders of Israel clothed themselves in sackcloth, a sign of humbling themselves. They bowed face down before God. David confessed his sin, acknowledging he deserved judgment but asked God to spare the people. The Angel of the LORD commanded David to build an altar. He immediately obeyed and went to the threshing floor of Ornan, offering to buy the place to offer sacrifice there. The price was paid. The sacrifice was made. David prayed, and the Lord answered with fire from heaven. The Angel of the LORD sheathed His sword. God had revealed Himself in judgment and in mercy. David walked in a deep fear of the Angel of the LORD and offered his worship with renewed zeal there at the threshing floor. Later, Solomon built the Temple at that same place. God had revealed Himself to David there, and Solomon recognized it to be the chosen place God wanted for sacrifice and worship (see 1 Chronicles 22:1; 2 Chronicles 3:1). The Angel of the LORD made clear His will, how David and His people should walk dealing with sin, and how they should worship in careful obedience.

The Angel of the LORD appeared many other times after David. One of those instances is very instructive of the Lord's care. We find it in the life of Elijah.

At the direction of the Lord, Elijah prayed for a drought in the land of Israel; this was God's way of dealing with their rebellion and idolatry. Then, the Lord instructed him to challenge the prophets of Baal to a meeting on Mount Carmel. First Kings 18 records the tremendous victory as the fire of God fell on Elijah's sacrifice after which the people turned back to the Lord and the prophets of Baal were executed. Elijah then prayed for much-needed rain, and the Lord answered. Then, he heard of the threats of Jezebel and ran.

📖 Read 1 Kings 19:1–8. What was Elijah facing, and how did he respond to his circumstances?

_____

_____

_____

Did You Know?

WHAT IS SACKCLOTH?

Sackcloth is a very coarse fabric made from goats' hair. Wearing sackcloth was a sign of contrition of heart or of mourning over one's sin. The cloth was somewhat irritating and the discomfort was sobering, a continual reminder of being needy, even desperate. It was often accompanied with fasting, prayer, and renewed seeking after God. God loves to see a contrite heart, not because He wants people to be uncomfortable or miserable, but because He wants to see hearts humble before Him. He delights to see dependence on Him and delight in His will alone, not in some inadequate substitute, some deceptive second-best that can in no way match what He wants to do and can do with those who will follow and obey Him. For us today, at times a "sackcloth heart" would be appropriate as we seek to follow wholeheartedly, ever watchful of things that distract and detour us from God and His will.

Did You Know?

THE FIRE OF GOD

David saw the fire of God fall on the sacrifice on the altar at the threshing floor of Ornan (see 1 Chronicles 21:26), like the fire that fell on the altar before Aaron (see Leviticus 9:24), the fire on the Temple altar in Solomon's day (see 2 Chronicles 7:1), and the fire on the altar in Elijah's day (see 1 Kings 18:36–38). Gideon saw God's fire (see Judges 6:21). The fire of God was displayed in judgment in Leviticus 10:1–2; Numbers 16:35; and 2 Kings 1:10, 12.

What did the Angel of the LORD do for Elijah?

_____

_____

_____

_____

What do you discover about the Angel of the LORD, His actions and His ways, in meeting and dealing with Elijah at this point in his life?

_____

_____

_____

_____

What was the result of this encounter?

_____

_____

_____

The Angel of the LORD met Elijah in his weariness, woke him, gave him food and drink, let him sleep some more and then fed him again. He knows what we need.

Elijah ran in fear from Jezebel. When he reached the wilderness, weary and worn, he prayed to die. He fell asleep. The Angel of the LORD met Elijah in his weariness, woke him, gave him food and drink, let him sleep some more and then fed him again. He knows what we need. What He provided gave Elijah strength for the next forty days. Then at Mount Horeb, Elijah encountered the Lord once again and was given his new assignments—all part of the Lord's plans for Elijah and for Israel.

In the Old Testament, the Angel of the LORD comes to assure the fulfillment of His will. In so doing He is ever aware of the needs of His people. He knows how to fight for us, protect, and provide for us. He does not necessarily scold us for the "down times," but He is always truthful in those times. Sometimes, the best thing, even the most "spiritual" thing is rest and a good meal. That was the case with Elijah, and this meal helped better prepare him for the next assignment, the further accomplishment of God's kingdom plans. What more can we learn about the Angel of the LORD and His ways?

📖 In 655 BC, Sennacherib, king of Assyria, invaded Judah and threatened to overrun Jerusalem (see 2 Kings 18). How would Hezekiah deal with this? Read 2 Kings 19:1–13. Summarize Hezekiah's situation.

_____

_____

_____

_____

📖 What did Hezekiah do according to 2 Kings 19:14–19?

_____

_____

_____

When Hezekiah heard the threats of the Assyrian army, he humbled himself in sackcloth and went before the Lord. He sent word to Isaiah concerning the threats of Rabshakeh and the Assyrians. Isaiah told the people that there was no reason to fear the enemy, for the Lord would deal with the Assyrians. Yet the threats intensified, and Hezekiah spread the ominous Assyrian letter before the Lord and prayed. He prayed for the reputation of God to be clearly revealed—"...*deliver us from his hand that all the kingdoms of the earth may know that Thou alone, O LORD, art God.*"

📖 Read the word given through Isaiah in 2 Kings 19:20–34. What did God promise, especially in verses 32–34?

_____

_____

_____

📖 Look at 2 Kings 19:35. What did God do about Sennacherib and his threats?

_____

_____

_____

What insights do you see about the Angel of the LORD in this incident?

_____

_____

_____

God heard Hezekiah's prayer. He promised protection for him and Jerusalem and assured him that Sennacherib would not so much as shoot an arrow there. The Angel of the LORD dealt decisively with the Assyrian threat by slaying 185,000 troops in a single night. Sennacherib went home in disgrace, and Jerusalem was safe. Again we see the Angel of the LORD fighting for His people, protecting, and providing in order to accomplish His purposes.

Though God delivered the Jews from the hostile intentions of the Assyrians in this instance, the sins of God's people opened the door for their eventual captivity. Years later, when the people of God were released from Babylonian captivity and journeyed back to Israel, they had much to do to rebuild Jerusalem and the land of Israel. To encourage them, God sent word through the prophet Zechariah, who records two different visions in which the Angel of the LORD promised to be at work protecting, defending, and restoring His people (see Zechariah 1:7–17; 3:1–10). He also spoke of the future days of Israel when the nation's strength would be clearly seen—a nation with the Angel of the LORD leading them (see Zechariah 12:8).

The Angel of the LORD proved Himself powerful and faithful in the lives of His people throughout the Old Testament. The testimony of His works remained on the hearts of His people as they awaited the coming of the Messiah. He would bring the promised and prophesied deliverance. The Angel of the LORD did indeed come—Christ was born in a manger in Bethlehem to save His people from their sins. . . . and the rest is history, or perhaps we should say that the rest of history is being carried out according

Put Yourself In Their Shoes

DANIEL AND THE THREE HEBREWS

The Angel of the LORD is ever watchful and aware of His people. We see this even in the midst of His judgments and corrective discipline on the nation. In Daniel 3, three young Hebrew men who were part of the Babylonian captivity faced the wrath of Nebuchadnezzar because they would not bow to his idol. They respectfully declared, *"If it be so, our God . . . is able to deliver us from the furnace of blazing fire . . . but even if He does not . . . we are not going to serve your gods or worship the golden image. . . ."* They were thrown in the furnace and there God *"sent His Angel,"* most likely another appearance of the Angel of the LORD who protected and delivered them. Not even the smell of smoke was on them (3:27–28). When Daniel was about 80 years of age he faced opposition from some of his fellow workers (6:1–28). As a result of their scheming Daniel was thrown into the lion's den, but the Lord *"sent His angel and shut the lions' mouths"* protecting Daniel and once again revealing His care so His people might accomplish His purposes.

to His perfect plans. He continues to work in His people's lives to accomplish His purposes. What about in our lives today? We will see some personal applications concerning the Angel of the LORD in Day Five.

The Angel of the LORD *is indeed the Leader, Protector, Provider, and Conqueror, the Warrior like no other, a friend in the truest sense of the word, and He is LORD.*

FOR ME TO FOLLOW CHRIST

We have seen many appearances and encounters with the Angel of the LORD. What was often a mysterious appearance of Christ in the Old Testament was always a clear revelation of His will. He is indeed the Leader, Protector, Provider, and Conqueror, the Warrior like no other, a Friend in the truest sense of the word, and He is Lord. How does His life and ministry apply to us today? The Angel of the LORD is Christ, God who became Man, our LORD and Savior. As we consider His ways in the Old Testament, we can apply those to our lives today. What does He want us to know about His will?

Many times we wonder about God's will for our lives. Should I go to college or not? If so, where and when? Or, what career path is right for me? Should I move or not move to this city or take that job? What about marriage and family? Should I change careers? How should I be involved in church? What about this or that ministry area? These and a myriad of other questions about God's will arise as we walk through life. To better know the answers to those questions we need to make sure we are obeying the "we-know-for-sure" will of God already revealed in Scripture.

Consider each of these scriptures in the chart below. Read each and in the left column record the clear will of God for your life, then in the "Apply and Pray" column, give some of the ways you see how this **has been applied** in your life, how it **is being applied** in your life, or ways it **should be applied**. You may also wish to write **an appropriate prayer in this column**.

THE WILL OF GOD	APPLY AND PRAY
I Timothy 2:4 and 2 Peter 3:9	
I Thessalonians 4:3–8	
Ephesians 5:15–18	
I Thessalonians 5:16–18	
Romans 12:1–3	
I Peter 2:13–17	
I Peter 3:13–17	

While we may face some foggy days in discerning God's will for our lives, many aspects of God's will are very clearly revealed in Scripture:

1) **(1 Timothy 2:4; 2 Peter 3:9)** God wants us to know Him as Lord and Savior through coming to Him in repentance and faith and then walking in faith.

2) **(1 Thessalonians 4:3–8)** Our walk with Him is to be a walk in sanctification, our whole lives, spirit, soul, and body, being set apart to holiness and His purposes, never to uncleanness and selfishness.

3) **(Ephesians 5:15–18)** He wants us making the most of our time on earth, every day on earth. To do that we must walk in the fullness of His Spirit and the fruit He produces in the heart and in the lifestyle, in words and deeds.

4) **(1 Thessalonians 5:16–18)** Our focus is the Lord. Therefore we rejoice in Him (even in difficult circumstances). We should maintain an attitude of gratitude and give Him thanks in everything, and we are to continually pray, always looking to Him in all circumstances and in every relationship.

5) **(Romans 12:1–3)** Our daily worship to Him involves our becoming a living sacrifice, offering our surrendered lives to Him, not to the world and its ways. Being transformed by the renewing of the mind *is the will of God,* and it is *the path to* further knowledge of the will of God. We have the opportunity to prove by experience *"what the will of God is,"* and when we do, we discover that His will is indeed *"good"* or beneficial, helpful. It is *"acceptable"* or *"well-pleasing."* It is the <u>best</u> choice among all choices. His will is *"perfect,"* the Greek word conveying the idea of reaching the right goal, hitting the right target in life.

6) **(1 Peter 2:13–17)** The issue of God's will also applies to every authority with which we deal—at home, in the church, in school, and with government. God's will is that we do right in every arena, which includes submitting to those in authority over us or who give leadership to some area of our lives. It is the Lord's will that in doing right we give a clear, consistent witness (verbal and lifestyle) of the lordship of Christ over our lives and of the hope we have in Him.

7) **(1 Peter 3:13–17)** Sometimes this consistent witness involves suffering for *"doing what is right."* When that is the will of God, we also discover the enabling power of God at a new level.

We know these things are God's will. You may be asking, "What else is God's will? Especially in my life, in my daily walk?" If you are walking in what you know is the will of God, you can be assured the Lord will guide you, provide for and protect you, even correct you to get you or keep you in the path of His will. As we saw in our studies this week, each time God revealed Himself as the Angel of the Lord, He proved this. In His revelation as the Christ, as Jesus, as our Lord and Savior, He has shown this time and time again. He will be faithful in your life as well.

APPLY One final truth related to God's will should help us in walking in His will. It is the issue of **surrender.** Jesus wants us to surrender to His will **before** we know <u>what it is</u>, **because** we know <u>who He is</u>. Surrender to His will is first surrender to Him. His will is not so much about tasks as it is about trust, not so much about where we should be or what we should be doing as it is about whom we know and are walking with. Reflect on your surrender to Jesus Christ, The Angel of the LORD.

If you are walking in the will of God, you can be assured the Lord will guide you, provide for and protect you, even correct you to get you or keep you in the path of His will.

Extra Mile
SURRENDER

Jesus wants us to surrender to His will:

■ before we know what it is

■ because we know who He is

Surrender to His will is accomplished by first surrendering to Him

SURRENDER

Read and think through the words to the hymn, "Take My Life and Let It Be," by Francis Ridley Havergal and reflect on your surrender to Jesus Christ, The Angel of the LORD.

Take my life, and let it be
Consecrated, Lord, to thee;
Take my moments and my days,
Let them flow in ceaseless praise.
Let them flow in ceaseless praise.

Take my hands, and let them move
At the impulse of thy love;
Take my feet, and let them be
Swift and beautiful for thee.
Swift and beautiful for thee.

Take my voice, and let me sing
Always, only, for my King;
Take my lips, and let them be
Filled with messages from thee.
Filled with messages from thee.

Take my silver and my gold,
Not a mite would I withhold;
Take my intellect, and use
Every power as thou shalt choose.
Every power as thou shalt choose.

Take my will and make it thine;
It shall be no longer mine.
Take my heart, it is thine own;
It shall be thy royal throne.
It shall be thy royal throne.

Take my love; my Lord, I pour
At thy feet its treasure store;
Take my self, and I will be
Ever, only, all for thee.
Ever, only, all for thee.

Write your thoughts or a prayer about your surrender to God and His will.

_____

_____

_____

_____

_____

_____

Lord, thank You for revealing Yourself as the Angel of the LORD, for showing Your power, Your compassion, and Your ability to fight for Your people and for Your will. Thank You that You do not give up on Your people in spite of their waywardness. I praise You for Your faithfulness in dealing with Your people in the details of life. Thank You for showing Your care and concern through Your provision, Your protection, and Your clear guidance. I praise You for being a purposeful Lord, One who has a focused plan, and who diligently works to accomplish all Your will. Thank You for including me in Your purposes, Your plans, and Your will. Thank You that though today I do not see all the details about tomorrow, You do see and have already planned how all will fit into Your design. I praise and honor You, acknowledging Your power to see Your will accomplished in spite of all the obstacles we see and experience all around. Thank You for daily bringing Your will to pass. I look forward to seeing how You will fulfill all to our good and to Your glory and honor. In Jesus' name. Amen.

In light of all you have seen about the Angel of the Lord, write your prayer to the Lord or make a journal entry in the space provided.

_____

_____

_____

_____

_____

_____

_____

_____

_____

_____

_____

_____

_____

_____

_____

The Angel of the LORD
CHRIST REVEALING AND ACCOMPLISHING HIS WILL
The Angel of the Lord is considered a Christophany, an appearance of Christ in the Old Testament

SCRIPTURE	EVENT	PLACE
Genesis 16:1–15 (note verses 7–13)	The Angel of the LORD found Hagar and Ishmael in the wilderness running from Sarai's harsh treatment. He delivered them and asked them to return to Sarai.	Wilderness near Shur
Genesis 17:1–22	*"The Lord appeared to Abram"* in some form when Abraham was ninety-nine years old and promised him a son, Isaac.	By the oaks of Mamre near Hebron
Genesis 18:1–33	The LORD came to the home of Abraham in the form of a man with two angels who were also in the form of men. He spoke to Abraham and Sarah about their coming son Isaac and to Abraham about the coming judgment of Sodom.	By the oaks of Mamre near Hebron
Genesis 21:8–21 (note verses 17–18)	The Angel of God met Hagar and Ishmael in the desert and provided water for them.	Wilderness of Beersheba
Genesis 22:1–19 (note verses 11–19)	As Abraham was offering up Isaac on Mount Moriah, the Angel of the LORD stopped him, spoke to him, and gave him many promises.	Mount Moriah (modern Jerusalem)
Genesis 28:10–22; 31:11, 13	The LORD appeared to Jacob in a dream at Bethel, promising him the land, many descendants, and a seed through whom the earth would be blessed. This same LORD appeared to Jacob as the Angel of God twenty years later.	Bethel
Genesis 31:10–13	The Angel of God spoke to Jacob in a dream instructing him to leave Haran and return to Canaan.	Haran
Genesis 32:22–32; Hosea 12:4–5	The Angel of the LORD wrestled all night with Jacob and blessed him at the Jabbok River.	Jabbok River
Genesis 48:3, 16	In Egypt, while blessing the sons of Joseph, Jacob testified before his family of *"the Angel who has redeemed me from all evil"* (NKJV). He invoked this *"Angel"* to *"bless the lads,"* something only God could do.	Egypt
Exodus 3:1–6 (note verse 2); Deuteronomy 33:16; Acts 7:30–34; Mark 12:26; Luke 20:37	The Angel of the LORD appeared to Moses in a flame of fire in the midst of a bush in the desert of Midian.	Mount Horeb (also known as Mount Sinai)
Exodus 4:24–26	The Lord met Moses and sought to kill him for failing to circumcise his son. This was possibly the Angel of the LORD.	On the way to Egypt
Exodus 14:19–20; Isaiah 63:9	The Angel of God appeared in the Pillar of Cloud and of Fire, guiding and protecting the children of Israel from Pharaoh's army.	At the Red Sea
Exodus 19—20 24:12–18; Acts 7:38	The Angel of the LORD gave the Law to Moses on Mount Sinai.	At Mount Sinai
Exodus 23:20–23	Moses received God's promise that He would send the Angel of the LORD to guide Israel into Canaan. (*"My name is in Him." "My Angel will go before you."* [NKJV])	At Mount Sinai
Exodus 32:34; 33:1–6, 12–16	The Lord told Moses that He would send a representative angel before the people, not the Angel of the LORD, for He Himself would not go with them because of their sin. Moses interceded and God promised, "My presence shall go with you."	At Mount Sinai
Numbers 22—24 (note 22:22–39)	The Angel of the LORD met Balaam and his donkey on the journey with the princes of Moab to meet Balak.	The Plains of Moab
Joshua 5:13–15; 6:1–5	A "man," the Commander of the army of the Lord, met Joshua near Jericho and instructed him in how to conquer the city.	Near Jericho in the land of Canaan
Judges 2:1–6	The Angel of the LORD rebuked Israel for disobeying Him in not dealing with the Canaanites as He had commanded.	Bochim (means "weeping")
Judges 5:23	The Angel of the LORD cursed the people of the town of Meroz for not fighting with the people of God against the Lord's enemies in northern Israel.	Meroz

SCRIPTURE	EVENT	PLACE
Judges 6:11–24, 25–27	The Angel of the LORD appeared to Gideon calling him to lead Israel against the Midianites.	Ophrah
Judges 13:1–24	The Angel of the LORD appeared to Manoah and his wife, promising them a son and then ascended in the flame of their burnt offering.	Zorah
2 Samuel 14:17,20	A woman of Tekoa spoke to David about the Angel of God *"discerning good and evil"* and being marked by *"wisdom . . . to know everything that is in the earth"* (NKJV).	Jerusalem
2 Samuel 24:10–25 (note verses 15–17) 1 Chronicles 21:1–30 (note verses 12–20, 27, 30	The Angel of the LORD was involved in judging David's sin of numbering the people (probably to assess his military might or to pridefully boast about his kingdom's potential.	Israel and Jerusalem
Psalm 34:7 (with 1 Samuel 21:10–15)	David celebrated the protection of the Angel of the LORD in the danger he faced from Achish, king of Gath.	Gath, city of the Philistines
Psalm 35:5, 6	David prayed for the help of the Angel of the LORD against an enemy who was against him without cause.	Israel
1 Kings 19:7	The Angel of the LORD touched Elijah and instructed him to eat in preparation for the journey ahead.	Wilderness south of Beersheba
2 Kings 1:2–17 (note verses 3, 15–16)	The Angel of the LORD instructed Elijah to go and deliver a message to Israel's King Ahaziah.	Samaria
2 Kings 19:35–36; Isaiah 37:36	The Angel of the LORD struck 185,000 Assyrian troops, bringing Sennacherib's threats to naught and delivering Hezekiah and the people of Jerusalem.	Near Jerusalem
Daniel 3:19–30	God *"sent His Angel"* and delivered Shadrach, Meshach, and Abed-nego from the fiery furnace. To Nebuchadnezzar, this fourth "man" in the furnace appeared *"like the Son of God"* (or "a son of the gods") (3:25, 28 NKJV).	The Plain of Dura in the province of Babylon
Daniel 6:1–28, (note verse 22)	When rescued from the lion's den, Daniel testified, *"My God sent His angel and shut the lions' mouths."* This phrasing *"sent His Angel"* is the same as Daniel 3:25–28	The city of Babylon
Zechariah 1:7–17 (note verses 11–12)	The Angel of the LORD appeared in Zechariah's first vision as the Commander-in-Chief of the angelic hosts, riding on a red horse of judgment seeking to bring mercy and restoration to Israel.	Israel and the Earth
Zechariah 3:1–10 (note verses 1–2, 3–4, 6)	The Angel of the LORD appeared in Zechariah's fourth vision, rebuking Satan and declaring Jerusalem and the nation (represented by Joshua the High Priest) as the cleansed and restored people and priesthood of God. With this declaration, comes the promise of the coming Messiah (Servant, Branch, Stone) and His kingdom.	Israel
Zechariah 12:8	Zechariah prophesied about the future of Israel when the nation will be strong like David or like a nation with the Angel of the LORD leading them.	Jerusalem and the area surrounding it

Lawgiver and Judge

CHRIST GIVING AND FULFILLING THE LAW OF GOD WITH PERFECT LOVE AND HOLINESS

James 4:12 says, *"There is only one Lawgiver and Judge, the One who is able to save and to destroy. . . . "* That Lawgiver and Judge is Jesus Christ. When He gave the Law He did so with perfect love, holiness, wisdom, and grace. He gave the Law because He knew man needed to hear and understand Him and His ways, to know His heart and His will for all of life. As the Lawgiver, Christ is also the one who evaluates all according to that Law, according to the design and desire of His heart. As people stand in relation to **His** standard, so they stand in relation to the heart of Christ. Their standing determines their station for all eternity—will it be salvation or damnation, to be saved or destroyed? In this lesson we will discover the many dimensions of Christ as the Lawgiver and Judge. We will see that the Lawgiver is also the grace giver, the One who expresses His heart through the Law, expects obedience to the Law, is willing to show mercy to the lawbreaker, and gives grace and power to obey His Law His way. In receiving the grace of Christ, one receives the Law-obeying life of Christ and thus has the potential to exhibit His life and love every day in every relationship.

How does the Law fit into the scheme of God? The Law is the heart of God in print. It is the heartbeat of God for daily life—in all relationships, in business, in worship, in government, in education, in every facet of everyday life. Paul said, *"the Law is holy, and the commandment is holy and righteous and good"* (Romans 7:12). Does that mean if I obey the Law, I will be holy and righteous and good? Can I obey the Law? Can I actually live by the dictates of the Law of God? Do I have the power and will to do that? If not, then how am I to honor the Law and the Lawgiver today? What does Christ have to say about His Law, about my relationship to it, and how it affects my relationship to Him?

What does this Law mean to the believer today? What does it mean to follow God in light of the Law given by the Lawgiver? Does He require meticulous attention to the minute details of the Law? If not, then where does the

WHO IS THE LAWGIVER?

The Lawgiver is also the Grace giver, the One who expresses His heart through the Law, expects obedience to the Law, is willing to show mercy to the lawbreaker, and gives grace and power to obey the Law His way. In receiving the grace of Christ one receives the Law-obeying life of Christ and thus has the potential to exhibit His life and love every day in every relationship.

Law fit into our daily walk? These and many other questions will be studied in this lesson. We will come to see the heart of Christ in fuller measure and hopefully see His life and His law worked out in and through our lives in greater grace.

CHRIST, THE LAWGIVER

We find the Law presented in the book of Exodus. How was it presented? As Moses tended his flocks around Mount Horeb (Mount Sinai), he came upon a bush that burned but was not consumed. The Angel of the LORD spoke to him from that bush and called Moses to join Him in delivering the children of Israel out of Egypt and into the promised land of Canaan. The Angel of the LORD identified Himself as "I AM WHO I AM" (Exodus 3:14) and told Moses He would bring the people back to that very place that they might worship there (Exodus 3:12). Jesus identified Himself as the "I AM" in John 8:58, *"Before Abraham was, I AM"* (NKJV). What place did Christ, the I AM, have in giving the Law to Moses? What can we learn about Him and His purposes in this initial presentation of the Law? We will begin to see in today's scripture search.

📖 Read Stephen's account of the events at Mount Sinai in Acts 7:30–38. What specifics are mentioned in this New Testament passage regarding Moses and his interaction with the Angel of the LORD in verses 30, 32, 35, and 38?

_____

_____

_____

_____

The Angel of the LORD appeared to Moses, identified Himself as the God of Abraham, Isaac, and Jacob, and sent Moses to be *"a ruler and a deliverer"* with the help and guidance of *"the Angel"* (NKJV). This Angel also spoke to Moses giving him *"living oracles"* to pass on to the people. It is the Angel of the LORD who gave the Law to Moses and the people of Israel.

📖 Let's explore a little further. How does God identify Himself in Exodus 20:2? Compare what you have seen in Exodus 3 and look at Acts 7:35–38, especially verse 36. Who is the giver of the Law according to these verses?

_____

_____

_____

_____

God identified Himself to Moses saying, *"I am the LORD your God, who brought you out of the land of Egypt."* This is Yahweh/Jehovah, the I AM who spoke to Moses at the bush, who sent him to Egypt, and who brought Israel out of Egypt. Exodus 3 identifies the Angel of the LORD as the one speaking to Moses as does Stephen in Acts 7. The Angel of the LORD,

> *"For the LORD is our Judge, the LORD is our Lawgiver, the LORD is our King; He will save us."*
>
> *Isaiah 33:22 (NKJV)*

✏ **Did You Know?**

(?) **WRITTEN BY GOD HIMSELF**

The Scriptures record that when God had finished speaking with Moses on Mount Sinai, *"He gave Moses the two tablets of the testimony, tablets of stone, written by the finger of God"* (Exodus 31:18; see also Exodus 24:12; 32:15–16). After Moses crushed those tablets at the sight of the Israelites worshiping the golden calf, God engraved two more tablets (Exodus 34:1). Those were placed in the Ark of the Covenant in the Holy of Holies in the Tabernacle (See also Deuteronomy 4:13; 5:22; 9:10; Deut 10:2–5).

Yahweh/Jehovah, the I AM, and Jesus are one and the same calling, delivering, and giving the Law.

When Christ *"became flesh, and dwelt among us"* (John 1:14), how did He view the Law? What do you discover in Matthew 5:17–18?

_____

_____

_____

_____

What should be the attitude of others toward the Law according to Matthew 5:19?

_____

_____

_____

Jesus Christ had utmost regard for all the Law of God and for the prophets who spoke His Word. He did not come to *"abolish the Law or the Prophets."* On the contrary, He chose to honor the Law by fulfilling it, *"until all is accomplished"* or fulfilled. Jesus came to fulfill the Law in His person and in His works, fully obeying the Law in its true intent and fully picturing all the types and symbols embodied in the Old Testament Law. This included every offering, every feast, every regulation, and all that which is pictured in the Tabernacle/Temple and in the priesthood. Throughout the history of heaven and earth, the Law would have a place of utmost importance. In the strongest terms, Jesus declared that the smallest letter (the Greek *iȯta* or the Hebrew *yod*) or even a single stroke (a serif, one small part of a Hebrew letter) would in no way pass away until all had been completed.

In this passage of Matthew, Jesus calls all to honor the Word of God, to obey the Law and to guide others in obeying it. The one who disobeys, who breaks the Law, and leads others to break it will be considered least in the kingdom of heaven while the one who obeys and teaches others to obey is considered great in the kingdom. Does this mean one can be a part of the kingdom through simple obedience to the Law? No. Jesus is speaking of one's view of the Law, of *the heart* that obeys. Later, we will see *how* this is to be done.

How complete must obedience be? What do you see in Matthew 5:20? Read that verse and record your insights.

_____

_____

_____

_____

Jesus presented what seemed to be an impossible condition in the matter of obeying the Law. In order to enter the kingdom of heaven one must have a personal righteousness that exceeds that of the scribes and Pharisees. How could anyone exceed the righteousness of the scribes and Pharisees? After all, these men displayed meticulous devotion to the Law (at least to the externals of the Law the way they understood it). They had even added

"The commandment of the LORD is pure, enlightening the eyes. . . . The judgments of the LORD are true; they are righteous altogether."

Psalm 19:8b, 9b

Word Study
RIGHTEOUSNESS

The word "righteousness" is a translation of the Greek word *dikaiosúnē* which is rooted in *díkaios* meaning that which is right or just, that which conforms to the expectations of the one setting the rules or regulations. *Díkaios* is rooted in *díkē* which refers to giving what is due or what is expected according to certain standards. Biblical "righteousness," *dikaiosúnē*, focuses on giving what is due, what is right, to God and man. Law is the expression of what the Lawgiver expects, what God wants done for Himself and for one another. It is the guideline, the outline, the director as to what is right or wrong.

some external "helps" to make sure they knew who was and who was not "keeping" the Law. Jesus said kingdom citizens must have a greater righteousness than even the scribes and Pharisees possessed. What did Jesus mean by this? We will see as we walk through the Scriptures.

Three examples of Christ's teaching in relationship to the Law will help us see His view of the Law and what it means to truly keep it. Look at each of these examples from Matthew and note how Jesus approached each one.

The Law "You have heard…" Matthew 5:21, 27, 43	Jesus' Statement "But I say…" Matthew 5:22, 28, 44	The Full Intent and Meaning of the Law Your Insights…

Jesus used the phrases *"you have heard," "it was said,"* and *"but I say"* six times in Matthew 5. In each case, He clarified what the Law said by giving His fuller meaning. In the three examples listed in the chart, the commandment, *"do not murder,"* in reality tells us to avoid the heart of murder, which is anger. *"Do not commit adultery,"* includes abstaining from the heart of adultery, which is lust. *"Love your neighbor,"* means more than loving those with whom you agree. It involves loving and caring for your enemies as well. God does not want unrighteous anger, lust, or hatred to exist in the hearts of His kingdom citizens. In these and in the other three statements, Jesus made it clear that He is interested in the heart of the Law, not mere outward conformity. The Pharisees were good at outwardly following rules and regulations but ultimately fell far short of God's kind of righteousness. What does God's kind is of righteousness look like? We will see in Day Two.

Lawgiver and Judge

DAY TWO

CHRIST, THE LAW FULFILLER

Christ states very clearly in Matthew 5:17, *"Do not think that I came to abolish the Law or the Prophets; I did not come to abolish, but to fulfill."* How did Christ fulfill the Law He gave? How do we see Him living out the very Law He wrote and gave to Moses and the people of Israel? How did Christ approach the Ten Commandments, the heart of the Law of God? What did He think of them? How did He fulfill each of them? We will see in today's lesson.

Consider this truth: the Law pleases the Father because it reflects the heart of the Father. Remember that following the law means much more than just outward conformity to rules and regulations; it's all about the heart. When we think of the Ten Commandments, we must not think of simple outward conformity, saying, for example, "I've never murdered anyone." God revealed these commands to reveal His heart, to show us the kind of heart He wants to see in us. If a person fully obeyed the Ten Commandments, not just with outward conformity, but with a whole heart, fully carrying out the intent of each command, that person would be fully pleasing to the Father. Why? God has never been interested in mere external acts. He wants to see that heart desire, that internal delight in doing His will, walking His way. Fulfilling the Ten Commandments is more than just "not doing" certain things. It is both affirming and acting from the heart the full intent of each command. It is our heart agreeing with God's heart. With that in mind, let's look at the life of Jesus and see how He fulfilled each command.

Commandment One—Worship God Alone. What do you find in Jesus' life in Matthew 4:8–10 and Matthew 11:25a?

_____

_____

_____

_____

In this passage, when Jesus faces the temptation to worship Satan in order to gain the kingdoms of the world, He responds with a clear refusal as He quotes Deuteronomy 6:13—the expression of His heart to worship and obey the Lord alone. We see His worship in action in Matthew 11:25. Here Jesus publicly praises His Father as Lord of heaven and earth and rejoices in His ways.

Commandment Two—No Idols. Words reveal the heart. What do you discover about the heart of Jesus in Matthew 6:24? Jesus applies this truth to seeking food and clothing in Matthew 6:25–33. How does Jesus respond to the need for food at His temptation in Matthew 4:3–4?

_____

_____

_____

_____

Jesus knew the only true Master worth loving and serving was His Father in heaven. The false god. Mammon or riches, was no substitute. Jesus certainly did not serve riches or strive to gain for Himself. Even when He had a legitimate reason to create His own bread, He refused, choosing rather to wait on His Father's provision. The Father did indeed provide as Matthew 4:11 indicates. Jesus worshiped no substitutes for God His Father.

Commandment Three—Honor God's Name. What do you find in Matthew 6:9 and John 17:6, 26?

_____

_____

_____

_____

Word Study
"LAW"

The word 'Law" is a translation of the Hebrew word *torah* which means "teaching." It is rooted in a word picture related to "sending," that is, sending words. It is the same root word used when speaking of shooting (sending) an arrow or sending rain. Teaching is sending truthful words specifically targeted, like sending an arrow or sending a spring shower—purposeful and helpful. God's sending of His Law was intended to be helpful, purposeful, and a delight for life and relationships. The problem is not the Law, but sin in the heart that rejects and hates the Law as well as the Lawgiver. Christ gives us a new heart with His Law written on it, a heart that loves Him and wants to do His will His way.

Jesus taught His disciples to honor the Father's name. He Himself delighted to honor and value His Father's name because He knew how truly valuable He is. He boasted in His Father, in all He had done and all He promised to do.

Commandment Four—Honor the Sabbath—Read Mark 2:23–28; 3:1–6 and record your insights into how Jesus dealt with the Sabbath.

_____

_____

_____

_____

_____

Doctrine
JESUS IS LORD OF THE SABBATH

As Creator, Jesus designed the Sabbath at Creation (Genesis 2:4). As Lawgiver, He wrote the laws in the Ten Commandments (Exodus 20:8–11). As Son of Man, He appeared on earth to experience the Law. As Law fulfiller, He perfectly carried out every Sabbath of His earthly walk. As Teacher, He clarified what the Law meant. As Lord of the Sabbath, He freed up His followers so that each could walk in the joy of spiritual and physical rest and refreshment His way.

As Jesus and His disciples passed through a grain field, they picked some grain and ate it. The Pharisees considered Jesus' actions unlawful. According to their opinions (new interpretations), Jesus' disciples were "working" or "harvesting" on the Sabbath. Jesus reminded His critics of a time when David and his men had a need and ate the consecrated bread set aside for the priests. Then, He pointed to the purpose of the Sabbath—it was for man's benefit not for his enslavement to rigid rules about work and rest. Then Jesus boldly declared that He was Lord of the Sabbath. On a certain Sabbath, Jesus healed a man with a withered hand because it was the right thing to do. The Pharisees were so hard-headed about their opinion of the Sabbath, it made them hard-hearted toward this healing—to them it was "unlawful work." In spite of the Pharisees' hardness of heart—they would have stopped Jesus if they could have—Jesus healed the man and honored the Sabbath God's way.

Commandment Five—Honor Father and Mother—We find an example of Jesus' relationship to His mother Mary and Joseph in Luke 2:41–52. Read this passage, focusing on Luke 2:51–52. What do you discover? In addition, look at what Jesus did and said in John 19:26–27 and record your insights.

_____

_____

_____

_____

Jesus said of His relationship to His Father, "I speak these things as the Father taught Me.... I always do the things that are pleasing to Him." (John 8:28b, 29b)

At the age of twelve, Jesus clearly honored His father and mother. He _"continued in subjection to them"_ throughout His years. Even while dying on the cross, Jesus showed concern for His mother. He delighted in honoring His heavenly Father and his earthly stepfather and mother. He placed value on them as the God-given channels of life, provision, and training. He could say at the age of 33, _"I always do the things that are pleasing to [My Father]."_ (John 8:29b).

Commandment Six—No Murder. How did Jesus respond to others? What insights about unrighteous anger and its outcome, murder, do you find in 1 Peter 2:21–23 and Luke 23:34?

_____

_____

_____

At a time when Jesus had every human reason to retaliate in righteous revenge against His accusers and those who physically beat and tortured Him, He *"uttered no threats."* On the contrary, He entrusted Himself to His Father and prayed, *"Father forgive them."* There was no murder in His heart, in words or deeds.

Commandment Seven—No Adultery. What insights do you glean from Peter's statement about Jesus in 1 Peter 1:19?

_____

_____

_____

_____

_____

Jesus never married, but in His relationships with men and women there was never any impurity. Peter sums up Christ's life and character by noting that He died as *"a lamb unblemished and spotless."* *"Unblemished"* is a translation of the Greek word, *amomos,* which describes something that contains no internal blemish; whereas, the word *"spotless"* comes from the Greek *aspilos,* which describes something or someone without any external stain or defect. We know that in the six trials (three Jewish trials and three Roman) He endured before He was crucified, prosecutors could not find fault in anything He had said or done. Pilate said at least three times, *"I find no fault in Him"* (John 18:38; 19:4, 6 [NKJV]).

Commandment Eight—No Stealing. What do you find Jesus doing when given the opportunity to bypass a temple tax? Read Matthew 17:27 and record you insights.

_____

_____

_____

_____

_____

The Jewish law required a half-shekel tax from every Jewish male (age 20 and above). The officials asked if Jesus paid that tax. Peter told them "Yes." Jesus asked Peter if an earthly king would tax his own sons or just strangers. "Strangers," Peter replied, assuming that the king's own family would be exempt from taxation. Jesus attempted to explain to Peter that He as the Son of the King (God the Father) was technically exempt from Temple taxation. However, not wanting to offend any Temple officials who would fail to understand such divine logic, Jesus told Peter where to find a coin to pay His and Peter's tax. Peter caught a fish as Jesus had instructed and found a stater, a coin equal to the payment for two men. He paid the tax. Not only did Jesus never steal, He was always found giving, even in this situation of paying the temple tax.

Commandment Nine—No False Witness. Look at 1 Peter 2:22 and record what you find about Jesus' words. Also look at Jesus' statements in John 8:42–47 and focus on His statements about the truth of His words. Write down your insights.

Jesus never uttered a deceitful word. Never did He sin in word or deed. When confronting the unbelieving Jews, Jesus gave witness of His relationship to the Father and of the truth of His words. Unlike the devil, who is *"a liar and the father of lies,"* Jesus speaks only truth, the words of God. Later, in John 12:50, He declared, *"I speak just as the Father has told Me."*

Commandment Ten—No Coveting. In a unique message given on the coast of Miletus, Paul gives a clear testimony about himself, about Jesus and about this matter of coveting. Read Acts 20:33–35 and record your insights.

_____

_____

_____

_____

_____

In talking to the elders of the church of Ephesus, Paul gave his own testimony declaring, *"I have coveted no one's silver or gold or clothes."* (He worked hard as a tentmaker to care for his own needs as well as the needs of others.) The subject of covetousness reminded Paul of the words of Jesus, *"It is more blessed to give than to receive."* We do not know when or where Jesus made this statement, as it is not recorded in the Gospels. But Paul attributes the statement to Jesus, and the quote is in keeping with Jesus' heart and lifestyle (see John 21:25). Jesus lived a live of blessed giving, never coveting any man's position or possessions.

Jesus fulfilled the Law perfectly, not only the Ten Commandments but every other Law given by Moses and the prophets. Quoting from Isaiah 53:9, Peter declared that Jesus *"committed no sin"* (1 Peter 2:22) and Paul testified, *"He made Him who knew no sin to be sin on our behalf"* (2 Corinthians 5:21). Jesus is *"the Holy and Righteous One"* (Acts 3:14; see also 7:52; 22:14; 1 Peter 3:18; 1 John 2:1; 2:29; 3:7). Not only did Jesus withstand any temptation to sin, He did what was right in every word and deed. In loving His Father with all His heart, mind, soul, and strength, and in loving His neighbor as Himself, Jesus manifested the fullness of love required in the Law.

As the Lawgiver, He spoke truth in every detail. As the Law-fulfiller, Jesus perfectly revealed the righteousness of God. What more can we learn of Him? We will see in Day Three.

Put Yourself In Their Shoes

THOUGHTS ON COVETING

Paul testified that before he was aware of the Law, he was not fully aware of his sinfulness. When the Law confronted his life, sin was exposed. He gave the specific example of coveting. When he saw the law, "YOU SHALL NOT COVET," sin within rose up with all kinds of coveting (Romans 7:7–11). He came to Christ and, while still having to deal with sin within, Paul found Christ within to be greater. He had victory through Christ. To the Ephesian elders, Paul testified of his time of ministry in Ephesus, *"I have coveted no one's silver or gold or clothes"* (Acts 20:33). This is an example of God at work, fulfilling the desire of His heart in the heart of a believer.

Lawgiver and Judge

DAY TWO

CHRIST, THE LAW "IMPLANTER"

Christ gave the Law. He came to earth and fulfilled the Law in every detail. Now, how are we to relate to the Law? What does Christ's work **for** us mean **in** us, in our daily decision-making? Today, we will look at the place of the Law in the believer's life—what it can do, what it cannot do, and what Christ does to accomplish His purposes and His will in each of His children.

📖 What was the Law intended to be for Israel according to Deuteronomy 32:44–47?

_____

_____

_____

_____

Just before Moses died he composed what is commonly called "the Song of Moses," a prophetic panorama of the people of Israel (Deuteronomy 32:1–43). After the "song," we read Moses' final words to the people that focused their attention on *"all the words of this law"* that were intended to be their *"life,"* the guideline for prolonging their days in the Promised Land. In that Law was the heart of God, His directions for daily life, a blessed life— *if* they would only obey.

📖 What was the "problem" in this arrangement? What do you discover in Romans 7:7–13?

_____

_____

_____

📖 What additional insights do you find in Galatians 2:16

_____

_____

_____

Paul makes it very clear that *"the Law is holy, and the commandment is holy and righteous and good."* The problem is not the Law, but the human condition or "heart." When a person comes face to face with the Law, the sinful natures rises up to rebel and assert its own wayward will, its own deceitful desire. Wrong choices and the sinful actions that follow yield **death.** God designed the Law to reveal **life** His way; however, the heart of a man or woman in stubbornness and self-deceit wants to go his or her own way. The Law does not force a person to sin; it simply reveals the sin in the heart, and with that sin comes the penalty of death. Paul declares in Galatians 2:16 that no man, Jew or Gentile, can ever be justified by the works of the Law. Human beings cannot follow God in their own power, nor can they merit His approval. Only through faith in Jesus Christ and yielding to Him can one please Him and receive His eternal life and perfect righteousness.

📖 How did Paul apply these truths in Acts 13:37–39?

_____

_____

_____

Obedience to the Law of Moses could never free a man from the condemnation of the Law or from the guilt of sin. No one could ever obey every aspect of the Law, as every person is disobedient at *some* point. Even the smallest degree of disobedience results in death. However, Jesus died to pay the penalty for every act of disobedience so that men and women could be free from the penalty and power of sin. He gives *"forgiveness of sins"* to those who believe in Him. Each one can enter into a new relationship in Christ.

WORTH REPEATING

"By the works of the Law no flesh will be justified in His sight; for through the Law comes the knowledge of sin. . . . Knowing that a man is not justified by the works of the Law, but through faith in Christ Jesus, even we have believed in Christ Jesus, so that we may be justified by faith in Christ and not by the works of the Law; since by the works of the Law no flesh will be justified" (Romans 3:20; Galatians 2:16).

📖 God knew His Law, and He knew the heart of man. Read God's promise in Jeremiah 31:31–34. What unique promise does God make in verse 33?

_____

_____

_____

📖 How is this promise fulfilled in the New Testament? Read Hebrews 10:1–18 and record your reflections. You may want to read Hebrews 8:6–13 for added insights.

_____

_____

_____

Doctrine

CHRIST AND THE ETERNAL COVENANT

Hebrews 13:20–21 says,

Now the God of peace, who brought up from the dead the great Shepherd of the sheep through the blood of the eternal covenant, even Jesus our Lord, equip you in every good work to do His will, working in us that which is pleasing in His sight, through Jesus Christ, to whom be the glory forever and ever. Amen

How does this relate to the Law and the believer? Jesus, *"the Great Shepherd,"* laid down His life in a covenant agreement and *"the God of peace"* raised Him from the dead. By His blood we enter into a new kind of relationship with Him, no longer condemned by our failure to keep the Law. We receive His eternal life and experience His power and equipping for daily life as He guides us in *"every good work."* He is working in each believer what is *"well pleasing in His sight,"* fulfilling His heart's desire, seeing the Law He has written on each believing heart carried out in words and deeds of love to Him and others.

God promised Israel that He would make a new covenant, a covenant different from the old covenant that Israel broke. In the new covenant, God would place the law within them and write the law on their hearts, not on tablets of stone. This would create a new covenant relationship between God and His people in which each one would know the Lord personally and experience complete forgiveness of his or her sins. The importance of the words of Jeremiah 31:31–34 is evident as they are mentioned twice in the New Testament (Hebrews 8:8–12; 10:16–17). The message is clear. The blood of Jesus Christ *forever* removed the sin that the blood of bulls and goats could *never* take away. In His death and resurrection, Jesus assured the fulfillment of this new covenant. Understanding that this promise was first made to Israel, it is important to add a note here about Gentile believers. In Romans 11:17–24, Paul reminds the Romans that, in His kindness, God grafted in the Gentiles as a wild olive branch into the cultivated olive tree of Israel. By faith in Jesus Christ, Gentiles can also enjoy the new covenant promises of Hebrews 8, 9, and 10 and experience the law written on their hearts.

📖 What does it mean that we now have the Lawgiver and Law-fulfiller actually living within through the power of His Spirit? Read what Paul says in Galatians 3:5–14, 21–29; 4:4–7.

_____

_____

_____

_____

By faith in Christ, the Spirit of God has entered the life of each believer and, like Abraham, righteousness has been reckoned to his or her account. Each is right before God because of the righteousness of Christ credited to him or her. That blessing through faith includes deliverance from the well-deserved curse of the Law that we could never overcome. While we could never keep the Law, the Law continues to serve a good purpose. It works much like a tutor, a full-time guardian, showing us right and wrong, revealing our inadequacies and unrighteousness, and leading us to look to Christ and trust in Him. When we trust in Christ and use His Law as our guideline, we become clothed in righteousness, and we learn to know God as our "Abba" Father. We also come to the realization that we have an inheritance awaiting us! What a family we belong to! Today, God calls us to live and walk this Christian life by faith, ever listening and obeying.

Though God calls us to know Him, and His Spirit is at work in us, we continue to wage warfare against our fleshly desires. How can we win this war against Satan and our flesh?

According to Galatians 5:16–17, how do we keep the flesh under control and walk in line with God's heart?

_____

_____

_____

_____

What happens if we follow the flesh or try to deal with the flesh through a system of rules and regulations? What do you discover in Galatians 5:18–21?

_____

_____

_____

_____

What is God's design according to Galatians 5:22–25?

_____

_____

_____

_____

Like the Galatian believers, we still have to deal with the flesh, but we should never try to suppress our flesh by placing it under the subjection of any law. God has given us His Spirit. The Holy Spirit is God's power source in our lives. We must walk according to the Spirit, listening step by step as He guides us with the truth of God's Word in the direction of His holy desires. The "flesh" and the Spirit are constantly at war within us. When we want to follow the Spirit's desires, the flesh fights. When we want to follow the flesh's desires, the Spirit opposes. While we still deal with fleshly desires, verse 16 assures us we do not have to *"carry out"* these desires. By the Spirit, we can say "yes" to Christ and His Law-obeying Life and in so doing say "no" to flesh. We face tough choices every day. The Spirit will lead us against the desires of the flesh and guide us to walk in Christ's overpowering life.

Galatians 5:18 assures us if we follow the Spirit, we do not have to subject ourselves to some system or "law." This verse does not refer to "the Law" but to any kind of "law," system, or fleshly regulation (religious or otherwise). It is ridiculous to think we can place the flesh under any kind of "law," trying in the energy of the flesh to defeat the flesh—such attempts are always a losing proposition! If we buy into the notion that we can overcome the flesh in our own power, whether through some religious law, through legalism, or through some "self-help" law either we or someone else has concocted, we are seriously deceived. We will still end up acting fleshly. Wayne A. Barber has categorized the works of the flesh in Galatians 5:19–21 as "deceptions," things people do in the energy of the flesh because they have deceived themselves that their method, "law," or "rule for life" is right. Such deceptions never provide ultimate satisfaction.

It is ridiculous to think we can place the flesh under any kind of "law," trying in the energy of the flesh to defeat the flesh—such attempts are always a losing proposition!

These *"deeds of the flesh"* include sexual deceptions (*"immorality, impurity, sensuality"*), superstitious deceptions (*"idolatry, sorcery"*), social deceptions (*"strife, jealousy, dissensions, factions, envying"*) and sensual deceptions (*"drunkenness, carousing"*).

In contrast, when we surrender to Christ and are led by His Spirit, we walk in truth. We find our joy and true satisfaction in the perfection of Christ—in His moral purity as opposed to immorality, in pure worship instead of idolatry, in peacemaking instead of striving, and in the pleasures of His heart as opposed to fleshly thrills. Such satisfaction is, in essence, the fruit of the Spirit—we love God, and part of loving God is observing God's Law. Our love is marked by true joy, genuine peace, real patience with people, genuine kindness, a goodness that builds others up, a faithfulness to God and to one another, a measure of gentleness appropriate for the needs before us, and an attitude of self-control because we are Spirit-controlled. This fruit of the Spirit defines the life God designed for us to live from the start. Those who know Christ began their Christian life saying "no" to the flesh and its *"passions and desires."* Since each believer is now alive by the Spirit, he or she can walk following the Spirit with His "law," His teaching and direction for life that is written on our hearts.

 Are you living this way? How is the work of the Lawgiver, the Law Fulfiller, and the Law "Implanter" being seen in your daily decisions? Think of this: the Law "Implanter" is also the Law "Empowerer" in your life. Pause and pray. Ask the Lord to show you one truth that you can apply from today's study.

Lawgiver and Judge   **DAY FOUR**

Doctrine
JESUS, THE CREATOR, REDEEMER, AND JUDGE

In his address to the men of the Areopagus in Athens, Paul proclaimed the true God as Creator and Redeemer. He pointed to Jesus as the one who died and rose again, who will one day judge the world—*"He has fixed a day in which He will judge the world in righteousness through a Man whom He has appointed, having furnished proof to all men by raising Him from the dead"* (Acts 17:31). Some in Athens believed and received this Jesus as Lord and Savior. Others now await that coming Day of Judgment.

CHRIST, THE JUDGE

What is the function of a judge? We usually think of a judge evaluating the facts in a case, deciding who is right or wrong and then confirming blame or giving reward. When we turn to the pages of Scripture, we find Abraham addressing the Lord in prayer concerning Sodom. He affirmed, *"Shall not the Judge of all the earth deal justly?"* (Genesis 19:25). Proverbs 15:3 states, *"The eyes of the Lord are in every place, watching the evil and the good"* (see also Proverbs 5:21). He views all that has occurred and knows not only who is right or wrong, but also knows all the motives and manners. How does God deal with the offenses against His perfect righteousness and holiness? We have seen that no one can stand justified in God's sight by the works of the Law. Paul states in the face of the Law of God that *"every mouth may be stopped and all the world may become guilty before God"* (Romans 3:19 [NKJV]).

Scripture has revealed that God the Judge condemns all sin and calls for just punishment and payment. However, Jesus has already paid that price. *"For what the law could not do in that it was weak through the flesh, God did by sending His own son in the likeness of sinful flesh, on account of sin: He condemned sin in the flesh"* (Romans 8:3 [NKJV]). He cleanses the guilty who place their faith in Him and now calls people to come by faith and be cleansed or face judgment on their own merits. He also acts as Judge of believers. How do all these factors tie together? We observe several actions relating to Christ as Judge in today's study. Note: it is important to remember as we review the

Scriptures that sometimes "judgment" refers to the activity of evaluating good or evil, while other times it refers to the sentence of condemnation.

📖 First, what were Jesus' thoughts about judgment? Look at John 3:14–21 and record your insights.

_____

_____

_____

_____

Jesus clearly revealed His heart. He did not come to judge the world but to lay down His life to save people from their sins. In His great love, the Father gave His Son. He would be lifted up as Moses lifted the serpent in the wilderness. Those who looked in obedience would subsequently be healed. Those who believe in Jesus receive eternal life. Those who refuse to believe face the judgment brought on by their unbelieving hearts. Most choose evil and darkness rather than the light Jesus brings, and they stand condemned by their choices. The one who comes to Jesus, who receives the truth, the word spoken by Him, receives eternal life.

📖 Jesus knew judgment would be inevitable. What did Jesus reveal about the judgment of God and about Himself as the Judge in John 5:22–30? Write down what you discover.

_____

_____

_____

_____

How does one escape the judgment of Jesus Christ? What does a person receive instead of judgment?

_____

_____

_____

_____

The Father has *"given all judgment to the Son."* He is the Judge before whom every man or woman will stand. What will be the verdict of each one's judgment? That depends on how one has responded to the truth spoken and lived out by Jesus Christ. If one hears Jesus' word and believes in Him as the one sent by the Father, that one will receive eternal life. He or she will not be condemned but will have passed out of death into the life given by the Son.

📖 According to John 5:28–29, who will stand before Jesus the Son of Man?

_____

_____

_____

_____

> "For while we were still helpless, at the right time Christ died for the ungodly. . . . But God demonstrates His own love toward us, in that while we were yet sinners, Christ died for us."
>
> Romans 5:6, 8

> "And if anyone hears My saying, and does not keep them, I do not judge him; for I did not come to judge the world, but to save the world. He who rejects Me, and does not receive My sayings, has one who judges him; the word I spoke is what will judge him at the last day."
>
> John 12:47–48

What is the source for Jesus' evaluation of each man or woman according to John 5:30?

_____

_____

_____

_____

Doctrine
ISAIAH SAW CHRIST AS JUDGE

In John 12:27–50, Jesus speaks of judgment, *"Now judgment is upon this world; now the ruler of this world shall be cast out"* (12:31). That statement refers to Jesus' coming death and resurrection. John 12:41 states that Isaiah saw the glory of Jesus and spoke of it. He also saw the seraphim around the throne, the trembling thresholds of the Temple, and smoke filling the Temple (Isaiah 6:1–13). In that encounter Isaiah faced the judgment on his own heart and cried out, *"Woe is me."* God cleansed him and called him to proclaim His message, a message of judgment on unbelieving hearts with the promise of a believing remnant. Jesus is the King and Judge whom Isaiah saw. In John 12 Jesus also deals with unbelieving hearts, calling them to believe, confident that some will come.

There are two groups who will stand before Jesus—those who have chosen to trust Jesus and His Word and those who have not. Those who have placed their faith in Jesus and His Word have done right by choosing the good Jesus offers, the good of His life, death, and resurrection. He has given them His new life and in the possession and power of that life they do the good deeds He commands. The other group consists of those who have rejected Jesus and what He has offered. He counts their deeds as evil and sentences them to face a resurrection of judgment. Jesus judges or evaluates each person based on what He hears from the Father. Jesus never varies from doing or saying what the Father wills. He only seeks the Father's will as He has revealed it. That, of course, is revealed for us in the written Word spoken by God and found in the Scriptures. It is absolute truth. According to that Word, Jesus will judge all.

What kind of Judge is Jesus? The apostle Paul expressed his confidence and joy at the thought of standing before Jesus. Just months before his execution, he penned the letter of 2 Timothy. Read 2 Timothy 4:1–8, noting especially verses 1 and 8. What do you discover about Jesus and His work as Judge?

_____

_____

_____

_____

"So then each one of us shall give account of himself to God."

Romans 14:12

The Lord Jesus Christ, who will soon judge all men is the righteous Judge, true in everything He says, accurate in every evaluation He makes. When He returns, He will judge the living and the dead. There are three judgments associated with His appearing and His kingdom: the Judgment Seat of Christ, the Judgment of the Nations, and the Great White Throne Judgment. We will see those in more detail later. Paul looked forward to *"that Day"* when he and *"all who have loved His appearing"* will be rewarded the crown of righteousness by Jesus, the righteous Judge. What a glorious day for Paul and others who have been faithful in following Christ—fighting the good fight, finishing the race, and keeping/guarding the faith.

We mentioned three distinct judgments. Let's look at each of these. The first is the Judgment Seat of Christ for Christians. It occurs after the rapture of the Church. What do you discover in 1 Corinthians 3:10–15? Record your insights.

_____

_____

_____

_____

_____

What additional insights do you glean in 1 Corinthians 1:4:1–5, particularly verse 5?

_____

_____

_____

_____

Look at 2 Corinthians 5:9–10. What do you discover in those verses?

_____

_____

_____

_____

Christ is the foundation of the church and each believer is building on that foundation in the ministries and avenues of service given him or her by the Lord Jesus. Each should be careful in how he or she builds. We can use *"gold, silver, precious stones,"* the materials given by God and representative of a Christ-filled walk, materials that last and bring Him glory, or we can build with *"wood, hay, straw,"* the materials representative of the corrupt efforts of the flesh, that which grows out of a fallen earth. The fire of God's judgment will test the quality of each person's work—one revealed as lasting and rewarding while the other is shown to be smoke and ashes and loss of reward. Each is saved but each is not equally rewarded. When the Lord examines every detail, *"the good or bad,"* *"the things hidden"* and the *"motives of men's hearts,"* then *"each man's praise will come to him from God"* and each will be *"recompensed for his deeds in the body."*

The Judgment of the Nations occurs after Jesus' Second Coming, between His appearing at the end of the Tribulation and the beginning of the Millennial Kingdom. Look at Matthew 25:31–46 and record your insights.

_____

_____

_____

_____

The Son of Man will come in His glory just as He told Caiaphas the night before He was crucified (26:57–64). That will occur at the end of the Tribulation. He will set up His throne and judge the people of all the nations according to their deeds, separating them as a shepherd would separate sheep from goats. The sheep, those who have followed Christ, whom He calls *"the righteous,"* will then enter *"the Kingdom prepared for you from the foundation of the world."* During the Tribulation years, these showed their righteous hearts by their righteous deeds, works of genuine love toward others. All others failed to walk in genuine righteousness and love and will be sentenced to the judgment of *"eternal fire"* and *"eternal punishment"* with the devil and his angels.

Doctrine

THE DAY OF VENGEANCE

When Jesus introduced His ministry in hometown Nazareth, He read from Isaiah 61:1–2 which begins, *"The LORD has anointed me to bring good news...."* Isaiah 61:1–2a is quoted by Jesus in Luke 4:18–19. While addressing people in a synagogue, Jesus read these words from a scroll containing the book of Isaiah. After He finished reading the first half of verse 2, *"To proclaim the favorable year of the LORD,"* He then closed the scroll (see Luke 4:19). Why? Jesus came the first time to bring good news, to lay down His life to save and give eternal life. Isaiah 61:2 says, *"To proclaim the favorable year of the LORD, and the day of vengeance of our God..."* [emphasis added]. Here, Christ prepares us for a day of judgment, a period in which He will deal with the ungodly and all evil. One of the pictures of this "day" is found in Revelation 19:11, *"And I saw heaven opened; and behold, a white horse, and He who sat upon it is called Faithful and True; and in righteousness He judges and wages war."* Jude 14-15 also pictures the Lord Jesus coming to *"execute judgment."* Today is the day of "good news," but Christ the Judge is bringing a "Day of Vengeance."

Scripture also talks about the Great White Throne Judgment, which occurs at the end of the Millennium and before the New Heavens and New Earth. Read Revelation 20:11–15. Who is there? What is the outcome of that meeting?

_____

_____

_____

_____

The Lord revealed to the apostle John *"a great white throne"* and the Lord sitting upon it. The dead, *"the great and the small,"* the "important" and the unimportant, the noteworthy and the "nothings," will stand before this throne. The many *"books"* of the deeds of men will be opened and read and judgment will be rendered according to what is found in those books. From this it appears there will be degrees of judgment based on the degree of wrong in those deeds. All are worthy of judgment in some measure. The final determining factor is *"the book of life."* If one's name is not found written in that *"book"*—anyone who has not believed in Jesus and received the eternal life He alone can give—then that one will be *"thrown into the lake of fire."* How important that we continue calling people to come to Christ!

Jesus is the righteous Judge, and He calls us to follow Him, knowing we will be evaluated by His all-knowing gaze and His all-understanding heart. He knows what we have done and why we have done it. In all of life, it is vital that we walk in real faith, trusting Him, listening, and obeying day in and day out. In Day Five we will look and evaluate this matter of real faith.

"It is appointed for men to die once and after this comes judgment"

Hebrews 9:27

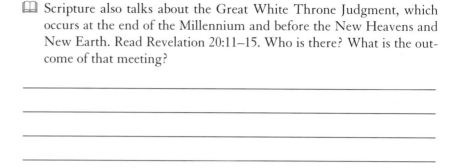

Lawgiver and Judge **DAY FIVE**

Put Yourself In Their Shoes

JESUS, THE LAW, AND FAITH

To Moses, He gave His handwritten copy of the Law, specifically seen in the Ten Commandments. This Law reveals His heart and will, His desire and design for all of life and for every relationship. In giving the Law, He knew that man with his sinful nature and sinful heart bent on self-direction and self-preeminence, could not and would not obey. People want to go their own way; their hearts want to go astray, to go their own self-chosen, self-centered way apart from God's perfect way. Jesus came to fulfill the Law, to pay the penalty for man's disobedience, and to give man a new heart to fulfill His will His way. That way is the way of Faith in Christ—The true believer **starts** by faith, **walks** by faith, and **finishes** by faith.

FOR ME TO FOLLOW CHRIST

Speaking to believers, Paul said, *"whatever is not from faith is sin"* (Romans 14:23). God wants us walking in a trust relationship throughout life, in all the details of life. We know that faith in Christ is the start of our new life, but we are also called to an obedient daily walk in that faith. Following Christ is all about walking by faith. From time to time, it is important that we honestly evaluate our walk. What does this faith we need look like? There are at least three vantage points from which to view real faith. We see faith first as **starting** faith that trusts God and His Word. Our second look at faith reveals **walking** faith that loves with God's kind of love. The third is **finishing** faith that is filled with hope.

First, let's look at starting faith. Read Romans 4:1–25 and 5:1–2. This is the starting point of our walk of faith. What does God want each of us to believe, to trust Him for according to verses 24–25?

_____

_____

_____

_____

What is the result according to Romans 5:1–2?

_____

_____

_____

_____

Abraham came into a saving relationship with God by faith not by works, especially not by the works of the Law nor by any act of circumcision, nor through any other rituals (since neither the Law nor circumcision were yet given [Genesis 15:1–6]). He believed God and what God said. By His grace, God declared Abraham righteous. God declares anyone righteous who places his or her faith in *"Jesus our Lord,"* the One who died for our sins and rose from the dead. Like Abraham, we can be confident that what He has promised He will perform. His salvation is sure—we can stand before Him justified, knowing *"peace with God through our Lord Jesus Christ."*

 Do you know God through the Lord Jesus Christ? Have you placed your life in His hands by faith? Have you trusted Him to save you, to forgive you, and give you eternal life?

📖 Look at James 2:14–24. Here we find **walking** faith that always goes with true **starting** faith. What was the proof that Abraham had genuine faith in his daily life? How did this also show genuine love?

_____

_____

_____

"Walking faith" refers to the daily walk of trusting in God—listening and learning from what God says, obeying what He commands, and following where He leads. Genuine faith is always accompanied by godly actions, deeds that reveal God's work in our hearts. Those deeds also reveal His love and care, His holiness and purity, as well as other characteristics of His heart. Abraham revealed his faith through works of obedience to God—specifically, the call to offer up his beloved son, Isaac. He responded in obedience and showed his love for God—Jesus said, *"If you love Me, you will keep My commandments"* (John 14:21). In James 2:21, 24, the phrase *"justified by works,"* when traced back to the Greek language does not mean "made righteous by His works," but the language emphasizes the idea of one "shown to be justified" or "shown to have genuine faith"—the works show that real faith is present. The works do not justify apart from faith. The works must be there to reveal the faith. The works must be present, or there is no way to see faith. It is not a matter of mere emotions or the accumulation of intellectual facts; even demons "believe" the facts about Christ and *"tremble"* with emotion (NKJV). Walking faith must have accompanying actions, and those actions show love for God and for others.

 Does your faith have accompanying actions in daily life? Is it a real walking faith? What recent steps of obedience can you point to that reveal genuine faith and genuine love?

_____

_____

_____

"But without faith it is impossible to please Him, for he who comes to God must believe that He is, and that He is a rewarder of those who diligently seek Him."

Hebrews 11:6 (NKJV)

> *"As it is, they desire a better country, that is a heavenly one. Therefore God is not ashamed to be called their God; for He has prepared a city for them."*
>
> Hebrews 11:16

True faith is **finishing** faith. Look at Hebrews 11:8–16. What insights do you see about this aspect of Abraham's faith? What marks of finishing faith and of genuine hope do you see in the testimony of his walk?

_____

_____

_____

_____

Abraham obeyed God when He called him out of Ur of the Chaldees. He lived in Canaan trusting God to fulfill all the promises He had given. He knew God was giving him a lasting nation and lasting blessings, but he did not see the fullness of those promises during his lifetime. Abraham trusted God throughout his life—he had finishing faith. He believed God would be faithful throughout life and that, ultimately, the *"heavenly"* country and the prepared city would be his inheritance. He had a confident expectation in God—a genuine hope that God would fulfill all His Word to him.

 Are you trusting God with the details of your life as well as the finish-line factors? Are you walking with finish-line faith that sees beyond today into eternity, into your heavenly home, the city prepared for you? Are you living in true hope?

_____

_____

_____

_____

> *Lord Jesus, You are the Righteous Lawgiver and Judge, the One who knows what is best for every area of life, every relationship in life.*

 Lord, thank You that You are the righteous Lawgiver and Judge, the One who knows what is best for every area of life, every relationship in life. Thank You for giving us a record of the Law and helping us understand Your heart, Your will for us. Thank You also that You knew we are but dust, frail, faltering, and unable to walk Your way apart from Your enabling. Thank You for Your clear judgment on all our sin, all my sin, for condemning every unjust action, word, thought, or motive. I also thank You for paying the penalty for that sin. What would have been the just punishment placed upon me, You took on Yourself on the Cross. I praise You as the Just One dying for me, the unjust one. Thank You that You have written Your Law on my heart by Your Spirit so that I can know and walk in Your will, being led by Your Spirit in line with Your heart. Thank You also for the written Word that continually instructs me as I read and meditate and pray. I praise You that knowing You is a faith journey all the way into eternity. What an awesome destiny we face living in Your presence, with Your heart fully expressed and exhibited for all to see and experience. May I walk each day in the fullness of Your Law, Your heart, by the energy of Your Spirit. Thank You for the freedom You give as I walk bound to You, not as a forced slave but as a bond-servant, willingly following, delighting to obey. May Your righteousness be clearly seen *in* me and *through* me as You fill, control, equip, and energize me to do Your will. In Jesus' name. Amen.

Christ The King

FOLLOWING THE KING OF KINGS

Psalm 10:16 says, *"The LORD is King forever and ever."* He has always been and always will be the ultimate authority in life. Yet He has always wanted to share the glories of Himself and His kingdom. That's why he created Adam and Eve. He placed them as the first king and queen of creation and gave them clear responsibility to "rule" over all the earth (see Genesis 1:28) in fellowship and harmony with Him. He wanted them to reign like Him, reflecting His image and bringing forth a family who would reflect His image—His love, His justice, His care, His wisdom—throughout all the earth. They were not to rule autonomously, but to rule under His rule. They were not to take the place of God in creation, but to make sure that God's will was followed in creation. What a wonderful kingdom that would be! What a wonderful place to live! Imagine having a ruler in the image of God with His character. Imagine a king who would reign with the wisdom of God's Word and will.

Imagine having a ruler in the image of God with His character. Imagine a king who would reign with the wisdom of God's Word.

JESUS CHRIST: THE TRUE KING

4000 BC	2050 BC	1892 BC	1081? BC	6 BC	30 BC	Any Day!	1000 Years	Forever
Adam Eve	Abraham	Jacob	David	Mary	The King of Israel	The Returning King	The Reigning King	The True King Forever
Promise of the Seed of a Woman	*Promise of the Seed of Abraham*	*Prophecy of the Scepter of Judah*	*Promise of the Seed of David*	*The Seed is Born* **Jesus**	**Jesus Christ** *Crucified Risen Ascended Reigning*	*"When He comes to be glorified in His saints on that Day."*	*"They . . . reigned with Christ for a thousand years."*	*"The throne of God and of the Lamb . . . forever and ever."*
Genesis 3:15; Isaiah 7:14; Matthew 1:18–25	Genesis 22:17–18; Galatians 3:16; Hebrews 2:14–18	Genesis 49:8–12; Numbers 24:17–19; Hebrews 1:8; Revelation 5:5	2 Samuel 7:12–17; Luke 1:31–33; John 7:42; Romans 1:3; 2 Timothy 2:8	*"Son of Man" "Son of Abraham" "Son of David"* Matthew 1:1, 17; 16:27–28 Luke 1:26–38, 46–55; 2:1–40;	John 1:49; John 18—20; Acts 1:1–11; Romans 1:2–4; 1 Timothy 3:16; Hebrews 1:1–13	1 Thessalonians 4:15–18 2 Thessalonians 1:6–10; Revelation 19:1–16;	Revelation 20:4–6	Revelation 21:1–27; 22:1–5

However, Adam and Eve failed. They chose to disobey God's Word and were expelled from the Garden of Eden. Instead of reigning, Adam and his children became enslaved to sin and selfishness. The first Adam failed to be the kind of king God wanted on earth. But that was not the end of the story. God was not through with man or His plans on earth. The Lord is King forever, and His kingdom stands forever. The rule he first placed in the hands of Adam will one day be placed in the hands of His Son, the last Adam.

The Kind of King God Desires

Did You Know?
? JOB DESCRIPTION FOR A TRUE KING

A true king should serve to provide, protect, and lead his people in righteousness. That means a kingdom fully supplied, at peace, and marked by purity in relationships. The Garden of Eden had all these characteristics at the start. The True King, the Lord Jesus, will bring these things to bear when He reigns on the earth. He wants us following Him as our True King so that we experience these things with Him right now.

The period of the kings began at a dark time in Israel's history. It was birthed out of the dismal period of the judges when *"there was no king in Israel; everyone did what was right in his own eyes."* Mankind needed leadership. They needed authority and accountability. And yet, that leadership had to be exercised under the umbrella of God's rule and reign. In 1 Samuel 8:4–9 we see that God was not pleased when Israel asked for a king. It wasn't that it was wrong for Israel to have a king—they needed a ruler. But apart from a total commitment to following God, a ruler would not always be a blessing. You see, Israel wanted a king *"like all the nations"* (like the Gentiles). But the rulers of the other nations were not the kind of king God wanted. They ruled as autocrats, accountable to no one but themselves. God wanted Israel to have a king who would see himself as a servant of the people and a follower of God as the ultimate King. In 1 Samuel 8:7 the Lord says that Israel had *". . . rejected Me from being king over them."* God gave them Saul, the kind of king they wanted, so they would learn to want the kind of king He wanted. When they learned their lesson, God gave them David, a man with a heart after God's heart who would do God's will instead of his own. As we look back over the kings we have studied, it is obvious that those kings who ruled well are those who submitted themselves to God as king. Those who ruled badly are those who went their own independent way. God does not simply want people to rule, but people who will rule under His rule.

The first human king mentioned in Scripture is Adam. Though he is not called a king, clearly that is his function, for in Genesis 1:28 he is called to "rule" over creation. Yet he failed to rule as God intended, and by his rebellion, he forfeited part of his kingdom to Satan's control (see 1 John 5:19). Once sin entered the picture, God revealed a new facet of His plan for planet earth.

📖 We have seen Genesis 3:15 and God's promise in a previous lesson. Read that verse again, thinking of a coming king. Identify who God intended to use to deal with Satan.

_____

_____

_____

_____

Immediately after mankind's fall, God communicated to Satan that from the woman would come a "seed" with whom his offspring would have enmity. Notice that the seed is singular. Ultimately, it points not to all of Eve's descendants, but to a specific individual. This is the first mention in Scripture of the

Lord Jesus. Eve understood this, for when her first child was born, she named him Cain ("the gotten one") and what she literally said was "I have gotten a man, the Lord." She was looking for the promised deliverer. But Cain was not to be that deliverer. That would happen further down the line. When the promised seed finally arrived, Satan would one day "bruise" that seed on the heel. This foreshadows the crucifixion. He, in turn, would bruise (literally "crush") Satan's head. He would rid man of the curse of death, bring him eternal life, and reveal His power as Lord and King. All of that hasn't happened yet—but it will.

📖 Another of the first kings we meet is the king of Salem (later Jerusalem), a man named Melchizedek. His name means "king of righteousness." What can we learn from him, especially about following God (and about a king following the true King)? Read Genesis 14:14–24, the story of Abram's rescue of his nephew Lot. What do you discover about Melchizedek?

_____

_____

_____

_____

Melchizedek was king of the city of Salem ("peace"). He was also a priest of El Elyon ("God Most High"), possessor of heaven and earth. As king of Salem, Melchizedek acknowledged that it was God Most High who was king over all, and who gave victory to Abram. He blessed Abram by the name of God Most High. To bless someone in a name is to bring to bear the character of that name in a person's life. In this case, it was to speak the blessing of El Elyon for Abram, including provision and protection. Abram gave a tenth of all the spoils, acknowledging that El Elyon was indeed the possessor of heaven and earth and deserved to be honored as such. He would honor Him as his God. As a priest, Melchizedek served God and received the offering on His behalf. Abram was careful to take nothing from the king of Sodom. He wanted it to remain clear that he saw God Most High as his Provider, Protector, and King.

The promised seed of the woman would also be the seed of Abraham.

 Are you looking to God as your Provider, Protector, and King? Are you bowing to Him daily as Lord and King? Is there anything you need to turn over to His sovereign care?

_____

_____

_____

In Genesis 22:17–18, the Lord came to Abram and promised him a seed [singular] that would *"possess the gate of his* [masculine singular in KJV] *enemies"* and that *"in thy seed all the nations would be blessed"* (see Acts 3:25 and Galatians 3:16)—characteristics of God's kind of king, a victor and a blessing to others. After God entered into a covenant with Abram, his name was changed to Abraham. Isaac, was born to Abraham and Sarah, and became the father of Jacob and Esau. Jacob's name was changed to Israel, and Jacob (or Israel) had twelve sons, the heads of the twelve tribes of what became the nation of Israel. According to Genesis 49:10–11 the rulership—"the scepter"—of Jacob was to be seen in the tribe of Judah. This Ruler is worthy of obedience, and the scepter never departs from Him.

What do you find about the "scepter" and the place of Jacob (and Edom or Esau) in Numbers 24:17–19? (This is the prophecy of Balaam given in the presence of Balak, king of Moab [ca. 1405 BC].)

_____

_____

_____

_____

A star and a scepter shall come from Israel and crush the head of Moab. Edom (or Esau) will also be a possession—conquered by Israel. *"One from Jacob shall have dominion. . . ."* In other words, Jacob will rule as king through this "One" to come.

The Lord revealed His strong hand in bringing Israel out of Egypt and into the land promised to Abraham and his descendants, the land of Canaan. What did the Lord want for His people when He brought them into the land of Canaan? What revelation did He give through Moses before they entered the land, concerning a king for the nation of Israel? Deuteronomy 17:14–20 (recorded by Moses around 1405 BC) gives us the guidelines under which a king should reign. Read that passage, and record the Word of the Lord in regard to a king in Israel.

_____

_____

_____

_____

If Israel would be what God desired them to be, they must be led by His Word. If they were to have the leadership they needed and that God wanted for them, they must follow Him in His choice of king. This was not an office a man would choose for himself. God wanted them to have the king He would choose. That was of utmost importance. **God's choice of king would lead the people in surrender to Him and in a true walk of faith and obedience.** The Lord gave other guidelines as well. He had to be an Israelite, not a foreigner. He was not to be a self-seeking man, seeking military might by multiplying horses, nor political might by the alliances that came with many wives. Neither should his goal be personal wealth. The Lord wanted a man who would seek Him, not money and power. That meant following Him through His Word and leading the people to do the same.

Around 1105 BC, Samuel was born and arose in Israel as the last of the judges and the first of the prophets. He ruled well and clearly spoke the Word of God to the people. When he appointed his sons to take care of some of the needs in Israel, they did not do well. They were corrupt and unjust (1 Samuel 8:3). At that point, the people of Israel came to Samuel asking for a king.

Read 1 Samuel 8:1–22, and record what you discover.

_____

_____

_____

_____

THE PRAYER OF HANNAH, SAMUEL'S MOTHER

"Those who contend with the LORD will be shattered; Against them He will thunder in the heavens, The LORD will judge the ends of the earth; And He will give strength to His king, And will exalt the horn of His anointed." (1 Samuel 2:10)

The people of Israel certainly did not want Samuel's sons ruling over them. They wanted a king like the other nations. When Samuel brought their request before the LORD, God made it clear that they were not rejecting Samuel. They were rejecting God as their king. They would rather follow a man than follow God. They would rather walk by sight than by faith. They would rather be like the kingdoms of the world than like the kingdom of God. God gave them what they wanted, a man named Saul.

THE PROMISED COMING OF THE TRUE KING

S aul came to power and ruled Israel in the folly of his own wisdom. He had no heart for God. The Lord then chose David, a man after His heart who would do His will. First Samuel 16:1–13 tells the story of God's choosing David as king over Israel. As we look at the full picture of Scripture we recall that in Genesis 3:15, the Lord promised a "seed" [Hebrew singular] to come and deal with the evil on earth. In Genesis 22:17–18, He promised Abraham a "seed" [singular] who would rule and bless the nations of the earth. In the midst of David's reign God revealed yet another piece of the puzzle of His design for a king in Israel and a king on earth. God promised David a "seed," [singular] and He promised to establish the kingdom of that seed of David forever (see 2 Samuel 7:12, 16). In 1 Chronicles 22:7–13, we read that Solomon was God's choice to succeed David. God chose to rule Israel through the descendants of David.

📖 What do you discover about God's promise to David in the account of Ahijah the Shilonite and Jeroboam I in 1 Kings 11:31–39?

_____

_____

_____

_____

_____

Did You Know?

❓ GOD CHOSE THE TRIBE OF JUDAH

David was from the tribe of Judah, but Jeroboam I was from the tribe of Ephraim. Psalm 78:67–68 made it clear: God "did not choose the tribe of Ephraim, But chose the tribe of Judah, Mount Zion which He loved."

The Lord told Jeroboam that He was going to tear the kingdom out of Solomon's hands and give ten tribes to Jeroboam. This arrangement of the division of Israel would not be forever—only for a time, in order to discipline Israel for the idolatry of Solomon and the people. In that message to Jeroboam, the Lord made it clear that David would always have "a lamp before Me," a man ruling on the throne in Jerusalem to carry out the covenant He made with David.

📖 Over eighty years after Ahijah's words to Jeroboam, Jehoram came to the throne in Judah (848–841 BC). Read 2 Kings 8:16–19, and record what you discover about the Lord's ways in the line of David.

_____

_____

_____

_____

The promise to David that the Lord would *"give a lamp to him through his sons always"* was the basis of the Lord's actions in the life of Jehoram over eighty years later. The Lord revealed His covenant faithfulness in the life of Jehoram king of Judah. In spite of the wickedness of the king and of Judah, the Lord remembered His promise to David.

The kings of Israel, and then of the divided Israel (Judah and Israel), ruled over a period of about 465 years (1051–586 BC). The first 120 years covered the united kingdom under Saul, David, and Solomon. The next 345 years saw the divided kingdom. In the time up to 722 BC, the Northern Kingdom (Israel) had 19 kings, all wicked in their reign. Over a period of 345 years (931–586), the Southern Kingdom (Judah) had 20 kings, eight of whom were righteous. In the midst of all this, God continued to show His faithfulness to the house of David and to the promise He had made. The promises remained—a righteous king would come.

📖 He also continued to speak through the prophets to the people of Israel and Judah about the true king who was coming. What do you find in Isaiah 9:1–2, 6–7?

_____

_____

_____

_____

The true King is the Word, the eternal expression of the mind and heart of God, God Himself: "In the beginning was the Word, and the Word was with God, and the Word was God" (John 1:1).

At a dark time in Israel's life when the threat of Assyria loomed on the horizon, Isaiah spoke words of hope. Assyria first came and captured the land of Zebulun and Naphtali in the area of Galilee. Isaiah promised that one day a light would dawn in Galilee. A child would be born, specifically a son, who would rule in strength and peace. He would bring light to a people in darkness.

The prophet Micah, a contemporary of Isaiah, ministered in Judah and revealed several things about this coming king. Micah first warned of judgment against Samaria and Jerusalem because they refused to obey the Lord and His word. He also spoke of glorious days to come. His greatest word was the announcement of the birth of the ruler of Israel in the town of Bethlehem.

📖 Read Micah 5:2–5. What do you see about Bethlehem? About this ruler?

_____

_____

_____

_____

Bethlehem is too little to be among the clans of Judah—insignificant to all but God. The ruler would be born there. He will go forth *"for Me (the Lord)"* as ruler in Israel. *"His goings forth are . . . from the days of eternity"* (5:2). He will be a shepherd to His flock in the strength and majesty of the Lord. He will be recognized for His greatness to the ends of the earth, and this one will *"be our peace"* (5:5a).

Many other prophecies were spoken about the coming king, the Messiah of Israel. There are over 300 prophecies related to the first coming of the

Messiah, and they were all fulfilled in exact detail in the person of Jesus Christ. We find those in the New Testament record of Jesus Christ. Just how does Jesus Christ fit in with the promises to David? After David had conquered his enemies and established his kingdom with the strength and wisdom of the Lord, God made a covenant with David that the throne of his kingdom would be established forever. David's throne was passed to his son Solomon, and to a descendant of his as long as Judah continued as a nation.

📖 Read Luke 1:31–33, and identify how Jesus relates to the throne of David, and where and how long His reign will be.

_____

_____

_____

_____

It is evident that the line of David never died out. Both Joseph and Mary were descendants of David. When God meets with Mary, she is told that the son she will bear is to be called Jesus (from the Hebrew, "Joshua" which means "Jehovah is Salvation"), and that He will be given the throne of His father, David. She is also promised that Jesus will rule over the house of Jacob (Israel) and that His kingdom will have no end. That was the king God had in mind for Israel. He was from the tribe of Judah, the tribe given the scepter forever. His throne and His kingdom would be established forever, and He would reign as the Son of David.

📖 As we have seen, God did not leave Himself without clear witness as to His desires and His design. He spoke through many prophets about this coming King, the Messiah. Over 230 years after David, Isaiah spoke of a coming Servant-King who would bring forth justice to the nations. We have noted how He would be a descendant of David (see 2 Samuel 7:12; Matthew 1:1). Read Isaiah 42:1–4 and Matthew 12:9–23. Notice the connection Matthew and the people make to Jesus as the Son of David. What does this say about Jesus as the King? (see John 1:35–51, especially verse 49, as it gives further light on the revelation of Jesus.)

_____

_____

_____

_____

Jesus fulfilled the prophecies of Isaiah and all the prophets. His ministry was aptly described by Isaiah. He had the marks of the long-awaited Son of David. Jesus was the promised king. In another incident, when Nathaniel met Jesus, he realized that this Jesus was the Son of God and the King of Israel.

The promise to Eve, Abraham, David, Isaiah, and Micah (and many, many others) came true. The seed of woman, the seed of Abraham, Isaac, and Jacob, and the seed of David, was born in Bethlehem. This Jesus grew up in Nazareth, and at age thirty came to be baptized by John the Baptist who was announcing the coming Messiah (see Isaiah 40:3). Jesus began the ministry the Father had for Him (see Isaiah 9:1, 6; 11:1–4a; 50:4–10; John 4:34; 5:19, 30; 8:15–18, 28–29), and many recognized that He was the Messiah. The Messiah, the Christ, the King of Israel, had indeed come. He was fulfilling

Did You Know?

THE SAME PROMISE

In 2 Samuel 7:12, 16 the Lord promised David a seed, a house, a kingdom, and a throne . . . forever. This same promise was then made to Mary, the mother of Jesus, in Luke 1:31–33. The promise began to be fulfilled in the birth of Jesus.

SON OF THE MOST HIGH

Jesus is the son of *El Elyon*, God Most High, the God that Melchizedek and Abram honored as their God and King (see Genesis 14).

the Father's will, but there was yet much to do and much to proclaim. Before the full revelation of the King's presence and power, He had to go to the cross to die for the sins of the world (see Isaiah 53:1–12). Then, in His resurrection, He revealed the assurance of the forgiveness of sin and the cleansing He had purchased with His blood. By faith in Him and His finished work one could have His very life and His Spirit within their heart and life (see Jeremiah 31:31–34 with Ezekiel 36:25–27 and Hebrews 8:8–12).

We also learn from the New Testament record that He has chosen to rule the earth ultimately through the Son of David, Jesus Christ. God has not yet fulfilled **all** His desires for the kind of King He wants in Israel and on this earth. We can see that more fully when we discover some of the battles that have gone on in the war against the true King. Then we will see how He has worked and is working to bring the coming King to earth.

All rebellion is rooted in a desire to raise our own throne above God's so that we can be our own god.

THE WAR AGAINST THE TRUE KING

Spiritual warfare began when Satan decided to rebel against God's rule in his life. In Isaiah 14:13–14 we see his rebellious heart reflected when he says, *"I will ascend to heaven; I will raise my throne above the stars of God, And I will sit on the mount of assembly In the recesses of the north. I will ascend above the heights of the clouds; I will make myself like the Most High."* He wanted to replace God, and sit on the throne of his own life. Throughout time, he has sought to seduce man into joining his rebellion. The Serpent has not stopped fighting God nor man, and sinful man has joined in the war against the true King. We must see the reality of the opposition toward the throne, toward God's desire and plan for His king in Israel and on the earth. At its core, this rebellion is rooted in a desire to raise our own throne above God's so that we can be our own god.

The Serpent defeated Adam, the first king of the earth. Opposition to the Lord's kingship and true worship were seen throughout the years in men like Cain and in the men of Noah's day (see Genesis 4:1–17; 6—7). In Nimrod, king of Babel, we see further opposition to the true King. Nimrod, whose name means "rebel," was the founder of Babel and Nineveh (see Genesis 10:8–12).

📖 Read Genesis 11:1–9, and record what you find about the purpose of the people of Babel.

_____

_____

_____

The main aim of the people of Babel was to make a name for themselves and to rule themselves in pride from their position of control. They had no thought of filling the earth as the Lord had directed both Adam and later Noah (see Genesis 1:28; 9:1). Instead, they wanted to stay together in Babel and pursue their own will. God saw that their unified language had allowed them to go unrestrained in accomplishing their will in opposition to His. Therefore, He confused their language, in part, to restrain them in their proud efforts and to get them to scatter over the earth.

This war did not stop with the confusion of the languages at Babel. It continued, and Babel became the foundation of the nation of Babylon, the enemy and destroyer of Judah, Jerusalem, and the Temple in 586 BC (2 Chronicles 36:5–21). Nineveh, which was also founded by Nimrod, was the capital of Assyria, the nation that conquered and scattered the kingdom of Israel in 722 BC (2 Kings 17). God decreed His judgment on both kingdoms, Babylon (Jeremiah 50—51) and Assyria (2 Kings 18—19; Nahum 1—3). In Revelation 17—18, we find the Lord bringing ultimate defeat to Babylon and all associated with it. The foes of the King of kings, Jesus Christ, will not stand.

Throughout history, Satan has attempted to destroy God's deliverer before he was old enough to deliver. He attempted this in Moses' day when the king of Egypt decreed that every male Hebrew child was to be put to death as soon as he was born (Exodus 1:16). He was fearful of the Hebrews and wanted to remove any possible threat to his throne and rule. But not only did Moses survive this scheme, but God worked it out so that Pharaoh paid to feed, clothe, and educate him. In the period of the kings we see another such attempt.

📖 Read in 2 Kings 11:1–3. What did the wicked queen, Athaliah, do to hold power? Why do you think she did this? What was Satan ultimately trying to achieve through using Queen Athaliah?

_____

_____

_____

The foes of the King of kings, Jesus Christ, will not stand.

Athaliah was the daughter of the wicked king, Ahab, and his evil wife, Jezebel. When her son, Ahaziah, died, she led a coup for the throne and had every one of the royal descendants of King David put to death. She wanted to be rid of anyone who could lay claim to the throne because she wanted to rule on her own. Through her, Satan tried to wipe out the line of David from whom the Messiah would come. If he had succeeded, there could be no deliverer to threaten his rule over the kingdom of earth. But God would not let his wicked plan succeed, and the priests rescued one infant son, Joash, and protected him until he could take the throne and continue the line of David.

There is another thread of opposition that runs through much of the history of Israel. Remember, the nation of Israel is simply the accumulated descendants of the man, Israel (Jacob). His twelve sons became the "twelve tribes" of Israel. But Jacob had a brother named Esau. When her twins were struggling in her womb, God told Rebekah that the older (Esau) would serve the younger (Jacob) (see Genesis 25:21–26). Esau was not a willing servant. He didn't want anyone else ruling his life. The descendants of Esau, the Edomites, were often a grief and an enemy to Israel. Esau was often a challenger to the rightful rule of Jacob (Israel).

📖 Moses faced the opposition of the Edomites as he led the people of Israel in the wilderness. Read Numbers 20:14–21, and record what you discover about the people of Edom.

_____

_____

_____

_____

Isaac prophesied that his son Esau would serve his son Jacob, but would also break Jacob's yoke from his neck (see Genesis 27:39–40). This was seen in the continual fighting of the Edomites against Israel.

Did You Know?

HEROD WAS AN IDUMEAN (EDOMITE)

Herod was known for his murderous ways. He called himself "king of the Jews" and zealously fought any threat to his throne, real or imagined. He executed hundreds of people during his reign: forty-five of the seventy members of the Sanhedrin when he first began to rule, his brother-in-law Aristobulus, his wife Mariamne (Miriam), her mother, her grandfather Hyrcanus, his two oldest sons, the children two years old and under within and around Bethlehem (because of the threat of a newborn king), and his oldest living son, Antipater, five days before Herod himself died. Finally, at his order, several prominent citizens of Judea were imprisoned to be executed upon his death, so that the people would mourn when he died. History records that his descendants continued their Edomite ways.

When Israel sought to go through the land of Edom, the Edomites stubbornly opposed them. They would not let them pass and even came out against them armed for battle—an example of Edom's opposition toward Israel.

When David ruled as king he conquered the Edomites for a time, and they were his servants (2 Samuel 8:14). David's son Solomon faced opposition from Hadad the Edomite who, as a descendant of the conquered king of Edom, sought to reestablish his authority and reign. In so doing he was an adversary to Solomon and caused much trouble (1 Kings 11:14–22, 25). Other kings faced opposition from the Edomites (also known as the sons of Mount Seir, where Esau had settled).

God raised up prophets to decry the ways and actions of Edom and to pronounce His judgment against them. During the period of the kings of Israel and Judah, we see the marks of the hand of God at work to fulfill His promises. Amos called all nations to an accounting with God (Amos 1—2). Included in that list was Edom, whose slave trade included the selling of Israelites and whose warfare with Israel was marked with intense rage and no compassion (1:9, 11–12). The entire prophecy of Obadiah (21 verses) announces God's coming judgment on Edom for their pride and wickedness, particularly against Israel. They rejoiced over the invasion of Jerusalem and the captivity of Judah. Edom joined in looting Jerusalem in 586 BC and hindered any escape by the Israelites (verses 11–14). Obadiah assured them that in spite of their actions, Zion would be established by the Lord and would rule even over Esau (verses 19–21). Isaiah 34:1–6 told of the Lord's judgment on the nations and on Edom. Ezekiel spoke of God's judgment on Edom (25:12–14; 35:1–15; 36:1–5). Psalm 137 lamented the days in Babylon and remembered the hatred of Edom during Jerusalem's destruction (verse 7).

What does this have to do with Jesus as King? Consider these historical facts. Judgment came in the fifth century BC when the Nabatean Arabs invaded and defeated Edom. The refugees fled from the invasion to the region south of Judea. This area became known as Idumea, the Greek name meaning "land of the Edomites." Here is one historical fact we must not miss: King Herod was from Idumea. He was an Idumean—an Edomite. What would such a man think of the Israelites? Knowing that the prophets had declared that a king would be born who would reign in Israel, why should Herod be afraid? Herod's work and reign in Israel constantly revealed his jealousy for his throne and his honor and glory. Consider all his glorious building projects—the Temple and Temple Mount, the city and port of Caesarea, Herod's Palace in Jerusalem, the Palace and Fortress at Masada and the Herodian Palace near Bethlehem. In light of this, it would be good to read the account of Herod and the wise men in Matthew.

Considering Herod and his background, what would the Bethlehem manger mean to him? Read Matthew 2:1–12, 16–18, and record your thoughts.

_____

_____

_____

_____

_____

Jesus was born in Bethlehem in the days of Herod the king. Magi from the east came to worship Him. They had seen His star—a sign to the men who studied the stars that a king had been born. They considered Him to be the King of the Jews. The religious leaders knew and could quote the Old Testament prophecy about where the ruler/shepherd of the people of Israel was to be born. While Herod was busy investigating this, the Magi were busy seeking the infant king, Jesus, to worship Him. God led them, warned them and guided them. With Herod determined to squelch any rival ruler, Bethlehem became a place of mourning once again, for he was fearful of any threat to his place of rule. As it had mourned the death of Rachel, wife of Jacob, so now Bethlehem mourned the death of the male children two years old and younger from the city and surrounding region. The war continued against the "seed," the true King, but God would not let this wicked plan succeed. We must remember this: No attempt to dethrone the true King ever succeeds!

📖 One other incident will document this war against the true King. We pick up the story on the night before Jesus' crucifixion just after Gethsemane and the trial before Annas and Caiaphas. Read John 18:28–40; 19:1–22. See the war going on, the battle over who is king. What did Jesus say about the true King, His kingdom, and about following Him?

_____

_____

_____

_____

_____

_____

Pilate questioned Jesus about being the King of the Jews. Jesus made it clear that He is indeed a king with a kingdom not like any in this world. He literally said, "My kingdom is not from here." It's source is not the world and its evil system. He does not gain His kingdom like the world—no fighting, no political maneuvering. His kingdom is from above, from the Father, by the power and purity of His Spirit. He confidently declared _"for this I have been born, and for this I have come into the world"_ (18:37). His purpose for leaving heaven as the Son of God and being born on earth as the Son of Man—the God-Man—was to be a king, the true King. As that true King His purpose is to reveal truth and lead His followers in truth, to reign in truth forever. All those who come to Him, who want to follow Him, who look to Him as their true God, their source of truth, walk with Him in truth. They hear His voice, and (the implication is) they follow Him as their true King.

Jesus died and rose from the dead as the triumphant Lord and King. We know from Scripture and from history that God has not fulfilled all His plans for the reign of the true King in Israel and on earth. The disciples knew that too. We can see that more fully when we discover how He has worked and is working to bring the coming reigning King to earth. That is why we still pray, _"Thy kingdom come, Thy will be done on earth as it is in heaven."_

No attempt to dethrone the True King ever succeeds!

"You say correctly that I am a king. For this I have been born, and for this I have come into the world, to bear witness to the truth...."

John 18:37

THE COMING, REIGNING KING

With the Babylonian captivity, the period of the kings came to an end. Though Israel would gain some measure of freedom, they ceased to be an independent nation. They watched as one kingdom after another ruled the known world, and ruled them as well. Babylon would give way to domination by the Medes and Persians, who were the main world power from 539–331 BC. Next, they watched as the Greeks stepped to the forefront under Alexander the Great. At Alexander's death in 323 BC, the Greek empire was divided among four of his generals. Jerusalem and Judea fell under the rule of the Ptolemies of Egypt and enjoyed some measure of liberty from 323–204 BC. Then Antiochus III conquered Egypt, and Jerusalem and Judea came under Syrian dominance with less freedom. When Antiochus IV (Epiphanes) took the throne, he set out to destroy Judaism and force Jews to worship Zeus. He outlawed all Jewish rituals. He destroyed copies of the Law and prescribed the death penalty for any found hiding one. He also desecrated the Temple by sacrificing a pig on the altar and erecting a statue of Zeus in the Holy Place. This led to the Maccabean revolt in 165 BC, a military action led by priests who eventually recaptured Jerusalem and restored the temple.

The descendants of the Maccabees ruled Jerusalem until 63 BC when it was conquered by Pompey of Rome. In 40 BC, Herod was made "king" of the Jews as a favor from Rome. Herod's people, the Idumeans, had been forced to convert to Judaism during the Maccabean reign, but he was not devout, and lacked the respect of the people. They were waiting for the coming king who would throw off all foreign rule and return Jerusalem to its days of former glory. This is what the people expected Jesus to do when they shouted "Hosanna" at His triumphal entry to Jerusalem. A week later, He died on a cross, and their hopes were dashed. Even after the resurrection uncertainty abounded. What would the Messiah do? For forty days after His resurrection Jesus appeared to His disciples, to over five hundred in one instance (see Acts 1:3–11; 1 Corinthians 15:1–8 [note verse 6]). On the fortieth day, Jesus met the disciples on the Mount of Olives. There they awaited further word from Him about the days ahead.

📖 What was uppermost in the thinking of the disciples that day? Read Acts 1:1–6, and record their question. What does this tell you about their expectation?

_____

_____

_____

_____

_____

The disciples were expecting Jesus to begin His reign as the King of Israel. They wanted to know if today was the day. He had spoken to them for forty days about *"the things concerning the kingdom of God,"* and it was natural for them to ask this question especially in light of all they knew from the Old Testament scriptures about the promised Messiah and His kingdom.

> "Lord, is it at this time You are restoring the kingdom to Israel?"
>
> Acts 1:6

📖 Jesus told them that the Father had fixed certain times and epochs to fulfill all the kingdom promises. To what can we look forward, and how are we to live today? What did Jesus tell His disciples? In the answer He gave them we find the answers we need for our daily walk. Read Acts 1:7–11, and record your insights.

_____

_____

_____

_____

Jesus commanded that after they were empowered by His Spirit, they should bear witness to Him throughout the earth until He returns. Then He ascended, and the angels assured them He would return in the same way. The Holy Spirit did come ten days later on the Jewish holy day known as Pentecost, and the church was born. The early church knew the presence and power of the Lord through the indwelling Holy Spirit, and they proclaimed His gospel of forgiveness and new life (Acts 2:38–39; 4:33; 5:30–32; 9:31; 10:34–43; 13:52). They also spoke of the coming kingdom of the Messiah. They were sure He was coming back to earth to reveal the fullness of His Lordship to all the earth. He promised to complete His work and His promises to Israel, to judge the nations that rejected Him, and to establish His reign on the earth for one thousand years (the millennial kingdom). They read these truths written by the prophets, they had heard them from Jesus Himself, they received revelation from the Holy Spirit, and penned those things in the New Testament.

📖 Read the Scriptures given, and describe the character and work of the Messiah.

In His First Coming—Isaiah 11:1–4a

_____

_____

_____

_____

_____

Isaiah spoke of a shoot from the root of Jesse, David's father. In other words, a descendant of Jesse and David would be born and on Him would rest the Spirit of the LORD, _"the Spirit of wisdom and understanding, the Spirit of counsel and might, the Spirit of knowledge and of the fear of the LORD"_ (11:2, NKJV). Jesus walked in the power of the Spirit and in the fear of the Lord, ever-following His Father's desires and will. He ministered to the poor and needy, the physically and spiritually needy, and He did so with perfect righteousness.

In the Tribulation and Second Coming—

Isaiah 11:4b–5 _____

_____

_____

_____

> *The disciples were sure Jesus was coming back to earth to reveal the fullness of His Lordship to all the earth.*

Romans 11:25–27 _____

_____

_____

_____

Zechariah 12:10 _____

_____

_____

_____

Revelation 19:15–16 _____

_____

_____

(For further study, see 2 Thessalonians 1:6–10; Psalms 2:4–9; 89:24–29.)

(For further study, see 2 Thessalonians 1:6–10; Psalms 2:4–9; 89:24–29.)

Word Study
THE COMING OF THE LORD

In the first century, the Greek word *parousia* was translated "coming," "arrival," or "presence" (see Matthew 24:3; 1 Corinthians 15:23; 1 Thessalonians 2:19; 3:13; 4:15; 5:23; 2 Peter 1:16; 3:4). This technical term referred to the official coming of a king or official to a region or town. At his coming he would right all wrongs and establish peace and order. Great preparations were made for his arrival including special gifts and a celebration of praise. Some cities proclaimed a holy day or even constructed buildings or minted a coin in honor of his coming. For many, expectations were high at the thought of his coming and expressions of joy abundant.

The Scriptures are clear that the Lord Jesus will return to deal with the nations of the world, with the wicked, with all who will not bow to Him as Lord and King. But they are equally clear that God is not finished with Israel either. In the seven-year period of great distress on earth (the "seventieth week" of Daniel 9:24–27), He will deal with His people Israel so that they finally turn to Him as their true King. All the earth will see and know that the earth is rightfully His and that He alone is worthy to reign, though many will still stand opposed to Him as their king.

In the Millennial Kingdom—

Isaiah 11:6–10 (in light of verse 5) _____

_____

_____

_____

Revelation 20:1–6 _____

_____

_____

_____

(If you want to study this further, see Isaiah 2:2–4; 60:3–5; 65:20–25.)

(If you want to study this further, see Isaiah 2:2–4; 60:3–5; 65:20–25.)

With Jerusalem as His capital, the Messiah and true King will reign over all the nations of the earth for one thousand years, a millennial reign. He will lead the nations in truth, judge with righteousness, and establish a lasting peace. Even the world's animal kingdom will live in peace and harmony, and children will be unharmed by any of them. The nations will rejoice over the reign of the true King, for He will order things on earth as they should be. Israel will prosper at the hands of the nations as the Lord Jesus oversees them. Many who are born in the millennium will come to the Lord Jesus and walk in His light. In addition, those born at this time will live long and fruitful lives protected by their King and enjoying the work of their hands. The people of the Lord will know a relationship with Him that is marked by wonder and awe.

APPLY Because of Christ's First Coming we can live in confidence and expectancy day by day and rejoice in His Second Coming. Paul wrote in Romans 15:12–13, *"And again Isaiah says, 'There shall come the root of Jesse, and He who arises to rule over the Gentiles, in Him shall the Gentiles hope. Now may the God of hope fill you with all joy and peace in believing, that you may abound in hope by the power of the Holy Spirit.'"* Are you filled with joy in believing and abounding in hope? Think of your walk now as you apply what you have learned in this lesson about God's choice of King and how He is fulfilling His kingdom plans.

FOR ME TO FOLLOW CHRIST

 **DAY FIVE**

Kings come and kings go. History records life as a constant change from one leader to the next. But behind it all, God rules. Nebuchadnezzar was king in Babylon while Israel was in captivity. It was he who brought the period of the kings of Israel and Judah to an end when he conquered what was left of the nation in 586 BC. He ruled over the most powerful nation on earth. His every whim was law, and Israel was subject to him. He had no respect for the God of Israel. But when three Hebrews, Hananiah, Mishael, and Azariah (renamed Shadrach, Meshach, and Abednego), violated his order to bow in worship before his golden idol, he learned that his was not the highest law. He witnessed first-hand the power of Jehovah supernaturally delivering those who would bow to no other God. Though he developed a higher view of God from this experience, his view was still not high enough. God warned him by a dream in which he was a magnificent tree that had to be chopped down in order to recognize the Most High as the true ruler of the earth. A year passed, and yet he was unrepentant.

📖 We pick up the story in Daniel 4:28. Read 4:28–30, and write what you observe about Nebuchadnezzar's attitude and lack of reverence for God.

_____

_____

_____

_____

_____

_____

Ask yourself: "Who is King of my life? Is my life characterized by self-will, self-effort, and self-glory?"

Even though Daniel interpreted his dream and called Nebuchadnezzar to repentance (Daniel 4:27), a year later we find Nebuchadnezzar patting himself on the back and glorying in his position, not recognizing God at all. In 4:30 we see all the manifestations of one consumed with self. We see self-will instead of surrender to God's will and way (He says, *"Is this not Babylon the great, which I myself have built. . . ?"*). We also see self-effort instead of trust in God (*". . . which I myself have built . . . by the might of my power . . ."*). Finally, we see self-glory instead of giving the Lord the honor and credit He deserves (*". . . for the glory of my majesty"*).

📖 Read Daniel 4:31–33, and identify how God deals with Nebuchadnezzar's pride and why.

_____

_____

_____

While Nebuchadnezzar's boasting was still in his mouth, God spoke, and his sovereignty was removed. He lost his mind and wandered like a beast eating grass like a cow for seven years. This judgment had one goal in mind: for Nebuchadnezzar to *". . . recognize that the Most High is ruler over the realm of mankind."*

📖 Take a moment to read through Daniel 4:34–37. What brought Nebuchadnezzar's humiliation to an end, and what lesson did he learn?

_____

_____

_____

_____

It was not until Nebuchadnezzar *"raised his eyes toward heaven"* that his reason returned to him. Further, it was after he *"blessed the Most High and praised and honored Him who lives forever,"* acknowledging that it is God, and not he, that rules. Once he recognized that he was accountable to God, his kingdom was restored. Now he could be the kind of king he ought to be, ruling under the authority of *"the King of heaven."* He learned a hard lesson about who was the true King, and that *". . . He is able to humble those who walk in pride."*

As we consider these truths, we see much about the right and wrong ways to exert our authority and influence. You see, each of us has a kingdom apportioned to us. It is the realm of our lives and influence. Some of us have others whom we are responsible to lead by serving. Yet however large or small our kingdom may be, it is not ours alone. It is our part of God's kingdom, and we must recognize that He is the ultimate ruler of all.

 Take a moment to reflect on the list below, and identify the components that make up your own kingdom.

___ House	___ Job	___ Car
___ Spouse	___ Children	___ Grandchildren
___ Business	___ Employees	___ Subordinates
___ Church office	___ Community office	___ Governmental office
___ Other_____		

Now take the time to reflect on each one, and honestly identify which of them you rule and manage as Nebuchadnezzar did—with self-effort, self-will, and self-glory.

_____

_____

_____

Put Yourself In Their Shoes

JESUS IS LORD, THE MOST HIGH GOD

Melchizedek, Abraham, and Nebuchadnezzar all acknowledged the Most High as their King. Jesus is the Son of the Most High (see Luke 1:32), our Lord and King (see 1 Timothy 1:17). What response will you have to the Lordship of Jesus Christ?

- The Response of Apathy: simply ignoring Him.
- The Response of Anxiety: too afraid to trust Him.
- The Response of Anger: constantly rebelling against Him.
- The Response of Awe: acknowledging your King with gratitude, trust, and surrender.

_____

_____

What about the components of your personal life? In the space provided, mark with an "S" those areas of your life that reflect a true surrender to God, and with a "W" those that are withheld from Him and controlled by self.

___ Friendships   ___ Finances   ___ Use of time
___ Hobbies   ___ Use of talents   ___ Family relationships
___ Possessions   ___ Thought life   ___ Plans for future
___ Work   ___ Christian service   ___ Other_____

Whatever we have, whatever we hold, whatever we do, whoever we are, we must all come to grips with the reality that heaven rules (see Daniel 4:26). If we are living our lives independent of God, we may prosper for a time, but in the end we will fail. The most important application of this study is that everything must be surrendered to Him. In Luke 6:46 Jesus asks a penetrating question: *Why do you call me 'Lord, Lord,' and do not do what I say?"*

In the life of every believer there is a throne and a cross. The throne is a place of ruling; the cross is the place of dying. The true disciple is called to *"take up his cross"* and follow Jesus. If Christ is to be on the throne of my life, I must be on the cross, dying to my own will and way. If I insist on sitting on the throne, ruling and reigning in my life, then Christ is not reigning, and I am not experiencing His resurrection life.

If you need to surrender, here are the steps:

1. Confess any sins of which God has convicted you in this lesson.
2. Repent of running your own life—do so area by area.
3. Yield each area of your life to Christ.
4. Trust Him moment by moment with the details of your life.
5. Deal with it quickly if you try to retake control over any area of your life.

(APPLY) *Lord,* I praise and exalt and honor You as the true King of heaven and earth. All your works are true, and all your ways are just. Your dominion is everlasting, and your kingdom has no end. Forgive me for those times when I have ruled my own life independent of You and Your will. Take Your rightful place on the throne of my life and lead me in Your ways. Help me to trust you with all of my worries, and help me to be quick to turn back to You every time I stray. Amen.

Write your own letter to the King:

_____

_____

_____

_____

_____

_____

> **In the life of every believer there is a throne and a cross. If Christ is to be on the throne of my life ruling, I must be on the cross, dying to my own will and way.**

> **Lord Jesus, take Your rightful place on the throne of my life and lead me in Your ways.**

_____

_____

_____

_____

_____

_____

Jesus is the King who gave His life for us, that we might be a kingdom of priests to God the Father. He has given His life that we might walk with Him and reign with Him forever. Follow Him! Look up, for He is the coming King. Maranatha! (see 2 Corinthians 16:21–23; Revelation 1:4–7; 22:16–21).

Christ the Prophet

PROCLAIMING TRUTH–LEADING US INTO TRUE WORSHIP

When we think of the prophets of the Old and New Testaments, certainly none rival the majesty and power of the Lord Jesus Christ. He opened the Scriptures as no man ever could and spoke as no man ever spoke (see John 7:46). He prayed as no man ever prayed and walked as no man ever walked. He walked in truth and spoke truth in all He did. Jesus Christ fulfilled the prophecies of the Old Testament that spoke of **The Prophet to come**.

The call of any prophet was to listen faithfully to God and speak His word, nothing more, nothing less, and nothing else. Any added opinion was disobedience to the Lord and a distortion of His message. That message was always to bring people to a right relationship with the living Lord, to genuine

> *"And this is eternal life, that they may know Thee, the only true God, and Jesus Christ whom Thou hast sent."*
>
> **John 17:3**

WHO IS "THE PROPHET"?

The Lord Promised Moses in Deuteronomy 18:18–19 . . .	Jesus Christ Is . . .	The Scriptures Speak . . .
"I will raise up a prophet	"THE PROPHET"	*"This certainly is the Prophet."* John 7:40; 4:19; 6:14; Acts 3:20–26
from among their countrymen like you,	"THE SON OF ABRAHAM" "THE SON OF DAVID"	*"The son of Abraham . . ."* Matthew 1:1; 27:37; John 4:9
and I will put My words in his mouth,	"THE SON OF THE FATHER" "THE SON OF MAN" "A DISCIPLE"	*"I speak these things as the Father taught Me."* John 8:26, 28; Isaiah 50:4
and he shall speak to them all that I command him.	"THE MESSIAH" "THE ANOINTED ONE"	*"He anointed Me to preach the gospel . . ."* Luke 4:18; John 1:38, 49; 12:49–50; 20:16
And it shall come about that whoever will not listen to My words which he shall speak in my name, I myself will require it of him."	"MY BELOVED SON" "MY CHOSEN ONE" "JUDGE	*"The Father . . . gave to the Son . . . authority to execute judgment. . . . As I hear I judge."* John 5:26–30, 43; Matthew 12:18–81; 17:5; Luke 9:35; Acts 17:30–31

worship in spirit and truth. Just before the eventful Passover week when Jesus prepared to give His life as the Passover Lamb, He gave this testimony of His life and ministry: *"For I did not speak on My own initiative, but the Father Himself who sent Me has given Me commandment, what to say, and what to speak. And I know that His commandment is eternal life; therefore the things I speak, I speak just as the Father told Me"* (John 12:49–50). That was true of the Lord Jesus in His life and ministry. Though we live 2,000 years later, through His Word we too can hear Him speak the Father's will, and through that we can come to worship Him in spirit and truth.

Christ the Prophet

DAY ONE

A Prophet like unto Moses

The Lord has always wanted His people to walk in truth. That is His nature. He is the Truth and walking in truth is as natural to Him as breathing is to us. He speaks truth, lives truth, and delights in truth. Lies and deception have no part in His ways, His character, or His Kingdom. It is not just that He does not lie, Scripture teaches us that He **cannot** lie (see Titus 1:2). When He chose Israel as His own people, He wanted them to walk in truth. All the laws He gave Moses were to help them walk in the truth and experience the freedom truth always brings. As He walked them out of Egypt and through the Wilderness, He sought to show them how they could encounter the blessed experience of following Him. When people did not walk in line with the truth, He dealt with them and showed Moses and the elders how to do the same. In the midst of those journeys, He made a promise to Moses. Today, we will look at that promise and see how that can help us walk more fully in the truth.

📖 Read Deuteronomy 18, and answer the following discussion questions.

What is the main point of verses 9–14?

_____

_____

_____

_____

What is the main point of verses 20–22?

_____

_____

_____

In general terms, how do verses 15–19 relate to verses 9–14 and verses 20–22? Is there a connection?

_____

_____

_____

_____

Put Yourself In Their Shoes

WHAT IS A PROPHET?

A prophet:

• is raised up by God

• is able to hear God

• speaks what He has heard from God

• is always true in what he says

The Lord warned the people about the abominations of the nations then inhabiting the land of Canaan, practices so detestable and unlawful they required the immediate removal of those nations from the land. The Canaanites were guilty of child sacrifice, witchcraft, consulting mediums (psychics), sorcerers, and spiritists and things associated with all these. The Lord wanted His people to walk following Him in truth, not in the lies and deceptions of the occult. The Lord wanted His people to listen to **Him**, not to false teachers and spiritists. The Lord promised to raise up a Prophet who would lead the people in truth, in all He said. They must ever be cautious of one who would speak presumptuously out of his own thinking or out of the lies and superstitions connected with the gods of Canaan and the surrounding nations.

In looking at Deuteronomy 18:15–19, what was God's promise to Moses about **The Prophet** (18:15)?

_____

_____

_____

Where would He come from (18:15)?

_____

_____

The Lord promised to raise up a Prophet from among their brethren, the chosen people of Israel. He would be a man like Moses raised up by God for them, to lead and guide them as Moses had done.

What was God's reasoning in providing for this **Prophet to come**? How were the people connected to this promise (18:16–17)?

_____

_____

_____

_____

When the Lord spoke at Horeb (Mount Sinai) the people were intensely afraid in the presence of the awesome majesty and holiness of God. The fire and smoke on the mountain, the flashes of lightning, and the thundering voice of God from the cloud caused them to fear for their very lives (see Exodus 19:16–20; 20:18–19). In this intense encounter with the holiness and power of God, they asked Moses to be their mediator between God and them (see Deuteronomy 5:23–33). This is the role every prophet of God fills.

What would be the chief characteristic of this Prophet that God would raise up (18:18)?

_____

_____

_____

What authority would this Prophet have (18:19)?

_____

_____

"I will put My words in His mouth, and He shall speak to them all that I command Him."
Deuteronomy 18:18b

The Lord promised to put His words in the mouth of this Prophet so He would speak all that God commanded Him. He would speak in the name of the Lord, with the authority of the Lord. This would not be a self-promoting prophet; He would be God-centered and faithful to deliver only the messages God the Father gave Him to speak.

What would happen to the one who would not listen to this Prophet (18:19)?

_____

_____

_____

The man or woman who heard this Prophet would be held accountable to answer to the Lord for how he responded to Him. Would people respond to Him with obedience or apathy or willful ignorance? All who listened to Him would have to answer for the way they responded to all they heard, implying accountability for how they obeyed. This not only refers to hearing the sound of this Prophet's voice, but to obeying from the heart the Lord's intent in the messages, the commands, and the statutes given.

What contrast does the Lord present in verses 20–22?

_____

_____

_____

_____

> "'Let him who has My word speak My word in truth. What does straw have in common with grain?' declares the LORD. 'Is not My word like fire?' declares the LORD, 'and like a hammer which shatters a rock?'"
> Jeremiah 23:28-29

📖 Read Jeremiah 23:9–32. Compare the message God gave through Jeremiah to God's message in Deuteronomy 18:20–22.

_____

_____

_____

_____

_____

Some would presume to speak for the Lord, while others would boldly declare that their messages were from other gods. Such prophets should surely die. By checking their accuracy, one could be sure whether the prophets were speaking presumptuously or from their own imagination. One hundred percent accuracy was the requirement. Therefore, if a prophet's prophecy did not come true as it had been stated, this prophet was a false prophet, an imposter whose message should be ignored. Jeremiah describes the messages of false prophets as straw that offers no benefit whatsoever, while he describes the Lord's words as grain that feeds, nourishes, and strengthens.

The Lord told Moses that He would raise up a Prophet and would give Him the words to say. That Prophet is Jesus Christ (see Acts 3:22), and God His Father gave Him the words He spoke on earth. How did that work out in the life of Jesus? We will see that in Day Two.

"I Will Put My Words in His Mouth"

A prophet speaks for God. This is what every true prophet has done through the ages. But all of the Old Testament prophets were precursors to the One that God promised to raise up. How would **this Prophet** know what to say and when to say it? The Lord told Moses that He would be faithful to give this Prophet the message He was to speak, *"I will put My words in His mouth, and He shall speak to them all that I command Him"* (Deuteronomy 18:18). To speak for God, a Prophet had to hear from God. We will see that process at work in today's lesson.

There are over three hundred prophecies concerning the coming of the Messiah, and they speak of His various roles. Some speak of Him being the King, others of Him being our High Priest, and still others speak of Him being the Prophet.

📖 Read the messianic prophecies in Isaiah 50:4–9. What do you see in verse 4 concerning what this Messiah will speak?

_____

_____

_____

How was the Messiah to receive His instructions (50:4–5a)?

_____

_____

_____

The Messiah would be one who spoke as a disciple, or a learner. He would learn from His Teacher and speak those words to the weary and downtrodden so that they would be sustained. The Hebrew word (*'uwth*) translated *"sustain"* refers to running to the aid of others, to support them and help them. Though He was God in the flesh, in His humanness the Messiah would learn by personal experience how to teach others, how to encourage others, how to run to the aid of others. He would learn this as He was awakened morning by morning to *"listen as a disciple"* (or learner). The ear of the Messiah, the God-Man, would be opened to hear and obey all the commands God the Father would give.

What is revealed about the heart of this Messiah (50:5–6)?

_____

_____

_____

Where was His confidence (50:7–9)?

_____

_____

_____

PROPHET, PRIEST, AND KING

Jesus Christ came as the promised Prophet, Priest, and King:

- **Prophet**—the one worthy and able to live and speak the truth in every situation
- **Priest**—the one able to be the mediator between God and man
- **King**—the one able to reign in righteousness and peace

Doctrine

THE "WORD" JESUS SPOKE

The Hebrew word, *dabar,* translated "a word" in Isaiah 50:4, is used 225 times in the Old Testament to speak of the *"word of the LORD,"* the word of prophetic revelation. The Messiah in Isaiah 50 would also be the prophesied Prophet raised up by the Lord.

The Messiah in Isaiah 50 is revealed to have a heart of obedience and submission even to the point of humiliation, a humiliation the New Testament graphically pictures in crucifixion. He would be surrendered to the Father, confident in His help. He would walk into death knowing He would come out of His tomb in glorious resurrection.

📖 Read Mark 1:35–38, and answer the questions below.

What do you discover about Jesus in Mark 1:35? (Note this was after a very long day of ministry in Capernaum.)

_____

_____

_____

_____

How does Mark 1:35 relate to Isaiah 50:4? What was Jesus' reply to their suggestion concerning the day's schedule (Mark 1:36–38)?

_____

_____

_____

_____

Jesus arose while it was still dark, and went out to a lonely place outside the city of Capernaum, perhaps somewhere along the shore of the Sea of Galilee or in the hills surrounding that lake. There He spent time with His Father listening with a learner's heart as described in Isaiah 50:4. When the disciples found Him, they informed Him that there were many yet in Capernaum who expected Him to minister there again that day. Jesus was quick to respond that He and they must go to other villages and proclaim the message the Father had given Him. This declaration of the truth was the purpose of His coming. Jesus followed the designs of His Father, listening to Him and obeying all He commanded.

📖 Read Luke 5:16. What is significant about this verse?

_____

_____

_____

📖 Read John 7:14–18 and 8:28–30, and record what you discover about Jesus.

_____

_____

_____

_____

Jesus often slipped away to uninhabited areas away from the crowds and village businesses in order to spend time with His Father. Christ's relationship with the Father was His delight and the source of His ministry. The people (including some of the leaders) were amazed at what Jesus taught, wonder-

> *"For I did not speak on My own initiative, but the Father Himself who sent Me has given Me commandment, what to say, and what to speak. And I know that His commandment is eternal life; therefore the things I speak, I speak just as the Father has told Me."*
>
> *John 12:49-50*

ing where He acquired such insight and how He taught with such power. Jesus made it plain that all He taught did not originate with Him but, in fact, came from God the Father. All that Christ said was true and righteous. In everything, He had the goal of pleasing His Father and bringing glory to Him. He wanted people to see and to know Him for who He was and surrender their lives to Him in worship and obedience.

 John 8:30 tells us many came to believe in Him because of what He taught. What was at the heart of all Jesus spoke and taught? Read the next two verses (John 8:31–32), and write your findings.

_____

_____

_____

_____

Jesus heard from the Father what to speak, and He faithfully proclaimed the message His Father gave Him. He spoke the truth and promised that those who chose to abide in His word (those who would receive and live by His word) would know the truth and walk in freedom. Lies only divide and bring bondage. Truth sets a person free and leads to oneness. Jesus wanted His disciples walking in that freedom and oneness, so He came as a Prophet declaring the truth. As a result, those who followed Him and His word could be free—open, transparent, and unhindered in their relationship to the Father and others.

 Are you walking in the freedom Jesus desires for you? Are you open, transparent, and unhindered in your relationship with Him? What about your relationship with others—your spouse, your parents, your friends, fellow Christians? Is there an area of division, bondage, lack of oneness? Ask the Lord to reveal the truth that is missing in that relationship or that area of your life. He wants you walking in truth and freedom.

_____

_____

_____

> *"It was for freedom that Christ set us free.... who hindered you from obeying the truth? ... For you were called to freedom...."*
> *Galatians 5:1a, 7b, 13a*

What else can we learn of this Prophet? As we look at His words to a woman wrapped up in many lies, we begin to see some added details in our portrait of this Prophet who spoke the words of God. We will discover those details in the Day Three discussion.

"I Perceive That You Are a Prophet"

Christ the Prophet **DAY THREE**

Would you know a prophet if you saw (or heard) one? What would he be like? The Lord said that the Prophet He would raise up out of Israel would *"speak to them all that I command Him."* (Deuteronomy 18:18). As we look through the photo album of the New Testament, we see several settings in which **this Prophet** did just that. Jesus Christ came as **The Prophesied Prophet**, able to live and speak the truth in every situation, faithfully speaking what the Father gave Him to say. We see one of the clearest examples of His ministry as **The Prophet** in an incident near the Samaritan village of Sychar, an occurrence that would forever change that village and its people.

📖 Read John 4:1–42, and answer the questions throughout this Day Three discussion.

BRIDGING BARRIERS

There were several barriers that Jesus bridged to reach out to the Samaritan woman: **Racial and Religious**—Jew and Samaritan, **Gender**—Man and Woman, and **Character**—Prophet and Adulteress.

Let's establish the background of this incident. What did the woman from Sychar notice about Jesus in her first encounter (John 4:7–9)?

_____

_____

_____

_____

This incident came in the fall of AD 27 during the first year of Jesus' ministry. With His ministry growing in popularity and with the potential for controversy with the Pharisees in Judea, He chose to leave Judea and travel to Galilee. Christ chose the shorter route through Samaria, and approached the village of Sychar around noon. While the disciples went to gather some food, Jesus stayed at Jacob's well outside town, and there at the noon hour a woman from Sychar came to draw water. Jesus asked her for a drink. She recognized that He was a Jew and responded with surprise, perhaps even offense—a Jewish man asking a Samaritan woman for a drink was not the norm, *"for Jews have no dealings with Samaritans."*

Jesus was not offended by her response. Where did He direct her attention (4:10)?

_____

_____

_____

Did You Know?

SAMARITANS AND JEWS

The Samaritans were the race that originated from the intermarriage of the Assyrians with the Israelites after the Assyrian conquest of Israel in 722 BC. The Samaritans were despised by the Jews because of their continual idolatry and adaptation of foreign culture. With the intermarriage came many compromises of the Mosaic Law in family and society.

What was the woman's response (4:11–12)?

_____

_____

_____

_____

Jesus directed the woman's attention to God, specifically on what He wanted to give her—*"the gift of God"*—and on Himself as the one who could give her this gift. He spoke to her of *"living water."* She wanted to know where this living water was found and how He could give it to her since He had nothing with which to draw from the well. Was He greater than Jacob himself who gave the well, a well that was able to provide so abundantly for Jacob's family as well as for many generations since that day?

How did Jesus answer her question? Where was His focus (4:13–14)?

_____

_____

_____

What was the woman's concern in John 4:15? Where was her focus?

_____

_____

_____

Jesus spoke of water that would forever quench thirst, versus the water of Jacob's well that satisfied temporarily. Jesus promised a source of Living Water that would be like a perennial fountain satisfying forever, picturing everlasting life. Jeremiah 2:13 spoke of the Lord as a fountain of Living Water that Israel rejected. Here Jesus was offering a fountain of Living Water in Himself, but that point had not yet become clear to the woman. She was still thinking of literal water (H_2O). She was very interested in this kind of water that eternally quenched thirst since she was evidently thirsty and tired of coming to the well every day.

Upon what idea did Jesus focus in John 4:16, and how did the woman answer Him (4:17)?

_____

_____

_____

_____

What was the woman's response to Jesus' piercing statement (4:17–20)?

_____

_____

_____

_____

Note the woman's new focus in John 4:20. What did she bring up?

_____

_____

_____

Jesus began dealing with the woman's barriers to this Living Water. He pointed to a spiritual boulder stopping up the well. The woman admitted she did not have a husband and left it at that, but Jesus did not leave it there—she had to deal with her past and present sin, the five husbands and the current live-in boyfriend. Because of her sinful life, Jesus' pointed analysis of this Samaritan woman was a sore subject to her. Jesus dealt with her sin, but she decided she wanted to change the subject and talk about theology. She correctly perceived He was a prophet, for no ordinary man could analyze her life like Jesus had just done. Since He was a prophet they could talk about "prophet things" like which was the best place to worship, Jerusalem or Mount Gerizim.

"For My people have committed two evils: They have forsaken Me, the fountain of living waters, to hew for themselves cisterns, broken cisterns, that can hold no water."
Jeremiah 2:13

With pinpoint accuracy, the Lord Jesus had a message for this woman (and for us). What did Jesus say about her worship (and Samaritan worship [4:21–22])?

_____

_____

_____

_____

📖 What was the heart of the message from **this Prophet,** Jesus (4:23–24)?

_____

_____

_____

_____

Did You Know?

MOUNT GERIZIM

Located in the Judea mountain range in central Israel, Mount Gerizim and Mount Ebal stand opposite one another with the site of Shechem resting in the valley between them. When Abraham first came into the land of Canaan, he built an altar at Shechem (see Genesis 12:6–7). Mount Gerizim (with Mount Ebal) was the place of the reading of the Blessings and Curses of the Law when Israel entered the land under Joshua (see Deuteronomy 11:29–20; 27:11–12; Joshua 8:30–35). The Samaritans placed a temple there since they considered this the best place for worship, not accepting Jerusalem as God's chosen place for the Temple (see 2 Chronicles 3:1–2; 6:4–11).

Jesus took the woman's focus off the **place** of worship, or the externals associated with any place, whether Mount Gerizim or Jerusalem, and focused her on the **Person** of worship, God the Father. Jesus confronted her doubts about what the Scriptures taught, and about the fact that the Jews truly did have God's revelation concerning salvation. The Samaritans, who only accepted the Pentateuch (Genesis—Deuteronomy), had corrupted their worship and refused what God had spoken through the many prophets and writers of the Old Testament. They did not know the truth. They worshiped a lie.

Jesus directed her attention on true worship of the Father and the fact that *"the hour"* was present for *"true worshipers"* to *"worship the Father in spirit and truth."* That *"hour"* was His death on the cross that would provide redemption and open the way to the Father for this woman and for any who would come and accept this redemptive gift of salvation. At the heart of Jesus' words was the truth that God is Spirit, and a relationship with Him must be on a spirit to Spirit level—from the heart and based on truth. The Father is seeking those who will worship Him based on the revelation of Scripture and the revelation of Jesus Christ, who is the Word and the Truth (see John 1:1–5, 14; 14:6). The depth of our relationships is always based on the truth of revelation. The greater the understanding between two people and the stronger the commitment to truth in their relationship, the deeper the relationship can grow.

What do you find in the woman's statement in John 4:25? Compare this with what she told her fellow villagers in John 4:28–29.

_____

_____

_____

_____

What is significant about Jesus' response and revelation in John 4:26?

_____

_____

_____

She quickly understood that He knew all about her, and the words He spoke about true worship being *"in spirit and truth"* pierced her heart. She believed (as did many other Samaritans) that a Messiah was coming. This Messiah would know and explain all that was necessary. **This Prophet** in her midst certainly told her all the things about her that would convince her of her need for Him. Then Jesus clearly stated who He was, literally, *"**I** who speak to you am He"* (emphasis added), pointing to Himself as the Messiah and using the language emphasizing the "I AM" as He did on several other occasions. He revealed who He was, and He revealed who she was. As a matter of fact, the way He exposed the condition of her heart as it truly was became the heart of her testimony to the townspeople—*"Come, see a Man who told me all things that I ever did"* (4:29).

📖 What did the townspeople come to believe (4:30, 39–42)?

_____

_____

_____

_____

_____

This Christ, the Messiah, the Prophet who speaks truth and leads people to know the truth, is the Savior of the world. He brings people to a true understanding of who God is in His nature and character. He reveals the meaning of all the Lord has said through the many prophets He has sent and through whom He has spoken in the Old Testament. He also reveals to men and women the truth about their own hearts, their true condition before God and what He requires of them, and He leads them to true worship of the one true God. Unlike the Old Testament Prophets however, Jesus doesn't only speak truth, He **is** truth—*"the way, the truth, and the life"* (John. 14:6).

"He Who Receives a Prophet"

Christ the Prophet DAY FOUR

What do you do with a prophet? Throughout the ages, prophets were controversial figures. Their messages required change, and not everyone wanted to change. No one was more controversial than Jesus, **The Prophet**. Quoting the Old Testament, Peter called Him a Stone to stumble over (see 1 Peter 2:8). The issue God addressed with Moses in Deuteronomy 18 (and in many other passages) was the issue of refusing and receiving—refusing what is a lie (that which takes a person further and further away from the true God), and receiving the truth (that which brings one into a right relationship with God). Truth builds relationships and brings one into closer fellowship and friendship, while lies divide and destroy—sometimes eating away at the relationship like cancer, and at other times slicing the relationship in two as with an enemy sword. When Jesus came proclaiming what the Father taught Him, He knew the life and death nature of what He said, and how important it was that it be received. Today we will look at the importance of receiving **this Prophet** and His word.

THE SEVEN "I AM" STATEMENTS OF JESUS

I AM . . . the Bread of Life (John 6:35), . . . the Light of the World (8:12), . . . the Door of the Sheep (10:7, 9), . . . the Good Shepherd (10:11, 14), . . . the Resurrection and the Life (11:25–26), . . . the Way, the Truth, and the Life (14:6), . . . the True Vine (15:1, 5).

Near the end of His second year of ministry (fall of AD 28), Jesus sent out the Twelve instructing them about ministry and its rewards (Matthew 10:1–42). Read Matthew 10:40–41. What did Jesus say about a prophet in these two verses?

_____

_____

_____

_____

Doctrine
WHO IS THE "SON OF MAN?"

Jesus asked *"Who do people say that the Son of Man is?"* The disciples replied, *"Some say John the Baptist; and others Elijah; but still others, Jeremiah, or one of the prophets."* Then Jesus asked, *"But who do you say that I am?"* Peter answered, *"Thou art the Christ the Son of the Living God"* (Matthew 16:13–16).

Jesus promised that those who received the Twelve as His messengers (as they would receive a prophet) would receive a prophet's reward. In Matthew 10:40–41 Jesus used the word *déchomai,* which is translated *"receives."* This word refers to one who receives wholeheartedly, readily, and deliberately. It is literally, *"he who is receiving,"* with the idea of an ongoing reception and welcoming of the prophet and his message, not just a "tip of the hat" nod.

In light of the full meaning of *déchomai* (*"receives"*) in Matthew 10:40–41, how would Jesus want to be received as **The Prophet**?

_____

_____

_____

_____

How does this compare with Deuteronomy 18:19?

_____

_____

_____

_____

Extra Mile
A PROPHET WITHOUT HONOR

How did the people of Nazareth (Jesus' hometown) receive Him the first time He returned there after His ministry had begun? Read Luke 4:16–30 to discover their reception of, or reaction to, Jesus.

If someone would be given a prophet's reward for receiving **one sent by Jesus,** then how much more would one be rewarded who **received Jesus** readily and deliberately with a whole heart. To receive Him as **The Prophet** sent from the Father was to receive the Father and His message of truth. At the same time, to reject Jesus and His message was to reject the Father as well. He stated in Deuteronomy 18:19, if anyone does not *"listen to My words which He shall speak in My name, I Myself will require it of him."*

What about Jesus' own family? How did His brothers and sisters receive Him? Jesus came to Nazareth for the first time in the early part of AD 28, near the beginning of His second year of ministry. He came once again in the fall of AD 28.

Read the account in Mark 6:1–4. Who is present?

_____

_____

_____

_____

What happened? What did Jesus do?

_____

_____

_____

_____

What was the response of the crowd?

_____

_____

_____

_____

_____

Jesus came to Nazareth, and on the Sabbath went into the synagogue, as was His custom. The townspeople were there, including Mary, His four brothers, and at least two sisters. (There is no mention of Joseph at this time.) Jesus taught and obviously performed some miracles since miracles are mentioned in verse 2. Regardless of the wisdom of His teaching and the power of His miracles, the crowd took offense at Him.

What did Jesus say concerning the whole incident?

_____

_____

_____

_____

What does this tell you about the family situation, at least among His brothers and sisters?

_____

_____

_____

_____

_____

> **"Jesus said to them, 'A prophet is not without honor except in his home town and among his own relatives and in his own household.'"**
> **Mark 6:4**

Jesus spoke forthrightly. A prophet has no honor in his hometown, among his own relatives, and in his own household. This statement sums up the whole crowd **including** Christ's own family. They did not believe in Him as the Messiah, and they were offended at what He taught. Only the power of God could change their hearts. The next time we hear of Jesus' brothers it was about a year later in the fall of AD 29 as they mockingly told Jesus to go up to the Feast of the Tabernacles and show Himself to His followers. Jesus told them His time had not yet fully come (John 7:1–9). In light of their rejection of Him, Jesus would trust His Father to draw them to Himself.

📖 How did the religious leaders receive Jesus as the Prophet? Read Matthew 23:29–39, and summarize what you find.

_____

_____

_____

_____

_____

What was the heart of Jesus toward the people of Jerusalem (Matthew 23:37–39)?

_____

_____

_____

_____

Anyone can know forgiveness of sins and new life within by the presence and power of the Holy Spirit, if he or she will receive Jesus and the truth He has proclaimed.

Some of the multitudes who heard Jesus and saw His miracles considered Him to be a prophet, some even considered Him to be **The Prophet** who was to come (see Matthew 21:11, 46; John 6:14; 7:40). Philip, a disciple of Jesus, saw Him as **The Prophet** (see John 1:45). Even Herod Antipas the tetrarch over Galilee saw Jesus as a prophet of some sort (see Matthew 14:1–2). However, the Pharisees and chief priests did not share these opinions or convictions; they saw Him as a threat to their political and religious power. Jesus rebuked their unbelieving hearts. He also wept over Jerusalem because she would not receive those sent to her by the Lord, nor would she receive **The Prophet**, the Lord Jesus. As a result judgment would soon come, but judgment would not have come to the people of Jerusalem if only they had believed the message of the prophets and the message of Jesus Christ.

So it is with us today. The Lord has spoken His Word, which we have recorded in the Old Testament, in the Gospels and Acts, in the Letters written by the Apostles, and in the prophetic Revelation to John. Will we receive and heed His Word? In the early days of the Church, the apostle Peter told the leaders and people of Jerusalem, _"TO HIM YOU SHALL GIVE HEED in everything He says to you,"_ for He was sent by God _"to bless you by turning every one of you from your wicked ways"_ (Acts 3:22b, 26b). In turning from sin to Jesus Christ, they could know forgiveness of sins and new life by the power and presence of His Holy Spirit, the Spirit He had promised and prophesied just months before. That same promise holds true for us today, if we will receive Him and what He has said.

 If you do not know Jesus Christ as your personal Lord and Savior, now is the time to settle that issue in your life. It is as simple as **receiving Him** into your life **readily, deliberately,** and **wholeheartedly**. You can turn to the end of this workbook to the section entitled **"How to Follow God"** and find step-by-step instructions on how to begin the journey of knowing and following Jesus Christ.

FOR ME TO FOLLOW CHRIST

Jesus always spoke truth. Truth was behind every word He said, as it is in any word of inspired prophecy, whether it **directs** someone regarding what they should do in the present or whether it **reveals** what is to come in the future. The issue of receptivity coincides with the issue of truth. Will I, will you, receive **The Prophet's** words of command, or exhortation, or instruction? What about the words of things yet to happen? Will we live in the light of what He has revealed? Will we prepare? God will hold us accountable for the way we receive the message of **The Prophet**. Deuteronomy 18:19 states, *"And it shall come about that whoever will not listen to My words which He shall speak in My name, I Myself will require it of him."* We must answer to the Father and to Christ as both Prophet and Judge.

 Are you hearing Him? Are You heeding Him? When do you spend time in His Word?

☐ In the morning   ☐ At night
☐ On my lunch break   ☐ Sometimes during the week
☐ Usually on Sunday morning   ☐ Rarely
☐ I need to start spending more time in His Word.

Has God spoken to you about some things through this lesson? Have you heard Him clearly? Are you heeding what He has said?

_____

_____

_____

Is your relationship with the Lord clear? Do you need to make restitution to someone, for something you have done or promised to do and have not yet done? Do you need to ask forgiveness for something you have said?

_____

_____

_____

_____

_____

Is there an area of disobedience in your life that He has pinpointed?

_____

_____

Hear and heed what He has said to you. You will discover that as you apply truth to your life; you will experience the joyous freedom that He wants for you. *"You shall know the truth, and the truth shall make you free"* (John 8:32).

We get a glimpse of the wonders of the salvation the prophets proclaimed when we turn to Revelation 19:1–2, *"Hallelujah! Salvation and glory and power belong to our God; BECAUSE HIS JUDGMENTS ARE TRUE AND RIGHT-EOUS. . . ."* As John saw and heard the proclamation of the Lord's salvation

Doctrine
TRUTHFULNESS IN THE INNER MAN

God has always wanted truthfulness from the innermost part of a man or woman. The first question posed to Adam after he sinned was *"where are you?"* implying more than location. The Lord wanted Adam to admit where he was in his relationship with the Lord. He wanted Adam to admit why he was hiding and covering himself with fig leaves. God essentially asked Adam, "Where are you? What is true of you, Adam, in the inner man?" David declared, *"Behold, Thou dost desire truth in the innermost being"* (Psalm 51:6a). John 4 reminds us that the Father seeks those who will worship Him in spirit and truth—from the heart with a cleansed conscience. Ephesians 6 tells us the first piece of necessary armor is the belt of truth, which implies truthfulness, or an open, honest heart. God wants truthfulness to exude from our innermost being.

As Moses and Samuel were both Prophet and Judge, so we see the same in Jesus—We read in Exodus 18:13–26 how Moses served as a judge for Israel in the wilderness. Speaking of the way the Lord knew Moses face to face, and the way he performed so many mighty works, Deuteronomy 34:10 says: *"No prophet has risen in Israel like Moses."* In 1 Samuel 3:20 we read, *"Samuel was confirmed as a prophet of the LORD,"* and 1 Samuel 7:15 declares that *"Samuel judged Israel all the days of his life."* The Lord Jesus is also Prophet and Judge (see Matthew 13:57; Luke 13:33; John 5:24–30; Acts 17:31; Revelation 19:11). Read John 5:19–47 and see how Jesus spoke of Himself as the Son of God, Son of man, Judge, and the one about whom Moses wrote.

The goal of Christ the Prophet, the One sent by the Father, is to bring us to worship and obey Him in spirit and truth.

he was tempted to worship the angel who brought him the message, but the angel focused his attention on the heart of the message the Old Testament prophets gave—**"worship God"** (19:10). Then the angel pointed him to the heart of all prophecy, *"For the testimony of Jesus is the spirit of prophecy."* Jesus is both **The Prophet** and **The Message**.

We know the Lord Jesus prophesied of many things to come—His Return for His Church, His judgment of the nations, etc. How are we to live in the light of all He has prophesied?

📖 Read Revelation 22:6–9. What do you find about the words of God?

_____

_____

_____

What does the Lord Jesus promise in verse 7?

_____

_____

_____

What command did the angel give John in verse 9?

_____

_____

_____

With the prophecy given in the Revelation to John, the Lord concluded His prophetic tapestry, and is now working to carry it through to fulfillment in history. All these words given by God are *"faithful and true,"* never failing, never deceiving, never bringing someone into bondage. His words guide us in paths of righteousness and peace. He is continually bringing us into a walk of freedom. The theme of salvation was behind all the prophets He sent and all the messages they proclaimed. Jesus Himself promised *"I am coming quickly,"* and those who heed His words will be *blessed* (fully satisfied within [22:7]). This is the picture He painted of the day of His return when the Jews will say, *"BLESSED IS HE WHO COMES IN THE NAME OF THE LORD"* (Matthew 23:39). Second Thessalonians 1:7–10, on the other hand, paints a picture of both judgment and worship:

> *. . . when the Lord Jesus shall be revealed from heaven with His mighty angels in flaming fire, dealing out retribution to those who do not know God and to those who do not obey the gospel of our Lord Jesus. And these will pay the penalty of eternal destruction away from the presence of the Lord and from the glory of His power, when He comes to be glorified in His saints on that day, and to be marveled at among all who have believed—for our testimony to you was believed.*

The goal of all truth, all prophecy, all that God has spoken is to bring people to worship and obey Him. The goal of **Christ The Prophet**, the one sent by the Father, is to bring us to worship and obey Him in spirit and truth.

In this week's lesson, what is the message you have heard from Christ the Prophet? Are you believing in Him, receiving His Word as truth? What difference has obedience made (or will it make) in your life? What truth do you think Christ is seeking to explain to you and express through you? In what way is Christ focusing your worship of the Father so that it is more fully in spirit and truth?

Spend some time with the Lord in prayer right now.

 Lord, I honor You as **The Prophet**, the One who ever speaks the truth. Thank You for the freedom that comes as I apply Your Word throughout the landscape of my life—dealing with myself, in my family, in my relationships, in my finances, in my workplace, with other brothers and sisters in Christ, and with those who do not know You nor Your truth. May I always surrender to Truth, knowing You cannot lie. Open my eyes to see what Your Spirit reveals, and teach me to clearly hear and fully heed all You reveal. Teach me to walk in the light of Your true Word for today as well as in the light of what You have prophesied concerning the future. May I worship You in spirit and truth openly and transparently, surrendering to You every detail of life and experiencing the joyous freedom You came to give. In Jesus' Name, Amen.

In light of all you have learned this week write your own prayer to our Lord and Savior Jesus Christ, **The Prophet** who ever speaks Truth.

_____

_____

_____

_____

_____

_____

_____

_____

_____

_____

_____

_____

_____

_____

_____

_____

_____

_____

Notes

Christ the High Priest

BRINGING US INTO TRUE WORSHIP AND FELLOWSHIP WITH GOD

The Old Testament is filled with the work of the priests, especially the High Priest. We see pictures and patterns for worship God's way throughout the Old Testament record. The Tabernacle in the Wilderness and the Temple in Jerusalem were marked daily by the ministry of many priests who worshiped there and led the nation in worship there.

God purposed that when we look at this ministry of the priests, we see the need to approach God in Spirit-filled worship and remain in His presence in fellowship. The epistle to the Hebrews tells us that the Tabernacle is a shadow of the heavenly Tabernacle where we have our High Priest, the Lord Jesus Christ, who intercedes for us daily. His blood continually speaks of our cleansing before God and of our access to the Father. We have continual access to His throne, which includes confident and continuous prayer, unbroken fellowship with Him, and reliance upon His strength and power for liv-

 *Doctrine*
JESUS THE HIGH PRIEST

Jesus Christ is *"a merciful and faithful High Priest"* (Hebrews 2:17); *"High Priest of our confession"* (3:1); *"a great High Priest"* (4:14); *"High Priest after the order of Melchizedek"* (5:10); *"a High Priest forever after the order of Melchizedek"* (6:20); *"a High Priest, holy, innocent, undefiled, separated from sinners and exalted above the heavens"* (7:26); *"a High Priest who has taken His seat at the right hand of the throne of the Majesty in the heavens"* (8:1); *"a High Priest of the good things to come"* (9:11); *"a Great Priest over the house of God"* (10:21).

THE SUBSTANCE OF THE SHADOWS IN THE TABERNACLE (HEBREWS 8:5; 10:1). JESUS CHRIST IS . . .

The Tabernacle	Our High Priest	Our Offering And Sacrifice	The Blood	The Veil	The Holy of Holies	The Mercy Seat	The Shekinah Glory
John 1:1, 14 ("dwelt" or "tabernacled," Greek—*skénoó*); Revelation 21:3	Hebrews 2:17; 3:1; 4:14–15; 5:5–10; 6:20; 7:26–28; 8:1, 3; 9:11; 10:21	Hebrews 7:27; 9:14, 28; 10:10, 12; John 1:29, 36; 6:51; 10:15–18; 1 Peter 1:19; 1 Corinthians 5:7; Ephesians 5:2	Hebrews 9:12-14; 10:19; 13:12; 20; 1 Peter 1:19	Hebrews 10:19-20 [Note: Matthew 27:51; Mark 15:38; Luke 23:45]	John 2:19-21 [Greek—*naos*]	Hebrews 2:17; 9:5; Romans 3:25; 1 John 2:2; 4:10 [Greek—*hilastérion*]	John 1:14; 17:22, 24; 2 Corinthians 3:18; 4:4, 6; Matthew 17:2; 2 Peter 1:16–18

ing a faith-filled, Spirit-powered life. We can experience this life of worship by experiencing His presence and walking in His power. He came as High Priest to bring the fullness of His Spirit into our lives. In this lesson we will see what it means to follow and experience Christ as our High Priest.

"Since therefore, brethren, we have confidence to enter the holy place by the blood of Jesus, by a new and living way which He inaugurated for us through the veil, that is, His flesh, and since we have a great priest over the house of God, let us draw near with a sincere heart in full assurance of faith, having our hearts sprinkled clean from an evil conscience and our bodies washed with pure water." (Hebrews 10:19–22)

Christ the
High
Priest

DAY ONE

📖 Word Study
EXACT IMPRESSION

Hebrews 1:3 speaks of Jesus as *"the exact representation of His nature."* The words "exact representation" are translated from the Greek word, *charaktér*, meaning "a stamp or impression." The word was used in the first century to refer to the character or impression made by a seal or a die cut, like an engraving that makes an exact impression of a letter or a seal. Jesus is exactly like His Father and revealed the Father when He walked on this earth. He said in John 14:9, *"He who has seen Me has seen the Father."*

🖋 Did You Know?
THE SCEPTER

The scepter was a symbol of the power and authority of a king. The ruler used it to indicate his decisions and held it out as a sign of approval or to allow one to approach his throne. Hebrews 1:8 says concerning the Son, *"the righteous scepter is the scepter of His kingdom."* Every thought Jesus has, every decision He makes, every direction He takes is righteous in every detail. His kingdom is right in every way.

OUR SOVEREIGN HIGH PRIEST

What do the Scriptures reveal about Jesus, who is called *"a merciful and faithful High Priest"* in Hebrews 2:17? In the book of Hebrews, we are introduced to the person and ministry of this High Priest, and we see how His ministry should apply to our everyday lives. From the beginning of Hebrews, we see a majestic portrait of Jesus, a portrait that spans time and eternity and brings us into the very presence of our sovereign Lord.

📖 The book of Hebrews paints a remarkable picture of Jesus in the first four verses of chapter 1. Read Hebrews 1:1–4 with 4:14, and describe what you discover about **who Jesus is.**

_____

_____

_____

_____

Jesus is, first of all, the Son of God, exactly like His Father in His nature and one with the Father in all His purposes. He is the heir of all things, and all things are placed under His Lordship. This Jesus is the radiance (the outshining) of the Glory of God, the clear manifestation of God in the flesh. As a man, He is the incarnation of the *Shekinah* glory. He is God Himself in every detail and, at the same time, fully man. He has the very nature of God and knows what it is to be a man in every way. He is greater than any angel—after all, He created them—and has a name greater in honor and excellence than all of them.

In Hebrews 1:1–4, 10 and 4:14, what do you find about the work Jesus did and now does?

_____

_____

_____

_____

📖 We also learn about Jesus' work in John 17 (sometimes called the High Priestly prayer of Jesus). Hebrews 1:1–2 tells of God's speaking through His Son. What do you see in John 17:1–8 about the work of Jesus and about what He has spoken?

_____

_____

_____

Jesus is the creator of the heavens, the earth, and the ages—all that is—and is now sustaining and upholding all things. He came as the God-Man, died on a cross, and made purification for our sins so that we can know His personal forgiveness. He arose from the dead and ascended through the heavens. He finished the work the Father gave Him to do. Therefore, He now sits at the right hand of the Majesty on high. In His work as the God-Man, He has done all the Father gave Him to do and has spoken all that the Father gave Him to say. Because of what He has done and what He has said, we can know God and the eternal life He gives.

📖 What added insights about Jesus do you see in Hebrews 1:8–9?

_____

_____

_____

Jesus, the Son, is the sovereign Lord. He is God, and His throne is forever. His scepter is a righteous scepter, which means that His reign is marked by righteousness in every way—everything He does, everything He says, every decision He makes. He always loves righteousness and hates lawlessness.

📖 What are the angels commanded to do according to Hebrews 1:6?

_____

_____

_____

The angels, who are part of "all things" the Son created and now upholds, have always known that the Son is **God** and have worshiped Him. When the Father brought Him into the world as the "firstborn," the angels were commanded to worship Him then as well. As a man, He was still God and worthy of worship, not only by the angels but by us as well.

📖 In light of who Jesus is and what He has done, what are we called and commanded to do according to Hebrews 2:1–3?

_____

_____

_____

As the sovereign Lord, Jesus is able to bring about all He has promised. We must pay close attention to all that Jesus has said and all He has done. He wants us to listen to Him and know by personal experience the salvation He bought—the salvation revealed in the Word He spoke. We have written for us in the Old and New Testament scriptures the "salvation" of which He spoke first through the prophets, then through His earthly ministry, and finally through what was spoken and written by those who heard. As we lis-

---

"And the Word became flesh, and dwelt among us, and we beheld His glory, glory as of the only begotten from the Father, full of grace and truth."

John 1:14

Did You Know?

THE FIRSTBORN

In Scripture, the term "firstborn" does not necessarily mean born first. Psalm 89:20, 27 speak of David as firstborn though he was not born first. These verses ultimately refer to the Messiah as God's firstborn, *"the highest of the kings."* It is a term that refers to preeminence, to an exalted position, and in Jesus' case refers to His position as the God-Man, God in the flesh, who is Lord.

ten to our sovereign Lord and follow Him, we will not drift into neglect in our walk or into unbelief in our relationship with Him.

We have a sovereign Lord who is our High Priest. He is the all-powerful Creator, worthy of worship by all His creation. Not only is He powerful, but He is also good and righteous in every way.

DAY TWO

OUR SYMPATHETIC HIGH PRIEST

"Jesus is Lord" was a foundational confession of the early Church. In that short confession is the truth that Jesus is the sovereign God and that our sovereign Lord is Jesus the Man, the God-Man. The epistle to the Hebrews is very clear on this truth and paints a dynamic portrait of the Lord Jesus as the God-Man who understands us and sympathizes with us. We can learn much as we look at our Lord who is also our **sympathetic** High Priest.

📖 What do you discover about Jesus in Hebrews 2:9–10?

_____

_____

_____

_____

Word Study
PROPITIATION

Jesus made "propitiation" for our sins (Hebrews 2:17). The words *"make propitiation"* are translated from the Greek word, *Hiláskomai*. The word *Hiláskomai* comes from the root word *Hilasmós*, which describes the means by which one is satisfied or appeased. According to *The Complete Word Study Dictionary New Testament* (©1992, AMG Publishers, pp. 768–770):

Jesus Christ . . . becomes *Hilasmós*, the means which is acceptable to God to satisfy His righteousness or His justice. . . . [Therefore Jesus] provides the satisfaction demanded by God's justice whereby the removal of sins is attained. . . . *Hilasmós* refers to Christ as the One who not only propitiates but offers Himself as the propitiatory sacrifice. He is both the sacrifice and the officiating High Priest.

For a little while, Jesus was made lower than the angels and had to face the suffering of death. He tasted death for everyone in fulfilling the Father's plan to bring many sons to glory, to the place of reflecting the character and nature of God. God designed for His children to become mature sons who walk in the fullness of the life of God, that is, in the reality of His glory. Recall how we have seen in the study of the Tabernacle that He clearly showed His glory to Israel in the wilderness, especially in the Tabernacle. He wants to show His glory now with each of His children, each being a "temple" or "tabernacle" of His Spirit. It was necessary for the Lord Jesus to experience suffering in becoming the mature man His Father wanted Him to be. Although Christ suffered greatly, at no time did He ever lose His sinless perfection. He remains sinless to this very day and will forever remain sinless. The word "perfect" refers to being mature, to completing a course, to reaching the intended goal.

📖 Read Hebrews 2:14–15, 17, and 18, and write a description of Jesus' time on earth? What did He face as a man, and what does it mean to us?

_____

_____

_____

_____

_____

Jesus partook of flesh and blood as a man. He was made like us in every area. He had the feelings, the physical needs, the weariness, and the temptations of a man. Those temptations were part of His sufferings. Because He never yielded in the slightest measure to any temptation He faced, He bore the full weight of every temptation, the full pressure each could bring. Jesus knew about the sins men faced from a man's perspective *and* from God's perspective. Therefore, when it came time to offer Himself as the sacrificial substitute and die for those sins, He went to the cross with a full knowledge of our sin and our need for atonement. He was willing to show mercy and was faithful to His Father and to us in His death. He died as a merciful and faithful High Priest. In dying on the cross as the sinless sacrifice, Jesus fully satisfied the justice of God, removing our sin debt and thus removing our death sentence. We need no longer fear death since Christ has taken our sin judgment on Himself, delivering us from enslavement to the fear of death and judgment.

What do you find about our High Priest in Hebrews 4:15?

_____

_____

_____

Jesus can sympathize with each of us because He was *"tempted in all things,"* in all areas of life. This does not mean He faced every single temptation that we have ever faced or will face. For example, Jesus was never tempted to "run a red light" or commit any other traffic violation. However, He was tempted to go past the authority of His Father and turn stones into bread after forty days of fasting (see Matthew 4). Each of the temptations Jesus faced was rooted in a legitimate desire—bread for a hungry man, protection from harm, and the opportunity to rule the world. All of these desires were things that would come His way in the Father's will and in the Father's perfect timing. The temptation was to do the right thing but in the wrong way, in the wrong timing, for the wrong reason, under the wrong authority. Jesus faced the devil's arsenal of doubt, deceitful thoughts, and presumption on the Word of God, but He never budged an inch from His Father's will. He followed His Father in every choice, and He can lead us in following Him as well.

We must understand this truth. Jesus faced **every type** of temptation we face. However, there is one big difference—we are tempted according to the desires and weaknesses of our sinful flesh. Jesus did not have a sin nature, nor any sinful flesh. He was born of a virgin with no earthly father. He was conceived *"of the Holy Spirit"* (Matthew 1:20). That meant He did not inherit the sin nature of Adam (see Romans 5:12, 19; 1 Corinthians 15:22), rather Jesus fully expressed the nature of His Heavenly Father, who could do no evil (see James 1:13; 1 Peter 2:22). Jesus said in John 14:30 that the prince of this world (Satan) *"has nothing in Me."* There was and is still no connection between Satan and Jesus. When Satan tempted Jesus, he could find nothing in Jesus that corresponded to any sin or to the nature of sin.

Think of this picture. Temptation is like moving a magnet over several metal objects. If there are pieces of iron, it is the nature of that iron to be drawn to the magnet. However, if the magnet moves over a piece of aluminum, nothing happens! It is not the nature of aluminum to be drawn to the magnet. In the same way, we are born with a sin nature that is drawn in certain ways to the magnet of temptation. We can even increase that drawing force by repeated yielding, by giving in to temptation. Jesus was born of His Father and the virgin Mary. He had the nature of His Father. He had no sin nature passed down from Adam to Him. There was nothing in Him that ever responded to

We need no longer fear death since Christ has taken our sin judgment on Himself.

When Satan tempted Jesus, he could find nothing in Jesus that corresponded to any sin or to the nature of sin.

any temptation. It was not His nature to desire any wrong or to sin in any way—thought, word, or deed. It was His nature to hate evil in every form. Jesus also has a full understanding of sin because no sin ever dulled His spiritual senses. Like a healthy person who can quickly sense the smell of rotten food, Jesus knows what is sinful and what is not by the "stench" or repulsiveness of that sin. A sick person can be dulled in his or her senses. Like a leper who cannot feel any pain in his hands or feet because the nerve endings have died, so a sinner is insensitive to sin until he is "healed" and awakened to the wretchedness of sin. Jesus was always aware and awake to anything that was sinful. This heightened awareness of sin added to His suffering on the cross. His sensitivity to sin was greater than any man ever knew or will ever know. While Jesus knows what we face and sympathizes to the fullest extent, He never condones our sin or treats it lightly. He came to die for that sin, to crush evil and to deliver us out of sin.

📖 Read Hebrews 2:18 and 4:15–16. What do those verses tell you about our sympathetic High Priest? What should be our response to Him according to those verses?

_____

_____

_____

_____

_____

Because Jesus has been tempted in the things He suffered, He understands the tests and temptations we face. Not only does He understand, but He also sympathizes. He identifies with us and is ready and able to come to our aid in those temptations. He desires to help us and knows **how** to help us; Jesus has been where we are. He calls us to come to Him, to the throne of grace (not the throne of judgment). There we will find mercy and grace, that is, the enabling power of God. His promise is that He will give well-timed help—help that comes exactly when we are facing the temptation.

📖 Hebrews 5 talks about how the earthly priests lived and acted toward those who came to them. Read Hebrews 5:1–2. What characterized the priests? In light of what we have seen about Jesus thus far, how much more can Jesus guide us?

_____

_____

_____

_____

_____

The priests at the Tabernacle and at the Temple were beset with weakness; they dealt with their frailty throughout their lives. Because of their own weaknesses they could *"deal gently with the ignorant and misguided"* and were ever ready to offer sacrifices for the people. Can Jesus do that? He suffered. He was weary. He had human weaknesses, yet He was without sin. Jesus faced every type of temptation we face, so He knows more than anyone does what we go through. He can deal perfectly and gently with us in our ignorance and in our misguided ways.

Jesus sympathizes with our weaknesses (see Hebrews 4:15). The Greek word for "sympathizes" is **sumpathéō**, meaning "to feel with," "to suffer with," "or to experience something with someone." The idea in this word is more than a sympathetic thought. It is to actually feel the experience when we face it. Jesus not only understands us, He enters into our experience. He wants us to come to Him for His grace and mercy in our time of need.

Hebrews 3:1 calls us to "consider Jesus." He is our sympathetic High Priest who fully understands us, is always aware of our needs, and wants to come to our aid. Therefore, we must believe Him and trust Him rather than doubting Him or wandering in unbelief. Not only are we to consider our **sympathetic** High Priest, but Scripture calls us to know Him as our **sacrificial** High Priest. When we know Him in this way, we will be drawn to follow Him more closely than ever. We will see that in Day Three.

Our Sacrificial High Priest

When we begin to look at the sacrifice of our High Priest, we begin to see the greatest of contrasts. We see the contrast between the old covenant and the new covenant. We see the contrast of the Old Testament sacrifices and the sacrifice of Christ. We see the temporal results of one and the eternal results of the other. When we look at our everyday walk of following God, we see a new day—a day of ready access to the true Holy of Holies, where Christ sits enthroned. We see an open heaven and open fellowship for each of us.

📖 Read Hebrews 10 and answer the questions below that pertain to this chapter in the Bible.

What was the benefit of the Old Testament sacrifices in taking away sin, according to Hebrews 10:1–4, 11?

_____

_____

_____

The sacrifices of the Old Testament were a shadow of what was to come. They could neither bring cleansing to the worshiper nor removal of his sins. They could only remind one of sins year after year until the perfect sacrifice would come. The blood of bulls and goats, those sacrifices offered most notably on the Day of Atonement, could not take away sins. All the sacrifices of the old covenant could never take away sins.

How did Christ view the Old Testament sacrifices according to Hebrews 10:5–9?

_____

_____

_____

Christ knew that none of the sacrifices of the Old Testament could take away sins. He knew that His Father did not desire more and more sacrifices. There was no need for more burnt offerings and sin offerings day after day and year after year. The Father looked to that one sacrifice that could take away sins, the sacrifice of His only Son. Jesus knew His body was prepared to be that sacrifice; that was His Father's will, and He willingly went to the cross as that sacrifice.

> "For this reason the Father loves Me, because I lay down My life that I may take it again. No one has taken it away from Me, but I lay it down on My own initiative, . . . This commandment I received from My Father."
>
> John 10:17–18

What do you find about the offering of the body of Christ in Hebrews 10:10?

_____

_____

_____

Did You Know?

THE ASHES OF A HEIFER

The ashes of a heifer are described in Numbers 19 for the outward cleansing of defilement that comes from touching something dead. Hebrews 9:13 speaks of this sprinkling and cleansing. The ashes are the evidence that the sacrificial heifer was consumed in the fires of judgment on sin and impurity. Hebrews 9:14 parallels the blood of Christ with those ashes—the fact that Jesus' blood was poured out points to the fires of judgment on sin and impurity being fully quenched. We do not have to carry a burden of guilt or a dirty conscience. The application of the blood of Christ by faith gives inward cleansing of the conscience from dead works (all we have said or done apart from His Spirit). Jesus frees us to worship and serve God clean and guilt-free in the life and power and joy of His Spirit.

The offering of the body of Jesus was the will of God. Jesus gave that offering once for all, and His body is never to be offered again. By that offering, every believer stands sanctified, set apart to salvation. This is a radical contrast with the sacrifices of the old covenant.

What was the result of the sacrifice of Christ? In other words, what did He do after He offered Himself, and what does this mean according to Hebrews 10:12?

_____

_____

_____

Jesus offered Himself as the one sacrifice for sins for all time. Never would there be a need for another sacrifice. His sacrifice was totally sufficient; the work was finished! Therefore, Jesus sat down at the right hand of God. In the earthly Tabernacle and Temple, there was no place for the high priest to sit down because the work was never finished. How different is the picture in Heaven, where Christ sits enthroned—His work of redemption complete and His promises awaiting their proper fulfillment in history.

What was the **result** of the sacrifice of Christ as far as believers are concerned? Read each of these verses, and record your insights.

10:10

_____

_____

10:14

_____

_____

10:15–16

_____

_____

10:17–18

_____

_____

10:19–20

_____

_____

Doctrine

CHRIST "SAT DOWN"

Hebrews 1:3 introduces us to the exalted Lord Jesus, who _"sat down at the right hand of the Majesty on high"_ after making purification of sins. There was no place for Aaron to sit in the Tabernacle because his work was never finished. Jesus finished the work He came to do. Christ fully dealt with our sins as we see in Hebrews 8:1 (He _"has taken His seat"_); 10:12 (_"having offered one sacrifice for sins for all time, sat down"_); and 12:2 (_Jesus . . . endured the cross . . . and has sat down"_).

Through the offering of the body of Jesus, believers have been sanctified or made holy. This means that believers have been cleansed and set apart as a special people unto God and His purposes. The sanctification of believers is both a settled fact and an ongoing process. We **are sanctified** (set apart) and we are **being sanctified** (continually set apart and increasing in maturity). To fulfill His will in His children in daily life, God has written His law on their hearts and minds. He has given us a new spiritual genetic code, a new nature that corresponds with the nature of God and that stands in opposition to the "flesh" with which we war. The Spirit of God leads us in what is right, which includes putting to death the deeds of the flesh (see Romans 8:3–14). The Spirit directs His children, and that direction is **always** in line with the Word of God. The Spirit assures us that all our sins are forgiven and forgotten; they will never be brought up against us. The offering of Jesus paid for those sins—once and for all, opening the way for us to live in His presence knowing we are forgiven, cleansed, and welcomed. We can know freedom from guilt, judgment, and condemnation. We can know the exhilaration and joy of being accepted in Christ, walking in openness and welcomed in His presence.

Because of the Sacrifice of our High Priest, Hebrews 10:22–25 gives us three commands, each beginning with *"let us."* What do you find the Holy Spirit commanding us. . . .

In Hebrews 10:21–22?

_____

_____

_____

How can we "draw near" to God according to these verses?

_____

_____

In Hebrews 10:23?

_____

_____

_____

How can we hold on to our hope according to this verse?

_____

_____

In 10:24?

_____

_____

According to verse 25, how can we encourage others to *"love and good deeds"*?

_____

_____

Doctrine

REMEMBRANCE OF CHRIST

Should we remember or dwell on past sins if they have already been forgiven? The Lord says, "THEIR SINS . . . I WILL REMEMBER NO MORE" (Hebrews 10:17). In contrast, First Corinthians 11:23–26 speaks of the remembrance of Jesus—His body broken and His blood poured out for redemption and forgiveness. This is the remembrance He wants us to have, and we observe this remembrance in the Lord's Supper.

> *"This hope we have as an anchor of the soul, a hope both sure and steadfast and one which enters within the veil, where Jesus has entered as a forerunner for us, having become a high priest forever according to the order of Melchizedek."*
>
> **Hebrews 6:19–20**

Christ the High Priest

God wants us to draw near to Him with a true, sincere heart, confident in the completed work of Jesus our High Priest. As the pieces of the Tabernacle and the priests who served there were sprinkled outwardly, our faith can rest in Him, knowing that, inwardly, our hearts have been sprinkled clean. In the Tabernacle, we see open access to God for the priests. But unlike the priests who only had access to God during certain ritualistic occasions in the Tabernacle and Temple, we can now have that same access **at all times**. We can openly confess our hope and confidence in all God's promises, because Jesus is faithful in all He has ever done or said. With that confidence in Jesus, we can encourage one another to walk in faith, in love, and in good deeds, knowing He will faithfully guide and direct us. To do that we must spend time with other believers to be encouraged and to encourage them, especially in light of the approaching day when we must give an account for our faith and the behavior it produced.

Jesus opened the way for us to come into the Holy Place by His own blood. Hebrews 6:18 speaks of the *"strong encouragement"* we have because of our hope in Him. Hebrews 6:19–20 paints an ancient picture to help us apply His sacrifice to daily life and to strengthen our faith and hope in Him. In the harbors around the Mediterranean Sea, there were large stones (at least one, often more) firmly embedded at the edge of the shore. These stones, known as the *anchoria* (Latin) or *ágkura* (Greek), served as the anchor rock, a mooring for ships. Sometimes a ship could not come into port using its sails, and so a "forerunner" would sail ashore in a small boat, carrying a line from the ship. The forerunner then tied the ship to the *anchoria*. That line was tied to the bow of the ship and was sometimes called an *anchoria* because of its attachment to the rock. Once tied, the ship was *"sure and steadfast"* (Hebrews 6:19), not because of an ordinary anchor dragging the sea floor somewhere, but because of the solid hold of the *anchoria* in the harbor. Those on the ship could lay hold of the line, the *anchoria*, and with it draw near within the harbor. Jesus our High Priest has gone before us as our "forerunner" and tied us into the harbor *"within the veil."* We are anchored to live in His presence, fellowshipping in the Holy Place (see Hebrews 10:19–22).

OUR STRONG HIGH PRIEST

Our High Priest calls us to come near, to come with confidence into the Holy Place. There He wants us to fellowship with Him, to find grace and mercy for our needs, and to stand strong in faith, trusting Him in every situation we face. Hebrews 11 presents those who followed God, people who walked with God by faith. Hebrews 11:6 tells us that true faith, like that of Enoch, believes "God is," that God is **God** and that He is a rewarder to those who diligently seek Him. Those in Hebrews 11 looked to God for His strength as their God, as the rewarder, as the guide and guard of their lives. Even those who faced martyrdom continued to look to Him as their strength in life, knowing He would fulfill all His promises sooner or later. Those who trust God to **guide** and **guard** them along the paths of life seek the Lord and find Him to be faithful. They worship Him. When we look at the people mentioned in Hebrews 11, we see true faith and worship in action. Like those in Psalm 84 who dwell in God's house in Zion, they *"go from strength to strength"* (84:7). How are we to walk in that faith and His strength for our lives?

📖 Hebrews 11 gives the testimony of Abraham who *"grew strong in faith"* (Romans 4:20) as well as the testimonies of other men and women of faith. How did these people practice their faith, and what did they endure? Read Hebrews 11:8–10, 24–27, 32–40 and list the things these people endured as they were made strong in faith.

_____

_____

_____

_____

_____

_____

Abraham left his country not knowing fully where he would live or what turns the journey would take. He left the culture (and idolatry) of Ur to live in tents in the land of Canaan, as he looked for the fulfillment of all the promises God made to him. Moses had the opportunity to live in the affluence and power of the courts of Pharaoh, but chose instead to endure rough treatment with God's people. By faith, he saw the true riches of following God, confident there was a reward for him and all who followed by faith. His endurance came through *"seeing Him who is unseen,"* believing God's Word to him and waiting on the fulfillment of God's promises at their proper time. In addition to Moses, many others faced numerous difficulties—wars and battles, wild animals and wilderness wanderings as well as mocking, scourging, chains, imprisonment, death by the sword, stoning, or even being sawn in two (the report of Isaiah's death). Yet, what those in Hebrews 11 endured cannot be compared with the wonder that will come in the Resurrection, when with all God's children they receive their reward and the fullness of God's promises.

📖 Hebrews 12:1–2 shares the testimony or witness of **how** the men and women of faith endured in running their race. With the words *"let us also,"* Hebrews 12:1 introduces us to three characteristics of these witnesses that we are told to emulate. What are those characteristics?

_____

_____

_____

Like a runner in a race who would never wear needless gear, we must *"lay aside every encumbrance,"* anything that **slows** us in the race. This "encumbrance" may be something that on the surface appears harmless in and of itself, but it slows our pace; it causes us to lag behind. We must also jettison the sin that *"entangles us,"* that which **stops** us from making progress in the race. Sin is something that misses the mark of God's will. These entanglements or sins are wrong, unrighteous, and God wants none of them in our lives. Once we have taken care of the things that hinder, we must look to what will help us make progress. What will **strengthen** us in our race? To endure, we must look away from any thing on which we depend and focus on Jesus. As we look to Him, our faith is strengthened. In Him, we find the ability to bear up under the rigors of the race marked out for us. Jesus is our

"How blessed are those who dwell in Thy house! They are ever praising Thee. How blessed is the man whose strength is in Thee; in whose heart are the highways to Zion!"

Psalm 84:4–5

LOOKING UNTO JESUS

Christ and the writers of Scripture spoke of those who followed in faith, **looking to Jesus** (see Hebrews 12:2, KJV). Jesus said Moses *"wrote of Me"* (John 5:46), and Hebrews 11:27 says Moses *"endured, as seeing Him who is unseen."* Jesus stated, *"Abraham rejoiced to see My day,"* and John 8:56 tells us Isaiah *"saw His glory, and he spoke of Him"* (John 12:41).

AUTHOR AND PERFECTER

Jesus is the Beginner and Completer of our faith (see Hebrews 12:2). He starts faith, and He brings it to its full goal or completion. As He is the Alpha and the Omega, the Beginning and the End for all of human history, so He is the Beginner and the Completer of the faith in which we walk. As we look to Him, we can grow in faith.

Extra Mile

THE CRUCIFIXION

What insights do you see about Jesus and His crucifixion in Psalm 22 and the other accounts of the crucifixion in Matthew 26:47–68; Mark 14:43–65; 15:1–39; Luke 22:47–71; 23; John 18—19; and 1 Peter 2:22–23?

strong High Priest who understands what it means to endure, and He can give us His strength to endure.

Hebrews 12:2 tells us to endure, *"fixing our eyes on Jesus."* We have seen that Christ was tempted in all things yet never sinned and that He can come to our aid. What more can we learn about how strong our High Priest is?

📖 Read Hebrews 12:2–3 along with Matthew 27:11–51, one of the accounts of the crucifixion. What do the Scriptures show He "endured"?

_____

_____

_____

_____

Jesus faced great shame, hostility, and hatred in going to the cross. He was mocked and ridiculed in all the trials He faced (there were three Jewish trials and three Roman trials). He was scourged, given a mock scepter and a crown of thorns, a king's robe and mock praise. He was crucified naked on a Roman cross, bearing the shame of a criminal and the pain of our sin, forsaken by His own Father. He endured it all, trusting His Father and knowing there was great joy set before Him.

Moses endured, *"seeing Him who is unseen"* (11:27). We endure in the same way, *"fixing our eyes on Jesus."* Hebrews 12:3 says, *"For consider Him who has endured"* the cross and the hostility of sinners *"so that you may not grow weary and lose heart."* Those things can easily happen to someone running a race. The words *"grow weary and lose heart"* literally mean "to become weary and give up." What are you facing in the race?

📖 Hebrews 12:4–9 shows us the child-training ("discipline" or "chastisement"—Greek, *paideía*) God uses to strengthen us to endure. What else do you observe in those verses?

_____

_____

_____

_____

Looking at Jesus and all He faced will help us focus on the Father's ways with us. We have not come close to enduring what Jesus faced; we have not waged war to the point of bloodshed in striving against sin. We can easily forget the exhortation God has given us in His Word. To be a son of God, one must experience and respect the Father's child-training by never treating Him or the training lightly. When we are reproved and corrected by the Lord, we must guard against fainting or wanting to give up. His training, reproof, and scourging are all marks of His love as our Father. As we yield to Him and His training, we will grow strong. As we face the difficulties that can come with child-training, we know that we can call on Him for help, and He will answer. He does not just send help; He **is** our help and our strength. Knowing we are loved and linked to Him and His purposes gives us a sense of purpose in all of life. God is working throughout the lives of all who trust Him, training ("disciplining") us all along the way.

It is vital to understand that God trains us in many ways. He uses many circumstances and many people to influence us throughout our lives. Sometimes His training is **corrective** or **preventive**—to stop us in sin or to keep us from sin. Sometimes His training is **instructive**. Instructive training comes in the form of principles and guidelines that show us the way. God has a variety of ways in which He applies each of these types of training. Some situations in life include all three types of training: corrective, preventive, and instructive. He sometimes brings **barriers** into life—things that keep us from going the wrong way, things that block our way like a hedge of thorns, protecting us. Though these barriers may occasionally hurt us temporarily, they are never meant for our harm, only for our good. Such barriers can actually be very instructive. At other times **blessings** from God may be used as an instructive form of training. Sometimes God gives us an unexpected blessing that helps us know Him better. Blessings can also confirm God's will in a particular area or encourage us to endure. Both **barriers** and **blessings** are loving **boundaries** that the Lord places around our lives to train us in His holiness. They lead us to His best for our lives. Hebrews 12:10–11 speaks about this.

📖 What is the result toward which the Lord aims according to Hebrews 12:10–11?

_____

_____

_____

The Lord wants us to receive His training so we know and experience His holiness in all of life, experiencing what it means to be set apart to Him and His ways. We must cooperate with Him to be fully trained. As we see God's sovereignty explained from chapters 1 and 12 of the epistle to the Hebrews, we see how God can work things in our lives to train us that we may come to experience His holiness. God's holiness refers to His being set apart from His creation in a special way. It includes His total satisfaction with Himself, with His ways, with His wisdom, with who He is. God is always right, and all the actions and words that come from Him are right. He wants us to share that satisfaction of holiness with Him as we surrender by faith to Him and His ways. Surrender opens the way for knowing God's satisfaction and partaking of the _"peaceful fruit of righteousness."_ That includes the peace of right relationships—the peace and harmony that exists when we are right with God and with others.

How do we experience this to the fullest? How are we to walk in life experiencing our sovereign and sympathetic High Priest? How are we to know the full meaning of His sacrifice and live in His strength? We will see these things in Day Five.

FOR ME TO FOLLOW CHRIST

Christ the High Priest

DAY FIVE

We have looked at Jesus our High Priest and have seen what He has done for us. The Lord wants us to understand His priestly role in a very practical, daily way. He wants us to walk in the assurance of His sovereignty and strength, to know the joy of His presence

Word Study
A FATHER'S INSTRUCTION

Ephesians 6:4 speaks of _"the discipline_ [Greek—_paideía_] _and instruction_ [Greek— _nouthesía_] _of the Lord."_ _Paideía_ is the caring, corrective, and all-encompassing child training of Hebrews 12. _Nouthesía_ refers to instruction and admonition which can take one of two forms: words of encouragement that guide and direct as well as words of reproof that stop, correct, and redirect. Our Father encourages while He corrects us.

and the reality of His victory over sin. Remember, He is taking us to glory—to the fullness of His presence, the completion of His purpose, and the total satisfaction of His heart (Hebrews 2:10; 2 Corinthians 3:18). Even now we are moving from one level of glory to another; we are learning what it means to experience His presence as in the Holy of Holies (see Hebrews 10:19–22). How can we experience this more fully?

First of all, we must recall what God has revealed about Himself. He is the God who is **able** to accomplish His will in our lives as we follow and worship Him. Look at each of the verses listed below that deal with God's ability, then record what each verse is saying and how that verse can make a difference in how you worship and follow Him.

Hebrews 2:18—He is able_____

_____

_____

Hebrews 4:12–13—The Word of God is able _____

_____

_____

Hebrews 7:25—He is able_____

_____

_____

Jude 1:24—He is able_____

_____

_____

Ephesians 3:20—He is able_____

_____

_____

_____

It is evident that the Lord is able to come to our aid in any temptation or trial we face. As we walk with Him and pay attention to His Word, He shows us our hearts and motives, and then we receive a true evaluation of our thoughts and deeds. When we draw near to God, we discover that *"He is able to save [us] forever"* (Hebrews 7:25), or as some translate, "able to save us completely" in every way. That is His ability, and we can rest in Him to finish the salvation He has begun. We **are** saved from the penalty of sin; we are **being** saved from the power of sin; we **will be** saved from the presence of sin. We will one day know the fullness of His salvation as we rejoice in our resurrection bodies (see Philippians 1:6; 2:13; 3:20–21; 4:13). This is guaranteed because He has the power to keep us from stumbling and to make us stand before Him—*"in the presence of His glory blameless with great joy"* (Jude 1:24). Until that day, we continue to worship and follow Him, listening to Him through His Word and calling on Him in prayer. We are assured that His power will continue to work within us, showing us His sovereign hand and His sympathetic heart, applying the full power of His sacrifice as He trains us to trust and rely on Him. He is making us the children He wants us to be.

> Remember that Christ is taking us to His glory—to the fullness of His presence, the completion of His purpose, and the total satisfaction of His heart.

JESUS CHRIST, OUR HIGH PRIEST

Sovereign High Priest	Sympathetic High Priest	Sacrificial High Priest	Strong High Priest
Hebrews 1	Hebrews 2—5	Hebrews 6—10	Hebrews 11—13
We can rest assured of His sovereign power and care.	We can walk in His sympathetic care in every area of life.	We can know His forgiveness, His presence within, and enter into joyful fellowship with Him.	We can know His strength for every day, for every circumstance, in every place we go.

True faith and worship start with this clear revelation that "God is able." How then can this revelation become real in daily life? How is Jesus to be real as **my** High Priest? How do I access this ability of God in my life? How do I fulfill what Hebrews 12:12–13 commands? Those verses state, *"Therefore, strengthen* [literally, "make straight"] *the hands that are weak and the knees that are feeble, and make straight paths for your feet, so that the limb which is lame may not be put out of joint, but rather be healed."* Many of the people addressed in Hebrews were weary, tired of the race, facing rejection, dealing with doubts about Christ, and in danger of stumbling badly. The Lord wanted them to run a strong race, and He wants the us to do the same. How are we to do that?

Proverbs 3:5–6 speaks about the Lord making our paths **straight**. If we are to walk (or run) on straight paths (see Hebrews 12:12–13), we must know what those paths are. That means we must follow God in what He says, for example in Hebrews 12:1–11, especially the command in verse 2 to fix our eyes on Jesus.

 Proverbs 3 gives us some very practical guidance as to what it means to walk with God. Look at each of the commands from Proverbs 3:5–6? Read each phrase and the questions that follow below and consider how these phrases from Scripture apply to your life.

"Trust in the Lord with all your heart" [a command]—Are things getting in the way of your trust? What helps you trust or walk in faith? What helps your heart ("all your heart") focus on the Lord and the things of God?

_____

_____

_____

_____

_____

_____

"Do not lean on your own understanding"—"Lean" means "to depend upon" for support. Are you relying on God's wisdom? Are you guarding against depending only on your own understanding and opinions? [Note: This command does not say, "do not **use** your own understanding." It says *"do not **lean** on"* it.] Are you spending time in God's Word (His understanding)?

> True faith and worship start with this clear revelation that "God is able!"

Are there any situations you are facing which you are tempted to handle on your own?

_____

_____

_____

_____

"In all your ways acknowledge [know] Him" [a command]—Are you knowing or experiencing God in all your ways? What are some of the "ways" of your life in which you have seen God at work? What are some of your "ways" that need His touch? Are you spending time in prayer giving Him those "ways"?

_____

_____

_____

_____

_____

_____

The Lord promises that if one follows His commands in Proverbs 3:5–6, He will make the paths straight; He will remove the things that cause one to stumble. But how can we consistently walk on straight paths? Hebrews 12 tells us the Lord will "child-train" each of His children, but we must understand **how** He does that. We must understand His ways, especially His "training" ways.

We all know that no one is effectively trained in anything unless he or she cooperates with the trainer, listening with a learner's heart and applying the training to life. In order to follow God, we must learn to interact with our Trainer, the Lord. One of the ways to interact with the Lord is to ask the questions, "What are You saying in this situation, Lord? How should I respond in this situation? What is Your way in this? What are You teaching me in this?" Each of us should **interact with** the Lord in the circumstances of life **instead of reacting to** circumstances. Often, full of fear or doubt, we react to the circumstance, to the people involved, or even to the Lord, instead of interacting with Him in trust and worship.

This **interaction** is the essence of Proverbs 3:5–6. When verse 6 says to *"acknowledge Him,"* it uses the Hebrew word *yada,* which means to know by experience. The word is used in the Old Testament in the contexts of sailing a vessel, hunting wild game, playing a musical instrument, and of the close, intimate relationship of a husband and wife. The author of the proverb wants us to know or acknowledge the Lord, to experience Him in all our ways, and to trust Him to make our paths straight. God promises to give us a stable walk, an "unstumbling" walk. The paths in which He leads us and trains us require that we trust Him and lean not on our own limited understanding. God knows what will cause us to trip or stumble, so He leads us to watch each step. But to receive guidance from the Lord, we must continually interact with Him. We must live a life of drawing near, of trusting Him as our High Priest.

Each of us should interact with the Lord in the circumstances of life, instead of reacting to the circumstances.

When Jesus walked on this earth, He was the perfect High Priest in every way. When He was interrupted, He continually looked for what the Father was doing. What looked like an interruption was often one of the Father's appointments to fulfill His will. Jesus never "reacted" to the circumstances around Him without seeking His Father's will. Jesus always interacted with His Father and with the people who appeared on the surface to be an interruption (that is the way His disciples often saw them). For example, in Mark 5:21–43, Jesus was on the way to Jairus' house because Jairus' daughter was sick. As Jesus walked, a woman with an issue of blood came up, touched Him, and was immediately healed. Jesus knew this was no ordinary encounter. The people around Him failed to recognize what was taking place. Jesus stopped and talked with her, confirmed her faith, and rejoiced in her healing. Then some came saying that Jairus' daughter had died and that there was no need for Jesus to come. To Jairus, the interruption caused by the woman with the issue of blood must have seemed to be a delay of denial that resulted in his daughter's death. How could his daughter possibly be healed now? However, this was a delay of destiny for the woman and for Jairus' daughter. Jesus went on to Jairus' house and raised his daughter from the dead. Jairus' daughter and the sick woman are two examples of how Jesus revealed Himself as the sovereign and almighty Lord; as a man sympathetic to the needs around Him; as the one able to deliver from disease and death; and the one able to strengthen—regardless of the challenge.

Hebrews 10–13 shows us this interactive design of God throughout the history of His people as well as in our own day. We have been brought into the presence of God through the blood of Jesus our High Priest and Mediator. Whether pictured from the Holy of Holies (10:19) or from Mount Zion (12:22), Jesus our Mediator, our *Shekinah Glory*, speaks clearly to us. Do not lose heart or think of quitting in the race of faith. God has a guaranteed future when all that faith holds now will be unveiled, when His presence will be fully revealed and His promises fulfilled. Make sure you keep your feet on the path He has laid out for you, the straight path of His holiness. Keep looking to Him, listening to Him, being trained by Him. Keep on loving others, and encourage them to trust God. God will always be present with you to guide you by His Word and to strengthen you by His grace. Know the Way that is eternal, the Way of true worship. Worship Jesus Christ as King of kings and Lord of your life.

 As you think back over all we have seen in the life and ministry of Jesus, think of these final words about our merciful and faithful High Priest. Hebrews 13:20–21 encourages us with these words . . .

> *"Now the God of peace who brought up from the dead the great* [the **Sovereign**] *Shepherd of the sheep* [our **Sympathetic** High Priest, the One who sympathizes as a shepherd with His sheep] *through the blood of the eternal covenant, even Jesus our Lord* [our **Sacrificial** High Priest], *equip you in every good thing to do His will, working in us that which is pleasing in His sight, through Jesus Christ* [our **Strong** High Priest is doing the equipping and the strengthening to do His will], *to whom be the glory forever and ever. Amen."*

He wants His sovereignty, His sympathy, His sacrifice, and His strength made real to us. This is His will for us—nothing more, nothing less, nothing else. Won't you accept His will for your life today?

Make sure you keep your feet on the path that Christ has laid out for you—the straight path of His holiness.

Spend some time with the Lord in prayer.

Lord, I worship You as my High Priest and yield to You as my Sovereign Lord. Thank You for loving and caring for me, for showing me mercy time and time again as my sympathetic High Priest. Thank You for Your grace, Your power that enables me to face and overcome temptation. I know my salvation is only made possible through Your sacrifice on the Cross. You bought me with Your blood and brought me to Yourself, setting me apart for Your purposes. Thank You! Thank You! Thank You, dear Lord! You delivered me out of my self-destructive path and set me on the path to real holiness and purity, real satisfaction and joy, real love and real family with You as my Father. Your strength is real for daily life, and I am so grateful. I praise You for the equipping You are doing in my life so that I might do Your will to the fullest, that I might worship You in spirit and truth, and that I might walk in a manner pleasing to You. In Jesus' name, Amen.

Write your own prayer of worship to the Lord or make a journal entry that reflects your worship of Him.

_____

_____

_____

_____

_____

_____

_____

_____

_____

The Son of Man

CHRIST FOLLOWING HIS FATHER

Jesus Christ is **"the Son of Man."** That title carries with it two profound truths. First, it is a title for the Messiah, the One promised throughout the Old Testament and pictured in Daniel 7 as He who is given dominion over an everlasting kingdom. The second truth is found in God becoming a Son of **man**. Our Lord, Jesus Christ is called the Son of Man. He walked on the earth as a man, and as a man He faced all that men face—hunger and plenty, weariness and refreshment, sadness and joy, laughter and weeping, temptation and triumph. Yes, He did this as a man, but, more than that, He did this as the God-Man. Certainly this mystery of the God-Man is one of those truths we cannot fully grasp, but we can receive illumination by His Spirit so that we can truly come to know Him and walk in fellowship with Him—with the Son and with the Father.

> *The Son of Man is worthy to be worshiped and adored. He is worthy to be followed and obeyed.*

JESUS CHRIST: THE SON OF MAN

Prophecy	Ministry	Crucifixion	Resurrection	Coming	Reigning and Judging
Daniel 7:13–14	Matthew 9:1–8; 11:15–19; 16:13–20; Mark 2:23–28; Luke 19:1–10; John 9:1–41	Matthew 16:21; 17:22–23; Mark 10:32–34, 45; Luke 18:31–34; John 3:13–21	Matthew 12:38–41; 17:9; Mark 9:31–32; Luke 9:22; 24:1–49; John 12:23–28; 13:31–33; 20:9	Matthew 13:36–43; 24:3–51 Mark 13:3–37; 14:61–62; Luke 9:23–26; 12:35–40; 21:25–28 John 14:1–3	Matthew 19:28–30; 25:31–46; Mark 13:26–27 Luke 22:67–70 John 5:19–29 Revelation 1:12–19; 14:14–16

As we walk through the Scriptures and the life of the Lord Jesus, we will learn the full meaning of this title "the Son of Man," and in so doing we will discover the Friend who sticks closer than a brother, the One who faced temptation in all its furor, *yet without sin* (see Hebrews 4:15). This same Friend can come alongside to encourage, guide, and direct us in whatever we are facing. The Son of Man is worthy to be worshiped and adored, followed and obeyed. Our hope is that in walking through this lesson you will develop a deeper understanding of how to worship and follow Christ, **the Son of Man.**

The Son of Man | DAY ONE |

THE SON OF MAN IS LORD

What do we discover about the Son of Man in the Scriptures? In the four Gospels, the Lord Jesus referred to Himself as the "Son of Man" over eighty times. In those references He revealed Himself as Lord, as the Messiah, as the Savior of the world, and as the coming King who reigns over all the kingdoms of the world. To see the Son of Man as He is and how we are to follow Him, we must see Him first in the Old Testament.

📖 The key Old Testament passage where the phrase "Son of Man" is used is in the prophecy of Daniel. Read Daniel 7:13–14. What is given to the Son of Man?

_____

_____

_____

What do you learn about Him and His kingdom?

_____

_____

> **"One like a Son of Man . . . was given dominion, glory and a kingdom, that all the peoples, nations, and men of every language might serve Him."**
>
> **Daniel 7:13–14**

The Son of Man was given dominion or rulership by the Ancient of Days (God the Father). He was also given glory and a kingdom. As a result, "*all the peoples, nations, and men of every language* [will] *serve Him. His dominion is an everlasting dominion which will not pass away; and His kingdom is one which will not be destroyed.*" Christ's kingdom will last forever!

What does this dominion include? When we look at this description of the Son of Man we recognize One who rules over all kings and kingdoms. The New Testament readily applies this to the Lord Jesus. What applications to Him do we discover in the New Testament?

📖 The Gospel of John uses the term "Son of Man" thirteen times. In the first of these, a conversation between Jesus and Nathanael (see John 1:47–51), we find some revealing truths about this "Son of Man." What does Philip reveal about Jesus while talking to Nathanael (1:45)?

_____

_____

_____

How did Jesus greet Nathanael (1:47–48)?

_____

_____

What was Nathanael's reply (1:49)? What did he say about Jesus?

_____

_____

_____

Jesus made a promise to Nathanael in John 1:50. What was that promise?

_____

_____

Philip came to Nathanael, telling him they had found the One about whom Moses and the Prophets wrote. In many passages throughout the Pentateuch (Genesis through Deuteronomy), Moses wrote of the Messiah to come. Many prophets also spoke of the coming Messiah. Nathanael honestly questioned if any good thing could come out of Nazareth. When Jesus saw Nathanael, He acknowledged Nathaniel's forthright honesty, _"Behold, an Israelite indeed, in whom is no guile!"_ What did Jesus' statement mean? Nathanael wanted to know how Jesus knew about him. Jesus then revealed that He also knew Nathanael had been under the fig tree well before Philip had found him. To that evident supernatural ability Nathanael responded in awe-inspired faith, _"Rabbi, You are the_ **Son of God**_; You are the_ **King of Israel."** Nathanael felt that whoever knew what Jesus knew had to be the Son of God, and, if that were true, He had to be the Messiah, the King of Israel. Jesus then promised that he would see even greater things. What did Jesus mean? Let's continue searching the Scriptures.

Did You Know?

PROPHECIES CONCERNING THE SON OF MAN

Moses and the Prophets penned over 300 prophecies about the Messiah, all fulfilled in the Son of Man, Jesus Christ.

What word picture did Jesus paint in John 1:51? List the elements of which He spoke.

_____

_____

_____

📖 Now read Genesis 28:10–17, and note the parallels to what Jesus said.

_____

_____

_____

Jesus spoke of the heavens opening and the angels of God ascending and descending on the Son of Man. In Genesis 28 we discover that Jacob had a dream that pictured Jesus' description almost word for word. The angels of God were ascending and descending on a ladder or, more likely, a staircase like that which stood at the entrance of an ancient city. Jacob saw this place as the _"house of God"_ and the _"gate of Heaven"_ (28:17). At the top of the stair-case, where a city gate would be located, stood the Lord, the God of Abraham, Isaac, and Jacob. He promised Jacob a land with many descen-dants (a nation) and a seed in whom all the families of the earth would be

Caesarea Philippi, located at the base of Mount Hermon about 35 miles north of Capernaum and the Sea of Galilee, is known for its life-giving waters, rich fields and abundance of trees. During Old Testament times and during the Greek occupation of the area, the city housed many shrines to various false deities. Herod the Great built a white marble temple there in honor of Caesar Augustus. Herod's son Philip ruled from this city (4 BC—AD 34). Philip brought restoration and beauty to the area and named it "Caesarea" after Tiberias Caesar. To distinguish it from the Caesarea on the Mediterranean coast, this Caesarea was called Caesarea Philippi (after Philip). At this location known for its many gods, Peter confessed Jesus as the Christ, the Son of the Living God.

Extra Mile

SON OF MAN— SON OF GOD

The Gospel of John reveals Jesus as the Son of Man and the Son of God. Read John 1:1–18, and list all that you find about Jesus in that passage.

blessed. This promise of a "seed" to Jacob was the same promise of a "seed" that God had given to Abraham. Galatians 3:16 reveals that this "seed" was Christ.

How does the Son of Man fit into this? Who is the Son of Man in John 1:51?

_____

_____

_____

John 1:51 reveals that the Son of Man is the staircase, the connection between earth and heaven. When we look at the context of the conversation between Jesus and Nathanael, we see some other revealing truths. First, when Jesus spoke of Nathanael as one in whom there was no guile or deceit, many believe He was contrasting Nathanael with Jacob, whose name means deceiver. There was no "deceit" or no "Jacob" in Nathanael. Deceit and insincerity marked many in Jesus' day as the Gospels clearly reveal. By revelation, Nathanael saw Jesus for who He is, the Son of God and King of Israel. Jesus revealed Himself as the Son of Man, the One about whom the prophet Daniel spoke, but more than that, He pictured Himself not only as the King who would reign, but also as the bridge (staircase) between earth and heaven, between man and God. He revealed Himself as both Lord and Savior, and the revelation of Himself had just begun.

The events surrounding Nathanael occurred during the first part of Jesus' ministry. As the weeks and months progressed, Jesus revealed more and more of who He was and why He came. In the third year of His ministry, we find Jesus with the Twelve in the city of Caesarea Philippi around the spring of AD 29. Matthew 16 gives the account in which we see a more complete picture of the Son of Man. There Jesus asked His disciples *Who do men say that I, the Son of Man, am?* (16:13 NKJV).

📖 Read Matthew 16:14–17, and answer the questions below.

What was their first reply (16:14)?

_____

_____

What was His follow-up question (16:15)?

_____

_____

What do you discover about Jesus in Peter's answer (16:16)?

_____

_____

_____

What does Jesus reveal in response to Peter's answer (16:17)?

_____

_____

_____

Jesus asked His disciples *"Who do men say that I, the Son of Man, am?"* (NKJV). They replied that people thought He was John the Baptist, Elijah, Jeremiah, or some other prophet. To His question *"Who do you say that I am?"* Simon Peter quickly answered, *"Thou art the Christ* [the Messiah], *the Son of the Living God."* Jesus revealed that Peter's confession of Jesus as the promised Messiah **and** the Son of God was by the revelation of His heavenly Father, not by any teaching or skill of men. That matched what God revealed to Nathanael over two years before.

The Son of Man is the Christ, the Messiah. He is Lord. What more can we learn about this Son of Man? We will discover more in Day Two.

THE SON OF MAN CAME TO DIE

Before Jesus was ever born, an angel spoke to Joseph (the husband of Mary, Jesus' mother), and told Him that the child Mary would bear was conceived of the Holy Spirit. He was to give Him the name "Jesus" (the Greek form of the Hebrew word *"Yeshua"* or *"Joshua,"* meaning "Jehovah is salvation"), *"for it is He who will save His people from their sins"* (Matthew 1:21).

As Jesus walked on earth, He knew His mission—*"to seek and to save that which was lost"* (Luke 19:10). From the earliest days He knew the Father had a design for His life (see Luke 2:41–52), and He delighted to do His Father's will (see Hebrews 10:7–10). Near the beginning of His ministry, Jesus spoke to one of the Jewish leaders, Nicodemus, about the will of the Father and the purpose of the Son of Man. What do we learn from that conversation?

📖 Looking at John 3:13–15, what do you discover about the Son of Man?

_____

_____

_____

Jesus made it clear that He, as the Son of Man who had descended from heaven, *"must . . . be lifted up"* even *"as Moses lifted up the serpent in the wilderness."* The result would be *"that whoever believes may in Him have eternal life"* (John 3:13–15). In that statement we begin to see an unclouded picture of why Jesus came and what He meant by saving the lost. He wanted people to know the forgiveness of their sins and the eternal life that He alone could give.

📖 What do you see about the purpose of God for the Son of Man in the next three verses, John 3:16–18?

_____

_____

_____

Probably one of the most familiar verses in all of Scripture, John 3:16 clearly proclaims the purpose of God in sending His only begotten Son, the Son

Did You Know?

MOSES AND THE BRONZE SERPENT

Numbers 21:6–9 records the incident in which the Lord sent fiery serpents because of the complaints of the people against God and Moses. Many died for their acts of insubordination. When the people came to Moses admitting their sin and asked Moses to intercede, Moses did so. The Lord instructed him to make an image of a fiery serpent made of bronze. Moses set this serpent on a standard and the people were informed that, *"if a serpent bit any man, when he looked to the bronze serpent, he lived"* (21:9). Jesus explained that, as the Son of Man, he too must *"be lifted up"* even *"as Moses lifted up the serpent in the wilderness."* Any person who believes or, in essence, looks to Jesus receives eternal life! Look to Jesus and live!

Doctrine

THE SON OF MAN AND FORGIVENESS OF SINS

Matthew 9:1–8 records that at Capernaum some men brought a paralytic to Jesus who, seeing the man's faith, told him his sins were forgiven. Some of the scribes questioned Him in their minds and even accused Him of blasphemy. Jesus, *"knowing their thoughts,"* rebuked them and then healed the man. He again affirmed that the man's sins were forgiven. Here Jesus, the Son of God and the Son of Man, showed His power by revealing the thoughts of man, by healing the diseases of man, and by bringing healing to the deepest part of man—bringing forgiveness of man's sins. Jesus fulfills all that His name means—Savior.

Doctrine

"MY CHURCH"

The Church belongs to Jesus Christ. He bought it (see Acts 20:28) and started it (see Acts 1–2). He is building it (see Matthew 16:18) and, as His Bride, the Church is being made beautiful by her Bridegroom (see Ephesians 5:23–27). He is returning to *"receive"* His own to Himself (John 14:3) so that we will *"always be with the Lord"* (1 Thessalonians 4:14–17).

of Man (as verses 13 and 14 call Him). God loved the world. Therefore, He sent Jesus to be lifted up on a cross for our salvation. The account of the bronze serpent being lifted up in the wilderness to save the people from the deadly bite of the serpent was a prophetic picture of the Son of Man being lifted up (see Numbers 21). We know Jesus went to the cross at the hands of the Jewish and Roman leaders. He died the humiliating death of a Roman cross, *"despising the shame"* as Hebrews 12:2 states. He was sent to die, not to judge the world, but to save the world. The one believing on Him *"is not judged."* As Jesus says in John 5:24, *"Truly, truly, I say to you, he who hears My word, and believes Him who sent Me, has eternal life, and does not come into judgment, but has passed out of death into life."*

 How about you? Do you know the love of the Father and of the Son of Man? Have you come to the place where you know your sins are forgiven and you have passed out of death into life? If not, read the section at the end of this book entitled *How to Follow God.* Make sure you are fitting into God's purpose for your life—God's eternal purpose for you.

How do the truths of John 3 connect to Peter's confession of Jesus as the Christ in Matthew 16? In Matthew 16:18–19, Jesus said that His Church would be built on *"this rock"* (*petra*, a large rock or bedrock), referring to the truth of Peter's confession of the Son of Man as the Christ, the Son of the living God. [Peter is the *petros*, small stone.] The Son of Man, the one to whom all dominion is given, is the Christ or Messiah, the Promised Seed of Abraham and Jacob. He is the one who will be a blessing to all nations by the salvation He brings.

The King of the kingdom of heaven, the Christ, would build His Church, and nothing would stop Him. People would be able to come into the kingdom of heaven through the Lord Jesus, the staircase to heaven. How would that happen? Jesus began explaining to the disciples this very truth immediately after Peter's confession at Caesarea Philippi.

📖 What do you discover in Matthew 16:21?

_____

_____

_____

_____

The Gospels often present Jesus talking about the Son of Man suffering death. At Caesarea Philippi Jesus began revealing that He would go to Jerusalem to be killed at the hands of the religious leaders, but He would rise the third day. Not too many days after the events at Caesarea Philippi—as Jesus and His disciples were moving about in Galilee apart from the crowds—He spoke to His disciples again. In Matthew 17:22–23 Jesus told them that *"the Son of Man"* would be *"delivered* (or *betrayed*) *into the hands of men."* Then those men would kill Him. According to Matthew 20:17–19, the "men" He was referring to included the chief priests, the scribes, and the Gentiles to whom Jesus would be delivered. In each instance Jesus promised that He would rise on the third day, but the disciples didn't seem to hear or understand the words about His resurrection. They could only hear the words about His death, and they were deeply grieved.

📖 Read Philippians 2:5–11, and answer the questions below.

What was the attitude of Jesus as He faced the coming cross? The apostle Paul spoke of Christ's attitude and His mission in Philippians 2:5–11. What was at the heart of all Jesus did according to verses 6–7?

_____

_____

_____

What characterized Jesus according to Philippians 2:8?

_____

_____

_____

What do you discover about the Father's view of Jesus in 2:9–11?

_____

_____

_____

Central in the heart of Jesus was His willingness to empty Himself of His glory to serve as a bondservant. In doing this He did not stop being God. He always existed in the form of God; in His essence He was and is and ever will be God, being equal with God the Father in every way. However, He chose to become a man, and in the likeness of man He walked as a servant. In His outward appearance as man, everyone could see the attitude and the actions of a bondservant. As a man and a servant He humbled Himself, obeying all the Father's will even to the point of willingly giving His life to die on the cross. Obeying the Father's will was why Christ came. The Father has exalted Christ as Lord, revealing to us that the Son of Man indeed lives as Lord and Savior.

The disciples were slow to understand all Jesus was saying. They did not understand the fullness of the purpose of God in the cross, nor did they understand how that cross would impact them. Jesus sought to make it clear to them. We will see that in Day Three.

> *"And being found in appearance as a man, He humbled Himself by becoming obedient to the point of death, even death on a cross."*
> *Philippians 2:8*

THE SON OF MAN CALLS US TO COME AND DIE

The Son of Man **DAY THREE**

Intermingled with Jesus' words about His cross were words about the resurrection and about being glorified in His resurrection. At one of those times, Jesus illustrated His own surrender to the cross and the glory that would come from that. To glorify someone meant to form a good opinion or view of them. It meant to help reveal his worth and his excellence. How would Jesus be glorified? How would His worth be expressed?

> Read John 12:23–24. What is the picture Jesus paints?

_____

_____

_____

How does a grain of wheat show its value? How does one know if a grain of wheat is of good quality?

_____

_____

_____

Jesus was just days away from suffering on a cross. How did Jesus illustrate this truth about the grain of wheat?

_____

_____

_____

"Truly, truly, I say to you, unless a grain of wheat falls into the earth and dies, it remains by itself alone; but if it dies, it bears much fruit."
John 12:24

Jesus knew that the hour had arrived for the Son of Man to be glorified. He knew that the purpose for which He came into the world was at hand, the hour of His death for the sins of the world. He also knew that in His death He would reveal the heart of the Father as well as His own heart. All the world would clearly see His love, His servant's heart, His purity, and His holiness. He would go to the cross as a sacrificial lamb, the Lamb of God. As a result, many would experience His love and forgiveness. The picture in which He chose to portray this sacrificial love was the story of the grain of wheat. If a grain falls into the earth and dies, it brings forth much fruit for the benefit of many. If it stays out of the ground stored away, protected, and unused, it may look like a beautiful, plump, healthy grain, but it *"remains by itself alone,"* unfruitful, never knowing the life that comes out of death.

> How did Jesus apply the truth about the grain of wheat to His disciples in John 12:25–26?

_____

_____

_____

". . . for this purpose I came to this hour."
John 12:27

Jesus readily applied this truth to His followers. He knew He was about to go to the cross to die. Like the grain that dies, Christ's death would mean abundant life for millions, an eternal harvest that would bring rejoicing throughout earth and heaven. If any one of His followers wanted to know that abundant life, he must hate his life in comparison to the life that Jesus offered. We know that Jesus offers a life of forgiveness with His Spirit living within. If a man loves his own life and seeks to protect it and keep it safe, disregarding the call of Jesus, he will lose that life. If he tries to find abundance in his own resources, then he will lose, but if he repents and "dies to his self"—if he surrenders himself to Jesus to obey Him, follow Him, and serve Him—then he will actually keep his life and be honored by the Father forever.

This "death unto life" truth is what Jesus as the Son of Man revealed to Peter in Matthew 16. After Peter's verbal recognition of Jesus as *"the Christ, the Son of the Living God,"* Jesus began to give further revelation of His purposes as the Son of Man. As we have already seen, they included revelation of His betrayal, His crucifixion, and His resurrection. This revelation also included a foreshadowing of the disciples' own dying to self. What explanation did Jesus give His disciples about this matter?

📖 Read Matthew 16:24–26, and record what Jesus said about cross-bearing. What is the first reason He gives for cross-bearing (16:25)?

_____

_____

_____

What reason does He add in verse 26?

_____

_____

_____

Jesus cautioned that anyone who tried to save his life would end up losing it, but if anyone would lose his life for His sake, he would find abundant life through Christ. The word for life actually means "soul," referring to the heart of life or, if you will, the very core of who and what we are. One will find true satisfaction when he gives his life away to the Lord for Him to possess, guide, and save. A man who gains the whole world yet loses his soul has lost everything. He profits nothing. There is nothing more valuable than one's soul. No amount of wealth, prestige, or pleasure can fully satisfy a man, nor can these earthly things come close to being worth enough to exchange for one's soul. But there is more to be learned. Jesus goes on to speak of reasons why one should give Him his life.

📖 Why should one give his life away to Jesus? Why invest in Him? Why should one "lose" his life for the sake of Jesus, the Son of Man? Read Matthew 16:27, and write your insights.

_____

_____

_____

In speaking to His disciples, Jesus introduced a new aspect of the life and work of the Son of Man. He *"is going to come in the glory of His Father with His angels."* He will reveal His exalted position in the splendor of His Father, and He will appear with a multitude of angels. What will He do when He comes? He will *"recompense every man according to his deeds."* Does this refer to some kind of salvation by works? Not at all! Jesus is simply assuring us that we must answer for how we respond to the truth He spoke and the call He made.

Have you given Him your life? Are you trusting in the death and resurrection of Him who is both the Son of Man and the Son of God. Are you depending on His death as payment for your sin? Have you received His righteousness in exchange for your sin? When He comes, He will judge men and women based on their relationship to Him. He will judge whether

Put Yourself In Their Shoes

CRUCIFIXION

Crucifixion (death on a cross) is one of the cruelest forms of execution ever devised by man. It is a death marked by utter humiliation and shame, extreme agony, and intense pain. The Romans would not execute one of their own citizens in this manner. Jesus asked His followers to take up their crosses daily and follow Him (see Luke 9:23). Jesus wants us to take up our cross and die to ourselves at every level so that He can fill us with His life and accomplish His purposes **in** and through **us**.

A man who gains the whole world yet loses his soul has lost everything. No amount of wealth, prestige, or pleasure can fully satisfy a man, nor can it come close to being worth exchanging for one's soul.

LORD IT OVER

When Jesus talked to His disciples about following Him, He emphasized having His perspective and heart. He did not want His disciples to be like those who *"lord it over"* others. *Katakurieuo* is the Greek word translated *"lord it over"* or *"exercise dominion over."* The first part *kata* gives intensification to this word. *Katakurieo* refers to having full mastery over a place or the people of that place. In the context, Jesus focused on Gentile rulers who reigned with absolute power, some as tyrants with no thought of serving those over whom they ruled. Jesus wanted a different heart and different actions. He wanted His followers to be servant-hearted. Peter later used this word in 1 Peter 5:3 in speaking of being a shepherd of God's flock, something to which Jesus had specifically called him (see John 21:15–17)—*"shepherd the flock of God...nor yet as lording it over those allotted to your charge, but proving to be examples to the flock"* (1 Peter 5:2–3).

> "[We are] always carrying about in the body the dying of Jesus, that the life of Jesus also may be manifested in our body."
>
> 2 Corinthians 4:10

people gave Him their lives or if they kept their lives for self-centered use. He will judge whether people tried to save their lives by keeping and protecting them. If they have tried to preserve their lives rather then surrender them to God, then they will have only their own resources "to bank on" instead of the resources of the Son of Man. Those depending on their own resources will be bankrupt, since none of the currency of self is worth anything in the kingdom of the Son of Man. Only His righteous life accounts for anything.

Just a few days before Jesus and His disciples reached Jerusalem, where He would face the cross, Jesus spoke to His disciples of His approaching death. Near Jericho, He had to deal with James and John, who wanted the two best seats in His kingdom, one on His left and one on His right. (Their mother also joined in the request for her sons.) Remember that this was just days before His crucifixion. James and John certainly were not learning well. However, we should not judge them too quickly. The other ten disciples were *"indignant"* over this request because they too wanted those positions of greatness. How did the Son of Man respond? We find His response in Matthew 20.

📖 What was the Son of Man's view of this world, the Gentile world (see Matthew 20:25)?

_____

_____

_____

What did Jesus tell His disciples He expected of them (20:26–27)?

_____

_____

_____

What was His own example to them (20:28)? What do you discover about His purpose in coming?

_____

_____

_____

The Gentiles (referring to all those outside the kingdom of God) are known for their seeking to *"lord it over,"* to rule by continually seeking greater authority and more control. Those outside God's kingdom certainly do not seek to give up their lives or to die to self. Jesus said it was to be just the opposite among His followers. They were to outdo one another in serving one another. Greatness in His kingdom came from humility and service. First place went to those who sought to serve as slaves. This serving attitude is the attitude of Christ that we have already studied in Philippians 2. In other words, people who give of themselves wholeheartedly to the benefit of others are living like citizens of His kingdom. Giving yourself involves dying to self, becoming that grain of wheat in the ground, hidden, dying, with the life of God being manifest out of that death to self. That was how the Son of Man saw Himself and His mission. As a matter of fact, He said He came *"to give His life a ransom for many"*—to die for their sins. In doing so He would see many come to know the life only He could give. As He called them to

Himself, to deny themselves, take up their crosses, and follow Him, through their experiences of dying to self, they would come to know the abundance of the life that He freely gives.

What further purpose does the Son of Man have for His people and for this world? We will see more of His purpose in Day Four.

THE GLORY OF THE SON OF MAN

More than once, Jesus spoke of the day when the Son of Man would come in great glory. Just after the incident in Matthew 16:27, Jesus said that some standing there would not taste death until they had seen *"the Son of Man coming in His kingdom"* (Matthew 16:28). To what was Jesus referring? The answer to this question is found in Matthew 17.

📖 Matthew 17:1 follows directly after Matthew 16:28. Read Matthew 17:1–9. What happened in 17:1–2? (You may wish to read Luke 9:28–36 for some additional insights.)

_____

_____

_____

Who appeared with Jesus (v. 3)?

_____

_____

What was Peter's response (v. 4)?

_____

_____

_____

Matthew reports that six days after Jesus said that some would see *"His kingdom,"* He took Peter, James, and John up on a mountain. Luke adds that He did so in order to pray, and that while He was praying His appearance changed (9:28–29). He was transfigured before their eyes so that *"His face shone like the sun,"* and His clothes were as *"white as light."* Then Moses and Elijah, representative of the Law and the prophets, appeared and began talking to Him about *"His departure which He was about to accomplish at Jerusalem"* (Luke 9:31). Peter suggested that he make three tabernacles for Jesus, Moses, and Elijah. Perhaps he said that because he thought that this would be the perfect place to stay—with the Lord resplendent in kingdom glory and Moses and Elijah there—or perhaps Peter was thinking the kingdom had already come, especially in light of Jesus' statement just days before (see Matthew 16:28). He may have been remembering some of the promises of the Old Testament, especially those pictured in the Feasts of Israel. As the Feast of Passover symbolized the crucifixion of Christ our Passover Lamb, and as the Feast of Firstfruits symbolized the Resurrection of Christ, so the Feast of Booths or Tabernacles (celebrated in early October) prophetically

✎ *Did You Know?*
❓ MOUNT HERMON

Mount Hermon is believed by many to be the location of the Transfiguration since it is located near Caesarea Philippi in northern Israel. Mark 9:2 says it was a *"high mountain."* Mount Hermon is 9,232 feet in elevation and would have afforded Jesus and His disciples an undisturbed area for this time of prayer.

symbolized the coming of the Messiah when He would lead His people in a reign of peace.

As Peter spoke, the Father overshadowed them in a cloud and said, *"This is My* **beloved Son**, *with whom I am well-pleased; listen to Him,"* and then commanded them to *"listen to Him!"* The frightened disciples were raised to their feet by the Lord Jesus, and then they left the mountain with Him.

What did Jesus tell them as they came down the mountain (17:9)?

_____

_____

_____

Jesus told Peter, James, and John to tell no one what they had seen until *"the Son of Man has risen from the dead."* This experience on the mount of transfiguration in some measure certainly fulfilled Christ's prophetic statement of the disciples seeing a preview of *"the Son of Man coming in His Kingdom."* The prophecy in Matthew 16:28 may also find its fulfillment in John's visions in the book of Revelation. They saw the glory of the Lord and of the Father. They recognized Moses and Elijah and heard their voices as well as the voice of the Father. The phrase *"coming in His Kingdom"* could even be translated "coming in His royal splendor." Later Peter described this event stating, *"we were eyewitnesses of His majesty,"* and spoke of *"when He received honor and glory from God the Father"* (2 Peter 1:16–17).

This incident certainly revealed the glory of the Son of Man, but it did not answer all of the disciples' questions about Him. Another incident as they traveled gave them another glimpse of what it meant to follow the Son of Man. Not long before His crucifixion, Jesus encountered a rich young ruler who was unwilling to sell all and follow Him (see Matthew 19:16–26). After that encounter, Peter questioned Jesus about their own stance before Him. They had left all, and he wanted to know what sort of reward awaited them. Jesus did not rebuke Peter for his question. It was a valid question, and Jesus wanted them to understand what awaited them in their relationship with the Son of Man. What did Jesus tell them?

📖 Looking at Matthew 19:27–29, what will occur in the *"regeneration"*?

_____

_____

_____

What is the reward for the disciples who *"followed"* Jesus (19:28)?

_____

_____

_____

What is the reward for anyone who follows Jesus (19:29)?

_____

_____

_____

Did You Know?
CLOUDS

The Lord often manifested Himself in a bright cloud sometimes called the "cloud of glory" or the *"Shekinah,"* related to the Hebrew word meaning "to reside or dwell." The Father manifested Himself in a bright cloud at the Transfiguration, and Jesus often spoke of returning in the clouds of heaven with power. Acts 1:9 says Jesus ascended in *"a cloud,"* and the angels who stood there told the disciples Jesus would *"come in just the same way"* as He left. Revelation 1:7 speaks of Jesus *"coming with the clouds,"* and Revelation 14:14 pictures *"One like the Son of Man"* (NKJV), sitting on a white cloud and crowned with a golden victor's crown.

Jesus assured Peter and His other disciples that a time was coming *"when the Son of Man will sit on His* **glorious** *throne"* (or, "the throne of His **glory**" [emphasis mine]). This particular event is referred to as the "regeneration," a time when the Lord will reign on the earth and all will be restored. Acts 3:21 speaks of *"the period of restoration of all things,"* a time prophesied and anticipated by the prophets and the people of God for ages. In that time the disciples will sit on thrones judging or governing the twelve tribes of Israel. All those who have given their lives to Jesus Christ will additionally be rewarded many times over and experience the blessing of eternal life.

The Son of Man is spoken of in many passages. His glory is revealed in many ways. Matthew 24:29–31 speaks of the end times when *"all the tribes of the earth . . . will see the* SON OF MAN COMING ON THE CLOUDS OF THE SKY *with power and great glory."* Matthew 25:31–46 shows us that when the Son of Man comes in His glory He will judge the nations as sheep and goats. Even before Caiaphas and the Jewish leaders on the night before His crucifixion, when asked if He was *"the Christ, the Son of God,"* Jesus testified, *"It is as you said"* (NKJV). Then He added, *"Nevertheless, I tell you, hereafter you shall see* THE SON OF MAN SITTING AT THE RIGHT HAND OF THE POWER, *and* COMING ON THE CLOUDS OF HEAVEN" (Matthew 26:63–64). Are you ready for His coming? In Day Five we will explore how we can be better prepared for Christ's coming.

FOR ME TO FOLLOW CHRIST

 The Son of Man

What does it mean to follow the Son of Man? We have seen that He is Lord. Following Him as Lord means surrendering to His will His way. We have seen Him as the Savior who died for our sins, offering us forgiveness and eternal life. Following Him as Savior means receiving His death for us, His Life within us, and receiving His righteousness in place of our unrighteousness. We have seen that the Son of Man will come in His glory to reign over all. Following Him means being ready for His return. How do we do that day by day?

📖 The first question each of us must ask is "Do I have a right relationship with God?" Read 1 Timothy 2:4–6. What is the first priority on God's heart according to verse 4?

_____

_____

_____

According to verses 5 and 6, what has God done to make sure we come to know Him in truth?

_____

_____

_____

_____

APPLY Do you know Jesus Christ as **your mediator**? This is the question of **salvation**. Are you rightly related to Him through His salvation? (See the section "How to Follow God" at the end of this lesson if you are not sure.)

📖 Jesus said that the grain of wheat does one of two things. It either remains by itself intact and alone, or it falls into the ground and dies, producing more life. What kind of grain are you? Read James 4:13–16. What does James say your life is like on this earth?

_____

_____

What is James' counsel to you?

_____

_____

_____

> "For there is one God, and one mediator also between God and men, the man Christ Jesus."
>
> I Timothy 2:5

APPLY Your life is like a vapor, like a morning fog that will soon be gone. Are you living for the moment, for what you can get for yourself right now? Are you living your life for the temporal or the eternal? Are you giving yourself for the ongoing, ever-growing kingdom? These are questions of **surrender**. James says the daily cry of our hearts should be *"If the Lord wills, we shall live and also do this or that."* Is that the cry of your heart today?

📖 Read 1 Timothy 6:17–19. What is the counsel of the apostle Paul in verses 17 and 18?

_____

_____

What is the promise of verses 17 and 19?

_____

_____

What are we to *"take hold of"*?

_____

_____

Paul knew from experience what it meant to give His life to the Lord Jesus, to fall into the ground and die as a grain of wheat. He knew what it meant to die to self and what it meant to begin to see eternal fruit in the lives of those in whom he invested. His instructions to those *"who are rich in this present world"* cover a broad range of the *"rich."* His definition of "rich" is not just those with millions of dollars, but refers to those who have more than they need. His counsel is very wise; never rest in the things you have. Riches are never a certainty, but God's love is always certain. Rest your life in His hands. What should we do with our riches? We should look to the Lord to guide us in doing good, in being generous, making sure we are ready to share. In this way our "riches" can be an eternal investment. Giving our lives and our "riches" to the Lord is taking hold of *"that which is life indeed."*

Think of this truth as a question about our investments. How are we investing our lives? The events of life, especially death, continually speak a message about **eternity**—this life is not all there is. There is something beyond the present. Life's events also convey meaning concerning our **destiny**—we are all headed toward one of two destinations. We will either be with the Lord in heaven, in His wonderful presence forever, or we will be separated from Him forever in hell.

There is also a word about **opportunity**—we have a choice to make. Will we surrender our lives and rest our hope of salvation on Jesus Christ? Or will we "keep" our lives and try to "save" our lives ourselves? That is the question about our eternal destiny. With that we then have the opportunity to invest our lives in what lasts forever—knowing and following. We have the opportunity to invest our lives in Christ and in getting the Word of God to the lives of people. That means helping them know His Word in order to know Him and His love more fully and thus come to follow and obey Him more completely. In these choices we and those who follow His Word can have a glorious destiny and a wonderful eternity with the Son of Man!

📖 In 1 Corinthians 3:9–15, the apostle Paul paints a vivid picture of how we can invest our lives. Read those verses. What are the materials with which we can build?

_____

_____

_____

What materials pass the test of God's fire (3:12–13)?

_____

_____

What are the two possibilities for each man (3:14–15)?

_____

_____

In building *"God's building,"* believers can use *"gold, silver, precious stones, wood, hay, straw,"* two categories of materials that face fire in totally different ways. The first three pass through the fire unharmed. If anything, only the dross is burned. The precious metal remains. In the second three, everything is burned up. Only ashes remain. God's fiery gaze will test the **quality** of each man's work, not the quantity. More is not necessarily better. Those believers who have built with lasting materials will receive a reward, and those who have used the inferior materials will suffer loss of reward, though they themselves will be saved.

How do we assure ourselves that we are building with the gold, silver, and precious stones? We must surrender our lives to the Lord and let Him guide us in the building process. As we walk by faith, we are building with "gold." As we depend on His Spirit we are putting "precious stones" in place. As we follow Christ we are seeing "silver" placed where He wants it. Every time we walk by sight instead of faith, carry out the desires of the flesh, or follow "self" instead of Christ, we have stored up wood, hay, and straw.

"Take hold of that which is life indeed."
I Timothy 6:19

We must surrender our lives to the Lord and let Him guide in the building process.

APPLY How about you? How are you building? Stop for a moment, and spend some time in prayer. Ask the Lord to give you His perspective and His evaluation of where you are. Ask Him to show you how to follow the Son of Man as He followed His Father.

Lord, thank You for coming as the Son of Man. Thank You for showing me that You are indeed a gracious Lord and Savior. Thank You for being born a man and living as a man and the God-Man on this earth. I know You know all that I go through. You *"sympathize with* [my] *weaknesses"* (Hebrews 4:15). You know how I feel and what I face since You have been *"tempted in all things as* [I am tempted]*, yet without sin."* Thank You that I can draw near to Your throne of grace and speak with confidence, telling You all that is on my heart. I know You won't send me away but will give me *"grace to help in time of need"*—well-timed for **my** exact need (Hebrews 4:15–16). Thank You for Your compassion and mercy. Give me ears to hear You so that I listen carefully to all that You say. Then help me fully obey You. May I walk in such a way that I build with gold, silver, and precious stones, not the wood, hay, and straw of self-centeredness. I want to be ready for Your return, not ashamed at Your coming, but glad over the joy of seeing Your face, the face of the Son of Man. In Jesus' Name, Amen.

In light of all you have seen about the Son of Man and knowing His coming approaches, write your own prayer to Him in the space provided.

_____

_____

_____

_____

_____

_____

_____

_____

_____

_____

Christ in Prayer

THE PRAYER LIFE OF JESUS

When we turn the pages of Scripture to the life of Jesus, we discover one who considered prayer essential in everything He did. Jesus came as the God-Man, marked by the character, nature, and power of His Father, yet He was always dependent on His Father in prayer. This is one of the most amazing aspects of Jesus' life. Jesus prayed frequently and fervently. He prayed as no other man has ever prayed. We are often amazed that Jesus spent so much time in prayer, but that is because we often misunderstand the full meaning of prayer as well as the full ministry of prayer. Jesus understood both.

When we look at the lifestyle of our Lord, we find many ways in which He instructs us by example. We have already seen the ways He instructs us by His teaching and the commands of His Word. As we look at His life from boyhood through manhood, we will see a life saturated in prayer. When we look at His "growing up" years, we will see the central place prayer played in His life. Then we will look at how prayer played a crucial role as He began His ministry and how prayer continued to be His lifeline to the Father in those all-important ministry years. Jesus never tried to minister without time spent in prayer with His Father. His prayer life in the last days of His ministry will show us how He prayed facing the greatest trial anyone has ever faced. Seeing His ongoing prayer life—His intercession for us—will encourage us as we seek to follow Him.

As we look at our own prayer lives, we need to allow Jesus' example to encourage and challenge us. We need to let His walk with the Father instruct us. While Jesus had a very unique relationship to His Father, we can let His walk with the Father help us picture the kind of relationship the Father wants with each of His children. Jesus knew what it meant to live **praying God's way**. He will guide us to do the same.

We are often amazed that Jesus spent so much time in prayer, but that is because we often misunderstand the full meaning of prayer as well as the full ministry of prayer.

THE PRAYER LIFE OF JESUS IN THE "PRIVATE YEARS"

W hat kind of daily life did Jesus have? What would we expect to find on His schedule each day, especially in those first thirty years, those "private years" of which we know so little? As we look at the Scriptures, we find some clues as to what a day in the life of Jesus would look like. As we look at His lifestyle, we can see some of the struggles He may have faced. We can also see the pattern in which Christ was led by the Father down the dusty roads of Israel some two thousand years ago and discover some of the ways the Father leads in our own lives.

📖 The first glimpse of Jesus' life is found when He was twelve years of age. Read Luke 2:41–52. Describe the events in Jesus' life at this point. What stands out about Jesus?

_____

_____

_____

_____

_____

_____

_____

Read Luke 2:49 again. What insights do you glean from Jesus' question to Joseph and Mary? Does this say anything about His prayer life?

_____

_____

_____

_____

_____

_____

_____

In Luke 2, we get a glimpse of the life of Jesus as a twelve-year-old boy, celebrating the Passover feast with His family and others in Jerusalem. In the festive and crowded atmosphere of the Temple, we find Jesus talking to the teachers of the Law, those men learned in all the Old Testament Scriptures. Jesus was there listening, asking questions, and answering questions—and all were *"amazed at His understanding and His answers."* While He was doing this, His family was journeying back to Nazareth. When Mary and Joseph realized that Jesus was not on the return caravan, they traveled back a day's journey to Jerusalem. Then they searched diligently for Him for at least another day. Finally finding Him in the Temple was a relief and a surprise, but Jesus was surprised at their surprise. His question to them is literally,

"Did you not know that I had to be in the things of My Father?"—a testimony that Jesus understood the things of His Father and that His Father had revealed those things to Him. Those two facts reveal that the prayer life of this twelve-year-old boy was very real and vibrant.

What further insights do you find in Luke 2:52? What clues can you glean about Jesus' lifestyle? What would this say about His prayer life?

_____

_____

_____

_____

_____

From age twelve on, Jesus grew *"in favor with God,"* meaning His relationship with God the Father stayed healthy and growing. It would also seem from that statement that the prayer life of Jesus continued to grow, remaining ever vibrant and strong. This is a testimony that He stayed in close fellowship with His Father, always walking in the light. Nothing ever marred that fellowship. Concerning His relationship with His Father, His family, and His fellow man, Jesus never had a mark or stain of wrongdoing in His life. The way remained continually open for Jesus to talk to His Father—any time, any place, and any circumstance. In addition, His relationship with others continued to grow strong.

📖 We have looked at an informative verse in an earlier lesson, but it would be good to review it at this point. Look at Isaiah 50:4, a prophecy about the coming Messiah. What do you see that would apply to Jesus' lifestyle, especially to His prayer life?

_____

_____

_____

_____

> **"The Lord GOD has given Me the tongue of disciples, that I may know how to sustain the weary one with a word. He awakens me morning by morning, He awakens My ear to listen as a disciple."**
>
> **Isaiah 50:4**

From what Jesus said to Mary and Joseph, it is evident the Father had already been teaching Him many things, waking Him *"morning by morning . . . to listen as a disciple."* The teachers of the Law and all who heard Him in those days at the Temple were astounded at His understanding and ability to answer questions about the Scriptures. Jesus proved to be a good disciple of His Father, a good listener in prayer, and a scholar when it came to searching and learning the Scriptures. Think of what it must have been like for the boy Jesus to be in prayer to His Father, always eager to hear Him. Jesus, ever the obedient learner, wanted to know His Word and was ever-attentive in prayer, having the heart of a disciple to His Father. The Father wants us to know a similar delight as we listen to His Word and learn to pray God's way.

Is there a way to know the delight of praying God's way more fully? How do we know for sure what went on in Christ's earthly life, say from age 12 to age 30? We again find a clue in the Scriptures. Luke 3:23 says, *"And when He began His ministry, Jesus Himself was about thirty years of age."* That statement comes immediately following His baptism and before the account of His temptation in the wilderness. What can we learn from the events surrounding Jesus' baptism by John in the Jordan River? These precursor events give us another look into this Man, our Lord, and they reveal some wonderful truths about His lifestyle and His prayer life.

📖 Read the account of Jesus' baptism in Luke 3:21–22. What does Luke note about Jesus when John baptized Him?

_____

_____

_____

_____

What part did the Holy Spirit play in this event? (You may want to look at the testimony of John the Baptist in John 1:29–34 as well.)

_____

_____

_____

_____

Jesus came to be baptized by John and begin the ministry the Father sent Him to fulfill. As He was being baptized, **Jesus was praying**, revealing both His dependence on and His love for His Father. After Christ was baptized and while He was **still praying**, the Holy Spirit descended upon Jesus in bodily form as a dove. John the Baptist recounts that the Father had revealed this as the sign to look for to signal the Messiah.

What did the Father declare at Jesus' baptism? What thoughts do you gather from that statement?

_____

_____

_____

_____

_____

The Father spoke from heaven, *"Thou art My beloved Son, in Thee I am well-pleased."* The Father dearly loved His Son. What a delight it must have been for the Father to walk and talk with His Son in perfect fellowship and flawless communion. What a joy—how well-pleasing it must have been to experience every day that oneness of heart and mind with Jesus, always receiving from His Son the love that flowed from all His heart, soul, mind, and strength, a love of complete and unwavering trust. Jesus was well-pleasing to His Father.

At this point, we must ask some questions: What does it mean to be well pleasing to God? Is there something special we must do, or some secret we must know, or something we must own? How can we be well-pleasing to the Father? How does this relate to praying God's way? What pleases God about our praying? We will see this in Day Two.

> **As He was being baptized, Jesus was praying, revealing both His dependence on and His love for His Father.**

THE PRAYER LIFE OF JESUS AND THE BEGINNING OF HIS MINISTRY

We have seen at the very outset of Jesus' ministry that the Father declared He was well pleased with His Beloved Son. This was before He preached any messages, gave any parables, taught any lessons, or performed any miracles. What was the foundation of this well-pleasing life of the Lord Jesus, and where does prayer fit in?

To see the truth of a well-pleasing life we need to look at two testimonies from Scripture. These will help us see how we can be well pleasing to God and how prayer relates to that aim. The first Scripture is from the pen of the apostle Paul.

📖 Read 2 Corinthians 5:6–9. What does Paul highlight about his walk (and the walk of those who truly know the Lord)?

_____

_____

_____

_____

There is a connection between what Paul says in verse 7 with what he says in verse 9 concerning our earthly walk and life in our heavenly home. What does Paul emphasize in verse 9?

_____

_____

_____

_____

As Paul reflected on his ministry and his earthly walk in 2 Corinthians 4 and 5, he came to a summary statement in verse 7 of chapter 5. There, he speaks about walking by faith, not by sight, trusting that what God has said is true. He knew that one day his life on earth would end—his body or "earthly tent" would be "torn down"—and that one day, every believer in Jesus Christ would walk in the fullness of eternal life, with new bodies in a new home (5:1–5). The common element in our earthly walk and in our heavenly home is the desire to be pleasing to God. On earth, that comes through our walk by faith. Faith or confident trust in God pleases God. A walk in faith says to our Father, "We love You and trust You. We believe what You have promised." That is what Jesus did in His earthly walk, and what Paul did as well.

Walking by faith is essential to pleasing God as we walk on earth. In heaven, our faith will be complete, and all we do will be pleasing to Him. Revelation 22:3 says that we, His bondservants, *"shall serve Him"* unhindered by any distractions, any deceptions, or any darkness. The Lord Himself will *"illumine"* us, and we will walk in the light with Him—reigning with Him forever.

Doctrine
PLEASING TO GOD

At Jesus' baptism, the Father said He was well-pleased with the Son (Luke 3:22). Over two years later, the Father made the same declaration about His Son on the Mount of Transfiguration (see Matthew 17:5). Second Corinthians 5:7–9 and Hebrews 11:6 point to the necessity of faith to please God, while Romans 12:1 focuses on surrender to God as *"a living and holy sacrifice, acceptable to God."* That is an act of faith. Romans 14:8 speaks of being well-pleasing to God as members of the family of God who do not condemn one another, but rather love and build up one another. Paul taught the Thessalonians how to please God through a holy walk (see 1 Thessalonians 4:1–8), and he prayed for the Colossians believers to walk pleasing to the Lord *"in all respects"* (Colossians 1:10). As with Paul and his companions, may *"we have as our ambition ... to be pleasing to Him"* (2 Corinthians 5:9).

"Enoch ... had this testimony, that he pleased God. But without faith it is impossible to please Him, for he who comes to God must believe that He is, and that He is a rewarder of those who diligently seek Him.

Hebrews 11:5b–6 (NKJV)

There is another verse that gives us insight into what marks one who is walking in faith and thus pleasing God. Read Hebrews 11:6. What action is true of one walking in faith according to Hebrews 11:6?

_____

_____

_____

_____

The one who believes that God is God, who believes He is who the Scriptures say, will keep coming (present tense) to God, diligently seeking Him in prayer and desiring a walk of fellowship. The one coming to God in faith expects God to hear him and to answer him. Such faith pleases God. That was the mark of those who walked by faith, people like Enoch in Hebrews 11:5. That was the mark of Jesus throughout His life.

Think back to Jesus' baptism and what the Father said about Jesus' life. Luke 3:22 makes it clear that the Father was *"well pleased"* in His Son. Therefore, what characteristic can we conclude marked Jesus' life in those growing up years and into manhood?

_____

_____

_____

_____

Even as a child, Jesus pleased His Father because Jesus walked in faith, believing that He was who the Scripture says He is. Jesus was (and still is) God the Son, and, while on earth, He daily came to God His Father. (Don't lose the significance of this in the mystery of it all.) Jesus' practice of continually coming to the Father in prayer did not stop in childhood. All His days on earth, Jesus pleased His Father as He diligently sought the Father in prayer. After more than two years of ministry as He was on what became known as the Mount of Transfiguration, the Father declared again, *"My Beloved Son, with whom I am well pleased"* (Matthew 17:5). As He walked and ministered and prayed, Jesus knew His Father was a rewarder to those who would come to God, earnestly seeking Him day by day. Day in and day out, Jesus desired only to be *"in the things of* [His] *Father."* Jesus knew His Father's will as the Father revealed it. Everything the Father revealed, Jesus wanted to obey ... and did obey. He wanted to join His Father in the work He was doing. Jesus desired to accomplish all the Father sent Him to do. That faith walk, that walk of diligently seeking His Father, greatly pleased the Father.

How about you? Are you walking, pleasing the Father by diligently seeking Him? Perhaps now would be a good time to pause and talk to the Father about the work He is doing, about the assignments He has for you, and about how you can walk pleasing Him. Remember, by the Holy Spirit in you, the life of Jesus can be real to you. His Spirit can fill you with His life and teach you to pray and walk in such a way that the pleasing life of the Son is experienced and seen in you. Daily seeking the Father is well pleasing to Him.

As we look at Jesus in the days of ministry, we can learn much from His lifestyle. The first thing we need to look at is how He sought His Father in those days in the wilderness. How He walked through those forty days and how He began His ministry will help guide us in how we face trials and temptations—even when we are doing the will of God.

📖 What do you learn from Luke 4:1–2?

_____

_____

_____

_____

Luke tells us that Jesus returned from the Jordan River after His baptism *"full of the Holy Spirit."* The leadership of the Spirit marked Jesus moment by moment. The Spirit of God led Jesus about the wilderness for forty days as He fasted. Fasting in the Old Testament was always considered a time to humble oneself and seek the Lord. Jesus walked in humility, always depending on the Spirit and the Father to accomplish what the Father wanted. During those days, the devil tempted Jesus in a variety of ways. When the forty days ended, Jesus became hungry. Because He was under the guidance of the Spirit, Jesus responded to the devil's temptation in the power of the Spirit. What can we learn from Jesus about how to respond to temptation (even during a time of intense prayer)?

📖 Read Matthew 4:3–11. How did Jesus respond to the tempter? What common factor is true in each response? In Luke 4:14, what does Luke highlight immediately after this encounter?

_____

_____

_____

_____

_____

_____

_____

The tempter questioned whether or not Jesus was the Son of God and offered Him an opportunity to prove it while at the same time satisfying His physical need for food. Jesus responded with the Word of God, *"It is written. . . ."* and pointed out that it is more important to follow what God says than to follow one's physical desires, even the basic desire for simple bread. Following God and His Word will provide the true nourishment for the true life man needs. Satan then used the Word of God to try and lead Jesus astray from following the leadership of His Father. Jesus countered with the Scriptures that command never to put God to the test or to presume upon Him. Jesus was always more concerned about His relationship with the Father than with any external reality, be it bread or miraculous physical protection. When Satan offered the kingdoms of the world with all their glory, Jesus again focused on His Father's will and His Father's Word. Nothing is more important than worshiping Him, not even *"all the kingdoms of the world."*

Did You Know?

❓ JESUS' BIBLE KNOWLEDGE

Jesus countered each temptation from the devil with Scripture, by first describing God's words as the true bread needed by man. Jesus was quoting from Deuteronomy 8:3. In the other two temptations, Jesus responded from this very same book (see Deuteronomy 6:13, 16). Jesus was well versed in God's laws for His people and followed these commandments in His heart. He had read and heard and meditated on God's Word, and it became His bread, His inner strength, His sword, and His outer weapon at the moment of temptation.

Jesus stood firm because He stood faithful to His Father and His Word.

Jesus stood firm because He stood faithful to His Father and His Word. In constant humility, Jesus depended on the Spirit of God, the Word of God, and the guiding hand of His Father. The result was victory at every point, never defeat in any point. Immediately after this, when Jesus came into Galilee, He came *"in the power of the Spirit."* Here is another picture of His absolute dependence on the Spirit and His continued focus on His Father.

How then did Jesus live day to day? What marked His schedule? We will see in Day Three.

PRAYER IN THE DAYS OF JESUS' MINISTRY

It is vital to see how Jesus walked day in and day out after those forty days in the wilderness. How would His daily pattern differ with all the demands and needs of people all around Him? How would He deal with those needs as well as the needs of those not-quite-mature disciples, those men who failed to "get it" time after time? We will see in today's lesson.

📖 We looked at Mark 1:35–38 in an earlier lesson. Look again and summarize what you see there. (Recall what we have seen in Isaiah 50:4.)

_____

_____

_____

_____

_____

_____

Early in the morning while it was still dark, Jesus got up and went to a solitary place to pray to His Father, an example of the *"morning by morning,"* mentioned by Isaiah. There, the Father gave Jesus His directions for the day, the wisdom He would need for the many ministry encounters He would face.

📖 Luke gives us another glimpse at Jesus in prayer. Read Luke 5:16 and write what you discover in that verse?

_____

_____

_____

_____

_____

Jesus would *"often slip away"* to a deserted place, a place to be alone with His Father. There, He would spend time in prayer. *Proseúchomai,* the Greek word translated "pray" in Luke 5:16, is the general word for prayer, indicating both the heart attitude of bowing to the Father about all kinds of needs, but also offering to the Father praise and thanksgiving. A heart attitude of prayer, praise, and thanksgiving was certainly true of Jesus' earthly walk and is an excellent example for us to follow. We too often need to "slip away" to spend time with our Father.

Another aspect of Jesus' walk in prayer is the attention He gave to major decisions and turning points in His life. We have already noted that Jesus was praying at His baptism and that He spent forty days in fasting and prayer before He began His ministry.

📖 What do you find in Luke 6:12–16?

_____

_____

_____

_____

Sometime around the summer of A.D. 28, after about eighteen months of ministry, Jesus went up to a mountain to pray and spent the whole night in prayer. The next day He called twelve of His disciples to be His apostles, His "sent ones." They would live in a special relationship to Him, being trained as the leaders of the early Church. The implication in this passage is that Jesus chose the Twelve based on what the Father revealed in His prayer time. Most likely, this was not the only time Jesus spent the night in prayer. John 7:53 and 8:1–2 note that Jesus went to the Mount of Olives and spent the entire night there and came from there back into Jerusalem the next morning. The Mount of Olives was the location of the Garden of Gethsemane, where Jesus and His disciples often met together. It is likely that Jesus and His disciples often met here for times of prayer.

📖 What part did prayer play in His ministry in Matthew 14:13–21? Also read what Jesus did in John 6:11 (note also 6:23). Record what you find from these two eyewitnesses.

_____

_____

_____

_____

_____

The crowds wanted to be where Jesus was. Many came to be cured of their sicknesses. Others wanted to hear His teaching or simply see and experience His power and His miracles. Evening came, and the disciples suggested that the crowds disperse and go to the nearest village to find food— but Jesus had another idea. He asked the disciples to provide food, and they responded pointing to a mere five loaves and two fish. Jesus asked them to bring those, and then He took them, looked up toward heaven, thanked the Father, blessed the food, and began breaking it and giving it to the disciples to distribute. Miraculously, they kept distributing food until all had enough to eat, more than enough for the crowd of *"about five thousand men"* plus many women and children. (Recall it was a lad or small boy there who had the five loaves and two fish.)

> ## "But He Himself would often slip away to the wilderness and pray."
>
> ### Luke 5:16

We find another very instructive look into Jesus' life immediately after this incident of the feeding of the five thousand. What do you discover in Matthew 14:22–23? What happened then in Matthew 14:24–33?

_____

_____

_____

_____

_____

Immediately after the miracle of the loaves and the fish, Jesus sent His disciples into a boat to go to the other side of the Sea of Galilee. The crowds went their way, and Jesus stayed behind and went up to a mountain to pray. When evening came, He was there on the mountain praying alone while His disciples were on the sea struggling with the winds and the waves. Jesus stayed on the mountain for quite some time. He did not come walking on the water to where the disciples were until "the fourth watch," which was between 3:00 and 6:00 A.M. That means Jesus stayed on the mountain praying from around 6:00 P.M. to at least 3:00 A.M., a period of more than nine hours. After that, a series of miracles occurred. First, Christ walked on the water to where the disciples were struggling. Then He called Peter to come to him, and Peter walked on the water for a few moments. Then Jesus entered the boat, and the winds and waves stopped—and according to John 6:21, the boat was immediately at the shores of the land they were trying to reach. This was a night of prayer and miracles, revealing to the disciples that Jesus was indeed God's Son.

What was Jesus' own testimony about how He knew what to do and what to say? Read John 8:25–29 and 12:49–50 and record your findings.

_____

_____

_____

_____

Jesus made it clear that His Father set His agenda. Jesus did nothing on His own initiative. What He did and what He said came out of His time with the Father—listening and learning and then carrying out what the Father gave Him to do in the power of the Spirit. Jesus continually practiced the presence of the Father, confident that the Father was with Him and that He Himself only desired to please His Father. We can do the same as we learn to pray God's way.

Jesus was a child of prayer, then a man of prayer, then a man of prayer in ministry. He was a man who walked in that closest of relationships with His Father. That life of prayer did not end with His ministry days. His last days on earth would prove to be His greatest days of prayer, revealing the greatest agony any man has ever endured in prayer as well as the greatest triumph anyone has ever experienced.

"I do nothing on My own initiative, but I speak these things as the Father taught Me. And He who sent Me is with Me; He has not left Me alone, for I always do the things that are pleasing to Him."

John 8:28–29

PRAYER IN JESUS' LAST DAYS

The most significant days in the life of our Lord Jesus were the last days before His death on the cross. In those days we see the fervency and fire of His praying more than any other time in His life. We see His compassion and agony at their greatest intensity. We also see the wonder and the expectation of an awesome future and a glorious eternity. We can learn much as we walk through the events of Christ's final days on earth, so pay close attention as we examine the very heart of God.

📖 Look first at John 12:27–33. What was Jesus' condition and what was His concern, His request? Look for application points to praying God's way for your own life.

_____

_____

_____

_____

_____

The events of these verses in John's Gospel take place shortly after Jesus raised Lazarus from the dead and made a triumphal entry into Jerusalem. Scores of visitors were in the city in conjunction with the approaching Feast of the Passover. Some of these visitors asked the disciples if they could see Jesus. As Phillip and Andrew approached Jesus on behalf of these visitors, Jesus exclaimed that He had become troubled in soul. The word *"troubled"* is a translation of *tarásso,* which means to be stirred or agitated. It was used of water boiling. As the Passover was swiftly approaching and the crowds were growing, Christ knew that His moment on the cross was also approaching, and all that Jesus knew about His mission caused Him to be troubled. Jesus could have prayed, *"Father, save me from this hour,"* but He did not. Instead, He prayed, *"Father, glorify Thy name,"* or "reveal the fullness of who You are." Jesus was praying in essence, "make people aware of who You really are, of Your will and Your ways so that they honor You." At that moment the Father spoke in a thundering voice from heaven, *"I have both glorified it, and will glorify it again."* Through the Crucifixion and the Resurrection, the Father would fulfill all He had promised and would reveal Himself through His Son in even greater ways. Jesus knew that His Father would take care of Him and that what He was about to do would be the deathblow to evil, to the devil, and to the problem of sin. As a result of Christ's work on the cross, many would be drawn to Christ and to the eternal life He alone can give. Because He was willing to do the Father's will, we can live—and He can now live in us. He lives to show us the Father's will, and when we know and do His will, we glorify Him.

The applications to our praying are evident. While we do not face what Jesus faced, we do have times when we are agitated and disturbed, our circumstances and our souls boiling within. We may want to pray, "Father, remove this situation from me or remove me from it." Instead, we should pray, "Father, do what You desire, what will glorify Your name, what will reveal You more clearly."

Word Study

TROUBLED SOUL

"Troubled" is a translation of the Greek word *tarásso,* which means "to stir," or "to agitate," and can also mean "to boil" (water). It was used of Jesus being troubled in spirit over the weeping of many after Lazarus had died (see John 11:33), of His being troubled in soul while facing the Crucifixion (see John 12:27), and at the Last Supper as He contemplated the betrayal of Judas (John 13:21). *Tarásso,* was also used of the disciples being troubled in heart in John 14:1 and 14:27. Jesus overcame His troubled heart. He now gives us His peace to counter our own troubled hearts.

In John 12:27–33, we see Jesus agonizing over His impending betrayal and public execution. Christ's vexation of spirit did not end on this day, however. In fact, He continued to carry that burden for the next several days. Then the day before the Crucifixion, after Jesus met with His disciples in the "Upper Room," we see again the expression of His heart, but it is not all agony. After washing the disciples feet, dismissing Judas into the darkness, and celebrating the first Lord's Supper with His own, Jesus began to tell them of the wonderful plans He had for them—some immediate and some eternal. At the same time, He spoke to them of the sorrow they would face. He promised them they would know a new day in their prayer lives as they learned to ask in His name. Then, walking with His disciples toward the Garden of Gethsemane, still near the Temple, He stopped and lifted His eyes to heaven and began to pray. We read His prayer in John 17:1–26.

📖 Read John 17 and complete all exercises pertaining to this chapter of the Bible.

What marks Jesus' prayer in John 17:1–5? What is at the heart of what He prayed in those opening verses?

_____

_____

_____

_____

_____

_____

In Jesus' prayer, He first focused on His relationship to His Father and expressed His longing that He would be glorified in all He did so that the Father would also be glorified. Jesus was always focused on His Father and doing His Father's will. He desired and prayed that all those the Father gave Him would know eternal life by knowing the Father and the Son, Jesus Christ. He also prayed that He would be glorified along with the Father with the glory He had even before the world existed, returning to that fullness of glory with His Father. Pleasing and glorifying His Father, as always, was at the heart of what Jesus did. What did Jesus pray for His disciples in John 17:6–19?

_____

_____

_____

One of the major concerns over which Jesus prayed was their walk in the world after He left them. Jesus gave His disciples the Word the Father had given Him, and they received those words, knowing they were absolute truth and full of life. Jesus made it clear in John 7:63 that the words He spoke *"are spirit and life,"* and Peter declared, *"You have words of eternal life."* Jesus prayed that the Father would protect the disciples and make them one through their relationship to the Father (*"keep them in Thy name"*) and that they would be guarded from the world system and from the evil one (Satan). Jesus desired that His followers know His joy as they walked in truth on a daily basis experiencing the sanctifying, purifying work of the Word of God. Then, walking in that joyous relationship with the Father and the Son, He prayed that as they were sent into the world, they would be marked by the truth He spoke to them and by the oneness He desired for them. Jesus not only prayed for those disciples present with Him that night, He also prayed for all those who would believe in Him through their word, through their testimonies, preaching, teaching, and writing. What did Jesus pray for and promise you and me, according to John 17:20–23?

_____

_____

_____

_____

What can all believers know with confidence according to John 17:24–26?

_____

_____

_____

_____

Jesus prayed that those who believe in Him based on the word of the first disciples would all be one. He desired for each one to know and experience the eternal life that He alone could give. That includes you and me and all who have believed the message of salvation through Jesus Christ alone. He promised to indwell believers, making them one with Himself and with one another, sharing that common life and love of the Son. Jesus then prayed that all His followers be with Him forever beholding His glory. He desired intensely that we experience the fullness of His glory as well as the fullness of His presence and His love forever.

After Jesus prayed what some have called His "High Priestly Prayer" in John 17, Jesus crossed over the Kidron Valley and entered into the Garden of Gethsemane on the west side of the Mount of Olives. Here we view His agony as never before seen.

📖 Read Matthew 26:36–38. What do you discover about Jesus in these verses?

_____

_____

Jesus came to Gethsemane to pray. Here, He truly faced the struggles of being a man. This was no insignificant exercise on the way to the cross. This was a battle—a grieving, distressing, agonizing battle—a battle that brought Him to the edge of death even there in the Garden. Jesus wanted His disciples there with Him to keep watch and to pray with Him. What a picture of His humility and His anguish.

📖 What was His first cry in the Garden according to Mark 14:35–36?

_____

_____

_____

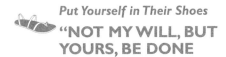

Put Yourself in Their Shoes
"NOT MY WILL, BUT YOURS, BE DONE

That has been the place to which God has brought many of His children. Abraham suggested to God that Eliezer or Ishmael could be counted as his heir, but God's will was for Abraham and Sarah to have a son named Isaac (see Genesis 15:2–4; 17:15–21). Jacob wrestled with the Angel of the Lord until all Jacob could do was hold on and receive God's will and blessing for his life—which included a limp in his walk from that day forward (see Genesis 32:24–32). Paul prayed three times for a thorn in the flesh to be removed, but God's will was for the thorn to remain and for Paul to discover the strength of God for his every weakness (see 2 Corinthians 12:7–10). God always wants us to pray the prayer His Son prayed, "nevertheless not my will, but Yours, be done" (Luke 22:42 NKJV).

PRAYER OF SURRENDER

Someone has expressed the prayer of surrender to God's will this way, "Father, Your will—nothing more, nothing less, nothing else." That attitude was the heart of Jesus, and should be the heartfelt attitude of His followers.

Jesus cried out to His Father, *"Abba! Father!"* the heart cry of a child in need. Jesus knew the Father could do anything, and, if possible, the Father could remove this cup of suffering. He knew He would face an agonizing separation from His Father as He paid for the sins of the world. Jesus, as always, revealed His strongest desire to only please the Father, *"not what I will, but what Thou wilt."*

📖 According to Matthew 26:40–46, what occurred after Jesus first prayed? What do you see about Jesus' prayer life?

_____

_____

_____

_____

After spending the first period of time in prayer, Jesus came back to where His disciples were and found them asleep. He urged them to watch with Him and to pray so that they would not enter into temptation. He went away and prayed as He did at first, again ending with, *"Thy will by done."* When He found His disciples asleep a second time, He went back and prayed a third time in the same way. He returned to find them sleeping once again, but He was ready to face His betrayer (Judas Iscariot) and the ordeal that lay before Him.

📖 Even though Jesus was betrayed, arrested, and underwent the gruesome pains of crucifixion, His praying did not stop. What do you discover in Luke 23:33–34?

_____

_____

_____

_____

_____

Did You Know?
ANSWERED PRAYER ON THE CROSS

While Jesus hung on the cross, He not only prayed for others, He also answered prayer. One of the thieves acknowledged Jesus as the King and asked Him to remember him when He arrived in His kingdom. Jesus replied, *"Truly, I say to you, today you shall be with Me in Paradise"* (Luke 23:39–43).

On the cross, Jesus looked down on those who had nailed him there, those who were gambling for His garments. Then, He prayed for them, *"Father, forgive them; for they do not know what they are doing."* Christ's compassion for mankind never ceased.

📖 What do you find in Matthew 27:45–50 and Luke 23:46?

_____

_____

_____

_____

_____

_____

After six hours on the cross, enduring the pain and the supernatural darkness that had been present from noon to three in the afternoon, Jesus cried out *"My God, My God, why have You forsaken Me?"* That was His agonizing cry of the separation He experienced bearing our sin, but it was also a cry that was looking to His Father to deliver Him. That is why He could pray with confidence, *"Father, into Thy hand I commit My spirit,"* knowing the Father had promised to resurrect Him. While on the cross He told John to take care of His mother, Mary, and He told the thief beside Him, *"this day you will be with Me in Paradise."* Perhaps these things along with all the events that accompanied the crucifixion that day caused one of the Roman leaders, a centurion in command of one hundred soldiers, to praise God declaring, *"Truly this was the Son of God"* and *"certainly this was a righteous Man"* (Matthew 27:54 and Luke 23:47 NKJV).

That Righteous Man truly was and is the Son of God who triumphed over sin and death. He lives today to live in us, to lead us in a walk with Himself and the Father by the power and presence of His Spirit. He wants us to experience the joy of that walk as He leads us in **praying God's way** and has assured us that we can experience joy by His power and work.

For Me to Follow Christ

W e have seen much about the prayer life of Jesus. Most remarkably, we have seen one who is the God-Man, the perfect Son of God, sinless, guileless, holy in every way, yet humbly and prayerfully dependent on His Father for every step of His earthly walk. He spent time in prayer as no one else has. He cried out to His Father as no one else has. He understands human need and divine provision as no one else has and today continues to intercede for us as no one else can. There is much we can learn from Him.

First, consider this truth—If Jesus spent time in prayer, then certainly we need to spend time in prayer and not make excuses for neglecting to pray. Below is an interesting article that I believe will prove to be helpful to you. Read this article and consider its meaning.

> Ours is a harder task than that which our fathers faced. Their conveniences and appliances were fewer, but they were not caught and often submerged in the rush of affairs as we are. We have many labor-saving and time-saving devices, but somehow we find it difficult to save time enough . . . for private meditation and prayer. . . . While we make our homes more beautiful externally than our fathers' with their limited means were ever able to do, can we make them also the abode of virtue, honor and love. . . ?

Does that sound like your life, your schedule, or your dilemma? Note this astounding fact: the paragraph quoted above appeared in a weekly Christian paper, the *Christian Observer* in the March 22, **1905** edition (page 7) as a reprint from another paper, the *Congregationalist*. Read it again. Have times changed? Perhaps. Have people changed? No! We make time **for what we think** is important.

Did You Know?

RESURRECTION PROMISES

Though some are veiled, some psalms and several prophecies speak of the resurrection and reign of the Messiah. In 1 Peter 1:10–12, we read how the prophets who *"predicted the sufferings of Christ and the glories to follow"* themselves *"made careful search and inquiry"* about these matters. Two are found in Psalm 22 and Isaiah 50. After speaking of many of the sufferings of the Messiah, Psalm 22:21c declares, *"You have answered Me,"* and Isaiah 50:9 adds, *"Surely the Lord God will help Me"* (NKJV). Jesus knew these truths and was confident His Father would raise Him from the dead.

Christ in Prayer | DAY FIVE

> *If Jesus spent time in prayer, then certainly we need to spend time in prayer and not make excuses for neglecting to pray.*

If there is anything Jesus' lifestyle should teach us, it is that we were never meant to "go it alone"—He prayed to His Father His entire life. He even urged His disciples to join Him in prayer at His hour of greatest need. We cannot nor should we even try to live the Christian life on our own power. We were made to be dependent. We came equipped with needs, needs that only our Father can meet and He has chosen humble, dependent, God-exalting prayer as one of the primary ways to meet those needs.

 We have seen . . .

➤ . . . We must **take time** to pray. Jesus did. **When** do you pray?

_____

When we consider our daily schedules or our future schedules, our needs now or upcoming, the needs of others, or how God wants to use us in His kingdom purposes, we must **make time to pray.** We need to pray over each of these areas. Are you spending some measure of time praying over these things? If not, why not start? If you don't have a set time or place, make one, and follow a pattern. (You may want to look back at Lesson 2, Day Five.)

➤ . . . When we face **major decisions**, we must devote **major time** to prayer. Jesus did. Are you facing any major decisions in your life? How will you focus prayer on that decision?

_____

_____

➤ . . . When we remember that Jesus lives in us by His Spirit to orchestrate our lives and our praying, we can be encouraged to know He will guide us in prayer **if** we will surrender daily, even moment-by-moment control to Him. Are you walking in the fullness and power of the Holy Spirit? Jesus did. Consider these truths: To experience the fullness of God's Spirit . . .

☑ Confess any and all sin to God. (Of course, Jesus was sinless and did not have to do this.) Confession is agreeing with God about sin; in other words, don't argue about it (see 1 John 1:9). Agreeing about the sin also means turning from it—repenting, not holding on to any part of it. When you agree with Him, you are walking in the fear of the Lord.

☑ Present yourself to God to be filled and controlled by His Spirit (see Romans 12:1–2). This means a heart and life yielded to Him. To surrender means to withhold nothing from Him.

☑ Ask Him in faith to fill you with His Spirit. He commanded us to be filled (controlled) in Ephesians 5:18, and so we know that is His will (see 1 John 5:14). He is not reluctant. Don't depend on feelings; depend on Him and His Word by faith. Expect Him to fill you as you obey His Word. Then walk in obedience to what He says.

Now let's think of how the Father wants us praying today. He wants us to come with confidence, with boldness, with humility, with an open heart to all He wants for us. We need to understand how openhearted He is and how open the way is to His throne.

Word Study
INTERCESSION

The Greek word, *entugchánō,* which is found in Romans 8:27, 34 and Hebrews 7:25, means, "to make intercession." Its fuller meaning is "to fall in with a person or to turn to or meet with a person, to come with free access on behalf of another" or even "to interrupt someone in speaking for the purpose of making a request for another." It means to make intercession for someone or to entreat on behalf of another. Romans 8:27 refers to the intercession of the Spirit on behalf of all the saints (all the followers of Christ). Romans 8:34 encourages us with the fact that Jesus Himself intercedes for us at the right hand of God the Father. Hebrews 7:25 speaks of Christ as our High Priest, forever making intercession for us.

📖 There are three passages that can help us understand our open access to the Father. These scriptures speak volumes of the triumph of Jesus' work on the cross and through His resurrection, and they speak of the ongoing work of the Father, the Son, and the Spirit on our behalf. Look at each of these and note the ongoing work of Jesus in particular. Summarize what you find.

Romans 8:31–34 (also note 35–39)

_____

_____

_____

_____

Hebrews 7:24–25

_____

_____

_____

_____

1 John 2:1–2

_____

_____

_____

_____

We can be confident of our relationship with the Father because He is _"for us"_ (Romans 8:31–34). He sent His Son to die for us, to give us His eternal life and multiplied blessings. We stand justified, not condemned. Jesus is at the right hand of God, a position of authority, power, and blessing. From that position, He intercedes for us. There He remains forever as our High Priest, not only opening the way to the Father, but keeping it open because of His sacrifice on the Cross then and because of His resurrection life now. His resurrection forever validates the adequacy of His life and death to bring us to the Father. He is now enthroned and _"always lives to make intercession for_ [us]_"_ (Hebrews 7:25). Jesus Christ is our advocate, defending us as if He were a benevolent trial lawyer determined to protect us against any accusations or charges. He, the Righteous One, is on our side, declaring our sins covered and paid for by His death and His blood. Such complete redemption is for anyone who comes to God the Father, trusting Him for salvation through the shed blood of His Son, Jesus Christ.

APPLY How should these truths affect your prayer life?

_____

_____

_____

_____

Jesus reigns as our loving Lord. He intercedes for us as our sympathetic High Priest. He defends us as our Righteous Advocate. He is for us! Therefore, the door is always open for praying God's way!

> **Jesus is for us and has opened the door for praying God's way!**

Jesus reigns as our loving Lord (see Romans 8:39)—there is none Higher. He intercedes as our sympathetic High Priest (see Hebrews 4:14–16; 7:24–25)—there is none more caring. He defends us as our righteous advocate (see 1 John 2:1–2)— there is none more righteous. We can come to the Father with confidence knowing we have open access made possible by the highest authority, encouraged by the most loving and caring High Priest, and guaranteed by the holiest judge. We do not have to make an appointment, wait for an appointment, nor fear having an appointment cancelled. We simply come and call on Him—humbly, open-hearted, dependent, surrendered, telling Him all that is on our hearts and minds, looking to Him to answer in His time, to accomplish His will His way. What a privilege we have! What a responsibility we have! What a joy we can have! Remember, He lives to lead us in **praying God's way**, so let's do that.

 Take some time to talk to your Father about what is on your heart, perhaps some issues concerning your walk or your wants or His will in your life. You may want to read and meditate on a passage of Scripture to help you focus your heart in prayer.

 Father, I thank You for sending Your Son, the Lord Jesus. Thank You that He always prayed Your will, and that He prayed for me! . . . that He is still interceding for me! Forgive me for my self-sufficient attitudes and actions. Thank You for providing forgiveness, cleansing, and an open door to the Father. Thank You for Your Word that guides me, teaches me, and focuses me in prayer. I praise You and thank You for being a loving Father and a compassionate Lord. Thank You for the way You give wisdom as I pray over my needs, as I face various trials, and as I pray for the needs and trials of others. I praise You that You are the Mighty and Victorious Warrior, able to win the battles I face. Thank You for placing me in Your Family, Your body of believers, and for teaching me about praying together with other believers. I praise You for praying for me, for continually interceding for me. I could never make it without You, but because of You, I am guaranteed to make it. Thank You! I pray with the Scriptures, *"Thanks be to God for His indescribable gift! . . . Thanks be to God, who gives us the victory through our Lord Jesus Christ. . . [I give thanks to You, Father, that You] qualified us to share in the inheritance of the saints in light. . . . Now to the King eternal, immortal, invisible, the only God, be honor and glory forever and ever. Amen."* (2 Corinthians 9:15, 1 Corinthians 15:57; Colossians 1:12; 1 Timothy 1:17)

This week we have sought to know what it means to live a life **praying God's way**. Think back over what God has shown you, how the Spirit has challenged you and changed you. Then, write your own prayer or make a journal entry in the space below.

_____

_____

_____

_____

_____

_____

_____

_____

The Prayer Life of Jesus

DATE	EVENTS	SCRIPTURE
Prophecy	The Father declared to His Son, *"Ask of Me, and I will surely give the nations as Thine inheritance."*	Psalm 2:8
Prophecy	Isaiah prophesied about the morning meeting between Jesus the Messiah and His Father. *"He awakens Me morning by morning."*	Isaiah 50:4
A.D. 7 ? Age 12	At the Temple, Jesus asked Mary and Joseph, *"Did you not know that I had to be in My Father's house,"* literally *"in the things of My Father,"* an indication Jesus had spent time in Scripture and in prayer with His Father.	Luke 2:49
A.D. 7–26? Age 12-30 In Nazareth	Jesus *"kept increasing in wisdom and stature, and in favor with God and men."* His relationship with His Father continued to grow as He grew in age and stature, indicating a continual prayer life.	Luke 2:51–52
All His life, to age 33	When Jesus came into the world, the prayer of His heart was to do the will of His Father, even to be the sacrifice offered once for all.	Hebrews 10:5–9; Psalm 40:6–8
A.D. 26 Age 30	When John the Baptist was baptizing Jesus at the Jordan River, Jesus was praying. *"While He was praying heaven was opened and the Holy Spirit descended upon Him in bodily form like a dove."*	Luke 3:21–22
A.D. 26	The Spirit led Jesus into the wilderness for a time (40 days) of fasting (and prayer) during which He was tempted by the devil.	Matthew 4:1–11; Mark 1:12–13; Luke 4:1–13
Early A.D. 28 Age 31	*"In the early morning, while it was still dark,"* Jesus *"arose and went out and departed to a lonely place, and was praying there"* (near Capernaum). This matches the prophecy of Isaiah 50:4 about the Father speaking to the Son *"morning by morning."*	Mark 1:35
A.D. 26-30 Age 30-33	Luke records a summary statement on the lifestyle of Jesus during His ministry years: *"He Himself would often slip away to the wilderness and pray."*	Luke 5:16
A.D. 27-30	Jesus often came to the Mount of Olives with His disciples *"as was His custom"* to a certain place, most likely the Garden of Gethsemane, to meet with His disciples and pray.	Luke 22:39–40; John 18:1–2
Summer A.D. 28 Age 31	Jesus spent the entire night in prayer after which He chose the twelve apostles.	Luke 6:12, 13–16
Spring A.D. 29 Age 32	When Jesus received the five loaves and two fish, He looked up toward heaven, and *"blessed the food"* (Matthew 14:19). John 6:11 adds, *"and having given thanks,"* Jesus began giving the food to the disciples. The disciples then distributed it to more than five thousand people (near Bethsaida).	Matthew 14:13–21; Mark 6:32–44; Luke 9:10–17; John 6:1–13
Spring A.D. 29	After feeding five thousand men (plus family members), Jesus sent His disciples across the Sea of Galilee. *"He went up to the mountain by Himself to pray; and when it was evening, He was there alone."*	Matthew 14:23; Mark 6:45–46; (see John 6:14–15)
Spring, A.D. 29	In the area of Decapolis, Jesus, again revealing His compassion for the multitudes, fed over four thousand people. He took seven loaves and some fish and gave thanks and blessed them, He began giving the food to the disciples to distribute. All had enough.	Matthew 15:32–39; Mark 8:1–10
Summer A.D. 29	Near Caesarea Philippi, Jesus was praying alone—with His disciples nearby. He then stopped and asked them, *"Who do the multitudes say that I am?"* This was just before Peter's confession of Jesus as the Christ, the Son of the Living God.	Luke 9:18–20; also Matthew 16:13–17
Summer A.D. 29	Jesus took Peter, James, and John *"and went up to the mountain to pray"* (Luke 9:28). This mountain was likely Mount Hermon. These three disciples witnessed the Transfiguration of Jesus.	Matthew 17:1; Mark 9:2; Luke 9:28
Summer A.D. 29	While Jesus was praying on the mountain, He was transfigured, and Elijah and Moses talked with Him. Then, in a cloud, the Father overshadowed Jesus and the three disciples and spoke, *"This is My Son, My Chosen One; listen to Him"* (Luke 9:35).	Matthew 17:1–8; Mark 9:2–8; Luke 9:29–36 2 Peter 1:16–17
Autumn A.D. 29	After the final day of the Feast of Tabernacles, Jesus went to the Mount of Olives (as He often did—[see Luke 22:39; John 18:1–2]) and apparently spent the night there, perhaps in prayer.	John 7:53; 8:1-2; also Luke 22:39–40; John 18:1–2

DATE	EVENTS	SCRIPTURE
Autumn A.D. 29	Jesus testified of time in prayer with the Father. *"The things . . . I heard from Him . . . I speak."* *"I speak . . . as the Father taught Me."*	John 5:19–20; 8:25–29; 12:49–50
Autumn A.D. 29	After the return of the Seventy from their mission, Jesus began to praise the Father for His work and His ways.	Luke 10:21–22; Matthew 11:25–27
Autumn A.D. 29	Once while Jesus was praying, *"after He had finished, one of His disciples"* requested, *"Lord, teach us to pray just as John also taught his disciples."*	Luke 11:1
Early A.D. 30	After Lazarus' death, Martha affirmed Jesus' life of prayer—*"whatever You ask of God, God will give You."*	John 11:22
Spring A.D. 30 Age 33	Some brought their children to Jesus *"so that He might lay His hands on them and pray; and the disciples rebuked them."* Jesus opened the way for the children and laid His hands on them.	Matthew 19:13–15
Days before Crucifixion	Jesus was troubled in soul and could have prayed, "Father, save Me from this hour." Instead He prayed, *"Father, glorify Thy name."*	John 12:27–33
Night before Crucifixion	Jesus assured Simon Peter that He had prayed for him that his faith would not fail when Satan tempted him and the other disciples. He encouraged him to strengthen his brothers.	Luke 22:31–32
Night before Crucifixion	Jesus promised His disciples He would *"ask the Father,"* and the Father would give them *"another Helper,"* the Holy Spirit.	John 14:16–17
Night before Crucifixion	Near the Temple and before going over the Brook Kidron and into Gethsemane, Jesus prayed His High Priestly Prayer to His Father.	John 17:1–26; 18:1
Night before Crucifixion	Jesus went with His disciples to the Garden of Gethsemane to pray. He then took Peter, James, and John with Him closer to His place of prayer. Jesus said *"My soul is deeply grieved, to the point of death; remain here and keep watch with Me"* (Matthew 26:38).	Matthew 26:36–38; Mark 14:32–34
Night before Crucifixion	Jesus prayed the first time, *"Abba! Father! All things are possible for Thee; remove this cup from Me; yet not what I will, but what Thou wilt"* (Mark 14:36). An angel appeared and strengthened Him. He continued praying in great agony, and *"His sweat became like drops of blood"* (Luke 22:44).	Matthew 26:39; Mark 14:35–36; Luke 22:41–44
Night before Crucifixion	Jesus came to His disciples and found them sleeping. He called them to watch and pray with Him. Then He prayed a second time, *"My Father . . . Thy will be done"* (Matthew 26:42).	Matthew 26:40–42; Mark 14:37–39; Luke 22:45-46
Night before Crucifixion	Jesus came to His disciples and found them sleeping a second time. He prayed a third time to His Father.	Matthew 26:43–44; Mark 14:40
Night before Crucifixion	Jesus came to His disciples and found them sleeping a third time. Judas then came and betrayed Jesus into the hands of the soldiers.	Matthew 26:45–46; Mark 14:41–42
Night before Crucifixion	Jesus *"offered up both prayers and supplications"* to His Father asking to be saved *"out of death"*—to be resurrected—and He was *"heard because of His piety"* or *"godly fear"* (NKJV).	Hebrews 5:7
Night before Crucifixion	Jesus made it clear that, if He chose, He could pray to His Father and the Father would send more than twelve legions of angels (72,000 angels) to deliver Him from the soldiers.	Matthew 26:53
Day of Crucifixion	Jesus prayed from the cross, *"Father, forgive them; for they do not know what they are doing."*	Luke 23:34
Day of Crucifixion	Jesus prayed from the cross, *"MY GOD, MY GOD, WHY HAST THOU FORSAKEN ME?"*	Matthew 27:46; Mark 15:33-36
Day of Crucifixion	After declaring, *"I am thirsty,"* and *"It is finished"* (John 19:28–30), Jesus prayed from the cross, *"Father, INTO THY HANDS I COMMIT MY SPIRIT."* Then Jesus *"breathed His last."*	Luke 23:46
Yesterday, Today, and Forever	Our resurrected Lord Jesus intercedes for us at the right hand of God. Jesus Christ the Righteous One is our advocate with the Father.	Romans 8:34; 1 John 2:1
Yesterday, Today, and Forever	Jesus, our High Priest, *"is able to save forever those who draw near to God through Him, since He always lives to make intercession for them"* (Hebrews 7:25).	Hebrews 7:25; 9:24

Christ, The I AM

CHRIST REVEALING HIMSELF AS THE ETERNAL GOD, LORD, AND SAVIOR

The first time Scripture reveals the Lord as the "I AM," we hear His words spoken to Moses, *"Do not come near here; remove your sandals from your feet, for the place on which you are standing is holy ground"* (Exodus 3:5). Moses *"hid his face, for he was afraid to look at God"* (3:6). So we too must approach the I AM with a serious and sober attitude, with a fear of God, with reverence and respect, and we must be ready to listen and obey. To surrender ourselves in the presence of the I AM is life changing, destiny changing. No self-exaltation or self-glory here, only God exaltation and God's glory. No self "agenda" here, only God's agenda. No stubborn self-will or insistence that our way be followed, only surrender to Him, His way, and His will. The Angel of the LORD, a revelation of Christ in the Old Testament, appeared to Moses in a burning bush and spoke His will for Moses and His people, Israel. When Jesus Christ the I AM speaks in the New Testament, we hear Him revealing His will for each of us personally and for His people corporately.

To Moses, God revealed His name—*"I AM THAT I AM,"* pointing to His self-existence, His eternal being, His self-sufficiency. God would be able to handle any obstacle and any opposition that Moses might encounter in dealing with Pharaoh and the Egyptians. He would lead Moses step by step in delivering His people out of Egypt into the land promised to Abraham, Isaac, and Jacob hundreds of years earlier. With an array of pictures, Jesus identifies Himself as the I AM, the Resurrection and the Life, the Good Shepherd, the True Vine. He spoke of Himself in this way on numerous occasions. Is there some significance in those words, "I AM"? If so, what is it? Does the meaning of those words or of that name speak to us today about obstacles and opposition to God's will like it spoke in Moses' day? What do these words, "I AM" mean for us today? How are we to relate to Jesus Christ as the I AM? We will explore these questions and many others in this lesson.

When Jesus Christ, the I AM, speaks in the New Testament, we hear Him revealing His will for each of us personally and for His people corporately.

As Christ opened the eyes and ears of His followers to reveal Himself as the I AM, so too our eyes and ears can open with new light and new insight as we search the pages of Scripture and walk before (and bow before) the I AM. Come along. Meet the I AM.

"I AM WHO I AM"

Exodus 3:14

THE I AM, OUR SOVEREIGN

God reveals Himself in many encounters throughout the Old Testament. What is significant about the revelation of God as the I AM? To Abraham, Isaac, and Jacob, He made Himself known as Yahweh/Jehovah (translated "LORD" and usually written in all capitals). Then, in Exodus 3:14, He gave to Moses the fuller revelation of Himself as *"I AM THAT I AM"* or *"I AM WHO I AM."* He linked that back to Abraham in the next verse, Exodus 3:15, *"Thus you shall say to the sons of Israel, 'The LORD* [YAHWEH/JEHOVAH], *the God of your fathers, the God of Abraham, the God of Isaac, and the God of Jacob, has sent me to you."* The same sovereign God, who revealed Himself as Lord in Genesis, revealed Himself to Moses and led in delivering Israel out of Egypt and into Canaan. He would ever be their God.

What is the significance of these revelations of His name? The name Yahweh translated *"LORD"* is related to the Hebrew word *hayah*, which means "to be" and is the root of "I AM." The emphasis in the name "Yahweh" and in the "I AM WHO I AM" is on God's self-existent being. He is the foundation of all being, the God who gives *"to all life and breath and all things"* (Acts 17:17). We could emphasize His name "I MYSELF **AM**" focusing on His everlasting being. He always "is"—ever the same, ever God. We could emphasize "I **MYSELF** AM" pointing to His ways and His holy nature—ever the consistent sovereign ruler, active in heaven and on earth, accomplishing His purposes according to Who He is. We can know He will always be who He has always been. His heart and character remain unchanged, His plans and purposes stay focused and firm. With those thoughts in place what else can we learn of God as the I AM?

📖 The prophet Isaiah exalts God for His person and for His purposes. Read these verses and record what you find about the Lord.

Isaiah 41:4

_____

_____

_____

_____

Isaiah 44:6

_____

_____

_____

_____

NONE BEFORE HIM

"You are My witnesses," declares the LORD, "and My servant whom I have chosen, in order that you may know and believe Me, and understand that I am He. Before Me there was no God formed, and there will be none after Me. I, even I, am the Lord; and there is no savior besides Me.... Even from eternity I am He...." (**Isaiah 43:10, 11, 13a**)

_____

_____

_____

_____

The Lord who has promised to care for Israel and be their God is the Lord, the "I am," declaring Himself as the first and the last, the one existing before the first generation and carrying all through to the last. He is God, the "I AM" before anything else existed, the everlasting, ever living God. There is no other. He is Lord and king whom none can overpower, the creator of the heavens and the earth, the creator of Israel, and the sovereign Lord over all.

When we turn to the pages of the New Testament, we find similar language coming from the Lord Jesus. John the Baptist was the first to testify of Him. He said in John 1:30 that Jesus *"existed before me,"* an amazing statement since Jesus was born six months **after** John was born (Luke 1:26, 36). What revelation did Jesus give to those whom He walked among? What can we learn from Him?

📖 Jesus understood very well who He was and what His Father sent Him to do. His understanding is made crystal clear in a confrontation recorded in John 8. Look at John 8:21–30. What did Jesus say about His relationship to His Father?

_____

_____

_____

Jesus continually appealed to His relationship with His Father to validate His person and His ministry. With two of His "hidden" I AM statements He made it clear who He was and where He came from—*"I am from above. . . . I am not of this world."* Unless the people believed this, that He is the "I AM," they would die in their sins. They did not understand what He meant. Jesus emphasized further that His Father had sent Him and everything He said He had received from His Father. When He would be lifted up, then they would recognize Jesus as the "I AM." Many began to believe His words, but not everyone did.

Many believed in part, but not wholly. Many continued to question Him.

📖 Read John 8:31–47? What is the mark of one who truly believes in Jesus according to verses 31–32?

_____

_____

_____

_____

The one who truly believes in Jesus abides in His word, listening to every detail, applying every aspect to daily living. When believers live this way, they understand the truth because they are taught of God. As a result, they begin to walk in the freedom Jesus promised instead of the bondage of lies.

Word Study
I AM

Ego eimí is translated *"I am"* throughout the New Testament. In this form, the words "I am" are emphatic. *Ego* is the word for "I" or "I myself." *Eimí* is often used without *ego* and is also translated *"I am"* but without the emphasis that *ego* adds. Emphasis is added when *ego* precedes *eimí* so that one can read "*I* (emphatic) am" or "I myself am." Jesus is quoted as saying *ego eimí* forty-eight times in the New Testament. His use of *eimí* alone is recorded ten times. The uses of *ego eimí* in the Septuagint (the Greek translation of the Old Testament) include the meeting with Moses in Exodus 3:14 as well as Isaiah 41:4, 10; 43:10 and 48:12.

What marked these who were arguing with Jesus? Note verses 37, 40, 42–43, 45–47 and summarize what you find.

_____

_____

_____

_____

Word Study
THE I AM BRINGS FREEDOM

Jesus, the I AM, brings freedom. Jesus spoke of His disciples hearing His Word and knowing His truth, and He promised they would walk in the freedom He alone could give. The Greek word translated *"make free"* in John 8:32 is *eleutheróō*, which points to "the truth" as a freeing agent in one's life. The emphasis of this word is on the clear manifestation of that freedom. Spiros Zodhiates points out in *The Complete Word Study Dictionary: New Testament,* "verbs which end in –oo generally indicate bringing out that which a person is or that which is desired" (AMG Publishers, p. 462). One who knows the truth will be shown to be free. He or she will walk showing that freedom; his or her redemption will be evident. In John 8, those to whom Jesus addressed made it clear that they were still enslaved to their sin and the lies of the devil, not free through faith in Jesus, the I AM.

The Jewish leaders who questioned Jesus' statements about being set free by His word had none of His word in them. They had no place in their hearts for Him or for what He said. They did not love Him or His word, the very truth of God. Instead, they wanted to kill Him, following the desires of their *"father the devil"* who was a liar and *"a murderer from the beginning."* They could not hear Jesus' word and would not keep His word.

These religious leaders continued to argue with Jesus, claiming their allegiance to Abraham. Jesus pointed out their inconsistencies and their unbelief. Then, He revealed further insight into who He was, as He focused on His relationship to Abraham. What do you discover in John 8:52–59?

_____

_____

_____

_____

These leaders did not understand what Jesus meant about believing His word and never seeing death. Abraham and the prophets died many centuries earlier. How could someone not die? Could Jesus be greater than them? Jesus responded by pointing first to His relationship to the Father and then to the fact that the Father would glorify Him and reveal His truthfulness and faithfulness to all generations. Jesus then focused attention on the fact that Abraham rejoiced to see His day—by faith Abraham had come to understand something of the coming Messiah, and he believed and rejoiced in that truth. To the continued unbelief of those standing before Him Jesus boldly declared, *"before Abraham was born* [literally, "came into being"], *I AM."* The Jews understood exactly what He meant and picked up stones to execute Him for claiming to be the I AM, but Jesus escaped from them.

"Before Abraham was, I am."

John 8:58 (NKJV)

📖 Jesus maintained His testimony of being the sovereign I AM throughout His ministry. The night before His crucifixion, His words were clear. Read the account of Jesus in the Garden of Gethsemane found in John 18:1–11. Summarize what you find.

_____

_____

_____

_____

Specifically what happened when Jesus declared, *"I AM"* in verse 6? What insights do you see in this event?

_____

_____

_____

When Jesus had finished praying to His Father in Gethsemane, He went to face the Roman soldiers, the officers of the chief priests and the Pharisees along with Judas, a crowd of hundreds. With their weapons and lanterns, Jesus faced them and asked plainly, *"Whom do you seek?"* When they said, *"Jesus the Nazarene,"* He declared, *"I am He"* or literally, "I AM." The force of His statement revealed the fact of His authority. *"They drew back, and fell to the ground."* He asked again, *"Whom do you seek?"* and they replied, *"Jesus the Nazarene."* Jesus then responded, *"I told you that I am He. . . ."* or "I told you that I AM." As He asked that His disciples be free to go, Peter drew a sword and cut off the ear of the high priest's slave. Jesus stopped Peter, who did not comprehend the power nor the plan of the I AM to fulfill all His Father's will. After that, they carried Jesus away.

📖 As He was tried that night, He continued to clearly reveal Himself. Read Mark 14:53–65 and record your insights into His statement found in verse 62.

_____

_____

_____

_____

In this second of three Jewish trials, the Jewish leaders sought to dig up some evidence with which to condemn Jesus. When Caiaphas the high priest asked, *"Are You the Christ, the Son of the Blessed One?"* Jesus replied plainly, **"I AM**; *and you shall see* THE SON OF MAN SITTING AT THE RIGHT HAND OF POWER AND COMING WITH THE CLOUDS OF HEAVEN" (emphasis added). With that statement, they falsely condemned Jesus to death, not believing He was the I AM.

Jesus not only stated that He was the I AM, our sovereign ruler, He proved it in His death and resurrection. He was also the I AM, our Savior. We will see more of this truth in Day Two.

> *"The high priest asked Him . . . 'Are You the Christ, the Son of the Blessed One?' And Jesus said, 'I am.'"*
>
> **Mark 14:61–62**

THE I AM, OUR SAVIOR

Christ, The I AM DAY TWO

While Jesus continued to reveal Himself to His disciples, He gave them several different word pictures that described Him and His mission. Some were very clear to the disciples, some not as clear. In Jesus' "I AM" statements, we find some of these descriptions. In today's lesson, we will focus on those statements in which Jesus pointed to Himself as **the Life** (Greek—*zoē*), each time emphasizing the specific life Christ gives. This life is always far beyond mere existence. It is God's life, eternal life, given by the I AM, our Savior.

📖 As Jesus ministered, the crowds began gathering in greater numbers to hear Him. John 6:1–14 records one occasion when a multitude began to gather near the shores of the Sea of Galilee. Jesus saw the need to feed them. What did He ask Philip according to verse 5? Why did He ask such a question (verse 6)?

_____
_____
_____
_____
_____
_____

Put Yourself In Their Shoes
JESUS' AUTHORITY

When Jesus was arrested in the Garden of Gethsemane, Peter grabbed a sword ready to fight. He cut off the ear of the high priest's servant. Jesus quickly stopped Peter, healed the ear and then pointed out that He could *"appeal to My Father"* and immediately have at His disposal *"more than twelve legions of angels."* A legion consisted of 6,000 troops. The cohort of Roman soldiers that came to arrest Jesus consisted of 600 troops. It could be that Jesus was revealing His overwhelming ability and authority to deal forcefully with this arrest if He so chose. Why twelve legions? He was speaking to Peter and perhaps He was saying He could provide more than enough angelic troops—at least one for Himself and one for each of the Eleven (Judas was no longer one of them). If that is so, each legion would outnumber the Romans ten to one. In any case, Jesus made it clear who was in charge—not the Romans, not the priests, not the Pharisees, but the I AM, our Savior, who willingly gave His life on the Cross. That stands as word of counsel and comfort, not only to Peter but to each of us.

"I am the bread of life."

John 6:35, 48

What did Jesus then do?

_____
_____
_____

As we have seen in other instances, Jesus knew what to do because of His constant communion with the Father. He asked Philip about feeding the crowds in an effort to test Philip, to see what he understood of Him and His ways. All the disciples could see was a lad's lunch. Jesus took that small lunch, gave thanks, then miraculously multiplied it and fed the crowd of five thousand men (plus five thousand to ten thousand women and children) and had twelve baskets left over! When the people saw what Jesus had done, they concluded that this was The Prophet about whom Moses had spoken.

Jesus left the crowds, not wanting them to force His hand to become king. He sent His disciples across the Sea of Galilee to Capernaum and later reunited with them in rather dramatic fashion by walking on top of the water to their boat (John 6:15–25). The next day the crowds were eager to see Jesus again. What words did Jesus have for their seeking hearts in John 6:26–27?

_____
_____
_____

What did He want from them according to verse 29?

_____
_____
_____

What did they want from Jesus? Record your insights from the interaction with Jesus found in John 6:30–35?

_____
_____
_____
_____

What potential problem did Jesus address in John 6:35–36? What did He require for someone to know His life?

_____
_____
_____

Jesus knew their hearts—they wanted free food, lots of free bread. He immediately focused their attention on the eternal dimension—He taught them they should seek from the Son of Man eternal life, not temporal bread. What work could they do to see God's miraculous works (and most likely get fed in the process)? Jesus again pointed to Himself and called them to believe Him—believe that He was sent from the Father and could give eternal life. They could not get their eyes off the possibility of food; hence they peppered Jesus with questions along the line of, "Where is some more bread like the manna our fathers ate?" Jesus said in essence, 'The Father is giving you bread out of heaven so you can have the life of heaven, eternal life.' They wanted this bread, but did not understand that Jesus **is** the Bread of Life and was standing before them ready to feed and quench their spiritual hunger and thirst. Their problem was unbelief. If only they would **come to Him, believe in Him,** and stop trying to get something **from Him,** something temporal and perishing.

What does it mean to know and experience the Bread of Life according to John 6:37–51, especially verses 47–51?

_____

_____

_____

_____

What is the promise Jesus gives in John 6:57–58 in spite of the confusion and debate of the crowd?

_____

_____

Jesus made clear statements about Himself again and again—*"I am the bread of life"*; *"I am the bread that came down out of heaven"*; *"I am the living bread."* That "bread" He spoke of was His flesh, His body that would be broken and given on the cross for the sins of the world. To all who received Him and what He did for their sins, Jesus promised eternal life. To any who would believe in Him—see Him for who He claimed to be and come to Him in whole-life trust, His life would become a living reality. The Father was at work drawing people to His Son, calling them, revealing truth to them. As anyone listened to the Father, received what He taught, and came to Jesus, that person would find Him to be the Bread that truly feeds the soul forever.

Many disciples (there were more than just the traditional twelve) did not understand, and many of these walked away from Jesus that day. Jesus talked to those who remained. He focused their attention on the eternal dimension—who He was and what He was doing and saying. He taught them that He would one day ascend back to heaven. To know Him and one day join Him there would take the work of the Spirit, giving eternal life. The flesh and all the bread in the world are of no benefit, of no profit in heaven, and they impart no spiritual reality. Therefore, we are to believe His words—they are spirit and life. They go beyond the temporal and impart eternal benefit (John 6:60–64). In spite of these teachings of Christ, some refused to believe.

Word Study
"THE LIFE"

In three of the "I AM" statements, Jesus spoke of "the Life"—the Bread of Life, the Resurrection and the Life, and the Way, the Truth, and the Life. The Greek language in each of these descriptions is emphatic, using the Greek article in each case (Greek—*he zoē,* "the Life"). This intensifies the meaning of "the Life" of which Jesus spoke. In addition, the Greek word *zoē* indicates a higher life than *bios,* a second Greek word translated "life." *Bios* focuses more on simple existence, the details and daily manner of life (see Mark 12:44; Luke 8:14; 1 Timothy 2:2; 2 Timothy 2:4). *Zoē* speaks more of the life of spirit and soul. It is "the Life" Jesus gives, everlasting or eternal life (see Matthew 7:14; John 3:15, 16, 36; Romans 6:4; Ephesians 4:18; 2 Peter 1:3). It is used in *"the tree of life"* (Revelation 22:2), *"the water of life"* (Revelation 21:6; 22:1), the *"aroma from life"* (2 Corinthians 2:16), and the *"life"* possessed by *"the Word"* Jesus and by the Father (John 1:4; 5:26; 1 John 1:1–2). The Spirit gives this *"life"* (John 6:63). All who come to Jesus believing in Him are given this *"eternal life."*

> ### "Lord, to whom shall we go? You have words of eternal life. And we have believed and have come to know that You are the Holy One of God."
>
> ### John 6:68–69

📖 What would the Twelve do? Would they walk away? How did Peter respond to Jesus' question concerning this? Look at John 6:67–69 and record what you find.

_____

_____

_____

_____

To the Lord's question, Simon Peter responded, *"Lord, to whom shall we go? You have words of eternal life. And we have believed and have come to know that You are the Holy One of God."* It was evident that they had *"heard and learned from the Father"* (6:45) and therefore believed in Jesus, all except Judas who later walked away from Jesus and betrayed Him. These eleven men truly believed in Jesus and proved it with their lives.

📖 The Father continually provided opportunities to reveal His Son as the I AM. We find another instance in John 11. Read the account of Lazarus in John 11:1–46. When Jesus arrived in Bethany, what were His first words to Martha (verse 23)?

_____

_____

_____

_____

What was the guarantee of those words according to verses 25?

_____

_____

_____

How could a person receive eternal life according to verses 25–26?

_____

_____

_____

> ### "I am the resurrection and the life."
>
> ### John 11:25

📖 Look at John 11:27. What was Martha's testimony about Jesus?

_____

_____

_____

When Jesus first saw Martha, He confidently declared, *"Your brother shall rise again."* As in other instances, Jesus began focusing attention on His gift of eternal life, a life beyond the ordinary, daily, physical existence on earth. Jesus promised that Lazarus would rise from the dead to which Martha readily agreed. (She thought Jesus was referring to the resurrection of the dead in the latter days.) Jesus then pointed to the present day. Standing before her He said, *"I AM the Resurrection and the Life"* (emphasis added). To know Him and the life He gives takes simple but wholehearted belief in Him. Martha confessed her belief in Jesus as the Messiah, the Son of God, and The Coming One (a messianic title).

📖 According to John 11:39–44, how did Jesus reveal His resurrection-and-life power that particular day?

_____

_____

_____

_____

Jesus had more to reveal to Martha, Mary, and to the rest of the people surrounding Jesus and this precious family. He went to the tomb of Lazarus and commanded people to remove the stone that sealed the entrance. Martha, of course, did not understand why the stone should be removed. Jesus urged her to believe Him. He prayed that those standing there would believe that the Father sent Him, that He was who He said He was. Then He called Lazarus to *"come forth,"* and to everyone's astonishment, Lazarus did exactly what he was told! Many who witnessed this miracle were persuaded to believe in Jesus as the Messiah, the Christ. Others still walked in their futile, fleshly opinions. Amazingly, some even wanted to see Jesus killed.

📖 The night before Jesus was crucified, He revealed yet another aspect of his saving work as the I AM. Read the account in John 14:1–11. What did He promise in verses 1–4?

_____

_____

_____

_____

What question filled Thomas' mind, according to verse 5?

_____

_____

After the event commonly referred to as "Last Supper" took place (see John 13), Jesus began talking to His disciples about leaving, going to His Father's house. He promised them He would prepare them a place there and return to receive them to Himself to live together forever. He assured them they knew the way; however, they did not yet fully understand His words—about **where** He was going or **the Way** there. They wanted to be clear about this Way of which He spoke.

📖 What did Jesus reveal about Himself to all of them in answer to Thomas' question in John 14:6–7? Read those verses and record your insights.

_____

_____

_____

_____

"I am the way, the truth, and the life."

John 14:6

To Jesus' statement about seeing the Father, Philip offered a question. What insights do you glean from his question and Jesus' reply in John 14:8–11?

_____

_____

_____

_____

_____

> "Jesus said . . . He who has seen me has seen the Father. . . . Believe Me that I am in the Father, and the Father in Me."
>
> John 14:9, 11

Jesus made Himself clear, "**I AM <u>the</u> Way**, _and_ <u>the</u> **Truth**, _and_ <u>the</u> **Life**; _no one comes to the Father but through Me_" (emphasis added). He is the way to the Father, the truth about the Father and reveals and gives the life of the Father to any who come to Him. Through knowing Jesus, we can know the Father. Jesus reveals the Father and makes Him real to us. Jesus told His disciples that they had already seen the Father. Philip questioned Jesus regarding His puzzling statement—after all, he did not recall any of them seeing the Father, though he was certain they wanted to do so. Jesus again emphasized His oneness with the Father—"_He who has seen Me has seen the Father._" His words were the Father's words. His works were the Father's works. In Jesus' earthly existence, His labor, and in all He said, He gave a clear explanation of the Father—His perfect will and His pure ways.

In all His statements about Himself as the I AM, Jesus revealed Himself as the Savior who gives eternal Life—He is the Bread of Life, the Resurrection and the Life, the Way, the Truth, and the Life. He is about life and giving life. In the original manuscripts of this passage of Scripture, a precise word for "Life" is used. It is the Greek word _zoē,_ which focuses on the life of the spirit and soul. The use of _zoē_ tells us that the Life Jesus speaks of here is more than just an existence. It is relational life, moral life, a higher level of life. Jesus came to guide us into His more abundant life.

APPLY Are you experiencing the Life Jesus gives? Simon Peter's question rings through the ages, "_Lord, to whom shall we go?_" We, like Peter, must acknowledge, "_You have words of eternal life._" If you have not come to know the eternal life that Jesus alone gives, now is the time. If you know Jesus as your Lord and Savior, is He real in your daily experience? Are you walking and talking with Him? Is He the "I AM" where you live? Is there someone you know who needs to come to Him and find life everlasting? Pray for them and tell them about Him.

Jesus is not only the I AM in the sense that He is our Savior, the eternal God who saves to the fullest; He is also the I AM in the sense that He protects us as the Good Shepherd. We will see how in Day Three.

DAY THREE

THE I AM, OUR SHEPHERD

A shepherd guides his flock. He guards and protects each one. He also feeds and nourishes the flock and rejoices in the fruits of his labor, foods produced from the flock such as milk and cheese and wool for making clothing. In the New Testament, Jesus revealed Himself as the Good

Shepherd. Understanding those words and listening to some of His related statements will help us profit today as we walk with the I AM, our Shepherd.

📖 What does it take to find your way on an unfamiliar path? One of the essentials is light. Jesus knew that and had some things to say about light. Read John 8:12–20 and record your insights from the words of Jesus.

_____

_____

_____

_____

To those walking in spiritual darkness and desperately needing someone to guide them, Jesus proclaimed Himself as the Light of the world. He promised, *"He who follows Me shall not walk in the darkness, but shall have the light of life."* He said this immediately after the close of the Feast of Tabernacles, the Autumn feast that celebrated the harvest and recalled the faithfulness of God in bringing the children of Israel through the Wilderness, led by the Pillar of Fire.

During this feast, in the Court of the Women in the Temple, four great lamps were lit at night to the sounds and sights of the people and priests singing and praising the Lord. In addition, they all knew the story of how the Lord had led them out of Egypt and into the Promised Land with a pillar of cloud by day and a pillar of fire by night. The celebration at the Temple recalled the light of His leading. It is quite possible that Jesus is capitalizing on their knowledge of this Exodus experience as He related to them that He was indeed *"the Light of the world."* Scripture shows that Christ was actually manifested in the pillar of cloud and fire that led the children of Israel through the wilderness after they departed Egypt. The Angel of the LORD, the pre-incarnate manifestation of Christ in the Old Testament, was the one who first appeared to Moses through the "burning bush" and also appeared to Israel in the Pillar of Fire that led them thereafter. Jesus wanted all to know they could now be led with *"the light of life,"* God's kind of life, and they no longer needed to walk in spiritual darkness.

The Pharisees refused to believe Him and for all intents and purposes called Him a liar—*"Your witness is not true."* Jesus made it clear that His witness about Himself and about His Father was absolutely true. Another incident would soon occur to point people to Him as the Light of the world. We find it in John 9.

📖 What additional insights about Jesus as the Light of the world do you glean from Jesus' encounter in John 9:1–11?

_____

_____

_____

_____

As Jesus was walking in Jerusalem, He and His disciples saw a man blind from birth. The disciples questioned Jesus about the man and revealed a false belief held in that day—they thought if someone was born blind or with some other defect, it meant that either the child or his parents had com-

Doctrine
JESUS, THE PROPHESIED LIGHT

When Jesus proclaimed, *"I AM the light of the world"* (John 8:12; 9:5), He was identifying Himself as the fulfillment of Old Testament and New Testament prophecies. Isaiah 42:6–7 speaks of the Lord bringing forth the Messiah *"as a light to the nations, to open blind eyes, to bring out prisoners from the dungeon, and those who dwell in darkness from the prison"* (See also Isaiah 49:6). In the New Testament, Simeon prophesied over the infant Jesus at the Temple, *"For my eyes have seen Thy salvation. . . . A LIGHT OF REVELATION TO THE GENTILES, and the glory of Thy people Israel"* (Luke 2:30, 32). Jesus used similar words when He commissioned the apostle Paul for his ministry of opening eyes that they might turn to the light and receive forgiveness through faith in Jesus (Acts 26:18).

"I am the light of the world."

John 8:12

mitted some sin causing this. Jesus saw things God's way. He revealed that this man's blindness was not the result of a sin problem. In the providence and mystery of God's will, God allowed the man's blindness to display His powerful works. Jesus had come to do those works of God while the opportunities were at hand, while the day remained. Night would soon come. Jesus knew He was the Light of the world and the world needed His works of light. As at Creation when Christ first brought light to the world and then to Adam's eyes after shaping him from clay, so now Jesus made clay from some dirt mixed with His spit and placed it on this man's eyes. After this man washed his eyes, he suddenly was able to see. His neighbors could not believe it, but the man continued to testify about what Jesus had done.

Read the remainder of the account in John 9:13–41 and summarize what you find. Why do you think Jesus spoke of Himself as the Light of the world? How did He bring light to this man and what difference did it make?

_____

_____

_____

_____

Jesus performed this miracle of sight on a Sabbath, so the Pharisees were upset and tried to dismiss the man and the miracle. They considered Jesus "a sinner" but the man continued to give bold testimony to the fact that Jesus had healed him. (The man's parents validated this as a legitimate miracle.) Trying to squelch the excitement that was ensuing, the Pharisees finally kicked the man out of the synagogue. When Jesus found him, He asked him if he believed in the Son of Man (a messianic title). He then revealed Himself as that Son of Man, and the restored man joyously believed and worshiped Jesus. As the Light of the world, Jesus came to bring spiritual sight to the spiritually blind who also have been "blind" from birth. He came to guide them into the truth and to show those who think they have sight and have no need of Him that they indeed remain blind in their sin. Without His Light, all is darkness. What more can we learn about Jesus as our shepherd and guide? The next verses in John reveal even more about the I AM.

📖 Jesus continued talking to the Pharisees and any others who would listen. He began talking about sheep. Read John 10:1–10. What **picture** did Jesus give first in His "I AM" statements (verses 7, 9)? What **promise** went with that picture (verse 9)?

_____

_____

_____

"I am the door of the sheep."

John 10:7

According to John 10:9–10, what problem could Jesus handle for any sheep that would follow Him?

_____

_____

_____

_____

Jesus described a typical day in the life of sheep—they have a sheepfold into which there is one door or gate. The shepherd calls the sheep by name and leads them in and out to pasture through that door. They follow him because they know him and his voice. The sheep run from any other who tries to lead them. Thieves must steal the sheep to get them out of the sheepfold. The sheep will not follow a stranger once they know the shepherd's voice. Those listening to Christ's analogy did not understand. Therefore, Jesus painted a clearer picture by saying, *"I am the door of the sheep,"* promising His care for His own. He would guide, guard, and nourish those who belong to Him. Sheep have one problem: they can easily stray or be harmed by any number of thieves and robbers who *"steal, and kill, and destroy."* One application of this truth concerns the devil, who is **the** thief and destroyer, as his names indicate. He is called Satan in numerous scriptures (meaning "adversary"), Apollyon in Revelation 9:11 (meaning "destroyer"), and *"a murderer"* (John 8:44), and those who follow his lies act his way. Jesus is the Good Shepherd who came to give total protection and abundant life forever.

📖 How would Jesus take care of the problems facing the sheep according to John 10:11–18? Who did He declare Himself to be in those verses?

_____

_____

_____

_____

> ## *"I am the good shepherd."*
> ## John 10:14

📖 What additional insights do you glean about the relationship between the sheep and Jesus and His Father according to John 10:25–30?

_____

_____

_____

_____

Jesus emphatically declared his protective qualities in His *"I am the door"* statement, but He also declared, *"I am the good shepherd,"* who cares for the sheep, even laying down his life to protect them. Jesus assured His listeners that He personally knows each of His sheep and they know Him, even as the Father and the Son know one another in a heart-to-heart relationship. As Jesus listens to and follows His Father, so His sheep listen to and follow Him. He would one day lay down His life as the Father commanded and thus assure eternal life to His sheep. His sheep are forever safe in His hand and in the Father's hand, a picture of detailed care and double security.

Jesus is the I AM—the Light of the World, the Door of the Sheep, and the Good Shepherd—who shepherds His people, guiding, guarding, nourishing them so they flourish in His abundant life. As He guides, He also sustains. We will see theses truths in Day Four.

THE I AM, OUR SUSTAINER

Jesus is the I AM, the self-existent One, the One who stands as Sovereign, who is our perfect Savior and who guides us as the Good Shepherd. As we follow Him, we find He is able to give us the wisdom, power, and grace we need for each set of circumstances, for each difficult situation. The disciples found that to be true in many ways. They discovered that He is the I AM, our Sustainer. In today's study we will see these truths more clearly.

📖 In Matthew 14:22–33 (also Mark 6:45–52; John 6:16–21), just after Jesus fed five thousand men and many more women and children, we find Him instructing His disciples to cross over the Sea of Galilee by boat ahead of Him. The events that were about to unfold would be yet another revelation of the great I AM. Read the account in Matthew and summarize what you find.

_____

_____

_____

_____

Look at Matthew 14:27 again. It is one of the hidden "I AM" statements of Jesus. Where did He focus their attention?

_____

_____

_____

> ## "Take courage, I AM; do not be afraid."
>
> ### Matthew 14:27 (literal translation)

Around 6:00 P.M., the disciples headed across the Sea of Galilee by boat, while Jesus went to a nearby mountain to pray. As the disciples journeyed across the sea, a strong wind struck, and they battled the relentless waves for hours. All the while, Jesus, aware of their plight, came walking on the water some time between 3:00 and 6:00 A.M. ("the fourth watch"). When they saw this ghastly visage, they were terrified. Immediately, Jesus responded, _"Take courage, it is I; do not be afraid."_ More literally He said, _"Take courage, I AM_ [Greek—_ego eimi_]; _do not be afraid."_ He was the Sovereign who could sustain them in the storm. Peter eagerly responded that he, too, wanted to walk on water and come to Jesus. Jesus commanded, _"Come!"_ and Peter walked on the water for a moment and then began to sink, pleading, _"Lord, save me!"_ Jesus immediately reached out and rescued Peter, and together they walked back to the boat. The wind suddenly stopped, and John 6:21 tells us, _"and immediately the boat was at the land."_ The disciples sat in awe of Jesus as they saw the power of one who could sustain them in the storm and then cause the storm to cease.

What added insights do you glean from Jesus' words to Peter in Matthew 14:31 and the comment about all the disciples in Mark 6:51–52?

_____

_____

_____

_____

Jesus pointed to Peter as one of *"little faith"* and questioned why he doubted. The term *"little faith"* is translated from *distazo*, a word picturing being pulled in two ways. In this case, Peter saw Jesus and the wind and the waves, yet doubted Him and His power. In the feeding of the five thousand men (not counting women and children), the disciples failed to learn the lesson of the loaves: Jesus is the sustaining I AM, able to provide more than enough bread and capable of protecting in the fiercest of storms.

📖 As Jesus walked with His disciples to the Garden of Gethsemane the night before He was crucified, He spoke to them about His sustaining ministry in their lives. Read John 15:1–8. What "I AM" statement do you find in these verses?

_____

_____

_____

_____

What is to be the relationship between the Vine and the branches? What can the branch do apart from the Vine according to verse 5?

_____

_____

_____

📖 What instructions did Jesus give His disciples on **how** to be a sustained branch? Record what you discover in John 15:7, 9, and 10.

_____

_____

_____

_____

📖 What are the results of the sustaining power of the Vine according to John 15:4–5, 8, and 11?

_____

_____

_____

Did You Know?

THE VINE AND THE TEMPLE

Adorning the four columns at the entry leading into the Holy Place in Herod's Temple in Jerusalem was an elaborate and beautiful golden vine. It was a symbol of Israel as God's vine (Psalm 80:8; Isaiah 5:7; Jeremiah 2:21; Hosea 10:1). The prophets often lamented the corrupt fruit of disobedience produced by the vine, Israel. It is possible that Jesus and the disciples passed by the Temple and could have seen that golden vine shining in the full moon of Passover. That night, Jesus pointed to Himself as the True Vine that produces righteous fruit which glorifies the Father. He called the disciples to abide in Him to see that same fruit manifested in their lives (John 15:1–8).

"I am the true vine."

John 15:1

As Jesus walked with the disciples from the place where they held their last supper together all the way to the Garden of Gethsemane, He focused attention on their relationship to Him—*"I AM the true vine."* He wanted them to understand they were like branches linked to Him and from Him they could receive His sustaining and abundant fruit-producing life. Apart from Him, nothing would come; nothing would be accomplished that truly mattered. Only in an abiding relationship could genuine fruit be borne. Such a relationship includes listening carefully and allowing His words to abide in the heart. Such listening in turn leads to God-pleasing prayer and God-given answers. The Father's kind of fruit is borne in such a relationship, and His fruit brings recognition and glory to Him. Therefore, an abiding relationship is a walk—a walk of obedient love, abiding in His love through obeying His word. This results in Jesus' kind of joy filling the life of a disciple.

Jesus promised His continued sustaining ministry after His resurrection. Read Matthew 28:18–20, what is commonly called "the Great Commission." What do you discover about the sustaining work of Jesus the I AM in those verses?

_____

_____

_____

_____

As the I AM, the resurrected Jesus could claim *"all authority . . . in heaven and on earth"* and with that authority He commanded His followers to *"make disciples of all the nations."* This involved evangelizing, baptizing, and teaching obedience to all He commanded. His promise: *"I AM with you always,"* literally, *"all the days."* The sovereign I AM is with us to save, to sustain, and to shepherd **always** and **everywhere**.

📖 Paul the Apostle experienced this sustaining ministry in *"all the nations"* to which Jesus led him. Read Acts 18:1–11 and record what you find about Jesus' work in the life of the Apostle Paul.

_____

_____

_____

_____

Note the hidden "I AM" (Greek—*ego eimí*) in verse 10. What significance do you find in this message to Paul? What did Paul do as a result, according to verse 11?

_____

_____

_____

_____

Paul left Athens (Acts 17) and traveled to Corinth where he joined Aquila and Priscilla in their tent-making trade and proclaimed the Scriptures in the synagogue every Sabbath. After Silas and Timothy came with financial support from the churches of Macedonia, Paul devoted his time *"completely to the word"* teaching and preaching the message about Jesus, the Messiah. However, the Jews resisted his message, and Paul began focusing on the Gentiles in Corinth, using the house of Titius Justus as a meeting place. Apparently, Paul faced a measure of opposition from the Jews and perhaps even from some of the Greeks. The Lord appeared to him in a vision encouraging him to not fear, but to speak boldly. How could he do this? The I AM would be with him, sustaining him, giving him power and protection. The Lord promised him many in Corinth would come to Christ. Paul let that word abide in his heart, and he obeyed, settling in and *"teaching the word of God among them."*

📖 We find the Lord Jesus speaking to the apostle John many years later. Again, Jesus revealed Himself as the I AM, our Sustainer. Read Revelation 1:9–19 and summarize what you find.

Put Yourself In Their Shoes
PAUL KNEW THE "I AM"

Jesus appeared to Saul (later known as Saul) on the road to Damascus in a blinding light that stopped Saul in his tracks. He revealed Himself to Saul, *"I am Jesus, whom you are persecuting,"* and *"I am Jesus the Nazarene"* (Acts 9:5; 22:8; 26:15). That encounter forever changed this man. Even his name changed from Saul to Paul. More importantly, he had a new heart, a new destiny, and a new ministry and mission of telling others about this Jesus, the "I AM." Do you know Him? Are you telling others about Him where you are?

_____

_____

_____

_____

Not only does Jesus reveal Himself as the I AM, our Sustainer in this chapter, but He also reveals Himself to John as the resurrected Lord, the sovereign I AM. Jesus appeared in majestic glory, clothed in readiness for judgment. His white hair speaks of His wisdom and honor. His flaming eyes speak of His piercing, discerning gaze able to judge with ultimate accuracy. His feet of burnished bronze show Him ready to walk in evaluation of the churches, and His voice is ready to speak with all authority and power, the power of the two-edged sword of judgment. John saw His brilliant, white face shining like the sun, like the holy, awesome Shekinah glory in the Old Testament Tabernacle. This is the living Son of Man, the I AM, the first and the last, triumphant over death and Hades. If He is able to conquer death and Hades, He is able to handle any lesser problem as well.

What specific word of encouragement and comfort does Jesus give John in verse 17?

_____

_____

What specific instruction does Jesus give him in verse 19?

_____

_____

Imprisoned on the Island of Patmos in the Aegean Sea off the coast of modern day Turkey, John saw the Lord Jesus and fell in great fear. The Lord laid His right hand (the hand of blessing) on John and commanded him, _"Do not be afraid"_ (literally, "stop being afraid"). Then He encouraged him, _"I am the first and last, and the living One"_ who can handle everything from first to last and all in between. Jesus called John to _"write therefore"_ all he had seen (the revealed Christ in 1:1–18), all _"the things which are"_ (the churches in Revelation 2:1–3:22), and the things yet future (Revelation 4:1—22:21). As the Lord called Paul to speak the message where God placed him, so He called John to write a message where God placed him. He would be with John to carry through all His will.

 What storms or fears are you facing? The I AM specializes in dealing with storms and fears, all the obstacles that try to get in the way of His will. He is sovereign over them and works His will in the midst of them. For the storms of sin He is the I AM, our Savior. He wants us to tell that message to others, to make disciples who follow Jesus, the I AM. For the fears of misdirection and confusion, He is the I AM, our Good Shepherd, able to guide the most wayward sheep in the right way. For the situations all around us—He is the I AM, our sustainer who calls to us, _"Do not fear, I AM"_ and asks us to believe He will sustain us and accomplish His will. Bring your situations to Him in prayer. Follow the I AM.

We began this lesson looking at Isaiah 41:4, 44:6, and 48:12, each of which points to the I AM as the first and the last. We close seeing Him once again,

> ## "I am the first and the last, and the living One."
>
> ## Revelation 1:17–18

the resurrected Lord Jesus who is the I AM, the First and the Last—the sovereign I AM, the saving I AM, the shepherding I AM, and the austaining I AM. How are we to walk with Him day by day? We will see in Day Five.

"Do not fear, for I am with you; do not anxiously look about you, for I am your God. I will strengthen you, surely I will help you, surely I will uphold you with My righteous right hand."

Isaiah 41:10

FOR ME TO FOLLOW CHRIST

What does it mean to follow the I AM? We have seen Him in the Old and New Testaments. Jesus not only claimed to be the I AM, He also proved His claim. He said, *"I am the resurrection and the life"* (John 11:25), and He proved it by raising the dead, and then He Himself arose, alive forever. He said *"I am the Light of the world"* (John 8:12; 9:5), and He gave sight to the physically blind and the spiritually blind. Over and over, Jesus revealed His awesome person, His perfect character, and His more than adequate power. As we follow Him, we can see Him at work in our lives as well, leading us in a walk of worship and surrender, insight and obedience, and faith and love. In today's study we will walk through some practical applications in trusting the I AM for all our days and in all our ways.

 Isaiah 41:10 presents us with one of the Old Testament "I AM" statements revealing a clear portrait of the I AM and His work on our behalf. Look at the statements from this verse given below and consider what application the Lord has for you. Each one is **a truth point** and **a trust point** in your life. Start your application with, "Lord, I trust You concerning _____."

God's Guarantee—His Truth Point: *"Do not fear, for I am with you"* (His presence **with you**)

My Trust Point:

_____

God's Guarantee—His Truth Point: *"Do not anxiously look about you, for I am your God"* (His power over circumstances **around you**)

My Trust Point:

_____

God's Guarantee—His Truth Point: *"I will strengthen you"* (His strength **within you**)

My Trust Point:

_____

God's Guarantee—His Truth Point: *"Surely I will help you"* (His help, power, wisdom, grace, and guidance **for you**)

My Trust Point:

_____

God's Guarantee—His Truth Point: *Surely I will uphold you with My righteous right hand"*—His Righteous Hand of Blessing, Security, and Strength **upholding you**

My Trust Point:

_____

Consider the seven main "I AM" statements below from the Gospel of John and the Great Commission in Matthew 28:18–20. Determine how each applies to your life or to someone with whom you could share these truths. Think through what you have learned and then fill in the statement, "Because this is true, I can be certain that _____." Thank the Lord Jesus for what it means to know Him and follow Him.

I AM the Bread of Life—Our manna each day and our fullness of life forever.
Because this is true, I can be certain that:

_____

I AM the Light of the World—Overcoming any darkness, lighting any path.
Because this is true, I can be certain that:

_____

I AM the Door of the Sheep—Our entryway into His abundant life and our guaranteed protection forever.
Because this is true, I can be certain that:

_____

I AM the Good Shepherd—Our guide and guard throughout life and eternity.
Because this is true, I can be certain that:

_____

I AM the Resurrection and the Life—Our guarantee to overcome death and enter into His new life.
Because this is true, I can be certain that:

_____

I AM the Way, the Truth, and the Life—Our clear path, our confident Word, and our guarantee of real life.
Because this is true, I can be certain that:

_____

I AM the True Vine—Our forever source for a life of joyful love and fruitfulness.
Because this is true, I can be certain that:

_____

"Go therefore and make disciples of all the nations. . . . and lo, I AM with you always. . . ."—Jesus is in us and with us to live the message and to tell the message.
Because this is true, I can be certain that:

_____

 Spend some time in worship of your Lord, the I AM. Pray for someone who needs to know the I AM. Pray for an opportunity to share the gospel of Jesus, the I AM, with someone.

"I am with you always."

Matthew 28:29

Lord, thank You for being the I AM, my Savior, for taking me where I was and for continually bringing me to where You want me to be—to Christlikeness.

Lord, I look to You as the I AM who is with me, who is my God, my strength, my help, and my support.

 Lord, I worship You as the I AM, the all-sufficient, all-powerful, all-wise God. I surrender to You as the sovereign I AM. Forgive me when I fret or fume over things that are not going my way. Remind me that Your way and Your will are always right, always best. Thank You for being the I AM, my Savior, for taking me where I was and for continually bringing me to where You want me to be—to Christlikeness. May I so abide in You day by day that I live out the new life You give. Please give me sensitivity to Your voice as I seek to follow You as the I AM, my shepherd. Thank You for the way You guide as the Good Shepherd through the storms and struggles. I am often amazed at the timing of Your turns in the road of life. I praise You for Your wisdom in leading and that You know me and all Your sheep in every detail. I also praise You for Your work as the sustaining I AM, for giving Your strength for each day. May I be reminded of that strength when I am tempted to hide or run in fear. I thank You for Your words through Isaiah, *"Do not fear, for I am with you; do not anxiously look about you, for I am your God. I will strengthen you, surely I will help you, surely I will uphold you with My righteous right hand"* (Isaiah 41:10). I look to You as the I AM who is with me, who is my God, my strength, my help, and my support. In Jesus' name, Amen.

Write your prayer to the Lord, the I AM or make a journal entry in the space below.

_____
_____
_____
_____
_____
_____
_____
_____
_____
_____
_____
_____
_____
_____
_____
_____
_____
_____

CHRIST IS THE "I AM"

I AM STATEMENT	SCRIPTURE	I AM STATEMENT	SCRIPTURE
CHRIST SAID, "I AM..." (GREEK EMPHATIC—*EGO EIMI*)			
the Bread of Life, the Bread that came down out of heaven	John 6:35, 48 John 6:41	the good shepherd	John 10:11, 14
the living bread that came down out of heaven	John 6:51	the resurrection and the life	John 11:25
the light of the world	John 8:12	the way, the truth, and the life	John 14:6
the door of the sheep	John 10:7, 9	the true vine. . . . the vine	John 15:1, 5
THE HIDDEN "I AMs" (GREEK EMPHATIC—*EGO EIMI*)			
I . . . am He (the Messiah/ the Christ)	John 4:26	I will come again, and receive you to Myself; that where I am, there you may be also.	John 14:3
[Jesus] *said to them*, "It is I [literally, "I AM"]; do not be afraid."	John 6:20; (see also Matthew 14:27; Mark 6:50)	I desire that they also, whom Thou hast given Me, be with Me where I am."	John 17:24
Where I am, you cannot come.	John 7:34, 36	. . .you may believe that I am He.	John 13:19
I am from above.	John 8:23a	. . .lo, I am with you always, even to the end of the age.	Matthew 28:20
I am not of this world.	John 8:23b; John 17:14, 16	And Jesus said, "I am; and you shall see the Son of Man sitting at the right hand of power."	Mark 14:62
I am He who bears witness of Myself	John 8:18	I am among you as one who serves.	Luke 22:27
Unless you believe that I am He, you shall die in your sins.	John 8:24	"Are You the Son of God, then?" . . . . [Jesus] *said* . . . "Yes, I am."	Luke 22:70
When you lift up the Son of Man, then you will know that I am He.	John 8:28	See My hands and My feet, that it is I Myself [I AM]	Luke 24:39
Before Abraham was born, I am"	John 8:58	Jesus the Nazarene. . . *said* . . . "I am He. . . ."	John 18:5, 6
If anyone serves Me, let him follow Me; and where I am, there shall My servant also be."	John 12:26	I told you that I am He. . . .	John 18:8

CHRIST IS THE "I AM"

(CONTINUED)

I AM STATEMENT	SCRIPTURE	I AM STATEMENT	SCRIPTURE
THE RESURRECTED CHRIST SAID "I AM" (GREEK EMPHATIC—*EGO EIMI*)			
To Saul on Damascus Road— *I am Jesus, whom you are persecuting. . . . I am Jesus the Nazarene. . . .*	Acts 9:5; 26:15 Acts 22:8	**To Paul in Corinth—** *Do not be afraid . . . but go on speaking and do not be silent; for I am with you. . . .*	Acts 18:9–10a
To John on Patmos— *I am the Alpha and the Omega, who is and who was and who is to come.*	Revelation 1:8; (see also 22:13a)	**To John at Patmos—** *Do not be afraid, I am the First and the Last. . . .*	Revelation 1:17; (see also Isaiah 44:6; Revelation 22:13)
Behold, I am alive forevermore [Greek, non-emphatic, *eimi*]	Revelation 1:18	*I am He who searches the mind and the hearts.*	Revelation 2:23
I am the Alpha and the Omega, the first and the last, the beginning and the end.	Revelation 22:13c	*I am the root and . . . offspring . . . the bright morning star.*	Revelation 22:16

Rabbi and Teacher

CHRIST REVEALING THE YOKE OF HIS LIFE AND TEACHING

"Rabbi"—what pictures does that word bring to mind? Does it conjure up images of a teacher, sitting out under a tree, instructing a small group of followers? Perhaps you think of a modern-day Jewish leader? Or maybe you picture Jesus with His disciples and the crowds around Galilee or in Jerusalem? A Rabbi, especially the Rabbi Jesus, is more than a teacher. He is a master-teacher, one whose followers give Him great respect and honor, even reverence. He is more than a man of knowledge or a lecturer or technician. He is not so much focused on facts and figures as on formation, heart formation. Jesus Christ is interested in molding minds and hearts to follow Him with all one's life, with every fiber of spirit, soul, and body.

How did people in Jesus' day view a Rabbi? Jesus was not the only Rabbi; there were many Rabbis active in New Testament days. A Rabbi was a man skilled in the Law of Moses and the Prophets who began teaching and training others in the Scriptures. Each Rabbi usually studied under another Rabbi or group of Rabbis and so had certain credentials within society. The apostle Paul studied under the highly respected Rabbi, Gamaliel, in Jerusalem (Acts 5:34; 22:3). Nicodemus declared to Jesus, *"Rabbi, we know that You have come from God as a teacher"* (John 3:2).

The primary function of a Rabbi was to impart a lifestyle. It was called a "yoke," a set of teachings under which a student placed himself. Each one listened and considered what was said, becoming more convinced of the call to follow and obey because this was the right way to live. Each pupil knew that through listening, learning, and following a Rabbi, he was taking his yoke upon himself. What kind of yoke did Jesus offer His followers? Was He any different from the dozens of Rabbis that proclaimed their ways to eager followers? What can we learn from Rabbi Jesus for our walk today? In this Lesson, we will discover His yoke and with it His ways in our lives—

> *"Rabbi, we know that You have come from God as a teacher. . . ."*
>
> **John 3:2 (Spoken by Nicodemus to Jesus)**

the process through which He takes us and the results He desires to see. Come, meet Christ, our Rabbi and Teacher.

Rabbi and Teacher | DAY ONE

Word Study
RABBI

The word **"Rabbi"** is rooted in the Hebrew word *rab* meaning "abundant," or "great." The Hebrew *rhabbi* means "a great one, chief, master" (*The Complete Word Study Dictionary, New Testament*, AMG Publishers, p. 1258). The word *Rabbi* has appeared in three forms in Jewish culture. *Rab* refers to an honored one, the first level of honor. The second, *Rabbi* (the letter "i" indicates "first person" case), means "my honored one" or "my master" and serves as a title of higher honor and dignity. The third level is the *Rabboni* which means "my great master, the most honorable of all" (*Complete Word Study Dictionary N.T.*, p. 1258). Only seven men in Jewish history were publicly given this honorable title. In Matthew 23:8, *Rabbi* is translated into the Greek *didaskalos*, "teacher." John the Baptist was addressed as "Rabbi" (John 3:26), while Jesus was addressed with "Rabbi" and "Rabboni." (Mark 10:51; John 1:38). He is **The Master Teacher** exalted above all others.

BEGINNING TO FOLLOW THE RABBI JESUS

What does a Rabbi relationship mean? There are **seven factors** recognizable in the relationship between a Rabbi and his followers. Let's see how those applied in the relationship between Jesus Christ and those who followed Him. **First**, the Rabbi must allow himself to be taught and trained in heart, ready to impart from His heart, expecting receptivity by the hearts of those who hear. Jesus was certainly qualified. He listened daily to His Father, allowed Himself to be taught and trained in heart, and then imparted what He learned to those ready to listen. **Second**, His followers had to have a heart to hear—humble, teachable, moldable. **Third**, Jesus the Rabbi gave a set of teachings to know, truth that sets free. **Fourth**, with the set of teachings came a learned lifestyle to willingly bear. This is known as the Rabbi's yoke. **Fifth**, He not only taught the yoke, He lived the yoke. He presented a way to walk—a way modeled after His words and in His example. **Sixth**, He gave a message to carry to others so they could know and enjoy the freedom of this yoke. **Seventh**, He promised a reward to receive—an accounting for what one heard, for how one responded, and for what one did with it.

Each of these components emphasizes knowledge that consumes the heart, not mere accumulation of information, theological or otherwise. How did Jesus reveal Himself and His Word to His disciples? What made them call Him "Rabbi"? In today's lesson we will be introduced to Jesus the Rabbi as His disciples were, and we will begin to see how He taught and trained them. We will also see how He works in teaching and training us.

We are first introduced to the Rabbi Jesus in John 1. Read John 1:19–39 to get the big picture. Who does John the Baptist say Jesus is according to verses 29, 30, and 34?

_____

_____

_____

What were the first words of Jesus to any of His disciples? What insights do you glean in that first interaction found in John 1:38–39?

_____

_____

_____

_____

Which of His followers do we meet in verses 37–51?

_____

_____

_____

John the Baptist made it clear that He was neither the Christ nor the promised Prophet. Instead, he indicated that Jesus was indeed Messiah. He called Jesus the Lamb of God, the one who existed before John, and the Son of God. Two disciples of John the Baptist, **Andrew** and **John** (the writer of the Gospel) sought to know more about this Rabbi. The initial words heard by these first disciples, were *"What do you seek?"* to which they replied *"Rabbi, where are you staying?"* Jesus then answered, *"Come and you will see."* This exchange between Jesus and Andrew and John was remarkably simple. Simple questions and simple answers, but an interaction that reveals the heart and ways of the Rabbi Jesus. He invited them to spend time with Him, and they did.

What they heard that day convinced them this was no ordinary Rabbi. They began to tell others. Andrew told his brother **Simon Peter**. Jesus met and called **Philip** to *"follow Me."* Each was willing to consider being a disciple of this Rabbi Jesus. Philip became convinced and called **Nathaniel** whose questions about this Rabbi caused Philip to simply reply, *"Come and see."* At this point they knew Jesus was a Rabbi and that John the Baptist had proclaimed Him as the Messiah and the Lamb of God. They, too, were considering Him as the Messiah as Andrew testified to his brother Simon Peter. Their evident hunger to know God and the reality of His promised Messiah led them to begin exploring the words and ways of this Rabbi.

📖 Early in Jesus' ministry, we see the Rabbi at a wedding celebration. There, Jesus revealed some uncommon truths about Himself and His ministry, what my son Josh calls "everyday glory." Read John 2:1–11 to see the full story. What are your first impressions? What strikes you in this series of events?

_____

_____

_____

_____

What does Jesus reveal about Himself to Mary, to the servants, and to the disciples? Note **how** He is beginning to "teach" His disciples.

_____

_____

_____

_____

What significance do you see in Jesus using the water purification pots for this miracle or "sign"? To what truth could He be pointing?

_____

_____

_____

_____

Jesus and His disciples along with His mother Mary were invited to a wedding in the small village of Cana. Most likely someone in the wedding party was a relative of Mary or a very close friend, since she seems to be helping

Did You Know?
BLIND BARTIMAEUS BELIEVED

As Jesus passed through Jericho, He passed near the place of the blind beggar, Bartimaeus, who began crying out *"Son of David, have mercy on me!"* (Mark 10:47). When Jesus asked him what he wanted, he revealed his faith in the Savior, declaring, *"Rabboni, I want to regain my sight!"* He called Him *"Rabboni,"* meaning "my most honored Master," believing Jesus was the Son of David, the promised Messiah, whom Scriptures promised would open blind eyes (see Isaiah 61:1; Luke 4:18). Bartimaeus was right. Jesus healed him, and he began following Him.

Did You Know?
WINE IN ANCIENT ISRAEL

The wine at the wedding in Cana of Galilee was a normal part of the festivities and of daily life in Israel. However, it should be noted that normally, the wine was highly diluted , as much as ten parts water to one part wine. Why? It was a common practice in ancient times to boil grape juice to preserve its sweet taste and to prevent fermentation. Water was then added to this syrupy product (note Proverbs 9:1–2). "Those were esteemed the best wines which were least strong." (Jacobus in William Patton, *Bible Wines: The Laws of Fermentation and Wines of the Ancients* [1871], p. 77, see also pages 42–48). *Oinos*, the Greek word translated "wine" in John 2, is a generic term which can refer to fresh grape juice, the diluted syrup, or to any other form of wine. This wedding celebration at Cana would not have been an occasion for drunkenness. Drunkenness and excess have always been condemned in Scripture (see Proberbs 20:1; 23:29–35; Isaiah 5:11–12, 22; Romans 13:13; and Ephesians 5:18).

with the wedding. A wedding celebration in that time and culture could last anywhere from several days to a week. In the midst of the festivities, the wedding couple ran out of wine, an offense that could mean trouble for them in this small village. Wedding celebrations were meant to be one of the highlights of the couple and the community. The groom's family was responsible for the feast and to run out of wine was considered socially unacceptable. The bride's family could actually bring a lawsuit for not providing for guests. This concerned Mary. She made Jesus aware of the problem, obviously hoping He would do something. Knowing Jesus as she did, was this her way of expressing her belief in Him as the Messiah? Perhaps she was aware that the Scriptures pointed to the time of Messiah's reign as a time when *"the mountains will drip sweet wine"* (Amos 9:13).

Jesus' response has puzzled many, but upon closer examination, we see He had a clear understanding of what needed to be done. His statement to Mary in verse 4 reveals four vital truths about Jesus, truths that help us see Him as Rabbi much more clearly. First, about His **person**—When Jesus said *"What do I have to do with you?"* He used a Hebrew idiom that can literally be translated, "What to Me and to you?" He did not treat Mary with disrespect or disfavor in this statement. He simply wanted her to see that His relationship with her now was more than just a mother/son relationship. He was the Son of God the Father, whom He must follow in everything.

Secondly, Jesus revealed a **process** here. When Jesus said, *"My hour has not yet come,"* He said in essence, "There is a process here, and I must follow it." It was not the appropriate time to reveal the fullness of who He was as the Messiah. Christ's death on the cross and his resurrection would occur before He revealed His full messianic reign. We also have a hint here of the process Jesus the Rabbi had in mind for His disciples, including what they would see on that miraculous day. As He took them through His training process, He would reveal more and more of Himself, His power, and His plans.

Thirdly, He revealed His **power**, the power to create. Here was an opportunity to reveal a measure of His ministry as Messiah. He told the servants to fill the water pots set aside for ritual purification. These were for washing hands during the feast, a very important ritual to the Jews of that day, though it only related to external cleansing. Jesus took that water and turned it into the best wine. Everyone recognized how good it was, but only the servants and the disciples knew that Jesus had just performed a miracle. This was the first outward *"sign"* that pointed to Jesus as the Messiah.

Fourthly, we see something of His **purpose**. Jesus reveals to us his heart in this incident. How so? Jesus presented His disciples with a message-filled miracle, a "sign" pointing to Him and His Kingdom. John tells us Jesus *"manifested His glory"* in the events in Cana. This idea of Christ revealing His glory also refers to Him revealing His grace. Jesus showed concern for the needs of this newlywed couple, but more than that He wanted His disciples to begin to taste His grace. We see this underlying desire in His choice of the purification water pots. When He turned all the water to wine, they had no other water for ritual washings. Jesus was always more concerned about matters of the heart, of showing His grace, than He was about external rituals, washings, and the like. He purposed to reveal a ministry of grace, an entire kingdom of grace. This wedding celebration was a good place to start, a place to see Jesus' *"glory as of the only begotten from the Father, full of grace and truth"* (John 1:14). How did the disciples respond? They *"believed in Him"* that day. But what else would they learn from this Rabbi?

Doctrine
THE EIGHT SIGNS

In the Gospel of John, the apostle John records eight miraculous "signs" for one purpose—*"that you may believe that Jesus is the Christ, the Son of God; and that believing you may have life in His name."*

The eight signs are:

- turning water to wine (2:1–13)
- healing the son of the royal official (4:46–54)
- healing the lame man at the pool of Bethesda (5:1–18)
- feeding the 5,000 men plus women and children (6:1–14)
- walking on the water and stilling the storm (6:15–21)
- healing "a man blind from birth" (9:1–41)
- raising Lazarus from the dead (11:1–45)
- Jesus Himself rising from the dead (20:1–29).

As we noted earlier, this Rabbi-disciple relationship developed out of simple conversations. A chronology of the Gospels reveals that these disciples walked with Jesus for several months after they were first introduced to him. Although, we do not have many details about Jesus' first year of ministry, we do know that the first disciples were with Him at Cana, then at Capernaum (see John 2:1–12), at the first cleansing of the Temple in Jerusalem (2:13–22), and in Sychar on their way back to Galilee. It was at Sychar where Jesus met the "woman at the well" and where many in the village acknowledged Christ as the Savior (see John 4). Some time after these events at Sychar, the disciples returned to their homes and to their fishing business. Why? Perhaps Jesus wanted His disciples to have a brief respite to digest what they had seen and heard. During this "lull," these fishermen could consider His claims. Meanwhile, Jesus traveled to Nazareth, where His own people rejected Him after hearing the claims He made in their synagogue. Beginning with His second year of ministry, Jesus moved to Capernaum, and subsequently, we see the development of a clearer call to His disciples to follow Him. We will begin looking at this call in Day Two.

ANSWERING THE RABBI'S CALL TO FOLLOW

W e read in the Gospels how Jesus first met and called His disciples to follow Him. It sometimes seems as if they simply walked away from everything to follow a man they had never seen until the day they met Jesus. However, when we compare the Gospel accounts, we find a different story. Jesus walked these men through a process. He allowed them to "come and see" first. He gave them time to consider His claims, to honestly evaluate Him and their relationship to Him. We will see more of this budding relationship in today's lesson.

Matthew 4:12–17 helps us understand the time frame of Jesus' ministry. John the Baptist was thrown into prison sometime during Jesus' first year of ministry. With that unrest and the opposition of the Pharisees in Judea (John 4:1–3), Jesus traveled back to Galilee. His move to Capernaum established a new base and new phase in ministry.

📖 Read Matthew 4:18–25. What do you see about Christ, His call, and the ministry He had?

_____

_____

_____

_____

Peter and his companions had known and followed Jesus during much of His first year of ministry. Afterward, they returned to their homes and businesses and had time to think about what they had seen and heard. Jesus moved to Capernaum, and there He encountered these men once again. This time, He now called them to come and follow, not just as observers, but as active participants in ministry. He told them He would make them *"fishers of men,"* a promise and a call to training and to fruitful ministry. Consequently, these fishermen left their nets and followed Him. The disci-

Did You Know?

? THE CITY OF CAPERNAUM

At the beginning of His second year of ministry, Jesus made Capernaum His home base, His "own city" (Matthew 4:13; 9:1). Once a small fishing village, it had grown into a prosperous city on the north shore of the Sea of Galilee. Peter and Andrew, James and John, and their families lived there. It was on the main trade route leading to Damascus, Syria in the north, Caesarea on the Mediterranean coast to the west, and Egypt in the south. The Roman government stationed a garrison there and had a tax office or customhouse, where Matthew served collecting taxes. (Matthew 8:5–9; 9:9). A God-fearing Roman centurion built the synagogue there (Luke 7:5). Jesus raised the daughter of Jairus, a leader of that synagogue, and there He healed the woman with the issue of blood (Mark 5:21–43). In spite of Jesus' many miracles, their unbelief brought His prediction of judgment (Matthew 11:23–24).

ples began to see even more activity throughout the region, as Jesus taught and proclaimed the good news about the kingdom of heaven. He healed all kinds of diseases and sicknesses and ministered to vast crowds. What were these disciples discovering?

When Jesus taught, everyone listened attentively. One example of His teaching is His famous Sermon on the Mount. What characterized Jesus' teaching according to Matthew 7:28–29? How did He compare to the scribes (or other Rabbis)?

_____

_____

_____

After Jesus gave His Sermon on the Mount, the people were astonished. He did not teach as the scribes did. Their teaching often involved quoting this or that rabbi, proving this or that point, or giving some tradition of the elders handed down to them though not specifically given in the Word of God. Jesus was different. He taught with *"authority,"* the translation of the Greek word *exousia,* which literally reads "out of the being." Jesus taught from within Himself what the Father had given Him, and He did so with the authority of God Himself. In the Sermon on the Mount, He had said several times, *"but I* [emphatic] *say to you,"* and the people recognized that authority.

📖 Jesus' authority became more evident to His disciples as well. Peter and the other disciples often accompanied Jesus and continued to grow in their relationship with Him. Read Luke 5:1–11 and record your insights.

_____

_____

_____

With Jesus' headquarters in Capernaum, it is likely that Peter and the others worked there from time to time, but that was about to change. Zebedee, the father of James and John, remained there and continued the fishing business with several servants helping. On one occasion, Jesus taught the crowds against the backdrop of the Sea of Galilee, and He used Peter's boat as a platform from which to speak. When He finished speaking, He commanded Peter to go out from shore and let down the nets to catch some fish. This kind of day-fishing made no sense to Peter, but he obeyed and was stunned at how many fish they caught. Even more was he awed by Jesus. After knowing Jesus for over a year, this incident of an evidently miraculous catch struck Peter with the holiness and authority of Jesus compared with his own sinfulness. He cried out *"Depart from me, for I am a sinful man, O Lord."* Jesus' message of grace continued to amaze and call His disciples and others to a more faithful following. Jesus said to Peter, *"Do not fear, from now on you will be catching men."* Of course Jesus meant that Peter would one day preach the life-giving message of Jesus Christ to scores of men and women. The Greek word *zogreo,* translated "catching," means to "catch alive." The kingdom of God is a living kingdom whose subjects live forever. Jesus wanted His disciples to be leaders in this kingdom. Peter and his companions responded. They *"left everything and followed Him."*

📖 Soon after this, Jesus called Matthew (Levi), a tax-gatherer who worked in the tax office in Capernaum. What do you discover about this call in Luke 5:27–32? What do you see about Jesus and His ministry?

The call, *"Follow Me and I will make you fishers of men,"* in Matthew 4:18 and the account described in Luke 5:1–11 are similar events but not identical. The sequence of events is different, and the chronology seems to indicate that the account in Luke 5 occurred a couple of months after the Matthew event. It is noteworthy that in Luke 5, Jesus did not issue the call *"follow Me,"* but gave the promise, *"Do not fear, from now on you will be catching men."* Jesus revealed the fuller meaning of fishing for and catching men.

_____

_____

_____

_____

_____

Jesus encountered Matthew at his tax office and called him to follow. Like the others, Matthew *"left everything behind"* and began following Jesus. His life was radically transformed. He wanted others to meet Jesus. First, he gathered his friends and business associates for a reception with Jesus at his house. When the Pharisees grumbled and questioned Jesus about His association with known "sinners," Jesus responded by focusing on His mission— *"I have not come to call the righteous, but sinners to repentance."* Matthew became a prime example to the other disciples of Jesus catching men and women alive as He advanced His kingdom. From this point forward, Jesus continued to catch men and women alive and reveal His heart and ministry of grace. He continues to catch men and women this very day!

📖 Jesus wanted His disciples to gain more than instruction. He had a mission for them. Read Luke 6:12–13 and write down your insights.

_____

_____

_____

_____

📖 What additional insights do you glean from Mark 3:13–16?

_____

_____

_____

_____

Midway into His second year of ministry, Jesus went into one of the mountains around Galilee and spent the night in prayer. The next day He called His many disciples to meet with Him and out of all of them called twelve to be *"apostles,"* literally "sent ones." He specifically purposed that these would *"be with Him."* Jesus would spend more concentrated time with these twelve men, during which He would teach and train them so that He could send them out to preach and minister as He did. These would become the leaders He needed to carry out His mission.

📖 Jesus had a clear understanding of His role as Rabbi and what He wanted for His disciples. Read Matthew 23:1–12. What main point did Jesus make about the scribes and Pharisees?

_____

_____

_____

_____

_____

Did You Know?
THE TWELVE

The twelve apostles are listed in Matthew 10:2–4; Mark 3:16–19; and Luke 6:14–16. The order of each list is slightly different, but in all the lists Simon Peter is first, and in each, the twelve are divided into three groups of four each. Andrew, James and John follow Peter in the first group. Philip heads the list of the second four (with Bartholomew, Matthew, and Thomas), James the son of Alphaeus heads the third list (with Thaddeus, who is named Judas the son of James in Luke, then Simon the Zealot (or Cananaean), and always last, Judas Iscariot, the traitor. Since the name Bartholomew does not appear in the Gospel of John, this could be another name for Nathanael who followed Jesus in John 1.

What was Jesus' role in the disciples' life?

_____

_____

_____

_____

What did He want to see in them?

_____

_____

_____

While the Pharisees sat in the "chair of Moses," explaining the Law, they failed to truly follow the Law.

Jesus warned His disciples as well as the listening multitudes about the scribes and Pharisees. While they sat in the *"chair of Moses,"* explaining the Law, they failed to truly follow the Law. Jesus acknowledged that all should obey what the scribes and Pharisees spoke from the Word of God, but He also warned people not to follow the religious leaders' example for these rulers did not truly obey God's Law. They burdened others with added man-made regulations. They were not interested in helping others, only in promoting themselves. They were masters of the externals, broadening the leather straps that tied the phylacteries on their forehead and arm. The Law commanded tassels on the corner of the outer garment (Numbers 15:38), but they lengthened them so others would be sure to notice their Law-abiding externals. They craved the best seats at banquets and in the synagogues and desired the most "respectful greetings," the exalted titles "Rabbi" ("my master"), "father," "Teacher." Jesus exposed this phony posturing for what it was and declared Himself to be genuine. He exclaimed, *"One is your Teacher. . . . One is your Leader,"* Jesus Christ. He pointed to one heavenly *"Father."* Jesus did not declare all human titles off limits. He simply pointed to the error of a proud walk, a life where one always seeks the approval of men and women and positions himself or herself for the public praise that exalts mankind to the exclusion of God and His work. Praise has its place. Jesus said that true exaltation awaits the one who will listen and follow Him as the "Rabbi," "Teacher," and "Leader." To do so with a humble heart, ready to act as a servant with a servant's heart, would fulfill His will and bring **His** commendation.

Jesus had much to teach His disciples. When we consider the process through which Jesus took His disciples, especially "the Twelve," we can trace a general pattern. The chart on the next page presents this pattern. In Days Three and Four, we will see this as it is worked out in the Gospels. For now, review the chart on the opposite page and consider how the Lord is working in your life, the process through which He is taking you.

After looking at the chart, write your thoughts or a prayer about His work and His processes in your life.

_____

_____

_____

_____

_____

APPROXIMATE DATE— TIME FRAME	JESUS' CALL TO HIS DISCIPLES	SCRIPTURE
December, 26 AD –January, 27 AD First months of ministry	*"Come, and you will see"* **Considering His Claims**	John 1:39 (1:46)
September, 27 AD Year One (Month 14)	*"Follow Me"* **The Call to Follow**	Matthew 4:19
Summer, 28 AD Year Two (Month 18)	*Be with Me* The Twelve **Companionship Training**	Mark 3:14
September, 28 AD Year Two, (Month 21)	*"Learn of Me"* **The Call to His Yoke**	Matthew 11:28–30
Summer, 29 AD Year Three (Month 31)	*"Take up your cross and Follow Me"* **Call to Crucifixion Living**	Matthew 16:24; Luke 9:23
April, 30 AD Year Four (Month 40)	*"Abide in Me"* **The Call to Christ-Life Living**	John 15:5–6
May, 30 AD Year Four (Month 41)	*"Witness of Me"* **Communicating and Living the Message**	Acts 1:8; 4:13, 33; 5:42; 6:7; 9:2; 19:9, 23; 22:4
Today! Everyday!	Watch for Me **Constant Watchfulness until He Returns**	Acts 1:10–11; Mark 13:32–37; Revelation 22:7, 12, 20

RECEIVING THE RABBI'S YOKE— LEARNING OF HIS CROSS

Rabbi and Teacher DAY THREE

Christ's revelation of Himself, His relation to the Father, His mission from the Father, and His destination at the cross were all taught to the disciples step by step. They did not hear it all in one day or one week or even one year. They discovered and digested truths about Jesus gradually. This Rabbi did not offer His followers an assortment of facts and raw data. What Jesus taught and how He led them were all tied to a personal relationship with Him. He wanted all that He said and did to connect to the mind and the will, to the head and the heart, to a genuine faith walk. Today, we will witness the disciples receiving more pieces of the puzzle as they begin to learn what it means to follow Jesus—the cost and the crown.

📖 Jesus saw various responses from the villages and cities in which He ministered. He continually called people to listen and follow, knowing many would not. He was not discouraged. He knew His Father was working. Read His words in Matthew 11:25–30. What do you discover from Jesus' prayer to His Father in verses 25–26?

_____

_____

_____

_____

What invitation did Jesus issue to those who would listen (verse 28)?

_____

_____

_____

Explain this yoke-relationship with Jesus. What do you see about Jesus?

_____

_____

_____

What do you see about those who follow Jesus, those who receive His yoke?

_____

_____

_____

Did You Know?

THE YOKE OF A RABBI

In New Testament days, people understood the workings of a yoke. Anyone with an ox dealt with yokes daily. They also knew about the "yoke" of a Rabbi or any teacher. Writings from the intertestamental times (400 BC—6 BC) spoke of this yoke. *Ecclesiaticus,* written about 180 BC, states in 51:26, "Put your neck under the yoke, and let your soul receive instruction." Many yokes were available, but that of Rabbi Jesus meant wisdom from above and true freedom.

Jesus' mission always followed His Father's will. He did all at the Father's initiation and with the Father's blessing. He loved and praised His Father and wanted His disciples to have a blessed relationship to the Father as well. It requires humble hearts willing to receive and heed instruction, similar to babies receiving nurturing. Any man or woman can know the Father and the Son as He reveals and opens the door to a relationship with Him. Jesus issued the invitation to all who would listen with His plea to *"come to Me."* Any willing to humbly admit they were continually *"weary"* and heavily burdened in soul, could receive *"rest,"* spiritual refreshment that only Jesus could give. Jesus emphasized the personal pronoun "I" when He exclaimed, *"and **I** will give you rest"* (emphasis added). Refreshment comes to those who come.

The "rest" Christ spoke of far exceeds momentary refreshment. He is describing **a life of rest,** eternal rest. In coming to Jesus, one meets the commands to *"take my yoke"* and *"learn from Me."* Here, Jesus the Rabbi is at His best, promising a "yoke" unequalled, unlike the yokes of others. To learn from Him means so much more than fact gathering and rule-keeping. Christ gives life and builds up life for those who rest in the Father's salvation and sovereign power—those who know His good will and experience His well-pleasing choices. Jesus is *"gentle and humble in heart,"* not harsh and proud. He is *"lowly in heart,"* meaning He meets us where we are. He gives life and builds up life. Jesus wants His followers to rest in His salvation and the Father's sovereign power, experiencing His good will and His well-pleasing choices.

With Jesus, we find true *"rest,"* marked by His grace, mercy, and wisdom. Here we are reminded of the LORD's words in Psalm 46:10, *"cease striving* (margin: *let go, relax) and know that I am God."* When we take on His yoke, we experience the truth that Jesus is indeed our God, the Lord and Savior who is sufficient for everything we face. We are called to simply surrender and obey. His yoke, the lifestyle He leads us in, is *"easy"* or *"kindly."* His *"load is light."* The Greek word translated "load" is *phortion*, which refers to what one can carry, one's personal responsibility, like a soldier's backpack. The life and the assignments Jesus gives fit who we are. It is *"light,"* not too heavy, not like the Pharisees' oppressive burdens, but just enough for us to carry in His strength.

📖 The disciples were in a yoke relationship with Jesus. In the summer of AD 29, Jesus asked His disciples some questions about their relationship to Him. What do you discover in Matthew 16:13–17?

_____

_____

_____

_____

Jesus asked simply, *"Who do people say that the Son of Man is?"* and then *"But who do you say that I am?"* In contrast to the crowds that spoke of Jesus as John the Baptist, Elijah, or Jeremiah, Simon Peter responded, *"Thou art the Christ, the Son of the living God."* This was a clear revelation from the Father to Peter and Jesus acknowledged that. It was time for them to know more about who He was and what He came to do.

What did Jesus reveal to His disciples in Matthew 16:21–23?

_____

_____

_____

_____

_____

How did the disciples respond, especially Peter? How did Jesus respond to Peter?

_____

_____

_____

_____

At Caesarea Philippi, Jesus made a definitive turn in His relationship with and His revelation to His disciples. He began to talk of the cross and His coming arrest, crucifixion, and resurrection. All the disciples heard were the sobering words, *"be killed,"* and Peter responded with *"God forbid it, Lord. . . . Never."* Jesus had to turn and rebuke Satan directly and Peter indirectly for the words Satan inspired him to say. He continued, *"you are not setting your mind on God's interests, but man's."* Jesus not only wanted His disciples to know what He faced, He wanted them to be ready for what His followers must face.

When we read the Scriptures, it is evident that there were many Rabbis teaching and training disciples. Each had his own version of teaching, a unique yoke. Jesus invited people to receive His yoke, leading to *"rest for your souls."* There were other yokes. Peter spoke of the yoke of the Law of Moses, *"a yoke which neither our fathers nor we have been able to bear"* (Acts 15:10). Paul called the law a *"yoke of slavery"* (Galatians 5:1). He referred not only to the Law of Moses but to any system of rules whereby one tries to straighten out his or her own life. In Jesus' day, people had to deal with the yoke of the scribes and Pharisees, heavy loads that the religious leaders themselves could not carry. Jews of that time also had to deal with the yoke of oppressive Roman rule and heavy taxation. Most of all, like us, they had to deal with the yoke of sin (Acts 13:38–39). Jesus came to deliver us from that yoke and give us His life, a yoke marked by forgiveness and abundant life.

What did Jesus tell them in Matthew 16:24-27? What promises accompany His troubling revelation?

_____

_____

_____

Did You Know?

JUDAS REJECTED THE YOKE

At the Last Supper meeting, when Jesus spoke of being betrayed, Judas said, *"Surely it is not I, Rabbi"* (Matthew 26:25). In Gethsemane, he came to Jesus and said, *"Hail, Rabbi!"* and kissed Him. Judas feigned being a follower, but he never truly received the yoke. Why did Jesus address him as *"Friend. . . ."*? The Greek word translated "friend" in Matthew 26:50 is *hetairos,* which refers to one who befriends for what he can gain, a parasite, a leech, an opportunist. Judas was only concerned for himself and what he could get out of his association with Jesus—in this case, thirty pieces of silver to go with the money he had often pilfered from the disciples' fund (John 12:6). (See full definition of *hetairos* in *The Complete Word Study Dictionary, New Testament,* AMG Publishers, pp. 662–665). This kind of "friend" is *hetéros,* "different," of a different spirit, not *állos,* not an ally. Jesus is not that kind of friend. He is a *philos,* one who unselfishly cares for the interests of others (Luke 7:34; John 15:13–15).

To follow Jesus would mean saying "no" to self and any self agenda, actually dying to one's own life by taking up one's *"cross,"* and with that point of surrender in place, follow Jesus in absolute loyalty and obedience. To try and protect, *"save,"* or gain life for oneself would mean actually losing in the end, but whoever loses his or her life, yielding to Jesus and His way, will truly find life everlasting. Losing life for His sake means finding life His way. The gift of life His way is true gain. This world is passing. There is a better world coming brought by the Son of Man. That is where one's energies and focus should be.

📖 Jesus began to speak of His cross about ten months before His crucifixion. Within a couple of months before that event, Peter had some questions about following Jesus. Read Matthew 19:27-29. What did Jesus promise Peter and all those who followed Him?

_____

_____

_____

Peter noted that all of them had *"left everything"* to follow Jesus. Jesus assured them that a greater kingdom was coming, one in which each of them would have a throne and a place of great responsibility. Not only would they be rewarded, but also *"everyone"* who has said "yes" to following Jesus—whatever the cost, *"shall receive many times as much"* and experience *"eternal life."* Jesus offers His yoke, the life and lifestyle to which He calls a man or woman, to those who humbly follow Him.

How would these disciples ever comprehend the cross? Surely they wondered how they could follow Jesus after His death, if He truly was sent to die. Christ's occasional references to His impending death bewildered them time and time again. How could they truly learn to follow Jesus if they did not comprehend and embrace the Father's will, including the cross? They simply needed to learn more from the Rabbi. He was not worried at this point with their lack of understanding. He knew what they must go through and how He would lead them.

Rabbi and Teacher   **DAY FOUR**

ABIDING IN THE RABBI'S LIFE— BEARING HIS FRUIT

The night before Jesus went to His death on the cross, He had a destiny-changing conversation with His disciples. Last words are always significant, and the words He spoke on this night would be His most important words yet, the link to the life He wanted them to experience and express throughout the world. He had more revelation to give them after His resurrection—that too would be life-changing and destiny changing. Today, we will consider His last words and His words for us related to the Last Days. Like the disciples, we will hear the Rabbi's destiny-changing words and will receive the opportunity to walk in a destiny-changing lifestyle, bearing His yoke.

📖 Read John 15:1–8. What is at the heart of all Jesus said? What do you discover in verses 5–6?

_____

_____

_____

_____

What kind of fruit did Jesus promise?

_____

_____

_____

Jesus began His ministry with the disciples with a simple *"Come and see."* Jesus essentially says, "Come and consider who I am and what I am saying." He gave them time to think over what He was doing. Then, He called them to *"follow Me,"* and they left all to do that. He chose twelve to *"be with Him"* in a special relationship. He urged them and others to *"learn of Me,"* to come to know and experience the yoke of His life and teaching. Then, He said, *"take up your cross and follow Me."* This command was a new and somewhat troubling revelation, but they stayed with Him, nonetheless. The night before His crucifixion, He gave them the link to how they could do all these things. He told them to **"abide in Me."** This is the same as saying, "Make sure your life is linked to Me like a branch to a vine, for I am **The Vine**." They would have to abide in His Word and let His Word keep penetrating their minds and hearts. With this reception of the Word must come prayer His way, making sure each was praying His will, or that which agrees with His Word. As they lived this way, His fruit would be borne in their lives, bringing pleasure to the Father. As He and others would see the expression of His Son's life in the lives of His followers, the Father would be glorified.

📖 After Jesus' resurrection, His Rabbi days were not done. He had more to reveal to His disciples. What do you discover in Acts 1:1–8? What did Jesus want them to do according to verse 8? How would they do that?

_____

_____

For forty days after His resurrection, Jesus appeared a number of times and taught His disciples many things. Christ delivered His most important teaching on the fortieth day, His last day with them, and just ten days before the Day of Pentecost (50 days after the beginning of Passover). On that day, He reminded them of the commission He had given. They were to be witnesses of Him in Jerusalem, Judea, Samaria, and to the uttermost parts of the earth. Only by the power of the Holy Spirit could they do this. He promised that the Holy Spirit who had been **with** them would soon be **in** them to guide and empower and give them the words to declare a powerful "witness of Me." That day, they watched Him ascend into heaven, doubtless carried

Put Yourself In Their Shoes

THE TIMING IN JESUS' LIFE AND MINISTRY

Galatians 4:4 says, *"when the fullness of the time came, God sent forth His Son, born of a woman, born under the Law."* Jesus showed a clear sense of the timing of His Father in all He said and did. He uses the term *"My hour"* in John 2:4, referring to the fullness of His revelation as the Messiah. The apostle John refers to Jesus' "hour" seven times (*"my hour"* [2:4], *"His hour"* [7:30; 8:20; 13:1], *"the hour"* [12:23; 17:1], and *"this hour"* [12:27]). Each of these references in John refers to the precise timing of the Father for Jesus' death, burial, and resurrection, and the glory that would be His when His hour had fully come. All that Jesus is doing in each believer's life is under His careful timing. He is Lord of time and timing, and we can trust Him for how He carries both to their fullness.

by the Shekinah cloud of glory mentioned often in the Old Testament. The promised Holy Spirit came on Pentecost Sunday, and the disciples began to be those witnesses, going first into Jerusalem, and within a few short years reaching into the remotest parts of the earth. What more were they to do? Let's look at one other word Jesus had given them.

📖 Rabbi Jesus had given clear direction about the Father's plans, but He did not give all the specific details. Yet what He gave was sufficient; it would take them through day by day until His Return. What further word do you discover in Mark 13:33–37?

_____

_____

_____

What should each day mean to a disciple, to one bearing the yoke of Jesus?

_____

_____

_____

Jesus gave a parable about His Return during the last week of His ministry in Jerusalem. He spoke of a master leaving his house in the care of his servants. They would be responsible for managing his goods and doing their assigned tasks. He promised he would return, but did not give any specific timetable. Therefore, the servants were to watch at all times. This parable tells all who follow Christ, "Be ready! Be on the alert!" His coming could be *"in the evening, at midnight, at cock-crowing, or in the morning."* In this passage of Scripture, Jesus calls His disciples and all believers to **watch for Him!**

 How are we to answer this call? Through God's word, Jesus is telling us, "Keep on **following** Me; **spend time with** Me; **take up your cross** daily, **learn** of Me, **abide** in Me, bear **witness** of Me, and **watch** for Me." This is the process of following God. Are you making progress in the process? Do not be discouraged. Remember, *"He who began a good work in you will perfect it until the day of Christ Jesus"* (Philippians 1:6).

We have seen much about the path and the process Jesus took His disciples through. Like them, Jesus is taking each of us who follow Him through that same kind of process—by opening up more of His Word to us, expanding our walk with Him, deepening our trust in Him, multiplying our ministry with Him, and increasing our expectation of His Return. How do we cooperate with Him as He expands our walk with Him? How do we follow Christ more faithfully and more fully? We will explore this realm in Day Five.

Rabbi and Teacher **DAY FIVE**

FOR ME TO FOLLOW CHRIST

The Rabbi Jesus revealed the yoke of His life and teaching, guiding His disciples into experiencing the fullness of His life. He led them to invest their lives wholly in Him and in His will. This was an eternal investment. Today, we hear much about investing—investing funds in stocks, bonds, mutual funds, real estate, or investing time in exercise, extra studies, or any number of hobbies and activities. In what or whom does Jesus want us to invest? Thinking of the yoke He gives—the lifestyle to which He calls us and for which He empowers us—consider four areas of **investing in eternity**.

Invest in the Eternal One. What is God's desire and command? Read Jeremiah 9:23–24 and Hosea 6:3 and record your insights.

_____

_____

_____

_____

What added insights do you glean from the apostle Paul's testimony in Philippians 3:8–10?

_____

_____

_____

The Lord warns against boasting in what is secondary—accumulated wisdom **(what a man knows)**, personal power **(what a man does or can do)**, or temporary riches **(what a man has)**. God wants us to have in-depth understanding and intimate knowledge of Him. Specifically, the Lord desires and delights in a person experiencing, expressing, and explaining to others who the Lord is by describing His loving kindness and mercy, His just rule, and His righteous character and ways. Hosea urged the people to _"know,"_ even to _"press on to know the LORD."_ That does not refer to formal intellectual knowing ("facts only" knowledge), but to an experiential heart-to-heart knowledge. Paul made it clear that such knowledge increases as we walk with _"Christ Jesus_ [our] _Lord."_ He wants us growing in knowing _"the power of His resurrection and the fellowship of His sufferings, being_ [continually and increasingly] _conformed to His death."_ Investing time in the Word of God and in prayer with God is investing in eternity, where we will enjoy the fruits of our walk with God forever.

Invest in Eternal Works—In His final week, Jesus gave a parable urging His followers to invest wisely and faithfully with what He has given to each of them. Read the parable in Matthew 25:14–30. What does the master do in this parable, and what are the servants expected to do? What characterizes the faithful servants?

_____

_____

_____

Works that matter for eternity are those in the center of God's will, the things He has called us to do. In the parable of the talents, the master gave his servants differing amounts of money to invest and use for his benefit. These "talents" were not abilities like speaking or singing. A talent can refers to a measurement of weight equivalent to approximately one hundred pounds. In this parable, the weight of money or number of silver coins given by the master matched his assessment of their abilities. Each servant took his assigned

Doctrine
JESUS' CARE FOR "HIS OWN"

John 13:1 says, _"Jesus knowing that His hour had come that He should depart out of this world to the Father, having loved His own who were in the world, He loved them to the end"_ [emphasis added]. Jesus loved "His own" to the end. He had prayed for them often. That same night, He told Peter specifically, _"Simon . . . I have prayed for you."_ Then in John 17, Jesus prayed for all of them, asking the Father to _"keep them in Thy name,"_ just as Jesus had guarded them those years. He prayed for them to know His joy, His protection from the evil one, the sanctifying work of the Father through the truth of His word, oneness with the Father and the Son and with one another, and to behold the glory of Jesus and to know the full love of the Father. Jesus loves us too—all those who have believed on Him through the disciples' word—and He prayed those same things for us, for we, too, are _"His own"_ and He will love us _"to the end."_

amount and either invested it or wasted the investment opportunity. When the master returned, he called for an accounting. One servant had earned five additional talents, while another earned two. They received the master's commendation—*"well done, good and faithful servant. . . . Enter into the joy of your lord."* In addition, they received the reward of rulership *"over many things."* But one man wasted his opportunity, showing himself to be a *"wicked and lazy servant"* who was no true follower of his master and hence, no true member of the kingdom. This man was immediately cast out. The Lord Jesus has given each of us an array of gifts and abilities. Most importantly, He gives us His life along with spiritual gifts for ministry, **all** of which are to be yielded to Him for His service. We have God-given opportunities to invest in the things that matter to Him. We will one day give an accounting and receive accordingly. May we hear from Him, *"Well done, good and faithful servant. . . . Enter into the joy of your lord"* (25:21, 23 [NKJV]).

Invest in Eternal Lives—In one of the most misunderstood parables in Scripture, Jesus gives us a word about investing in the lives of others. Read Luke 16:1–13. What do you discover about investing on earth in preparation for eternity?

_____

_____

_____

Jesus presented a parable about investments in which He presents one basic application. The story involves a steward or business manager who was accused of squandering a rich man's possessions and then was summarily fired. Immediately, the steward sought a way to protect himself once he was out of a job. He called his master's debtors and settled their accounts at a lesser rate. His master praised him for his shrewd business dealings—he recovered most of the debt, and he made friends of the debtors. Jesus made the application—believers should take this world's wealth, which is often used by *"the sons of this age"* for unrighteous purposes (aptly labeled *"the mammon of unrighteousness"*) and use it to invest in eternal relationships. Earthly wealth will not last, neither will this age, but the age of light is coming when *"the sons of light"* will live in *"eternal dwellings."* Those who have invested in making "friends"—in bringing others into the kingdom and building them in their faith—will be gladly and gratefully received by those converts in heaven. Investing in friends is part and parcel of the yoke Jesus gives His followers.

Invest in your Eternal Home—In Matthew 6:19–21, Jesus focused His listeners on heaven, the future home of His followers. How should each prepare for that home? How should each invest?

_____

_____

_____

What additional insights do you glean from 1 Timothy 6:17–19?

_____

_____

_____

_____

Doctrine
ETERNAL WORKS

Ephesians 2:10 says, *"For we are His workmanship, created in Christ Jesus for good works, which God prepared beforehand, that we should walk in them."* First Peter 4:10–11 focuses on God's grace gifts to believers and commands that those speaking should speak *"the utterances of God"* and those serving should do so *"by the strength which God supplies."* Paul reminds us that at the Judgment Seat of Christ each believer will be *"recompensed for his deeds in the body."* The works God has planned for us to do as part of His church, His Body, are God-designed, God-given, to be God-empowered, and will be God-rewarded. They count for all eternity.

Matthew 6:19 is one example of Jesus' call to not overemphasize this present, temporary life. An eternal existence awaits us, a home prepared by the Lord Jesus Himself. In John 14:1–3, Jesus promises His disciples He would go to prepare a place and return to receive them to Himself to forever live with Him in that home. While Jesus prepares this home, his followers are also to make preparations. Jesus called and commanded that one lay up lasting treasures in heaven. How? First, through focusing on loving and holding onto God and His priorities and not loving and serving *"mammon"* (Aramaic word meaning "wealth"). The Holy Spirit gave additional insights through Paul in 1 Timothy 6. We can easily be deceived by riches (they are marked by *"uncertainty"*), even to the point of being *"conceited"* with owning such riches. Instead, we should trust God for the wise use of those riches and the true joy He gives. We should also benefit others by good works and by generosity. This kind of "giving living" involves experiencing a richer, fuller experience of the life God gives and storing up treasure in heaven.

 How are your investments—the eternal ones? What is your "investment strategy"? Look back over the four areas of eternity and take some time to evaluate your **time,** your **resources,** and your **priorities.** Ask the Lord to provide some practical advice concerning your "investment portfolio." Maybe He will speak to you concerning all four areas of eternity. Perhaps it would help to record your prayer and the plan the Lord gives you.

_____

_____

_____

_____

My Prayer

_____

_____

_____

_____

God's Investment Strategy for Me

_____

_____

_____

_____

 Lord, I praise You as the Rabbi, my exalted Master and Teacher. I praise You because You are the Truth. Everything You say is Truth that sets me free. Thank You for your patience in the teaching and training processes, for the way You help me understand You, Your will, Your ways, and how my ways must continually adjust. Thank You for calling me to continually yield my agenda to you, so that I may take up Your agenda, Your yoke, Your way of walking. I am amazed at Your patience. I stand in awe of Your creativity in getting the point across to me time after time. Thank You for not giving up on me or Your perfect purposes for me. Thank You for including me

Doctrine
THE GIFT OF REST

In Mathew 11:28–29, Jesus promises to those who would come to Him, *"I will give you rest."* His rest is a grace gift, unearned, undeserved, but much needed and appreciated. In this invitation of Jesus, He goes on to call any who would come to learn from Him and *"find rest."* While His rest is a gift, it must be received to be experienced and enjoyed. Once received, one begins learning from Jesus and finds even more that Jesus' way is the way of rest. Jesus' words, *"You shall find rest for your souls,"* is from Jeremiah 6:16, which pictures one at a crossroads deciding which way to go. That verse speaks of "the ancient paths" and "the good way." To follow Jesus and His good way means finding rest rather than waywardness and judgment. The rest He gives is refreshing to the soul, a walk marked by His peace and grace. He wants to be to each the roadway of rest, the place to learn from Him and discover the joy and "rest" of His yoke.

YOUR INVESTMENT

Invest in:

- The Eternal One
- Eternal Works
- Eternal Lives
- Your Eternal Home

My Rabbi, my Teacher—I need You to give Your wisdom and understanding.

My Rabbi, my Yoke-Giver—may I truly walk with and rest in the Yoke You give.

in Your purposes. Thank You for continually bringing me to see that I cannot live the Christian life in my own strength or wisdom. You never said I could, and You never expected me to do so. I am a branch. You are the Vine and only You can give Vine-Life that brings wonderful Vine-Fruit. Thank You for the training exercises, the faith stretchers and faith builders You orchestrate in daily life to show me Your adequacy and sufficiency for my many inadequacies. Thank You that You are willing to reveal truth, to open my eyes to see and understand Your Word and Your ways so that I might walk with You in those ways. Thank You for not relegating knowledge of you to some theological corner, but for making the knowledge of You real in every day life—every area of life. Thank You for the process of growth, that You keep pruning, revealing falsehood to be replaced with Your truth, pinpointing sinful attitudes and actions to be repented of and replaced with Your righteous living. I praise You for giving the greater rest for my soul, for the deepening peace of knowing You and Your ways. May I be a clear and bold witness of who You are and what You can do in any life that will surrender to You, listen and obey. As I follow You in faith, may I continually exalt You as My Master—I need You to lead me, My Teacher—I need You to give Your wisdom and understanding, My Yoke-Giver—may I truly walk with and rest in the yoke You give. In Jesus' name. Amen.

Write your prayer or a journal entry in the space below.

_____
_____
_____
_____
_____
_____
_____
_____
_____
_____
_____
_____
_____
_____
_____
_____
_____
_____
_____

The Lamb of God

WORSHIPING AND FOLLOWING THE CRUCIFIED, RISEN, AND REIGNING LAMB

"The Lamb of God"? What pictures does that phrase bring to mind? What does a lamb have to do with the purposes and plans of God? What is the meaning of this lamb? Those questions and many more are answered throughout Scripture—from the beginning in Genesis to the believer's entrance into eternity in Revelation.

When we think of a lamb, many pictures come to mind. We think of a gentle creature, quiet and somewhat defenseless, or we sometimes think of a sacrifice and an altar and a flaming offering. We might think of one among a flock with a skilled shepherd, guiding, guarding, and feeding. Perhaps Psalm 23 comes to mind—*"The Lord is my Shepherd"*—and you think of yourself as the sheep in need of His care and guidance. What about the Warrior Lamb? This picture perhaps is a rare thought. What is a warrior lamb, you might ask? The Warrior Lamb is fierce and just and rules over His enemies, dealing with wrong and injustice. What about a lamb pictured as a king enthroned over a great kingdom, marked by great honor, glory, power, and majesty, ruling with wonder and awe? When we think of a lamb, this, too, is a picture seldom presented.

When we come to the Scriptures, all of these pictures arise to reveal The Lamb of God and our Lord Jesus Christ. He is gentle and quiet in character and conduct, yet that is not all He is. Sometimes, He is not so quiet. When it is time to deal with injustice and speak for the entire world to hear, He reveals His perfect holiness as well as His love, which is sometimes a fierce love. He made Himself defenseless before mere men and human courts, though He is the absolute judge, the ultimate commander, and the almighty, victorious warrior. He knows the flames of the altar and the fierceness of the wrath of God. He endured that on an altar known as the Cross—the place of the fires of judgment on sin, your sin and my sin. Because of His awesome mercy and His holy love, He willingly died and

Jesus is the Lamb of God, worthy of all honor and worship, all praise and adoration, all blessing and obedience.

purchased us for His purposes. Jesus is the Lamb of God, worthy of all honor and worship, all praise and adoration, all blessing and obedience. Come meet this Lamb and follow Him closely.

The Lamb of God **DAY ONE**

"WHERE IS THE LAMB?"

What do the Scriptures say about lambs? We first read of sacrifices from the flock in Genesis 4, not long after the creation and fall of man. Abel brought the *"firstlings"* from his flock, and Scripture records that God had regard for Abel and for his sacrifice. Hebrews 11:4 tells us that Abel offered to God a sacrifice by faith, and God was well-pleased. When Cain brought his offering of the fruit of the ground, perhaps grain, God was not pleased with Cain nor his offering. Evidently, Cain did not offer by faith and probably contradicted the revelation Adam and Eve had received about how to worship God. God wanted a living sacrifice, a sacrifice that portrayed the truth about sin and death, as well as the reality of God's justice and mercy.

For the next several hundred years, men offered many sacrifices on many altars. In today's lesson we will look at two pictures of the Lamb in the Old Testament. In Genesis 12, we read of a man named Abram who was called by God to come, worship, and follow Him as the one true God. God made many promises to Abram—promises of a land He would give him, a nation of descendants to dwell in that land, and the blessing of God, especially through his seed. Over the years Abram offered many sacrifices as he worshiped and followed God. Several years after Abraham's son Isaac was born, God asked him to offer a most unique sacrifice, his beloved son, Isaac. We find the account in Genesis 22, where we will also begin our journey looking for the Lamb of God.

📖 Read Genesis 22:1–8 and describe the events as they progressed.

_____

_____

_____

_____

_____

What was Isaac's question, according to verse 7? Why do you think he asked this question?

_____

_____

_____

_____

What was Abraham's response in verse 8?

_____

_____

Isaac asked, "Where is the lamb. . . ?" to which Abraham replied, "God will provide for Himself the lamb" (Genesis 22:7, 8).

Look at Genesis 22:9–13. What did God do at the place of sacrifice?

_____

_____

_____

_____

How did God provide a sacrifice in the place of Isaac?

_____

_____

_____

_____

God called upon Abraham to offer his son Isaac as a burnt offering on Mount Moriah, the location of modern day Jerusalem. Abraham left his home in Beersheba early the next morning with his son Isaac and some of his servants. This was a test, a continuous test of faith, as they journeyed for three days. On the third day, they reached Mount Moriah, and Abraham told his servants that he and Isaac would go up the mountain to worship and then return. Isaac, who was around 20–25 years of age at this time, carried the wood, and Abraham carried the fire and the knife. As they walked, Isaac asked the obvious question, *"Where is the lamb for the burnt offering?"* In faith, Abraham pointed to the Lord Himself as the provider of the lamb. As Abraham was about to slay his son, the Angel of the LORD stopped him, accepted his willingness to offer his son by faith, and then showed him a ram caught in the thicket. Abraham then offered this ram to God as a sacrifice. God tested Abraham's trust, and Abraham trusted God's test. Is there a fuller meaning to this event?

📖 Look at Genesis 22:14 and record your insights into Abraham's response and interpretation of this series of events.

_____

_____

_____

_____

After Abraham saw how the Lord had led him and how he had provided a ram to offer in the place of his son, he named that place *"The LORD Will Provide"* (in the Hebrew language "Jehovah-Jireh" or Yahweh-Jireh). The second part of verse 14 gives an explanation of that name, noting that for years after that day it was said, *"In the mount of the LORD it will be provided."* This explanation however begs the question: **"What** will be provided?"

Earlier in this chapter, Abraham told an unwitting Isaac that the Lord would *"provide for Himself the lamb"* (Genesis 22:8). After the Angel of the LORD prevented Abraham from sacrificing Isaac, the Lord indeed provided Abraham a ram, fulfilling what was needed that day, but also representing the provision of a lamb to come at a future time. A little Hebrew word study will help us clear up what is being said. The word *"provide"* is a translation of *raah,* which means "to see with perception and understanding." We could say, *"In the Mount of the LORD it will be* **seen.***"* What will be seen? In the context it appears that the lamb provided by the Lord will be **seen.** This is in essence a prophet-

Put Yourself In Their Shoes
TRUE WORSHIP

When Abraham took Isaac up Mount Moriah, he did so to worship. There on the Mount, the Angel of the LORD acknowledged Abraham's faith obedience and in so doing gives us a definition of worship. He pointed to three things in Abraham's heart and actions:

1. He acted in the fear of the Lord—true worship fears and respects the LORD only and always.

2. He withheld nothing from the Lord—true worship gives wholly and freely.

3. He obeyed the Word of the Lord—true worship obeys promptly and fully. How is your worship?

Did You Know?

? WHERE WAS MOUNT MORIAH?

First Chronicles 3:1 informs us that the place known as Mount Moriah was in the city of Jerusalem. There is where God chose to place the Temple in Solomon's day. It was on the piece of ground David purchased from Araunah (Ornan) the Jebusite (2 Samuel 24:18–25; 1 Chronicles 21:18–30; 22:1–5). The place the prophesied Lamb would be seen would be Mount Moriah in Jerusalem at the Temple area.

ic word given through Abraham—a lamb would be seen on Mount Moriah, provided by the Lord Himself. Later, we will see how this works out.

The Angel of the LORD spoke a second time to Abraham with a revelation related to the lamb to be seen as well as the seed to come. In the words, *"your seed shall possess the gate of their* [literally, "his"] *enemies,"* we see that out of Abraham's seed would come a ruler. Two promises are evident here, a lamb to come will be seen, and a ruling seed will come. Later in this lesson, we will see how these two mysterious entities will come together in one person, the one man who is both the Lamb of God and the ruling Lion. For now, what more can we learn of the Lamb of God?

The next significant mention of a lamb is found in Exodus 12, the record of the children of Israel preparing to leave Egypt after 430 years there. Read Exodus 12:1–13. (You may also want to read Exodus 11 to see the context of the Tenth Plague.) What was the first thing the children of Israel were to do according to verses 1–5?

_____

_____

_____

_____

The exodus from Egypt would be a life-altering experience. It was so significant that the month in which they were to leave became the first month in their calendar. On the tenth day of that month the children of Israel were to *"take a lamb"* for each household as a sacrifice and a meal. If a household was too small to eat an entire lamb, then they were to join with another household and divide the lamb among them. Specifically, the lamb was to be a male, one year old, without any blemishes or defects. Note how personal this became—it was *"a lamb"*; then it was called *"the lamb,"* referring to the specific one selected; then it was called *"your lamb"* for your need.

Note the time frame in verses 3 and 6. What were the children of Israel to do on the fourteenth day of the month?

_____

_____

_____

According to Exodus 12:7–11, what procedures did God instruct after the lamb was slain? (You may want to also read some of the details given in Exodus 12:21–22.)

_____

_____

_____

_____

_____

After the selection of the lamb on the tenth day of the month, each household was to keep it until the fourteenth day of the month. During that four-day period, they could observe the lamb to see if there were any hidden blemishes, and they could protect the lamb from being wounded or blemished in any way. On the fourteenth day, they were to kill the lamb at twilight. Then, they were to take some of the blood in a basin and brush it onto the doorposts and lintel of the houses where they would be eating the roasted lamb along with *"unleavened bread and bitter herbs."* Any of the lamb that remained was to be burnt with fire the next morning. The minute details of this night suggested a hasty departure was about to take place. Of course, God was about to deliver them from their Egyptian bondage. God commanded them to eat with their loins girded, sandals on, and staff in hand. What would transpire on this night?

📖 What was God's plan? Read Exodus 12:12–14, 23, 29–36 and record the events of that night. What was the significance of this night for Israel?

_____

_____

_____

_____

_____

God prepared the children of Israel for what He was about to do. At midnight, the Lord would pass over the land of Egypt and strike down the first born of man and beast, dealing a deathblow to all the gods of Egypt who were powerless to stop Him. All the homes where the blood had been applied would be safe and secure. He promised, *"when I see the blood I will pass over you, and no plague will befall you to destroy you."* Having obeyed the Word of God, the Hebrew children were protected by the covering of the blood of the lamb. Because they ate the Passover lamb, they walked out of Egypt in the strength of the Lamb of God. Not only were they protected, but in the midst of God's judgment on Egypt, the Hebrew children were also set free, after being supplied with all they needed and hurried out of the country by the Egyptians. This night of deliverance would become known as the Lord's "Passover" because He **passed over** the houses of His obedient children. They were to celebrate Passover at the same time every year in remembrance of the great deliverance God provided them through the sacrifice of an unblemished lamb. Exodus 13:21–22 reveals that the Lord Himself then led His people out of Egypt and into the wilderness with a pillar of fire by night and a cloud of glory by day.

What is the significance of these two Old Testament accounts of God's work among His people? What other Scriptures help us understand the events of Abraham on Mount Moriah or the events of Moses in the exodus from Egypt? The New Testament presents to us a very clear picture of the Lamb of God and how He fulfills what we have seen in the Old Testament. We will begin looking at these truths on Day Two.

Put Yourself In Their Shoes
A LAMB FOR WHO?

In Genesis 4, we see Abel's sacrifice, a lamb for **a man**. In Exodus 12 we see the Passover lamb, a lamb for **a household**. In Exodus 29:38–46 we see the daily burnt offerings, a lamb for **the nation** (one in the morning and one in the evening). In John 1:29 we see the Lamb of God, the Lamb for **the world**.

"Behold the Lamb of God!"

The Lamb of God ⬛ DAY TWO

"The Lamb of God"—what an image! A lamb seems in some ways to be too small a creature to convey who God is or what God's plan is. A lamb is not considered a strong animal or one that is particularly wise, but when we begin to see the full revelation of this Lamb in Scripture, we see amazing strength and wisdom as well as deep compassion, mercy, and love. To better understand the Lamb, we begin today by looking at the first days of the ministry of Jesus.

📖 John the Baptist presents a very clear testimony about the Lord Jesus in the New Testament. Read John 1:19–35. What was John's testimony about himself and about Jesus in verses 19–28?

_____

_____

_____

_____

What did John add in verses 29 to 36?

_____

_____

_____

John the Baptist was preaching and baptizing in the wilderness near the Jordan River, and many were asking him who he was, some asking if he were perhaps the Christ, the long-promised Messiah. Was he the promised Elijah, or was he the Prophet Moses promised long ago? To all these questions John clearly answered "No!" He was the voice crying in the wilderness, preparing the way for the one who was the Christ, the Messiah, the promised Prophet. John declared the greatness of this Messiah, far greater than him or any other prophet or teacher. The next day, John saw Jesus coming to him and boldly declared, *"Behold, the Lamb of God who takes away the sin of the world!"* He revealed that this man Jesus existed long before he existed, was of higher rank than he, had the seal of the Spirit of God upon Him, and was in fact the Son of God. What more can we find out about this Lamb of God?

📖 What do you discover about Jesus in the verses immediately following John's testimony? Look at John 1:37–51, looking specifically for descriptions of Jesus. Who was He—what did others say about Him?—what did He say about Himself?

_____

_____

_____

_____

_____

_____

Andrew and John, two disciples of John the Baptist, heard him declare Jesus to be the Lamb of God and they followed Jesus, seeking to know more about Him. They knew Him to be a Rabbi or teacher, but what more could they find out? Jesus invited them to come with Him and see. After this, Andrew reported to his brother Simon that they had met the Messiah or Christ, the one about whom Moses and the Prophets wrote. Nathaniel called Jesus *"the*

Word Study

BEHOLD, THE LAMB

The word "Behold" in John 1:29, is a translation of the Greek word *íde*. It is rooted in the word *eídō*, which, in turn, is connected with *horáō*, meaning "to see with perception." *Íde* is in the imperative tense, meaning it is used in the form of a command, as in, "Behold!" or "Look!" or "Observe!" In this context, the command to "behold" means so much more than offering a casual glance. It carries the idea of perceiving or grasping with clear understanding—"Look very carefully and understand the full significance of what I am showing you." When John the Baptist said, *"Behold the Lamb of God,"* he was pointing to something of immeasurable, spiritual, and eternal significance—"The Lamb of God is here! Don't miss what God is doing! Don't miss who this Man is and what this Man will do. He will take away the sins of the world—your sins and my sins. Make sure you understand and attach yourself to this Man who is the Lamb!"

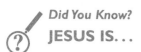

Did You Know?

JESUS IS. . .

John recorded the truth about who Jesus is. In chapter one alone he revealed Jesus as the Son of God, the Lamb of God, the Christ, the Messiah, the King of Israel, and the Son of Man (John 1:29, 36, 41, 49, 51). He is all this and more as John described in chapters 2—21, and he gave the all important application, *"these have been written that you may believe that Jesus is the Christ, the Son of God; and that believing you may have life in His name"* (John 20:31).

Son of God" and "*the King of Israel.*" Jesus called Himself "*the Son of Man.*" This Lamb of God was the Son of God and the Son of Man who came to take away the sins of the world. How would He accomplish this?

Fast-forward from the first week of Jesus' public ministry to the final week of Jesus' earthly life. It is the week of the Passover celebration. The Passover was to be celebrated on Thursday, the fourteenth day of the month Nisan (our months of March–April). Sunday was the tenth of the month, the day for the selection of the lamb for the Passover, followed by four days of examining the lamb for any blemishes or defects.

What happened on that Sunday according to John 12:12–16? What did they call Jesus?

_____

_____

_____

_____

_____

📖 Compare what you find in John 12 with what you discovered about Jesus in John 1. Write your insights.

_____

_____

_____

_____

On Sunday, Jesus left Bethany to go to nearby Jerusalem. There, a "*great multitude*" took palm branches and went to meet Him as He rode into the city on a donkey's colt. The palm branches were a symbol of the national hope in the coming of the conquering Messiah. The people began to cry out "*Hosanna!*" which means "bring salvation now" or "save now." They praised Jesus as "*the King of Israel.*" They saw Him as their Messiah—the choice as their deliverer. Everything Jesus was doing was at His Father's command—the time: the Sunday before Passover, the place: the city of Jerusalem. John recorded that Jesus was the Lamb of God in chapter one, and here in chapter twelve he makes it clear that Jesus is the King and the people's choice as Messiah who could "save now." Their idea of saving had more to do with getting rid of current Roman rule, Roman taxes, Roman idolatry, Roman influence and all else that went with it, but Jesus had something else in mind, something much greater, something eternal.

📖 How did Jesus see Himself and His mission? What is His testimony in John 10:10–11, 14–15, 17–18?

_____

_____

_____

_____

Doctrine
WHY THE EMPHASIS ON FORGIVENESS OF SIN?

When John the Baptist declared Jesus to be the Lamb of God he focused attention on His person—"*of God*" and His role—"*who takes away the sin of the world.*" Why did He say that? All the Old Testament sin offerings could not take away sins, as Hebrews 10:3–4 states. Those offerings and the "*blood of bulls and goats*" simply covered sin for a time, like a credit card covering a debt for a time, until someone can pay the full debt. No man could do that because all men's bank account of righteousness is bankrupt. Only Jesus lived a perfectly righteous life and in His death could pay for the sins of the world. In that death and in that payment, He took away our sins. Colossians 2:13–14 says He has "*forgiven us all our transgressions, having canceled out the certificate of debt. . . .*" Jesus removed our sins as far as the east is from the west (Psalm 103:12). He took them away and we can now know His forgiveness forever and experience His gift of righteousness.

Jesus came to give life, abundant life. Like a good shepherd, He willingly laid His life down for the sheep so that they could have that life. Not only would He give His life, He would also *"take it up again,"* pointing to His resurrection. Christ's spirit of surrender was in keeping with His Father's will and plan. How would this be carried out in light of the people's response on the Sunday of His Triumphal Entry (Palm Sunday)?

The gospels record that for the next four days, Jesus was tested in many ways. He cleansed the Temple of the greedy sellers and moneychangers on Monday, and on Tuesday the Jewish rulers challenged His authority to do what He was doing and say what He was saying. They tried to trap Him and discredit Him with their questions, but Jesus countered their every move, their every word. The rulers and religious leaders began seeking a way to put Jesus to death. Jesus had already told His disciples this day would come. Judas joined with the rulers against Jesus as Jesus continued to prepare His disciples for that coming day and beyond. Then on Thursday night, the religious leaders arranged for Jesus' arrest. Soon after, Jesus underwent three Jewish trials and three Roman trials, and then the Jewish leaders and the Roman authorities led him out to be crucified. What was the final verdict about this Man after this week of examination?

In the first of three Jewish trials, Annas could not produce a guilty verdict on Jesus and sent Him to the high priest, Caiaphas. Read this account in Mark 14:53, 55–65 and record the details. What did they find out about Jesus?

_____

_____

_____

_____

_____

What do you discover in Pilate's testimony in Matthew 27:24 and John 18:38; 19:4, 6?

_____

_____

_____

_____

_____

In the three Jewish trials, the leaders tried everything they could to find something to hang a guilty verdict on Jesus. In the second trial before Caiaphas, they sought someone who could accuse Jesus of wrongdoing, based upon anything He had said or done. In an attempt to assure success, they brought in witnesses to tell lies; however, these witnesses couldn't "get their lies straight." Nothing was working for this kangaroo court; the witnesses could not agree. Finally, the inquisitors asked Jesus if He was *the Christ, the Son of the Blessed One.* Christ answered this question in the affirmative, because it was indeed true. They accused Him of blasphemy, and on that false charge condemned Jesus to die. They then met with the Sanhedrin at daybreak to "officially" condemn Him to death (Matthew 27:1).

Did You Know?

THE TRIALS OF JESUS

After Jesus was arrested the night before He went to the cross, He underwent three Jewish trials and three Roman trials. The first Jewish trial was before Annas, former high priest and father-in-law of Caiaphas the current high priest (John 18:12–14, 19–24). The second trial was before Caiaphas (Matthew 26:57–68; Mark 14:53–65; Luke 22:54) and the third trial was before the Sanhedrin at daybreak (Matthew 27:1; Mark 15:1; Luke 22:66–71). This third meeting was necessary to make their judgment "official" since no trial was to be held under cover of night. In spite of their official word, none of the trials actually revealed any wrong on the part of Jesus. Then, there were three Roman trials, the first before Pilate (Matthew 27:2, 11–14; Mark 15:1–5; Luke 23:1–5; John 18:28–38), the second before Herod Antipas (Luke 23:6–12) and the third back before Pilate (Matthew 27:15–26; Mark 15:6–15; Luke 23:13–25; John 18:39–40, 19:1–16). Each of the Roman trials could produce no evidence that Jesus had done anything wrong and certainly nothing worthy of crucifixion. He was the Lamb tested and found without blemish (1 Peter 1:19).

When Jesus faced the Roman trials before Pilate and Herod Antipas, again the testimony was clear—no guilt, no fault found. Pilate said three times, *"I find no fault in Him"* (NKJV), and in the third Roman trial he even *"took water and washed his hands in front of the multitude,"* declaring, *"I am innocent of this Man's blood,"* but then He delivered Jesus up to be crucified.

📖 Peter wrote about Jesus' death bringing to light the full picture of His purity and righteousness and what His death meant. Read 1 Peter 1:18–20 and note your insights.

_____

_____

_____

_____

All who believe in Jesus Christ and who place their lives in His care as their Lord and Savior, experience His redemption. Each one discovers freedom from the bondage and enslavement, guilt, and condemnation of his or her sin. That redemption was not paid for by the prized treasures of earth—silver and gold—but with the most prized treasure in heaven and earth, the blood of Jesus. In the eternal plan of God, He died as a lamb, the *"unblemished and spotless"* Lamb of God—for you and me.

📖 There is yet another picture we need to complete. What do you discover about Christ in 1 Corinthians 5:7?

_____

_____

_____

_____

📖 Read 1 Corinthians 5:1–7 to see the context and Paul's application for the believers in Corinth. Note your insights.

_____

_____

_____

_____

What further word of exhortation did Paul give in 1 Corinthians 5:8?

_____

_____

_____

Word Study

UNBLEMISHED AND SPOTLESS

These two words in 1 Peter 1:19 describe the purity of Jesus, the Lamb of God. "Unblemished" is a translation of the Greek word *ámōmos*, made up of the negative particle *á-* and *mōmos*, the word for "spot" or "blemish." *Ámōmos* was used to describe a sacrifice without blemish and is found in the Septuagint (Greek Old Testament) in Exodus 29:1 and Numbers 6:14. *Ámōmos* is used several times in the New Testament speaking of Christ (Hebrews 9:14; 1 Peter 1:19) and of Christians cleansed by His blood (Ephesians 1:4, 5:27; Colossians 1:22; Jude 24). In 1 Peter 1:19, *ámōmos* is used with *áspilos* which refers to being "without spot." *Áspilos* is found in 1 Timothy 6:14; James 1:27; and 2 Peter 3:14, exhorting Christians to walk unstained. *Ámōmos* focuses more on the absence of any internal defect or blemish, whereas *áspilos* describes the absence of any external defect or spot. Jesus was pure within and without.

"Christ our Passover" gave Himself as a sacrifice for us in order to deliver us out of the bondage of our "Egypt," our enslavement to sin and death. As the Israelites walked free out of Egypt, so we are meant to walk in the freedom Christ gives, no longer slaves to sin. Paul applied these truths to the Corinthian believers who were ignoring the immorality of someone who claimed to be a believer. Paul pointed to this man's sin as leaven that was influencing and infecting the whole fellowship in Corinth. Just as the Israelites

cleaned out the literal leaven for the Passover, so the Corinthians should deal with any sin, any deception or deceptive influence, any wandering from the Word of God. As our Passover, Christ has died to forgive and cleanse and give new life. We have something to celebrate, but not with fleshly, sinful living— no malice or wickedness of any kind should be in our hearts or in our midst as a body of believers. Instead we are called to walk in *"sincerity and truth,"* obeying and following the Lamb individually and as a body of believers.

Let's connect the dots to see the full picture. Abraham prophesied that in the Mount of the Lord the lamb would be seen. Mount Moriah is the location of the ancient Temple in Jerusalem. At that place, many of Jesus' tests and trials occurred the week of Passover, in those days when the Passover lambs were under the watchful eye of the priests to find any blemish or defect. The people acknowledged Jesus as the Messiah on Sunday before Passover, lamb selection day, and then for the next four days the people tested, questioned, and tried Jesus. No one could find any fault or blemish. What about the Jewish and Roman trials? Absolutely none of these trials could find a scintilla of fault in Jesus, yet those conducting the trials handed Him over to be crucified. He died on a cross as the unblemished, spotless, innocent Lamb of God, provided by the Father. This gift of God, this prophesied Lamb was seen dying not just in the place of Isaac, but also in the place of you and me. He died taking away *"the sin of the world."* He is our Passover Lamb, delivering us from our disobedience to God's Law, from our enslaving sin, and from the wretched kingdom of darkness. He is the Lamb we partake of so that, like the Israelites, we walk in the will of God and in the strength of the Lamb. Behold that Lamb, Jesus, the Messiah, the Son of God and Son of Man! Worship and love Him. Follow and obey Him.

 Do you know by faith this Lamb as your Lord and Savior? He is God's gift to you. Are you giving Him your allegiance and love? Do you know someone who needs to know this Lamb? Share these truths. Introduce that one to the Lamb of God who can forgive his or her sin and give new life forever.

What more can we learn of this Lamb of God? There are many truths in the Scriptures, especially in the book of Revelation. We will begin uncovering those truths in Day Three.

"WORTHY IS THE LAMB!"

On the Island of Patmos, the imprisoned apostle John received *"The Revelation of Jesus Christ"* concerning the things which were occurring then and the things which would occur in the days and years ahead. That revelation revealed the fullness of God's plan of the ages as well as the fullness of His reign over all, all heaven and earth. Where does the Lamb fit into this scheme? We will see in today's lesson.

📖 The Lamb of God is mentioned in the book of Revelation 28 times, more than in any other book of the Bible. We are introduced to the Lamb in Revelation 5:6. Describe this Lamb according to verse 6.

_____

_____

_____

_____

What other description do we find about this Lamb in Revelation 5:5?

_____

_____

_____

In Revelation 5, the Lamb is enthroned, indicating His rule. Though having been slain, He is standing alive. He has seven horns. The horns of an animal provide protection and a means for self-defense as well as for establishing domain. They are indicative of strength and power. Seven is the number of completion. These seven horns point to Jesus' perfect strength and full ability to establish His domain over all the earth. His seven eyes *"which are the seven Spirits of God"* reveal His ability to know all that is in the earth. He sees all, understands all, has full comprehension, perfect knowledge, and impeccable wisdom. This Lamb is also the Lion of the tribe of Judah, fierce and powerful, the king of the wilderness. He is the Root of David, one who has descended from David and, like King David, has shown His ability to wage war and win. He has overcome sin, death, hell, and the grave. What an awesome Lamb!

What is the Lamb doing in Revelation 5? Read verses 1–7 and summarize what is taking place. (You may want to read Revelation 4 to see the full context.)

_____

_____

_____

_____

What has the Lamb accomplished according to verses 9–10?

_____

_____

_____

John saw the very throne of God in heaven plus the thrones of the twenty-four elders (representative of the Church). He saw all the splendor and majesty of God surrounding God's throne and heard the undiluted, never-ending praise and worship of the living creatures and the elders before the throne. In His right hand the Lord held a scroll, in essence the title deed to earth and all its kingdoms. The one who could open its seven seals could claim authority over all the earth and right all wrongs. No one was found worthy to claim that authority except the Lamb who is also the Lion. His worthiness is found in His mission accomplished—He was slain, and through His blood He purchased for God those *"from every tribe and tongue and people and nation."* Not only that, He made them into a kingdom of priests—changed from within to reign in royalty, purity, and loyalty alongside the Lamb. What an awesome work the Lamb has done, is doing, and will do!

Did You Know?

THE LION OF JUDAH

When Jacob blessed his sons at the end of his life, he gave a prophecy concerning the tribe of Judah and the One who would be born of that tribe. Jacob's words in Genesis 48:8–12 are an amazing portrait of the coming of Christ. Judah's ultimate descendant Jesus will receive praise and honor and His hand will be on the neck of His enemies. He is like a lion who rules over all. From Judah *"the scepter"* and *"the ruler's staff"* shall not depart. Through Judah *"Shiloh"* shall come, a reference to the Messiah. *"To Him shall be the obedience of the peoples."* His prosperity and success will become evident for all to see. That is certainly true of Christ who is both the Lion and the Lamb, whose success is evident in the record of "The Revelation" to John.

Word Study
LAMB

In the New Testament, there are two Greek words translated "lamb," but the emphasis is different for each word. The first, *amnós*, refers to a sacrificial lamb. It is used in John 1:29, 36 ("the [sacrificial] lamb of God who takes away the sin of the world"), Acts 8:32, and 1 Peter 1:19. The second word, *arníon*, is used of the living Lamb and His finished sacrifice in Revelation 7:14; 12:11; and 14:4. It is used to designate Christ the risen, exalted Lamb in Revelation 5:6, 8, 12–13; 6:1, 16; 7:9, 10, 14, 17; 12:11; 13:8; 14:1, 4, 10; 15:3; 17:14; 19:7, 9; 21:9, 14, 22–23, 27; 22:1, 3.

Did You Know?
THE SCHEME OF THE LAMB IN REVELATION

Revelation 6—19 reveals the outline of the work of the Lamb to bring justice to the earth and establish His reign. The broad outline is found in the seven seals on the scroll, the title deed to all creation. Within those are all the events of the Great Tribulation. Seven seals are opened, and the seventh seal contains the seven trumpets. The seventh trumpet brings forth the seven bowls that conclude with the Lamb's triumph over all evil and the establishment of His righteous rule.

What is the response of the twenty-four elders to this Lamb? Record what you discover in Revelation 5:8–10.

_____

_____

_____

_____

How do the angels and living creatures respond along with the elders according to Revelation 5:11–12?

_____

_____

_____

_____

The twenty-four elders each held a harp, signifying their ability to offer praise and to make proclamation like the prophets of old. Along with the harp they each held a golden bowl full of incense, signifying fervent and holy prayer and intercession. With these in hand they burst into song, a new song, a song of worship and praise to the all-worthy Lamb for what He has done and what He will fully bring to pass among the saints of all ages. An innumerable host of angels and living creatures joined the elders proclaiming *"with a loud voice"* the worth, the value, the praise, the recognition, and the honor due to the Lamb. They recognized and acknowledged His power, His riches, His wisdom, His strength, His honor, His glory, and His blessing—for He alone is worthy to be praised and adored at the highest level.

What additional insights do you find in Revelation 5:13–14?

_____

_____

_____

_____

Ultimately, all the created order declares the worth of the Lamb and His right to rule over all—to Him belongs all *"blessing and honor and glory and dominion forever and ever."* He is the highest, most honored, almighty King. No person or place is untouched by His rule, His power, and His dominion. The elders' response was *"Amen!"* which means, "So it is!" With wholehearted, joyful surrender, they worshiped Him.

 What is your response to the Lamb? The word "Amen" is a statement of affirmation, meaning, "So it is." Are you affirming with your life, your lips, your choices that He indeed is worthy"? Are you giving Him your highest praise, bowing in your most joyful surrender, walking in deepest reverence and fear? Are you offering your fullest measure of love, withholding nothing—all your heart, soul, mind, and strength? Are you yielding to Him with prompt, full, unquestioning obedience? Spend some time in prayer and worship the worthy Lamb of God.

In Revelation 15:1–4, we find another celebration to the Lamb along with a "song." It has to do with the final judgments at the end of the

Great Tribulation. The scene is in heaven. What is the setting, the events surrounding this "song" according to Revelation 15:1?

_____

_____

_____

_____

Who is singing the "song" according to verse 2?

_____

_____

_____

What is the title of the "song" being sung (15:3)? What is the focus of this "song" in verses 3–4?

_____

_____

_____

What does this "song" tell you about the Lamb?

_____

_____

_____

_____

In the scheme and design of the Revelation, chapter 15 introduces the seven last plagues poured out of the bowls of God's wrath. Here we see the final demonstration of God's wrath before Christ's second coming. In this context we read *"the song of Moses . . . and the song of the Lamb,"* as well as the been victorious over "the Beast" (antichrist) in spite of all his injustices. The song points to the greatness of the *"Lord God, the Almighty,"* as well as the magnitude of His righteousness and His rule. He rules as king over His saints in all the nations and brings about justice for them. He is worthy of great honor and glory. The nations will one day recognize His rule and declare the truth and righteousness of His judgments. It is evident that those in Heaven recognize the Lamb, not only for what He has done on the Cross, but for all He will do to complete His design and establish His rule of righteousness. The Lamb is also the Lion, who is indeed worthy of honor and obedience!

We follow a victorious Lamb. He is worthy of our praise and adoration, our allegiance and love, our daily surrender and obedience. What does it mean to follow this Lamb? What other truths do we find in the Scriptures? We will see in Day Four.

Extra Mile
SONG COMPARISIONS

Read the "Song" in Exodus 15:1–21 along with the "Song of Moses" in Deuteronomy 31:30; 32:1–44. Compare them with the "Song" in Revelation 15:3–4 along with the judgments of God on the nations in Revelation 16.

Doctrine
LAMB, LION, SERVANT, AND KING

"The Old Testament pictures of lamb and king are incomplete, and leave us wanting a king who can bring peace." (Josh Shepherd)—Jesus is the prophesied Lamb, dying for the sins of the world (Genesis 22:14; Isaiah 53:7; John 1:29). He is Jehovah's servant, yielding to His will in everything (Isaiah 49:5–13; 50:4–11; 52:13—53:12–15). He is also the exalted, reigning Lion, Lord, and King (Philippians 2:5–11; Revelation 5:5; 17:14; 19:16;). He is the perfect, prophesied Son of David—the Lion of Judah (Genesis 49:8–12) and the Servant-King, fulfilling God's promises to David (2 Samuel 7:8–29), bringing peace, and establishing His reign (Isaiah 9:1–7).

DAY FOUR

"FOLLOW THE LAMB WHEREVER HE GOES"

Following Jesus the Lamb is what we were created to do—for time and eternity.

What does it mean to follow the Lamb of God? First, consider a definition of the word "following," especially as it applies to following Jesus the Lamb and Lord. It means much more than simply taking orders from someone or getting directions to some place. It involves heart and head, instruction and direction, but, most of all, it involves a shared fellowship and a living relationship. It means listening to and learning from, meditating on what is said and applying that in word and deed. It is heart and lifestyle transformation, not just thought stimulation or intellectual information, though these elements are certainly part of the equation. **Following Christ** means going in the same direction **with Him** and leading others to do the same. It means avoiding the wrong direction and warning others of the snares and traps along the way. It is being confident of a sure destination with a Leader who will never forsake us. It means walking with a humble, teachable, moldable heart, hungry to know, grow, and go—going wherever He leads, knowing whatever He speaks, and growing in all the ways He directs. Following Jesus the Lamb is what we were created to do—for time and for eternity, and if we understand we are actually following the Lamb of God who is also the Lion of Judah, we will be secure in His love, certain of His care, and confident in His leadership.

What more can we learn about this Lamb we are following? If He is the most worthy being in all of time and eternity, in all of creation and beyond, then following Him must be the greatest privilege and blessing, the most magnificent adventure, the most humbling opportunity, and the most God-exalting surrender we could ever join in. It is also the costliest investment worthy of all our attention, our hearts, our souls, our energies, and efforts. It is costly to us in that we lose everything, yet He is worth all we could give. Remember that it was costly to Him as well, for did he not give everything? What can we gain from following Him if it costs us everything? In losing our life we gain Him, His eternal life and His joy, as He begins to gain the love, worship, and praise of which He is worthy. He gains a bride by His side forever, and we gain our home with Him. We also gain His heart with us, and the eternal joy of loving Him and walking with Him. What are some of the aspects of this following? We will begin to see in today's lesson.

Designed for Following

📖 What was in the mind of the Lamb long before time began? What did He want from His creation? What do you discover in Revelation 13:8 and 17:8? [Note the context contrasts those who worship the Beast {13:1–9; 17:1–8} and those who belong to the Lamb.]

_____

_____

_____

_____

_____

_____

We were made for following. Revelation 13:8 points to *"the Book of Life of the Lamb,"* the book containing the names of all those who know and follow the Lamb. The Greek text, which is well translated in the King James and

New King James versions, focuses on *"the Lamb slain from the foundation of the world"* (NKJV). The redemptive work of the Lord Jesus was in the heart and mind of the Father, the Son, and the Spirit from the beginning. Revelation 17:8 points to the Book of Life also being written since the foundation of the world. Both of these verses point to God's design—first of all, for the Lamb **personally giving life, His life,** for those in the world, His being counted as slain and risen from the beginning. Those who believe, follow, and obey Him experience His Life given **for** them and **to** them.

The *second* aspect of this destiny for God's people is found in them **personally knowing the life** of the Lamb. They truly experience a personal relationship with Him and know the power of His life. The Lamb's Book contains the names of all who belong to the Lamb. These have His life given to them. They experience this by grace through faith in Christ. They believe His Word expressed in the gospel. The phrase in the Greek language could be translated *"**the** Book of **the** Life of **the** Lamb,"* focusing on the specific book with the names of those who have the specific life of the Lamb in them, His kind of life, eternal life. What security each one has whose name is found in this book! Each one knows the Lamb as personal Lord and Savior and has *"the life of the Lamb"* given within. The word "life" in the term, *"the Book of Life of the Lamb,"* is a translation of the Greek word *zoē*, which implies relational life, not mere existence. All those listed in the Book of Life have come to know and experience the eternal life of the Lamb within. These people follow Him; they experience His life and share it with others, telling of the life the Lamb of God offers. They lead others into that knowledge of the Lamb as He calls, convicts, and converts them by the power of His Spirit.

The Duty and Delight of Following

In Day Two, we saw in our focus of 1 Peter 1:19 Peter's testimony about the Lord Jesus and about Jesus' death as a sacrificial lamb. In the six verses leading up to this verse, Peter makes several applications to the daily walk of a believer—our daily duty.

📖 Read 1 Peter 1:13–21. Knowing that the Lord Jesus died as the Lamb, what should be our response? What do you find in verse 13?

_____

_____

_____

_____

_____

What marks followers of the Lamb according to 1 Peter 1:14–16? What do you see about the delight of following Him?

_____

_____

_____

_____

In this passage, Peter looks forward to the hope of every believer, *"the revelation of Jesus Christ."* His coming will signal the final steps in completing God's eternal plan. We will enter into the joy of the Lord—**His joy** in fulfilling His will and **our joy** of being in His presence forever. For now, we are

Put Yourself In Their Shoes
THE CALL OF THE LAMB

Even now, the Lamb calls, *"Come to Me!"* (Matthew 11:28). The apostle John wrote, *"Let the one who is thirsty come; let the one who wishes take the water of life without cost"* (Revelation 22:17).

First Peter 1:18–19 states that we were *"redeemed . . . with precious blood, as of a lamb . . . the blood of Christ."* The Greek word *lutróō,* translated "redeemed," literally refers to bringing a ransom (*lútron*) to pay for someone. It is rooted in the word luo, "to loose" or release, set free. *Lutróō* refers to releasing someone through the payment of a ransom, like someone on the slave block in ancient times. Jesus set us free from oppression, slavery to sin, and ultimate condemnation by His own blood, His death as the Lamb of God.

called to be *"obedient children"* whose eyes are on the Father rather than on the world and its lusts. Before we knew the Father and followed the Lamb, those deceitful desires lied to us and led us astray. We foolishly followed them in our ignorance. We now have a new calling, the call to holiness—this is not a calling to a cause, but to a person; we follow the Holy One, and His holy purposes. We should live in a way that is different, set apart from the ordinary, set apart to God and His holy ways. He has made us holy, set apart to Him, and He empowers us to become holy in our behavior. Holiness includes being exemplary in all our relationships and dealings in life. He has given us His life so that as we surrender to Him "day in and day out," He can see His holy life manifested in and through our lives.

📖 What perspective should a believer have when he or she thinks of this relationship with the Father and the Lamb? What attitudes should be seen at the heart of a believer according to 1 Peter 1:17–19? (You may want to read 1:3–12 to see the fuller picture.)

_____

_____

_____

As *"obedient children"* we look to and call on our Father, knowing that we are accountable to Him for all we say or do. That should lead us daily to a reverential fear of the Lord—a cautious perspective, knowing He will evaluate all we have done during our brief stay on earth. We also walk with a sense of His love and security, for He is a Father who paid an inestimable price to purchase us for Himself. The redemption price Jesus paid secured our rescue. With that is a sense of expectancy—we are here for a brief time, stationed on earth temporarily. Though undeserved, there is more to come. Before He saved us, all we could boast about was a futile life and a futile past, but God sent Jesus to redeem us. We should walk with gratitude and joy—we have been purchased out of slavery to sin, out of the empty, meaningless life of our past and, as Peter exclaimed in 1:3–9, we are destined for *"an inheritance . . . imperishable and undefiled and will not fade away, reserved in heaven."* We are also *"protected by the power of God through faith for a salvation ready to be revealed in the last time."* What a Savior, what a salvation He gives, what a message we can share with others. Peter later urges his readers (and us) to be ready to tell others the reason for this hope we have (1 Peter 3:14–18). How wonderful is this work of the holy Lamb of God!

📖 Throughout the ages, millions of men and women have followed the Lamb as their Lord and Savior. In the Book of Revelation, we see many followers of the Lamb. When God calls someone to follow Him, what we see in that relationship should also mirror some of the things the Lord wants in our relationship with Him. In Revelation 14:1–5, we read of those who *"follow the Lamb wherever He goes."* What do you see in the relationship between the Lord and the 144,000 in those verses? List the characteristics you find in them that would be pleasing to the Father if found in your life.

_____

_____

_____

_____

_____

_____

_____

_____

The 144,000 belong to the Lamb, *"having His name and the name of His Father written on their foreheads."* They have been purchased by the Lamb and sing a song given to them by Him. These souls walk in purity and faithfully *"follow the Lamb wherever He goes"*—no arguments, no hesitation, just faithful following. They walk in truth and tell the truth, always living a blameless life, above reproach. While these 144,000 have a special place in the plan of God, they are also an example of the kind of relationship the Lamb wants with each of His children. The Lamb wants us to be faithful followers, obedient, knowing we belong to Him, valuing the great price He paid to purchase us. He wants us to have the flexibility to follow wherever and whenever. It is a "flex and obey" mindset that trusts the sovereign Lamb of God in all He says and does, *"wherever He goes."*

The Victory of Following

📖 The victory of following is the victory of surrender, of yielding to the Lamb. As believers surrender and follow Him, they discover the power of His victory. Read Revelation 7:9–17. What evidence of victory do you find in these verses?

_____

_____

_____

_____

John saw the evidence of the Lamb's victory in the multitude of redeemed souls from *"every nation and all tribes and peoples and tongues, standing before the throne and before the Lamb."* The palm branches in their hands were a symbol of the kingdom and were used in celebrating the Feast of Tabernacles, which also spoke of the establishment of God's kingdom. Those clothed with white robes, the robes of the righteous, praised the enthroned, reigning Lamb of God for the salvation He has brought. All in heaven responded in worship to God. One of the elders gave testimony of the victorious cleansing of the saints through the blood of the Lamb. These gladly serve the Lamb forever. Ironically, the Lamb of God serves as a shepherd to His flock; He joyously cares for them, protects them from harm, and leads them to *"living fountains of water"* forever.

📖 What elements of victory do you see in Revelation 12:7–11?

_____

_____

_____

_____

In a scene picturing Satan's defeat and demise, we see the overcoming, victorious power of Christ. The devil, who is the deceiver and accuser of the brothers, will one day be seen in total, inglorious defeat. The brethren overcame him and his accusations *"by the blood of the Lamb."* Christ's perfect sac-

> **The Lamb wants us to be faithful followers, obedient, knowing we belong to Him, valuing the great price He paid to purchase us. He wants us to have the flexibility to follow Him wherever and whenever.**

There are two types of crowns mentioned in Scripture. The *diádēma* is used in Revelation 12:3 referring to the dragon wearing seven diadems. Revelation 13:1 speaks of the beast with ten crowns, both verses revealing the earthly rule of various kingdoms. Revelation 19:12 shows Jesus Christ with "many crowns" (*polus diádēma*), indicating His supreme royalty and unchallenged rule. The *diádēma* is the royal crown. The word is rooted in *diadéō*, to bind around, and was used of the band around the tiara of a Persian king. It was like a turban made of silk, linen, or a similar material. The Septuagint translation of Esther 1:11 speaks of Queen Vashti's *diádēma* or royal crown. Another crown mentioned in Scripture, *stephanos,* appears 18 times and often refers to a victor's crown. In the first century, it was used of "the crown of victory in games, of civic worth, military valor, nuptial joy, [or] festival gladness. Woven of oak, ivy, myrtle, olive leaves or flowers, [it was] used as a wreath or garland" (Spiros Zodhiates, *The Complete Word Study Dictionary New Testament,* AMG Publishers, 1992, pp. 423, 1311—12).

rifice paid for all sin and brought full forgiveness and redemption. This simply means that all accusations against those who follow Christ are null and void. The testimony of His work of salvation is a testimony of victory and the basis of full surrender—a willingness to lay down one's life.

📖 What kind of victory does the Lamb win at Armageddon according to Revelation 17:14 and 19:11–16?

_____

_____

_____

_____

Ultimately, Christ the Lamb, the King of kings and Lord of lords will reveal Himself in full power and authority. He will defeat any and every foe and establish Himself as the valid victor over all, the sovereign Lord in command. We should follow Him. Picture the crucifixion with its brutal images. This picture is presented in striking detail in Matthew 27:27–31. In this passage, we are told that Roman soldiers, aided and abetted by a riotous crowd once shamed the silent Christ with a crown of thorns, a mock rod in the form of a reed, a borrowed robe, and the scorn of an unbelieving, mocking crowd. Yet, one day, this same Jesus will reveal Himself in His awesome resurrection glory, no longer silent, but wearing a ruler's crown and a king's robe, holding a rod of iron, and He will be praised by all His faithful followers. Every word He declares will stand. Every decision will be carried out. Every action will be honored. He will rule with a rod of iron—unbending and strong, impossible to be defeated. Jesus Christ is our victorious Lamb. Following Him means knowing the victory that surrender to Him brings and experiencing the joy He gives to surrendered hearts.

What do these truths mean for our daily walk? How can we follow the Lamb in day-to-day life? We will see in Day Five.

The Lamb of God **DAY FIVE**

FOR ME TO FOLLOW CHRIST

Picture a beautiful symphony. We have been called to join the "Symphony of the Lamb"—that is the Father's desire, delight, and design. How? First, He sent His Son, our Lord Jesus Christ, the Lamb of God, to live and die for us. He came to buy us and bring us to Himself, to bring a song to our hearts and to hear that song from our lips. We not only hear the song, we become part of the orchestra, offering praise and worship to the Lamb. And we call to others to join in. God has worked in our lives in great detail to make us followers of the Lamb, and He is working daily to bring others into the fold. Day by day He desires to use us in His Kingdom endeavors—bringing others to Him and helping them grow in knowing and loving Him. The Lamb's symphony is ever expanding; the sounds of praise and worship are ever increasing. His glory is being revealed in more hearts in more places throughout the earth. What is His design for us now as we look forward to the grandest symphony in heaven? How are we to follow the Lamb today?

The Lamb of God took away the sin of the world. He reconciled the world to Himself. This undeniable truth is the heart of the gospel, the heart of the message of the New Testament. We see this truth evident in many places and in many lives. The life of Paul, the Apostle is one example. What the Lamb did in this man's life dramatically changed him; it forever changed who he was and what he did. Paul gives testimony of this radical transformation in 2 Corinthians 5 and 6. In applying these truths to his readers and to others his readers would eventually touch and impact, he focuses on the salvation that Jesus offers. There are some clear applications in these chapters for us today. Let's see how this applies to following the Lamb.

📖 We read Paul's call in 2 Corinthians 5:14–21. What is to be the focus of every believer according to verses 14–15?

_____

_____

_____

_____

How are we to look at others according to verses 16–17?

_____

_____

As new creatures in Christ, what is God's plan, God's design for each of us, according to verse 18?

_____

_____

_____

_____

According to verse 19, what is at the heart of this "ministry"?

_____

_____

_____

_____

What is our "official" job description in verse 20?

_____

_____

_____

_____

📖 What reality and what message were on Paul's heart in verse 21? What does God want us to do with that message according to the next two verses, 2 Corinthians 6:1–2?

_____

_____

_____

Did You Know?
THE DAY OF SALVATION

In 2 Corinthians 6:2, Paul says, *"behold, now is THE ACCEPTABLE TIME, behold, now is THE DAY OF SALVATION,"* quoting from Isaiah 49:8 where we find the promise of God's salvation reaching around the earth. Paul applied it to the salvation offered in Jesus Christ and his desire that the Corinthians join in experiencing that and in bringing others to know Christ and His salvation. Reading from Isaiah 61:1–2a, Jesus spoke of His ministry as one of proclaiming *"the acceptable year of the LORD"* (Luke 4:18). The *"acceptable year of the LORD"* is equivalent to Paul's *"DAY OF SALVATION"* (Isaiah 49:8). Some also see here a reference to the Year of Jubilee (Leviticus 25) when a proclamation went throughout the land—all slaves, prisoners, captives, and indentured servants were set free, all debts were forgiven, all work ceased and the land had rest. That is certainly a picture of what the Lamb has accomplished for us—we have been set free, all debts forgiven, and we enter into His rest, His finished work of salvation. That is a message worth believing and proclaiming now!

How are we to follow the Lamb of God? How should what He has done make a difference in our lives? Think through the four summary truths from 2 Corinthians 5:14–21; 6:1–2 listed below and how the Lamb wants you to follow Him. Write your thoughts in the space provided.

1. Christ's love and sacrifice for us has given us new life. Therefore . . .
   <u>Live gratefully surrendered to Christ and His will. Follow Him.</u> (5:14–15)

2. Through His death and resurrection, He can change anyone. Therefore . . .
   <u>See people for who He can make them—new creations who can become faithful followers.</u> (5:16–17)

3. God has a service for each of us, a *"ministry of reconciliation,"* introducing others to Him, His forgiveness, and a right relationship with Him. Therefore . . .
   <u>Follow Him in His purposes and plans. Join with God in telling others what He has done to bring them to Himself and to new life.</u> (5:18–21; 6:1)

4. There is a time for hearing, receiving, and experiencing the grace of God. That time will one day come to a close. Therefore…
   <u>Now is the time to tell and the time to receive God's grace.</u> (6:1–2)

_____

_____

_____

_____

_____

_____

The Life of the Lamb

We have seen the life of the Lord, the Lamb, again and again. In the life of the Lamb is the essence of what the **Last Adam** gives—the image of God, the fruit and fruitful life God desires and the opportunity to reign in life through Christ Jesus. The life of the Lamb is at the heart of the **Seed**, Christ, and in His seed placed within us. It is His life manifested in the character and works of the **Angel of the LORD**. It is the outworking of Christ the **Lawgiver**, **Prophet**, **Priest**, and **King**. The **Son of Man**, the **I AM**, reveals the life of the Lamb. It is His life that comes through in all He says and does as the **Rabbi**, in the yoke of living He places upon us and in us. His life is seen in every act of **prayer** and devotion, every conversation with the Father, and ultimately in the fulfillment of all the Father's will as the crucified, risen, reigning Lamb of God.

 Give thanks to the Lamb for His Life and the Salvation He has brought. Think of His Life and what a change He **has** made, what a difference He **is** making, and what a difference knowing Him **will make** for all eternity. Read each statement and write a note of thanksgiving and praise to the Lamb in light of all He has done.

He gave His Life **for you**—

_____

_____

He gave His Life **to you**—

_____

_____

Consider what the Lamb has done for us: We were. . . .thought of by Him before time began, bought by Him in eternity and time, fought for by Him on the Cross, sought after by the Father, caught for Him by a faithful witness, brought to Him by the Spirit, taught by Him through the Word, fraught with blessings from Him both now and in eternity, wrought by Him as His Bride, naught but Grace have we received from Him. Therefore, we ought to worship Him, our worthy Lamb and Lord, Jesus Christ.

His Life is active **in you**—

_____

_____

His Life can be seen **through you**—

_____

_____

His Life can be shared with others **by you**—

_____

_____

His Life will ever be **with you**—

_____

_____

 Perhaps the hymn "Just As I Am" by Charlotte Elliott conveys a worthy response to the Lamb. Read and think through these lines. Allow them to form your own response to the worthy Lamb of God as you participate in the Symphony of the Lamb.

Just As I Am

"Just as I am, without one plea but that Thy blood was shed for me, And that Thou bidd'st me come to Thee, O Lamb of God, I come! I come!"

"Just as I am, and waiting not To rid my soul of one dark blot, To Thee whose blood can cleanse each spot, O Lamb of God, I come! I come!"

"Just as I am, tho tossed about With many a conflict, many a doubt, Fightings and fears within, without, O Lamb of God, I come! I come!"

"Just as I am, poor, wretched, blind—Sight, riches, healing of the mind, Yea, all I need in Thee to find—O Lamb of God, I come! I come!"

"Just as I am, Thou wilt receive, Wilt welcome, pardon, cleanse, relieve; Because Thy promise I believe, O Lamb of God, I come! I come!"

"Just as I am, Thy love unknown Hath broken every barrier down; Now to be Thine, yea, Thine alone, O Lamb of God, I come! I come!"

"Just as I am—of that free love, "The breadth, length, depth, and height" to prove, Here for a season, then above—O Lamb of God, I come! I come!"

Spend some time with the Lord in prayer.

 Lord, I worship you as the worthy Lamb of God, the One sacrificed on the Cross—for my sin and me. Thank You for dying, for rising, for reigning, and then calling me to Yourself. I praise You that I can know Your forgiveness, experience Your life, walk under Your lordship, and worship You. You are indeed the victorious Warrior Lamb, reigning over all Your followers and Your enemies as well. My days often seem so full of defeat. Thank You for giving me Your victory as

Lord, You are indeed the Victorious Warrior Lamb reigning over all Your followers and your enemies as well.

A POINT OF PRAISE

Read the lyrics to the hymn, "Crown Him with Many Crowns," by Matthew Bridges:

Crown Him with many crowns,
The Lamb upon His throne:
Hark! How the heav'nly anthem drowns
All music but its own!
Awake, my soul, and sing
Of Him who died for thee,
And hail Him as thy matchless King
Through all eternity.

Crown Him the Lord of love:
Behold His hands and side—
Rich wounds, yet visible above,
In beauty glorified.
No angel in the sky
Can fully bear that sight,
But downward bend his wond'ring eye
At mysteries so bright.

Crown Him the Lord of heav'n:
One with the Father known,
One with the Spirit through Him giv'n
From yonder glorious throne.
To Thee be endless praise,
For Thou for us hast died;
Be Thou, O Lord, through endless days
Adored and magnified.
Amen.

I allow You to overcome me day by day, moment by moment. My walk is so fragile. May I live so that You are the central focus of my waking and my walking. My mind is so feeble. May I comprehend more of Your greatness in a world that tries to hide that truth. My heart is so crippled. May I show You genuine love and devotion without hypocrisy. I thank You for Your fiercely jealous love that longs for Your best in my life and fights against anything less. My comprehension seems so empty. May I magnify and exalt You more and more as I grow to know You. Lord Jesus, may each Scripture portrait I see bring me a new vision of the salvation You give, a new sense of awe at Your majesty and beauty, a new understanding of Your wisdom and wonder, a new comprehension of Your perfect holiness and great love, a new depth of worship as I see Your worth, and a new song of praise from my heart. Then, let my comprehension of you overflow in my walk and in my talk so others can be introduced to You, to truly know You and follow You forever. You are worthy, O slain Lamb of God, to stand risen and reigning, and to receive all glory, and honor, and wisdom, and power, and blessing, forever. Amen.

Write your own prayer or perhaps a letter or journal entry to our Lord Jesus, the Lamb of God.

_____
_____
_____
_____
_____
_____
_____
_____
_____
_____
_____
_____
_____
_____
_____
_____
_____
_____

THE LAMB OF GOD
SCRIPTURE PICTURES, PROPHECIES, AND PROCLAMATIONS
ABOUT THE LAMB OF GOD FROM ETERNITY PAST TO ETERNITY FUTURE

EVENT	SCRIPTURE
"The Lamb slain from the foundation of the world" [KJV]—Jesus is the Lamb preplanned and counted as slain even before time began (*"the foundation the world"*). [God's eternal design is also noted in Acts 2:23; 4:27-28; 13:26–29; 2 Timothy 1:9; Titus 1:2; John 17:24; Ephesians 1:4–9; 1 Peter 1:18–21; and Revelation 5:6.]	Revelation 13:8; 1 Peter 1:18-21
"The Book of the Life of the Lamb" [The original Greek language emphasizes the specific Book and the specific Life (*zoē*) of the specific Lamb, Jesus Christ.] It contains the names of all who are chosen and belong to the Lamb, who have His Life given to them by grace through faith in Him and His Word expressed in the Gospel. Even now the Lamb calls, "Come to Me!"—John declares, *"Let the one who is thirsty come; let the one who wishes take the water of life without cost."* Revelation 22:17	Revelation 13:8; 17:8; 21:27; see also 3:5 and 20:12, 15
The Seed of the woman—The Lord promised Eve a *"seed,"* a man born of a woman who would crush the serpent's head and deal with the seed of the serpent and all evil. That "Seed" who would be wounded was Jesus Christ, the Lamb of God.	Genesis 3:15; Galatians 3:16
The Lord clothed Adam and Eve with animal skins slain because of sin. Perhaps the sacrifices were lambs serving as a picture of the atonement price to be paid one day by the Lamb of God.	Genesis 3:21; 1 Peter 1:18–20
Abel brought an animal sacrifice, *"the firstlings of his flock,"* very likely a lamb or lambs, and sacrificed them on the altar of worship. He offered by faith.	Genesis 4:4; Hebrews 11:4
"Where is the Lamb?"—As Abraham and Isaac ascended Mount Moriah to worship, Isaac asked the question, *"Where is the lamb for the burnt offering?"* Abraham assured Isaac that God would provide the lamb. The Lord provided a ram there which served as a picture of the Lamb God would provide on that same Mount Moriah in Jerusalem almost 2,000 years later. In this event Isaac served as a type of the crucifixion and resurrection of the Lord Jesus Christ.	Genesis 22:7–14; Hebrews 11:17–19
The Passover Lamb—God directed Moses and the people of Israel to *"take a lamb . . . the lamb . . . your lamb"* and sacrifice it as the Passover lamb for the deliverance of each heart and each household from certain judgment and death. This serves as a picture of Christ our Passover Lamb who has delivered His followers from judgment and death.	Exodus 12:3–5, 21; 1 Corinthians 5:7–8
The Burnt Offering—Everyday, twice a day (9:00 a.m. and 3:00 p.m.), the priests offered up a one–year-old lamb as a burnt offering in the Tabernacle in the Wilderness and later in the Temple in Jerusalem. On the Sabbath two additional lambs were offered. At the first of every month (new moon) the priests offered an additional burnt offering which included seven lambs. At the yearly Passover offering seven lambs were part of the burnt offering included in that celebration.	Exodus 29:39–41; Numbers 28:4–8, 9–10, 11–14, 16–21
Jesus died "as a lamb"—Isaiah prophesied that the Messiah (Christ) would die as a lamb led to the slaughter. Starting from Isaiah 53, Philip *"preached Jesus,"* proclaiming the message of Jesus' death and resurrection to the Ethiopian eunuch, an official of the court of Queen Candace. He believed and was baptized.	Isaiah 53:6–12; Acts 8:30–38
"The Lamb of God"—John the Baptist proclaimed Jesus as *"the Lamb of God who takes away the sin of the world!"*	John 1:29, 36
"A Lamb without blemish and without spot"—Jesus Christ fulfilled all the Old Testament Scripture pictures and prophecies in dying as *"a lamb unblemished and spotless."*	1 Peter 1:18–21
The Risen Enthroned Lamb—In the Book of the Revelation the Apostle John saw in heaven the risen, enthroned Lamb who had been slain. He had *"seven horns,"* symbolic of perfect strength and power, and *"seven eyes which are the seven Spirits of God,"* symbolic of the fullness of the Spirit as well as the perfect perception and wisdom He possesses. He is enthroned forever.	Revelation 5:6; 7:15, 17
Singing "Worthy are Thou"—The Twenty-four elders fell down before the Lamb and sang a new song, *"Worthy are Thou. . . ."*	Revelation 5:8-10

EVENT	SCRIPTURE
Saying "Worthy is the Lamb"—Myriads of angels, the living creatures, and the elders joined in saying, "Worthy is the Lamb. . . ."	Revelation 5:11–12
Blessing to the Lamb—Every creature in heaven, on earth, under the earth, and in the sea proclaimed to the Lamb *"blessing and honor and glory and dominion forever and ever."*	Revelation 5:13–14
The Ruler of the Scroll—John saw the Lamb break the first of seven seals on the scroll, revealing His lordship and His ownership of the scroll, the title deed to the earth and that which is the instrument of the display of His reign.	Revelation 6:1
The Wrath of the Lamb is revealed in the opening of the sixth seal.	Revelation 6:16
The Salvation of the Lamb—In the events of the Great Tribulation, John saw an innumerable host of saints from all over the world stand before the Lamb clothed in white with palm branches in their hands. They praise the Lamb for His salvation.	Revelation 7:9–10
The Blood of the Lamb—Those who come out of the Great Tribulation *"have washed their robes and made them white in the blood of the Lamb."* By His death on the Cross, the Lamb Jesus paid the full sin debt thus providing forgiveness and cleansing from all sin, stain, and defilement. Because of *"the blood of the Lamb,"* believers overcome the devil or Satan, *"the accuser of our brethren."*	Revelation 7:14; 12:9–11
The Shepherd Lamb—The enthroned Lamb is the Shepherd of those who come out of the Great Tribulation. He will be their Shepherd dwelling among them forever.	Revelation 7:13–17
The Lamb on Mount Zion—The Lamb stands triumphant on Mount Zion reminiscent of the prophecies of Abraham in Genesis 22:14–17 and of the Psalmist in Psalm 2:5–6, 7–12	Revelation 14:1; Genesis 22:14–17; Psalm 2:5–12
The Lamb and the 144,000—The 144,000 sealed messengers carry the name of the Lamb and His Father on their foreheads indicating they belong to the Lamb. They sing the song of the redeemed, walk in purity and *"follow the Lamb wherever He goes"* (14:4). They are *"purchased… as first fruits… to the Lamb."*	Revelation 14:1–5
The Lamb as Judge—Those who worship the beast face judgment forever *"in the presence of the Lamb."* Those who follow Jesus persevere in obedience and faith and never face the judgment of the Lamb.	Revelation 14:9–12
The Song of the Lamb—Those who were victorious over the beast *"sang the song of Moses . . . and the song of the Lamb,"* a song of praise to God for His *"great and marvelous"* works, His *"righteous and true"* ways, and the worship due Him by all the nations.	Revelation 15:2–4
The Warrior Lamb—The Lamb overcomes all those who wage war against Him at Armageddon. *"He is Lord of lords and King of kings."*	Revelation 17:14 with 16:14–16 and 19:11–21
The Marriage and the Marriage Supper of the Lamb—*"The Lord our God, the Almighty, reigns."* He is the Lamb and His redeemed Bride ("the saints") has made herself ready for the Marriage and the Marriage Supper of the Lamb, the ceremony that begins their reign together. The New Jerusalem is their ultimate home.	Revelation 19:1–9; 21:9
The New Jerusalem and its Temple, the Lamb—The twelve foundation stones have the names of *"the twelve apostles of the Lamb."* (21:14) *"The Lord God, the Almighty, and the Lamb are its temple,"* the temple of the New Jerusalem—In other words, the fullness of the Presence of the Lamb is the dwelling place of the redeemed and the angelic host forever.	Revelation 21:22
The Lamb is the Lamp of the New Jerusalem. The glory of God fully revealed in the Lamb illumines the city.	Revelation 21:23
The Life-giving, Eternal Throne of the Lamb—The *"river of the water of life"* flows from the throne of the Lamb. The *"tree of life"* is there, but no curse will ever be there. The bondservants of the Lord serve the Lamb, see His face, and bear His name. They live by His life, walk in His light, and reign by His side forever.	Revelation 22:1–5

How to Follow God

STARTING THE JOURNEY

Did you know that you have been on God's heart and mind for a long, long time? Even before time existed you were on His mind. He has always wanted you to know Him in a personal, purposeful relationship. He has a purpose for your life and it is founded upon His great love for you. You can be assured it is a good purpose and it lasts forever. Our time on this earth is only the beginning. God has a grand design that goes back into eternity past and reaches into eternity future. What is that design?

The Scriptures are clear about God's design for man—God created man to live and walk in oneness with Himself. Oneness with God means being in a relationship that is totally unselfish, totally satisfying, totally secure, righteous and pure in every way. That's what we were created for. If we walked in that kind of relationship with God we would glorify Him and bring pleasure to Him. Life would be right! Man was meant to live that way—pleasing to God and glorifying Him (giving a true estimate of who God is). Adam sinned and shattered his oneness with God. Ever since, man has come short of the glory of God: man does not and cannot please God or give a true estimate of God. Life is not right until a person is right with God. That is very clear as we look at the many people who walked across the pages of Scripture, both Old and New Testaments.

JESUS CHRIST came as the solution for this dilemma. Jesus Christ is the glory of God—the true estimate of who God is in every way. He pleased His Father in everything He did and said, and He came to restore oneness with God. He came to give man His power and grace to walk in oneness with God, to follow Him day by day enjoying the relationship for which he was created. In the process, man could begin to present a true picture of Who God is and experience knowing Him personally. You may be asking, "How do these facts impact my life today? How does this become real to me now? How can I begin the journey of following God in this way?" To come to know God personally means you must choose to receive Jesus Christ as your personal Savior and Lord.

- First of all, you must admit that you have sinned, that you are not walking in oneness with God, not pleasing Him or glorifying Him in your life (Romans 3:23; 6:23; 8:5-8).

- It means repenting of that sin—changing your mind, turning to God and turning away from sin—and by faith receiving His forgiveness based on His death on the Cross for you (Romans 3:21-26; 1 Peter 3:18).

- It means opening your life to receive Him as your living, resurrected Lord and Savior (John 1:12). He has promised to come and indwell you by His Spirit and live in you as the Savior and Master of your life (John 14:16-21; Romans 14:7-9).

- He wants to live His life through you—conforming you to His image, bearing His fruit through you and giving you power to reign in life (John 15:1,4-8; Romans 5:17; 7:4; 8:29, 37).

You can come to Him now. In your own words, simply tell Him you want to know Him personally and you willingly repent of your sin and receive His forgiveness and His life. Tell Him you want to follow Him forever (Romans 10:9-10, 13). Welcome to the Family of God and to the greatest journey of all!!!

WALKING ON THE JOURNEY

How do we follow Him day by day? Remember, Christ has given those who believe in Him everything pertaining to life and godliness, so that we no longer have to be slaves to our "flesh" and its corruption (2 Peter 1:3-4). Day by day He wants to empower us to live a life of love and joy, pleasing to Him and rewarding to us. That's why Ephesians 5:18 tells us to *be filled with the Spirit*—keep on being controlled by the Spirit who lives in you. He knows exactly what we need each day and we can trust Him to lead us (Proverbs 3:5-6). So how can we cooperate with Him in this journey together?

To walk with Him *day by day* means ...
- reading and listening to His Word day by day (Luke 10:39, 42; Colossians 3:16; Psalm 19:7-14; 119:9).
- spending time talking to Him in prayer (Philippians 4:6-7).
- realizing that God is God and you are not, and the role that means He has in your life.

This allows Him to work through your life as you fellowship, worship, pray and learn with other believers (Acts 2:42), and serve in the good works He has prepared for us to do—telling others who Jesus is and what His Word says, teaching and encouraging others, giving to help meet needs, helping others, etc. (Ephesians 2:10).

God's goal for each of us is that we be conformed to the image of His Son, Jesus Christ (Romans 8:29). But none of us will reach that goal of perfection until we are with Him in Heaven, for then "we shall be like Him, because we shall see Him just as He is" (1 John 3:2). For now, He wants us to follow

Him faithfully, learning more each day. Every turn in the road, every trial and every blessing, is designed to bring us to a new depth of surrender to the Lord and His ways. He not only wants us to do His will, He desires that we surrender to His will His way. That takes trust—trust in His character, His plan and His goals (Proverbs 3:5-6).

As you continue this journey, and perhaps you've been following Him for a while, you must continue to listen carefully and follow closely. We never graduate from that. That sensitivity to God takes moment-by-moment surrender, dying to the impulses of our flesh to go our own way, saying no to the temptations of Satan to doubt God and His Word, and refusing the lures of the world to be unfaithful to the Lord who gave His life for us.

God desires that each of us come to maturity as sons and daughters: to that point where we are fully satisfied in Him and His ways, fully secure in His sovereign love, and walking in the full measure of His purity and holiness. If we are to clearly present the image of Christ for all to see, it will take daily surrender and daily seeking to follow Him wherever He leads, however He gets there (Luke 9:23-25). It's a faithful walk of trust through time into eternity. And it is worth everything. Trust Him. Listen carefully. Follow closely.

Notes